The
Making of
Modern
Austin

Power, Money & the People

by
Anthony M.
Orum

Resource *Publications*

An imprint of *Wipf and Stock Publishers*
199 West 8th Avenue • Eugene OR 97401

Resource *Publications*
an imprint of Wipf and Stock Publishers
199 West 8th Avenue, Suite 3
Eugene, Oregon 97401

Power, Money and the People
The Making of Modern Austin
By Orum, Anthony M.
©1987 Orum, Anthony M.
ISBN: 1-59244-077-0
Publication date: October, 2002
Previously published by Texas Monthly Press / Gulf Publishing Co., 1987.

Contents

———

Acknowledgments

——

THE BOOKS I DO SEEM TO TAKE FAR TOO LONG AND far too much energy to complete. One reason that this happens, I suppose, is because I try to create a small world within the pages I write, a piece of life that is self-contained and comprehensive. In the case of this book on Austin, I also have created a small world of friends for myself. I owe to all of them a debt that I can never possibly repay, but I hope that the few lines here might serve as a start.

There are, to begin with, the 180 or so people who agreed to provide me with their memories and thoughts about Austin. All of these people are somewhere cited in the pages of my text, and I thank them for granting me the time and patience to put up with my questions. Some of them sat and talked with me for several hours, and I am especially grateful for their kind forbearance. I also want to single out a couple of people who became more than merely purveyors of memories for me, who became, indeed, good friends. They are Emma Long, a wonderful person and truly an Austin institution, and Janett Fish, Walter Long's daughter, who very graciously permitted me to ransack her father's files and records, which resulted in the discovery of about twenty oral histories that Long himself had done back in the 1950s and 1960s. I also am deeply grateful to Bill Livingston, vice-president for graduate studies at the University of Texas, for providing the financial support for this work when no one else would; and to my good friends, whom I shall dearly miss, Joe Feagin, Walter Firey, Dale McLemore, and Gideon Sjoberg, who gave me the kind of personal encouragement so necessary to a scholar who sets out on a different trek from that of virtually all his academic peers. Audray

Bateman, curator of the Austin History Center, along with several of her staff, particularly Linda Zezulka and Carlos Lowry, also provided more support in the course of my odyssey than they will ever recognize.

Scott Lubeck and Anne Norman of Texas Monthly Press also helped me to complete this work, particularly toward the latter stages when my well of enthusiasm had about run dry. Scott gave me hope that a finished book would see the light of day at a time when I, myself, had begun to entertain some doubts about the matter. And Anne was meticulous, upbeat, intelligent, cheery and altogether a good soul to work with as we prepared the manuscript for final publication.

Most of all, of course, there are those day-to-day companions who had to listen to my meanderings and put up with my complaints, only occasionally to be rewarded with a piece of inside information about the Austin past. To my large, extended family in Austin, otherwise known as the Runners' Group—we have run together regularly at the Town Lake Hike and Bike Trail for almost a decade— what can I say, except that you won't have to listen to my terrible jokes anymore: Rhoda Silverberg (and also Eric, Kristen, and Liese), Bob and Grace Lee, Betty McCreight, Dick Stanford, Martin and Elizabeth Turner, Evie Sullivan, and Margaret Weichert. You can, and will, never be replaced. Finally, to the continuing members and recent additions to my immediate family, thank you for all your patience (and also for not slamming the doors too often): Nicholas Orum, Hannah Jorjorian, Rebekah Jorjorian, and Susie, most of all, you. And, finally, to Mark, wherever you are. We all wish you, too, were here to celebrate this book.

Prologue:
Three Tales of a City

——

RIVER CITY. CITY OF THE VIOLET CROWN. THIRD COAST. These are some of the sobriquets bestowed on Austin. Everyone has some special sense of the place. All those who have been here have taken a piece of the hills and the countryside with them – if they have left. Most who come here never leave. For good reason. It seems ideal, almost. Beautiful countryside. Wonderful people. A great deal of hustle and bustle. Heavy-handed politics, of the good-old-boy variety. Wealth, lots of it. A unique setting. Dallas or Houston, with water, hills, and civility. Laid-back, calm. And hot, sultry hot from May until the brown days of October football at the university.

I could go on and on here, but I won't. I shall leave the many pictures to the chapters of the book. Here I want simply to tell you what the book is all about, and why I did it. Of course I did it because I love the place; that goes without saying. I really did it because I found some of the hustle and bustle quite fascinating, particularly the slapdash, come-hell-or-high-water, showy disorder of the 1970s and 1980s. I was not a student of cities when I began to study Austin, but I am now. Cities are marvelously disjointed social creations, held together seemingly by the sharp differences among their residents, given a purpose by otherwise lackluster city officials, furnishing a setting that for many of us can be only dimly noticed out of the corners of our eyes as we rush to work early in the mornings. Austin is on its way to becoming a great city, at least a great city of the Southwest. How it embarked on this venture, who gave it a semblance of direction and purpose – that is what this book on Austin is all about. Or, at least, partly.

Really there are three sorts of stories here. One is about growth. Another is about a Texas town filled with Texas-sized characters. And the last is about the urban struggle between big money and little people. The first, the main tale, has lingered in my head more or less coherently for the past six years. It began in a most undramatic fashion, prompted simply by mild curiosity. One day, in 1980, I was driving down from my home in the hills, west of Austin. Suddenly, it seemed, there were houses where none had stood before. A new highway had materialized, right in the middle of some dense cedar trees. Where once had stood a small hill, gracing some otherwise flat land, a shopping center now provided people with their daily goods. The changes had been quite gradual, of course; but they had transformed a rural, peaceful setting into a new civilization, becoming a metropolis. Since I was between academic writings, I thought I would do a little research into the growth of Austin. The little research has turned into this book.

The first story that you will find here, then, is one about why and how Austin has expanded. It is a story that traces the gradual rise of people and buildings, city boundaries and residential dwellings. But it is more. I try to explain why growth has happened to Austin, to pinpoint the ingredients that account for its increasing prominence among America's urban centers. Several elements, I found, proved essential to such growth. And they are things that happen to other mushrooming urban places, though perhaps not quite in the same way, nor all together. The first element is that of culture. I never thought that culture could promote expansion until I looked into the history of Austin. But culture played a central role, in two different ways. First, there has been in Austin, almost from its very birth, a strong vision of the future. Austinites constantly have spoken about such a vision, and about people who held it. Walter Long, manager of the Chamber of Commerce from 1915 through 1949, stuck by one guiding biblical precept throughout his public life: "Without a vision, the people perish." The vision, moreover, was not of any utopia, but of a particular one. It was a place in the future that would be bountifully supplied with all the good things of Western industrial civilization. These were, so many Austinites thought, industry, factories, and wealth. One can almost precisely date the late nineteenth, early twentieth century expansion of Austin from this dream. And, like all dreams, it was unnatural. But it was one that came to be accepted by the leading circles. Culture became implicated in the growth of

Austin in yet another fashion. The men and women who worked on behalf of the dream were driven to succeed and to capture the future. They were wealthy. More than that, they worked hard. Labor. Drive. Ambition. These became the cultural elements that provided meaning and direction to the lives of those who built modern Austin.

Not everyone in Austin possessed vision, nor were all compelled to dominate and to define the future. The people who had a hand in erecting modern Austin, in realizing the dream and in making it count, were people I call *urban entrepreneurs*. They are unique individuals, although they can be found in almost every city, fabricating designs for expansion. Such people perform a role that entails self-sacrifice, relinquishing today's wealth or simple personal ambition for the munificence of tomorrow's urban arena. For them, love and devotion to the idea of a place at times even come to substitute for love and devotion to other human beings. Several such urban entrepreneurs lived and loved and died in and for Austin.

There is even more to the tale of Austin growth. All the dreaming and all the hard work are fine, but there must be resources to make everything go. To turn the dreams into reality. Money and power—the things so often associated with Texas. Interestingly, at the very start of its twentieth-century boom, it was not any money that happened along. It was not, as you might expect, private fortune, not oil money, not cattle cash. It was money and power that came from the federal government. If Franklin Delano Roosevelt—along with Texans James Buchanan, J. J. Mansfield, Lyndon Johnson, and Tom Miller—and many associates had not used the resources of the state during the Great Depression to build dams, to pave sidewalks, to create new federal buildings, to make jobs—if, in short, they had not furnished people with a livelihood—I would not be writing a story about Austin today. It would be a nothing place, a spot set along the wayside of urban history like so many others, home to dreamers but not to multitudes of people.

The driving forces behind Austin expansion, both personal and financial, changed sometime in the late 1960s or early 1970s. The vision remained the same, as did the ambition and labor. But the source of building funds, and the kinds of people obsessed with a vision for the future expansion, changed markedly. The federal government, the state, no longer played the central role. The private marketplace gradually replaced the federal government, and prominent figures in the private sector began to rule the roost. In a phrase, the urban entrepreneurs of earlier decades were replaced by *market entrepreneurs*. Market entrepreneurs, many of whom hold fortunes based outside Austin, are as animated by the dream of expansion as the urban entrepreneurs. Yet they care considerably less for the place and much more for private fortunes. They want, quite simply, a piece of the action in Austin. A new economic vitality thus arose in the community in the 1970s and 1980s; ironically, it happened because many of those who promoted the growth of Austin cared little for community.

The tale of growth in this book, then, is about dreams, ambition, drive, people, and money. All of these elements made expansion possible. But what of the second story, the one of Texas? This is the history of Austin, and of all those special people who came to live here. It is a story of their foibles. And fables. And of their fame. I speak here not of Stephen F. Austin, for whom the site was named, nor even of Sam Houston. Instead, I have in mind people like Lyndon Johnson, who was launched on an extraordinary political career by his doings in late 1930s Austin, or even Tom Miller, late, great mayor of this city, who rose through the ranks of the FDR Democratic party to take on important national tasks, such as heading up, along with Creekmore Fath, the Texas presidential campaign for Harry Truman in 1948. I speak also of Thurgood Marshall, who came to Austin in 1946 to argue on behalf of one Hemann Marion Sweatt, who had been denied entrance to the University of Texas Law School simply because he was black. Marshall drew from that experience the ammunition so necessary to his brilliant Supreme Court victory over segregation in 1954. I speak here, too, of Texas populism and populists, in the form of the so-called liberals who through much of the second half of the twentieth century campaigned so hard in and from Austin, men and women like Emma and Stuart Long, Ralph Yarborough, and their many allies.

The second story is about the unique events that happened in Austin. It is about the founding of the Colorado River Association here, which twenty years later would create the social and political architecture for the Lower Colorado River Authority. It is about the history of the black community in Austin, and how the residential segregation of this community was politically fashioned by certain city fathers. It tells, too, of the exploits that helped to bring about the end of segregation, events that happened fully five years before the Reverend Martin Luther King, Jr., and his collaborators launched a nationwide civil rights movement with the bus boycotts in Montgomery, Alabama. Finally, this second tale relates some of the infamous anecdotes about the University of Texas, and how the university, and its Board of Regents, achieved universal renown. The second story, in brief, is about very distinctive Texas personalities and institutions.

The third and final story is about the continuing, episodic struggles between capitalism and democracy in Austin. This is a story that I truly did not anticipate when I set about writing this history. But it is one that becomes ever more apparent as one digs more deeply into the Austin past. And as one tries to realize that, in fact, there have been two great dreams struggling to make themselves real in the twentieth century. One is the vision of industry, great wealth, and private property. This is the dream of growth. It is the dream of big capital. The other is the vision that has emerged continuously to challenge the first. It is the dream to make the benefits of growth available to ever larger numbers of people, and to involve them in the very process of defining what the future in Austin will be. I call this second one the dream of democracy.

At least since the 1930s, various sets of people and the two different visions of the world have come into deep conflict in Austin. Proponents of the democratic vision arose first on the campus of the University of Texas, educated in the maverick populism of the likes of Bob Montgomery, Clarence Ayers, J. Frank Dobie, and others. This was the kind of democratic vision that detested corporate capitalism and yearned for more wealth and freedom for the common people. In the mid-1940s, these democratic populists joined others in Austin, consisting of union officials, minority blacks and browns, and some New Deal Democrats, to take up the cause on behalf of the "little people." Led by Emma and Stuart Long, these folks labored to gain benefit for all those people who had been left out of the main vision, the one for community expansion. People like Tom Miller, Walter Long, and other prominent business figures in the Austin of the 1950s and 1960s, those the populists referred to as "the Establishment," were targeted as the opponents of the dream of populist democracy. The clash was fascinating. Growth against democracy. A group of urban entrepreneurs aligned together against urban reformers. The conflict provoked some very nasty episodes. Like the firing of Stuart Long as newscaster at KVET. Or the dismissal of Ben White from his position as plant superintendent at Austex Chili. The entrepreneurs, and their allies, knew how to fight, and how to win.

But they were not completely victorious. Again, the late 1960s saw a similar struggle. Now it was a conflict over civil rights and property rights. Blacks and browns against affluent Anglos. The prize in this struggle became the policy of open housing. The populist democrats, many of them survivors from the earlier decade, fought for open housing. The Establishment cronies rallied behind the defeat of this ordinance. And again, not too surprisingly, those who wanted main-ly to see the city grow and to expand, those who bought the idea of growth lock, stock, and barrel, were victorious. As Nelson Puett, a realtor, would say in reprising the results of the vote over open housing, it was a "victory for property rights in Austin."

The third story, like the first one, continues to the present day. It is a matter of new wine in old bottles. Those who push now for expansion pursue the dream born a century ago, even though they are led today by market entrepreneurs and much of the capital for their fight comes from private sources. The democrats retain much of their old rhetoric and ideological slogans, but their concerns have broadened. Today those concerns revolve around the environment and neighborhoods. Beginning in the 1970s in Austin, neighborhood groups sprang up everywhere, more than a hundred in all. And everywhere those groups pursued a similar theme. Limit growth, limit expansion. Stop the commercialization of Austin. Bring big capital to its knees. But everywhere, too, the vision of growth continued vir-tually unimpaired. There may have been a victory here or there, an ordinance or two designed to forestall expansion. But such victories have proven to be merely temporary ones. And they give little com-fort to those who truly had hoped to involve all the little people, if not in the benefits of growth, at least, as the mid-1970s Austin Tomorrow program anticipated, in creating a workable vision for the future of Austin.

There are, thus, three different tales of Austin in this book, three different ways to read the chapters that follow. What ties them to-gether is that they are about the people of a place called Austin. Un-like many scholars, I believe that in the end the world turns not on abstract principles alone, but on the actions of everyday people, on their desires and their disappointments, on the richness of their am-bitions and the strength of their hopes. Over the past fourteen years that I have lived in Austin, I have come to love its people, for they, after all, are the community. It is to them that I dedicate this book.

1.

Between Wilderness and Civilization

——

There is something different about this country from any other part of the nation. The climate is generally pleasant, the sun is generally bright, the air seems to be always clean, and the water is pure. The moons are a little fuller here, the stars are a little brighter, and I don't know how to describe the feeling other than, I guess, we all search at times for serenity, and it's serene here. And there's something about this section that brings new life, and new hope, and really a balanced and better viewpoint after you've been here a few days.

Lyndon Baines Johnson
36th President of the United States[1]

AUSTIN IS AT A CROSSROADS. IT LIES SOMEWHERE near the center of the state, between north and south, east and west. It represents a geographical transition point, too, a bridge between the hills and the plains. In the past it was a transition from the heights of civilization to the depths of the wilds, at the fringes of the world. And today it lies at a turning point, between the rawness of its past and the grand cultural and economic accomplishments many of its residents have come to expect of its future.

It is March 1983. It have just returned from a brief tour, by car, of the hill country of central Texas. Austin lies at the edge of the hill country. A geological fault line, the Balcones Fault, runs directly through the city. On one side the land is hilly and wooded, and, if one goes west through this land, there is a continuous stretch of hills for many, many miles. On the other side the land is flat, with a few gentle rolls to its surface. As you would expect, those who are rich live in the hills of Austin, and those who are poor and must scrape for a living reside in the plains. This coincidence between geologic and social divisions in the city will not soon change. As Austin now grows, the big and fancy developments are rising in the western hills. As in Johnson's lifetime, as in the time of the Indians who lived here so long before the white settlers, there is something magical about those hills. Only today the magic must be bought for a stiff price.

Geologically, the fault line helps to make Austin special. Apparently because of this and other anomalies running through the city, Austin has become a magnet for all kinds of peculiar and wonderful things. Among others, soon to be discovered by new immigrants to the community, are an absolute rash of allergies, of all sorts and types. Even if one never before had an allergy, Austin's unique position, in the middle of Texas on the Edwards Plateau, traps the molds and spores and pollen of trees and flowers. In December, January, and February, a wondrous allergy comes alive, making itself felt in the nasal passages and in dripping noses and runny eyes. It is called cedar fever, and even in places elsewhere in America where there are cedars, one will never find such a malady.

But surely, as Lyndon Johnson claimed, the allergies, and even the hot, sometimes dry summers, are burdens to be endured for the great mysteries that arise here, in central Texas and Austin. The moons do indeed seem somewhat fuller, the stars are often so bright and clear as to give one a sense of being within the confines of some planetarium in New York City, and the sun, most definitely in July and August, always feels a good deal fuller and bigger and more intense than elsewhere. For people who have never been to this part of the world, there is a certain image held in the mind's eye about what it must look like. When I first arrived, in February 1972, on retreat from a deathly cold and overcast day in central Illinois, I had little idea of what to expect. There ran through my mind, I remember clearly, images of cactus and parched skulls and sand, and maybe a few cowboys here and there, under a hot sun at high noon. Of course, what I discovered was nothing like that. But other people seem to hold the same image.

I found a letter from a thirteen-year-old boy by the name of Paul Dombrowski, who in 1957 lived in Schenectady, New York. Paul wrote in February to Mayor Tom Miller, a major figure in this story of Austin, in order to secure some lizards from the "big, big, big, State of Texas" with which to populate his new terrariums. On the lower left-hand corner of his letter, occupying a big, big, big space, Paul drew his image of Texas, and Austin. There sits a very large cactus plant, in the middle of an empty space. And, in the background, we observe something like hills or mountains or a mesa. In Paul's mind, like my own and those of many others who arrive here for the first time, Texas was big and spacious, full of cactus plants, with a few mountains in the background. And also apparently full of lizards to populate the terrariums of young boys who lived in the cold, cold North.[2]

A good deal of Texas, especially west Texas, fits the picture Paul drew. But the country that abuts Austin on its various sides—that runs perhaps 100 miles direct from Austin as the center—is vast, and vastly different from Paul Dombrowski's mental image. The drive from Austin to the northwest, along the banks of the Colorado, to Marble Falls, thence to Kingsland and Lake Buchanan, is filled with hills. They are not steep hills. Often they rise no more than two or three hundred feet above ground level. But there are many of them. Some are homes for large numbers of scrub cedar, or juniper, trees. Such trees do not grow very tall, owing, I suppose, to the limestone and sandstone on which they must seek their livelihood. There are also some hackberries and oaks and other trees that reside on these hills. On the drive one will see a goodly number of cattle grazing the land, but few herds of dairy cows. There also are sheep, and some hogs. It is a lovely countryside, but often not very inviting. One can easily imagine these hills when the Indians roamed them. And, indeed, the historical records and the memories of grandchildren and great-children contain names of events and of men and women who fought battles with the Indian marauders on these hills back in the nineteenth century. Little did these folks fully appreciate or want to recognize, except in rare cases, that in the eyes of those "savages" they themselves were the marauders.

As one reaches points sixty or seventy miles northwest of Austin, the land, which had been limestone and sandstone, begins to turn a different color altogether. Here outcroppings of red and pink granite begin to arise, like red giants awakening from a long slumber. On the other side of Marble Falls, there is a large quarry where today great chunks of granite are lifted from the earth. Back in the late nineteenth century, prisoners worked this quarry to gather blocks for the new Capitol building in Austin. Today these outcroppings of

"Sunset Red" are shipped off to places like Los Angeles to construct courthouses, or to Minneapolis to build life insurance companies.[3] In the area surrounding Llano, in Llano County, the granite continues to surface in large blocks. One of the favorite recollections of the history books in this area is the time, back in 1906, when a huge block of red granite, weighing forty tons, was carved out of the earth, wrapped in many logs, and rolled down to the railroad to be hauled off to Austin.[4] It took six months to do the rolling. The mining of the red and pink granite was a major business in the nineteenth century, and even today a good deal of business is done with these rocks.

In fact, far below the surface, out of the reach of human sight, there lie streaks of iron and gold and silver. Some people up here thought that the iron would become a big source of wealth for the residents in the nineteenth century. Around 1892, there even was a "boom" in Llano, brought about by speculators who thought there would be iron, maybe even a little gold, in them thar hills. There wasn't, or at least not very much.[5] Llano's boom has since fizzled, while Austin lights up the skies, with its hand on gold that runs black and lies below the surface and makes it the capital of the richest state in the country.

The hills begin to disappear somewhat short of Kingsland, although every now and then there is some hill, or mesalike thing, popping up just to remind you that this is the hill country. One will also find lakes here, created by the great dams of the Lower Colorado River Authority. There is Roy Inks Lake, Lake Buchanan, and Lake LBJ, and together they and the heights here are known as the Highland Lakes area. Tourists now graze where herds of cattle once did, and homes on the lakes bring a fancy price. Still, even the poorest visitor or inhabitant of the region is free to take a car, or bike, through the countryside. Some of the soil here, among patches of rock and limestone, actually appears very fertile—black and, on this day, wet and rich as anything one could ever uncover in Iowa or Wisconsin. The land is flat. And one even spies a few herds of dairy cows, here and there. While the hills between Austin and Llano could not support much in the way of corn and wheat, or cotton in the nineteenth century, the fields here could. And they did. Those farmers who made their living off the fields then did so because of the crops of corn, wheat, and especially cotton they raised.

A different route from Austin, almost directly due west, tells a story of yet a different kind of land. The area west of Austin, stretching out as far as Fredericksburg and including Johnson City, is the area in which Johnson himself grew up. It, too, rolls. And like so many of the other people who operate businesses in this central Texas region, those who do so in this stretch of land want to appropriate the name, indentity, and commercial possibilities of "hill country" all for themselves. As in Llano, New Braunfels, Dripping Springs, and elsewhere the visitor will discover hill country insurance companies; hill country cafes; hill country Chevrolet, Ford, or Plymouth dealerships. The hills here are different. They are not quite so steep as northwest of Austin. And they are not quite so closely packed together. They are more densely forested, however, with a greater variety of oak, it seems, than in other sections. The early German settlers referred to portions of this land, around Fredericksburg, as "forested," even though Peter, his grandfather, and the bad wolf would have thought them wide open spaces.

Where one sees the short grasses and cream and black rocks that form into mealy soils around Marble Falls and Llano, here there is sometimes a reddish cast to the soil, such as one finds in Georgia. The clays are not quite so dense, and the redness lasts not quite so long, but for a moment, if you did not know where you were, you would think it Atlanta. Looking back from these lands, across to Austin, one can see miles and miles of rolling hills and forests. The land settles out, after a while, and large fields appear, and now and then herds of dairy cows. Some of this land, too, is quite black and quite fertile. Those early German farmers in Fredericksburg, equipped with their 10 acres of land in the settlement, or having gained large acreage outside, in parcels of 160 or 320 acres, were able to harvest crops like wheat and corn, raise cows, sometimes just a single milk cow for the family, or even have a herd of goats.[6]

There are no forests, and very few trees, south and southwest of Austin. At least, there are none to compare with those of Dripping Springs, or nearby Johnson City. Once more, the land turns a different shape, a different color. On the drive to Seguin, the sky opens up even more. If you let your eye rest on the horizon, it seems as though there are centuries between you and the end of the earth. This land is almost flat, reminding one of lands in eastern Iowa, or central Illinois. It is deeply rich land, too. The soil is as black as coal. Initially the settlers in this area, an ethnically mixed lot from lands like Germany but also from Tennessee and the Carolinas, took up residence far from these black soils. They believed this land to be less fertile and established their farms and large cotton plantations in the area of the clay loams. The loam soil reminded some of them of the lands they had left. Large cotton plantations arose here in the nineteenth century, with all that entailed, including large bands of black slaves.[7]

In the past, besides the cotton, there were fields of corn and wheat. Now there are fields of milo, the general crop of the region. In early March the soil is so rich and the weather so mild that the green of new crops runs swiftly across fields, announcing profits to be made soon. There are occasional tall trees here and there. But there is nothing like the trees of the Fredericksburg, or even Austin. A farmer transplanted from Iowa would never know the difference, except when December and January and February rolled around, and it was a mite too warm to be winter.

Central Texas is big. But more that that it is diverse. Besides the lakes that now dot the region, there are the many trees and pastures and lands. There is a Georgia here, and a Wisconsin, and an Iowa. There even is an England, in the eyes of some, as Lady Bird Johnson has called a small forest of live oaks on the Johnson ranch. In places this land is rugged, and some parts are inviting. Some of it gives you the impression that you can see for miles and miles, and some of it leaves you with the sense that the world stops only two blocks away. It is thickly populated with trees in parts. Yet you will not discover the stately oaks and elms of Wisconsin, or the majestic trees of a California redwood forest, or the tall poplars that line the roads of a French countryside. The trees here are not so very tall, no more at times than twenty or twenty-five feet high. The cedars give off a nice smell, particularly when you desecrate one for a small fire. But the smell is nothing like the rich odors of dark pine forests along a Wisconsin shoreline, or of the great pines of western Montana. The greens of the pastures are sprightly, especially in March and April, long before the sun has burnt signs of life to brown ash. But they are nothing compared to the greens observed in an English countryside, or south of Paris, near Avalon, just after a fresh spring rainstorm. The hills are often quite breathtaking, particularly in the early morning, when the sky is clear and pale blue. The bluebonnets and Indian paintbrushes sprinkled along the highways in early spring, sometimes blanketed across fields through which one can imagine Dorothy and her friends dancing off to a different Oz, give a bright color and a soft feel to the land. But the roll is nothing like the rise and drop of miles in the mountains of Colorado.

If we collate and file our perceptions, if we add them all up, and let our minds just absorb this land and countryside for what it is, it feels open, and wonderful, and clear. Even in the midst of great urban growth, of civilization, of politics and the fine art of money-making, one senses a natural and wild feeling. Only ten minutes from downtown Austin, the site of ever faster bustle and buildings that stretch up toward those bright stars, deer and wild turkeys and armadillos and raccoons still play upon the hills. Today's modern · adventurers here, who drive pickups, wear cowboy boots, and talk tough English, try hard to recreate the West. But the West, and the frontier, would still be alive without all these movie set fictions. And that is really the story of the hill country and Austin today. Today as yesterday, it is a confrontation of civilization with wilderness. It continues to offer people a frontier to explore. The great uncertainty, for Austin as for its inhabitants, is whether that frontier will be around fifty years from now.

Shortly after the founding of the Republic of Texas, in 1836, Mirabeau B. Lamar sent out from Houston a party of four men to locate a site for the capital. On April 13, 1839, they reported to the president the discovery of an ideal site. This document represents the first beginnings of Austin, at least for the white settlers. I reproduce it here in its entirety. As much as any single document could, it helps to give a feel for the land, and the times of the discovery.

Report of the Commissioners
City of Houston, April 13, A.D. 1839.

To his Excellency Mirabeau B. Lamar, President of the Republic of Texas:

The Commissioners appointed under the act of Congress dated January, 1839, for locating the permanent site of the seat of Government for the Republic, have the honor to report to your excellency that they have selected the site of the town of Waterloo, on the east bank of the Colorado river, with the lands adjoining, as per the deed of the sheriff of Bastrop county, bearing date March, 1839, and per the relinquishment of Logan Vandever, James Rogers, G. D. Hancock, J. W. Harrall, and Aaron Burleson by combining the greatest number of, and the most important advantages to, the Republic, by the location of the seat of Government thereon, than any other situation which came under their observation within the limits assigned them, and as being, therefore, their choice for the location aforesaid.

We have the honor to represent your Excellency that we have traversed and critically examined the country on both sides of the Colorado and Brazos rivers, from the upper San Antonio road to and about the falls, on both those rivers, and that we have not neglected the intermediate country between them, but have examined it more particularly than a due regard to our personal safety did perfectly warrant.

We found the Brazos river more central, perhaps in reference to actual existing population, and found in it and its tributaries perhaps a greater quantity of fertile lands than are to be found on the Colorado; but, on the other hand, we were of opinion with that the Colorado was more central in respect to territory, and this, in connection with the great desideratims [sic] of health, fine water, stone, stone coal, water power, etc., being more abundant and convenient on the Colorado than on the Brazos river, did more than counterbalance the supposed superiority of the lands, as well as the centrality of position, in reference to population, possessed by the Brazos river.

In reference to the protection to be afforded to the frontier by the location of the seat of Government, a majority of Commissioners are of opinion that object will be as well attained by the location upon one river as upon the other; being also of opinion that within a very short period of time following the location of the seat of Government upon the frontier, the extension of the settlements produced thereby will engender other theories of defense of lands now the homes of the Comanche and bison.

The site selected by the Commissioners is composed of five thirds of leagues of land and two labors, all adjoining, and having a front upon the Colorado river somewhat exceeding three miles in breadth. It contains seven thousand seven hundred and thirty-five acres of land, and will cost the Republic the sum of twenty-one thousand dollars or thereabouts, one tract not being surveyed. Nearly the whole front is a bluff of from thirty to forty feet elevation, being the termination of a prairie containing perhaps two thousand acres, composed of a chocolate colored sandy loam, intersected by two beautiful streams of permanent and pure water, one of which forms at its debouche into the river a timbered rye bottom of about thirty acres. These rivulets rise at an elevation of from sixty to one hundred feet, on the back part of the site or tract, by means of which the contemplated city might, at comparatively small expense, be well watered, in addition to which are several fine bluff springs of pure water on the river convenient distances from each other.

The site is about two miles distant from, and in full view of, the mountains or breaks of the table lands, which, judging by the eye, are of about three hundred feet elevation. They are of limestone formation, and are covered with live oak and dwarf cedar to their summits. On the site and its immediate vicinity stone in inexhaustible quantities and great varieties is found, almost fashioned by nature for the builders' hands; lime and stone coal abound in the vicinity; timber for ordinary building purposes abounds on the tract, though the timber for building in the immediate neighborhood is not of so fine a character as might be wished, being mostly cottonwood, ash, burr oak, hackberry, post oak and cedar, the last suitable for shingles and small frames.

At the distance of eighteen miles west by south from the site, on Onion Creek (a stream affording fine water power), is a large body of very fine cypress, which is also found at intervals up the river for a distance of forty miles, and; together with immense quantities of fine cedar, might readily be floated down the streams, as the falls, two miles above the site, present no obstruction to floats or rafts, being only a descent of about five feet in one hundred and fifty yards, over a smooth bed of limestone formation, very nearly resembling colored marble.

By this route, also, immense quantities of stone coal, building materials, and in a few years agricultural and mineral products, for the contemplated city can be obtained, as no rapids save those mentioned occur in the river below the San Saba, nor are they known to exist for a great distance above the junction of that stream with the Colorado.

Opposite the site, at the distance of one mile, Spring creek and its tributaries afford, perhaps, the greatest and most convenient water power to be found in the Republic. Walnut creek, distant six miles, and Brushy creek, distant sixteen miles, both on the east side of the river, afford very considerable power. Extensive deposits of iron ore, adjudged to be of very superior quality, are found within eight miles of the location.

This section of country is generally well watered, fertile in a high degree, and has every appearance of health and salubrity of climate. The site occupies, and will effectually close, the pass by which Indians and outlawed Mexicans have for ages past traveled east and west, to and from the Rio Grande to Eastern Texas, and will now force them to pass by way of Pecan bayou and San Saba, above the mountains and the sources of the Guadalupe river.

The Commissioners confidently anticipate the time when a great thoroughfare shall be established from Santa Fe to our seaports, and another from Red River to Matamoros, which two routes must almost of necessity intersect each other at this point. They must look forward to the time when this city shall be the emporium of not only the productions of the rich soil of the San Saba, Perdenales [sic], Hero, and Pecan bayou, but of all the Colorado and Brazos, as also of the produce of the rich mining country known to exist on those streams. They are satisfied that a truly national city could be no other point within the limits assigned them be reared up; not that other sections of the country are not equally fertile, but that no other combined so many and such varied advantages and beauties as the one in question.

The imagination of even the romantic will not be disappointed on viewing the valley of the Colorado, and the fertile and gracefully undulating woodlands and luxuriant prairies at a distance from it. The most skeptical will not doubt its healthiness, and the citizen's bosom must swell with honest pride when, standing in the portico of the capitol of his country, he looks abroad upon a region worthy only of being the home of the brave and free. Standing on the juncture of the routes of Santa Fe and the seacoast, of Red river and Matamoros; looking with the same glance upon the green, romantic mountains, and the fertile and widely extended plains of his country—can a feeling of nationality fail to arise in his bosom, or could the fire of patriotism lie dormant under such circumstances?

Fondly hoping that we may not have disappointed the expectations of either our countrymen or your Excellency, we subscribe ourselves your Excellency's most obedient servants,

> H. C. Horton, Chairman
> J. W. Burton
> William Menifee
> Isaac Campbell
> Louis P. Cooke

The actual site chosen for the seat of government by the commissioners, the town of Waterloo, consisted of a small number of residents at the time. Once the location had been settled on, an agent acting on behalf of the president was quickly selected. His task was to survey and to sell various parcels of land in the new capital. His name was Judge Edwin Waller. Judge Waller established the original boundaries of the new capital, which lay between Shoal and Waller creeks, and apportioned the initial pieces of land. The total size of the new community was 640 acres, half the size of residential developments on the outskirts of present-day Austin. Occupying the center of the original map of the town was the site for the Capitol building and grounds. The major street that ran up to the Capitol was Congress Avenue, and at its other end lay the shores of the Colorado River. Just north of the Capitol grounds was a site designated as College Hill. Eventually this became home to the University of Texas.

The land sold quickly: people were eager to move to what they expected to be a lively and active place in the Republic. After the first auction, in August 1839, 301 parcels of land had been sold for almost $200,000. Building and development in the town moved so fast that Lamar and his cabinet were able to move into the town in October, and the state archives were transported there at the same time. Battles remained to be fought to secure Austin as the official capital, however. In 1842, there was an abortive effort to transfer the state archives to Houston. And it was not until 1872 that Austin became the official and permanent capital of the state.[8]

Then as now Austin was a victim to its past. In the heart of Indian country, it truly was a wilderness town, despite the best efforts of the settlers to make it a cultivated one. There were a number of different tribes in the area, but the most notable, perhaps, were the Comanches. Even today, longtime residents can point to the places in Austin where the Comanches customarily traveled by horse and by foot. Portions of one path run along one of the major majestic peaks in Austin, Mount Bonnell, from which one can easily imagine Indian sentries long ago looking over the countryside and the Colorado River below.[9] The Indians, of course, roamed these parts long before the white settlers, well in advance of the Spanish and Mexican invaders of the sixteenth, seventeenth, and eighteenth centuries. If this land of rivers, hills, and grasses truly belonged in a primeval fashion to any group, it was the Indians – the Comanches, the Tonkawas, the Waco, the Lipans, and others.

As Frank Brown, writing in the nineteenth century, sympathetically observed:

> [The Indians] considered the country theirs by right of in-
> heritance, believing the game had been provided by nature, or
> Providence, or by the Great Spirit, for their sustenance. From
> time immemorial, they had set up lodges in the beautiful groves
> of the forest. Their children had played beneath the shade of
> the trees and swung upon the grapevines pendant from the
> branches.[10]

They had traveled the hills and plains more or less unimpeded for centuries. Conflicts took place, of course, among the different Indian tribes, each of which was intent on settling its own rights to the territory.

The invasion of the white settlers, the bearers of Western practices, changed all that. Displaced from lands they believed theirs, from areas that held a mystery for them, the Indians inevitably rebelled and sought to recover these lands. They revered many of these places as special sites for spirits and other things about which the white settlers could only speculate, and which many of them, even had they so wished, could never fathom. Some of these special spots remain with us today. Near Llano, where the granite is mined, there is a place called Enchanted Rock. This place was revered by the Indians because of the mysteries it held. It is a huge outcropping of solid granite, which stands almost five hundred feet high and covers a full square mile of surface. The Indians in the area, it is said, held various tribal sacrifices and rituals here. Some legends say that white women, captured during Indian raids of settlements, were offered as a sacrifice to appease the gods of Enchanted Rock.[11] Other legends tell of an Indian princess who cast herself from the rock to the grounds below when she saw her fellow tribesmen and women being slaughtered by another tribe. Her spirit, it was thought by the Indians, still hovers above Enchanted Rock and, on dark nights with no moon, gives off eerie sounds and whispers, able to frighten even today's most stalwart camper.[12]

An uneasy peace often reigned between the settlers and the Indians. There was not always open conflict, though many of the early stories of Austin and the surrounding countryside involve fights between the Indians and settlers.[13] Near Llano there is a monument to the fight on Packsaddle Mountain in 1873. The significance of this battle, to the pioneers and to their ancestors in Llano County, is that it signaled the last actual fight between the settlers and the Indians in this region. The Indians finally were driven from their lands and conquered.[14] A story deep in the history of Fredericksburg, however, tells of the pact arranged between the Comanches and John A. Meusebach, considered the founder of this settlement and a key figure in the establishment of the German immigrants in central Texas. Meusebach, originally known as Baron von Meusebach, made a pact with several Comanche chiefs in an area north of Fredericksburg, bordering the San Saba River. Once the treaty was made secure, when the Indians came in a month's time to Fredericksburg, an exchange of gifts and commodities took place between the Germans and the Indians. Subsequently relations remained generally friendly between the two groups, despite occasional raids on settler homes or camps.[15]

In and near Austin, even through the 1870s, there were accounts of troubles between residents and the Indians. While workers were rioting in Hay Market Square, down in Austin the settlers still battled the slings and arrows of those whom they sought to displace. In the first years of the Civil War, a resident reported that there were serious dangers from the Indians as well as from the Yankee soldiers. Where the University of Texas now stands, the Indians were encamped, and bands of Yankee soldiers roamed the streets of the Confederate town. Little girls, it was said, could take no bigger risk than to travel the streets, for fear they would be ravaged by those terrible Indians or, worse, by Yankees.[16] And there were also those various reports of Indian raids upon lone encampments or settlements, raids that lasted well into the period of Reconstruction.[17]

Sometimes the battles between the settlers and the Indians were intensely fierce, like the one that took place at Packsaddle Mountain.

Both the settlers and the Indians believed they had a right to the land, so both fought desperately to secure it. Perhaps it was the attachment to the territory that produced the Indian raids, usually described by whites as savage. In any case, the memories of settlers often were alive with stories of how Indians had perpetrated unbelievable acts against defenseless families.

Mary Fry, author of an especially readable history of Llano, records an interview with W. H. Roberts in 1941 in which the latter describes the details of an Indian raid about which he learned as a lad. In February 1866, he recalled, while her husband and male members of another family were in Austin, a number of Indians approached a Mrs. Friend in her house with several other women and a number of small children. The Indians broke down the door of the house, shot Mrs. Friend with arrows, and then scalped her. They took the remaining women and children as prisoners. Somehow Mrs. Friend made her way, despite an arrow that remained stuck in her breast, to neighbors nearby to report the tragedy. The next day a search party was organized to go after the Indians and to seek the return of the prisoners. They followed the trail of the Indians by locating the bodies of the captives. Young infants were thrown casually along the paths, with their bodies mutilated and heads scalped. One woman was found with her body badly mangled, and all the bones of her body apparently broken.[18] Besides countless stories like this one, there were the special tales spun of those settlers, often children, who had been captured by Indian tribes, returning many years later, by chance, fully transformed into a Comanche or a Waco.[19]

The early settlers in Austin had to battle many things in order to be able to survive. They had to learn how to grow crops and raise animals in surroundings that often seemed foreign and unfamiliar, too hot and too dry in the dead of summer. They had to fight disease, brought about by the unfamiliar difficult conditions. In Austin infants died of cholera or of something just described in the books as fever. Women died soon after childbirth. Old age often set in in the forties or fifties, when many people today are going through a mid-life crisis.

Most of all, the settlers had to battle the Indians, and sometimes, as in the early 1840s, the Mexicans, in order to determine the so-called rightful ownership to the land. This was a wilderness, and a wide expanse that previously had been unexplored and uncharted—but only by whites, not by the Indians who had lived there for centuries. Thus, when we speak and think today of these people settling and making a new life for themselves, establishing a new social structure and new community, we must remind ourselves that to succeed and to be prosperous these settlers had to conquer not only nature, but also other human beings, then often regarded as savages and less than human. This sense of being the conquerors, of overcoming obstacles and creating a new world for themselves, remained a trademark of these pioneers. But it left victims in its wake, victims whose story often remains untold only because we have had to reconstruct this world through the eyes of the victors.

While Indians were displaced, black men and women were enslaved. The census of 1847 reported a total population in Travis County of 2,584 – 2,140 of them white, 329 voters, and 444 slaves.[20] A number of the early residents in Travis County, and Austin, were people who were second- or third-generation Americans. Their parents had come from Scotland or England and settled in the hills of Virginia, North Carolina, and Tennessee. And when the opportunity arose, or circumstances compelled, they packed their bags, traveled west, and stopped in places like Austin.[21] They brought with them both the knowledge and need to grow certain kinds of crops, along with a set of predetermined social patterns that they would plant here in the soil, along with the seeds for new crops. Some areas of the hill country did not permit the planting of the old crops, or the easy resurrection of old customs. Thus, in and around Llano, where the soil sometimes only permitted wheat and corn to be grown, it was reported that there were comparatively few slaves.[22] In the neighborhood of Fredericksburg, as well as New Braunfels, there were slaves who worked on the settlements of the German pioneers. But there were not so many as in Travis County, or in and around Seguin, where the land and new immigrants fostered such enslavement.

The crop grown in and around Austin, throughout the rich and fertile flatlands of Travis County, the one that fostered the transplantation of slavery, was cotton. There appear to have been no vast plantations as in the states of the Deep South, but there were enough large ones to support small groups of black slaves, working for white masters and mistresses. Austin, in fact, quickly became something of a trade center for cotton in the nineteenth century and remained so well into the twentieth. Bales of cotton would be brought into Austin from as far away as Llano. The barter economy remained in effect for a long time, as farmers exchanged bales of cotton for linen, or finery. Speaking of rural families in the nineteenth century, Carl Widen says, "they would usually bring in a bale of cotton, and sell it, and they would use that money for buying the things they didn't raise on the ranch, like cloth, pepper, and coffee. They had their own mills to raise their corn, and they raised their own meat."[23]

Toward the end of the nineteenth century, the two main crops that were brought into Austin were corn and cotton. There was a public cotton market in the city where the cotton could be brought and sold. A number of Austinites in the twentieth century, among them M. H. Reed and Edgar H. Perry, became rich through dealing in the cotton business and trading abroad with the manufacturing enterprises in England. Indeed, there was talk, as late as the twenties, about establishing some sort of mill in Austin to refine the cotton.[24] Such a factory was intended to bypass the woolen mills of England, establishing in Austin the manufacturing process itself. But the plant never was built.

Cotton required people to pick it; and because they had done so in the lands of the South from which new immigrants to Austin and Travis County had come, blacks became the human implements through which the cotton was harvested. It is unclear whether the relations between blacks and whites in Austin and nearby were any more, or less, harsh than those in, let us say, Alabama or Virginia.[25] Certainly these relations were less well rooted by the time of the Emancipation Proclamation, having been in effect only two to three decades.

But the fact is that the social structure that arose here included, as part of its central dynamic, the subjugation of blacks to whites. And this influenced relations within the community for many years to come. Even when blacks were freed, and there was an active Freedmen's Bureau in Austin in the late 1860s, they were regarded by local whites as inferior and provided only the most menial forms of employment. This system of relations between blacks and whites in the area remained long in effect and received the sanction of the larger social and economic community. Among other things, it is notable that well into the twentieth century, the Austin Chamber of Commerce had a bureau whose task it was to recruit cotton-pickers in Travis County for the cotton farmers.[26] Those cotton-pickers were blacks, and, by this time, Mexicans, too.

This pattern of relations between blacks and whites adds yet another special wrinkle to the social fabric of Austin. The Indians were overcome and eradicated or, where not eliminated, confined to small pieces of territory and eventually put on reservations. But blacks continued to live with the frontier settlers and to do the work the settlers would, or could, not do. When the twentieth century rolled around, these blacks, and Mexicans in ever growing numbers, remained in and around Austin, employed as pickers, or servants, or barber assistants, or just running odd jobs. They were not treated badly; they were not subject, it appears, to the blatant cruelties inflicted on them elsewhere, as in Alabama or Georgia. Nevertheless, they were subjects, an unfree group of people. They, like the Indians, were not regarded as full and equal human beings. They lived in shacks along Waller Creek, in the flatbeds of East Austin. When the story of beautiful and friendly Austin was told in 1917 in the famous booklet "Austin, Texas: The City of the Violet Crown," we see pictures of the large Victorian mansions of Colonel Andrew Zilker and the magnificent home of D. C. Reed.[27] We can even see the new housing division of Enfield Park, on the outskirts of town. But no one bothered to take a picture of the homes of the black and brown Austinites living in East Austin.

There is a story I have run across in one of the priceless interviews conducted in the early 1960s by Walter Long that captures the reaction of both blacks and whites to the peculiar institution in Austin:

> I could mention something about the introduction of music into the Austin Public Schools, if you are interested in that. . . . We were getting quite a number of requests to do something, so one evening it was decided that we would put up $2,500 to buy instruments. Weldon Covington was our band teacher. Twenty percent of our scholastics were colored, and I made arrangements with J. R. Reed that we would buy $2,000 worth of instruments for the white band, and $500 for the colored band. The colored band was taught by a man by the name of Joyce. He was a tailor by profession, and part-time instructor, and was paid $40 a month. One evening at our school board meeting, Mr. McCallum read a letter that he had received from a colored boy, stating that he would like to play an instrument in the band. It started out "Dear Mr. School Board" and was signed "Your Obedient Servant." He said his

parents were poor and couldn't buy an instrument for him, and he worked on Saturdays and made $1 but that wasn't enough. Harris Gardner made the motion that the music committee be authorized to buy our obedient servant a horn. We were invited to attend the dedication of the horns of the Anderson High School at the Ebenezer Auditorium and the president of the Band Mothers club over there came out and was telling about the generosity of the school board, and a boy came out carrying a great big horn and she gave the retail price of it and you could hear oh's and ah's all over the room, and the next horn was a smaller horn, and they called that a B flat base, and the boy who carried that horn was our obedient servant.[28]

There is a famous argument put forth first by Comte Alexis de Tocqueville and subsequently echoed and refined by many other observers of the growth of America.[29] In case you may not be familiar with it, it says, in effect, that American society and communities were able to develop as they did because Americans, the pioneers here, did not face the oppressive circumstances and entrenched nobility confronted by their brothers and sisters living in Europe. In fact, of course, that is one reason for the emigration of so many of those Germans and Swedes and Czechs to Texas. There reigned, it was claimed by de Tocqueville, a state of equality in America: all people, equally unencumbered with financial burdens or advantaged with material wealth, faced a harsh and often unrelenting wilderness.

Even Frank Brown, that exquisite and meticulous record-keeper of the history of Travis County through the end of the nineteenth century, talks about the settlement of this area in words that sound like de Tocqueville, though I doubt he ever read him. "There was no distinction," Brown writes, "between families or individuals on account of wealth, or station, or education. All men, so to speak, were on a common level. The conditions of the Country demanded this.[30] There is a good deal of truth to this thesis. All people were equal, more or less, in this new land. Past advantages rarely meant greater or easier accommodation to the barren hills, or scrub forests. The settlers represented a new breed of culture, a mix of something of their past with a good deal of their present. The spirit that was created among them, the effort to make something new and strong out of thoroughly raw and natural materials, blossomed into the desire, simply, to expand and to grow.

But everyone was not free, much as many of the settlers would like us to believe that. Nature would suffer under the settlers' conquest. And, so, too would the blacks. Whites were free because blacks were unfree. The sense of conquest, over land and people, developed as ever more forests gave way to the axes of white settlers, and ever larger numbers of black people became subject to the orders of whites. A spirit, a point of view, came to prevail, some of which, as I shall argue later, emerged in the form of ideas about growth and expansion in the world. But the earth and other human beings paid a price for that spirit. And while the white settlers did not realize the debt incurred, several generations later, their descendants would.

Indians and settlers, whites and blacks, transplanted Southerners and frontiersmen, these were among the major groups and social distinctions in early Austin. But there is one more element in the social composition of the community we must take into account. A large number of the early settlers were people who were first-generation Americans. They often came from Germany, occasionally from Scandanavian countries, sometimes from eastern Europe.[31] Germans may have been the most prominent of these new immigrants. In the middle 1840s, about the time that revolutionary conditions were beginning to brew in Hanover, Berlin, and Prussia, an organization was created in Germany, the Society for the Protection of German Immigrants in Texas. Led by Prince Carl of Solms-Braunfels, the group learned of land in Texas and arranged for its purchase as well as for the immigration of many of their countrymen to settle in Texas. A number of these people were members of the nobility in Germany.[32] Beginning in 1845, they came by ship to Texas, landing first at Indianola. Slowly they made their way northward. Death and disease took their toll. Many of the people settled at a small site on the banks of the Guadalupe River, others nearby at Comal Creek, at a place they named New Braunfels. Others eventually made their way further north and created the small community of Fredericksburg. Though the Germans remained heavily concentrated in these two spots, some soon came to settle in Austin, too.

Austin became home in the nineteenth century to a sizable and very vital German community. Though nothing on the order of those communities that arose in such places as Milwaukee, Wiscon-

sin, the German settlers in Austin became prominent in a number
of different pursuits and organized a network of groups and associations that, among other things, assisted the German newcomers.
Today there is a very famous museum in Austin, called the Elizabet
Ney Museum. Within its walls are housed a number of busts and
statues made by Miss Ney, who was a famous sculptor and one of
Austin's most distinguished residents at the turn of the century. She
was a German immigrant to the United States and to Austin. She
was also something of an infamous eccentric, one of those about
whom people whisper under their breath and fashion ribald jokes.
Her manner of dress was, to say the least, unusual. She would deck
herself out, according to her friend, Max Bickler, "after the Graecian
style," sometimes wearing a black veil, and flowing drapery over her
body, long before it was the fashion.[33] Occasionally she would be
seen in public in the garb in which she worked, a jacket and something on the order of men's coveralls. A free spirit in an age and place
that was undecided about free spirits, she had few close friends in
Austin, apart from Bickler.

Other famous German settlers in Austin were Augustus Scholz and
his wife. Along with other German immigrants, the Scholzes first
arrived at Indianola and then came to live in Austin. He bought a
house, then a cafe, adding a zoo, a bowling alley, and gradually
expanding his property until it included an entire city block. The
property became known as Scholz Garten, after the fashion of the
famous beer gardens in Germany, and was the gathering place for the
large number of German settlers in Austin. Here among other things
they would hold the famous singing festivals, the *Sängerfest*. The *Sängerfest* was a direct import from the old country. Singing societies
were a favorite pastime of the Germans, who regularly gathered to
hear the tunes of their fellow countrymen. Contests were held, winners announced, and altogether the festivals were times of celebration
and good fellowship. Scholz and his wife became sponsors of many
of the newly arrived German immigrants to the area.[34] Today, the
Scholz Garten still inhabits the same quarters at Sixteenth Street and
San Jacinto, but it is mainly a watering spot for University of Texas
students. Their singing naturally is a good deal less polished but
about as robust as that of the German singers a century ago.

Max Bickler's father was another of the German immigrants to settle in Austin. Jacob Bickler, however, was a second-generation
American. His parents had settled first in Wisconsin, where Max

received a college degree from the University of Wisconsin at Madison. He came to Austin about 1870 and began a school here in the mid-1870s. The school, first known as the German school, catered both to girls and to boys. Eventually it came to include both primary and secondary grades, and it remained in operation well into the twentieth century. Children of the newly arrived German settlers attended it, but so did children from the leading and established families in Austin. As there was no public schooling available for a time, the Bickler school became a very popular one in the community.[35]

Germans may have been among the most prominent of the early immigrants to Austin, but there was a considerable mixture of other groups, too. There were people of Swedish ancestry, and those of Dutch. In the *City Directory* of 1872-73, for instance, we find this sparkling array of names: Petmecky, Paggi, Palm, Pulaski, Millican, Lundberg, Klappenbach, McCleland, Abrahams, Swenson, Bahn, Anderson, Amsler, Smith, Ryan, and De Cordova.[36] If you just read those names in a newspaper at the time, you might think you were in New York, Chicago, Philadelphia, or Cleveland. But this was Austin, and the ethnic flesh melted here just about as well as in those other places – if not better.

Austin also had a mix of people of different religious origins, and the community of the early settlers had places of worship of many different faiths. The first census in the community was conducted in January 1840. Among the almost 900 residents at the time, there were a goodly number of "professors of religion," 73 to be precise, among whom one could count Methodists, Presbyterians, Cumberland Presbyterians, Episcopalians, Baptists, and a sizable group of Roman Catholics.[37] By 1882, forty years later, there was a somewhat more colorful display of denominations in the community: Episcopalians, Presbyterians, Methodists, Swedish Methodists, Roman Catholics, and Methodist Episcopalians. Of course, there also were the "colored" churches, including the Fontaine Baptist, the Third Baptist, and the Austin Methodist Episcopal Church. And a synagogue was under construction. In 1885, it opened its doors to Austin as Congregation Beth Israel, complete with a rabbi.[38] In fact, a few of the most wealthy and prominent Austinites in the nineteenth century were Jews. The brothers Phineas De Cordova and Jacob De Cordova (a famous and powerful businessman who held and sold large quantities of land in central Texas), were Jewish, as were Henry and Morris Hirschfeld, German immigrants, who helped to found the

Austin National Bank in 1890.

The settlers, or pioneers, in this frontier town, then, were as diverse as the land around them. They came to America, and to this place, from a host of different backgrounds. These differences, as far as one can tell, did not produce a host of major diversions in the community itself.

The key social and economic differences were those between the settlers and the Indians and between "coloreds" and whites. Eventually they would be supplemented by those between the browns and whites. Otherwise there were no deep and substantial barriers among ethnic communities, such as grew up in the great metropolises of the North. Every white settler possessed an equal opportunity for success, depending on his or her skills and initiative. That which seemed to mark the successful frontiersman, whether farmer or merchant, on the edges of civilization, was, in fact, industry and thrift. Often, in the accounts of the earlier settlers, found in places like Fredericksburg, industry and thrift are singled out as among the principal virtues of the settler.[39] This must also have been the case in Austin. These early pioneers, it is reported, were people who prized not only individual initiative, but also contribution to the betterment of the community as a whole. Both Frank Brown, chronicler of Austin, and descendants of the early settlers in New Braunfels and Fredericksburg report that a pattern of individual initiative and willing contribution to the betterment of the whole community spontaneously arose among early residents. In Austin, as other towns on these frontiers, Brown writes, "[a] failure to ask a neighbor to a raising, a chopping frolic, a quilting, or other entertainment, was an indignity that required explanation. All were not only willing, but anxious, to contribute something to the general comfort, and were aggrieved if the opportunity to do so were withheld. This beneficent and unselfish disposition was the charm of a new community, and is yet witnessed on many rural places in country districts."[40]

The sense of a whole community, in the midst of religious and social diversity, is possible perhaps only in places that were as small numerically as Austin, Seguin, Manor, Castell, Fredericksburg, or Llano. More than that, however, the integrity is the obverse of the defeat of the Indians and Mexicans, the subjugation of the blacks, and the conquest of nature. For, as sociologists tell us, a sense of brotherhood, of oneness, often springs from battles carried on with a common enemy.[41] And there were many common enemies, both known and unknown, conscious and unconscious, found in Austin. The victory of the settlers meant, in particular, a growing sense of loyalty to the whole community, a sense of patriotism, as Frank Brown calls it, that often took priority over the differences that lay just beneath the surface. When the war with the Germans broke out in the early twentieth century, this spelled some trouble for the Germans in Austin. But the troubles were never enough to create a fracture in the town deep enough to render this sense of going-it-together fragile and impermanent.

No story of the life of early Austin would be complete without recounting some of the more colorful features that stand out in the memories of early Austin residents. These events represent the highlights for the community, the times of celebration and joy, the moments when attention could be turned from the chores of the day to companionship with friends or just plain entertainment. Among them were the circuses that came to town, to amuse young children and provide a day out. For many, the circuses were the chief amusement during the year. Schools were closed, and many people shut down business.[42] Horse races were held on some of the major thoroughfares, then, of course unpaved. On First Street in Austin, which runs along the shores of the Colorado, they held horse races. On Congress Avenue, the main thoroughfare of the city, leading up to the Capitol building, they held big parades of the various animals and circus performers. Max Bickler remembered the time when they had a parade, with the men carrying balloons, and a wagon got loose on Congress Avenue:

The most outstanding thing in the parade was when the old fellows were coming along selling balloons, and some of the boys enjoyed taking a rubber band and a pin and shooting those balloons, and one of those bent pins or a small staple missed and just then the big Bengal Tiger cage was coming around the corner and this pin or staple hit one of those animals and he jumped and growled and started jumping from side to side in his cage, and that scared the four horses to the animal wagon and two men always rode up on the driver's seat, and the driver was trying to hold his horses in and they began dashing up Congress Avenue and he put his brakes on but he just couldn't hold them and the man sitting with him couldn't hold them, and finally he was able to turn them in there in front of the Avenue Hotel against the sidewalk, and they bent one of those old iron gallery posts.[43]

Edna Besserer Kuse, granddaughter of Augustus and Mrs. Scholz, remembered the circuses equally vividly, as well as the vaudeville performers who showed their talents in the area of Austin known as Hyde Park, located adjacent to the university. Where rows of small houses and new condominiums, homes to many university faculty and students, now stand, they put on dances in a pavilion, with large bands that came to Austin from other parts. And they had rowboats that could be taken out by young men and ladies and rowed across a small lake in the area. On circus day, too, Charlie Morrison recalled, they held special shows in the Hancock Opera House, with various performers who treated the audience to special skits and routines. The performers, Morrison remembered well, had regular routines of jesting with young boys and girls, while up in the peanut gallery, in the upper decks, even younger boys would toss things on the stage at the sight of a bad skit.[44] Today, of course, it is easier: we can simply change channels.

Besides the circuses, there were the regular medicine shows that dotted the main streets of Austin, particularly Congress Avenue. These various healers of all sorts of ailments would come into town, proclaiming they had a cure for whatever ailed the local residents. Sometimes they performed their magical acts in public. Some medicine men served as dentists, for example. Without the aid of any anaesthetic, operating from their wagons decorated with pictures of their deeds and other wild paraphernalia, they would relieve the patient's malady. Seating the patient in a chair, the dentist would pull forth some God-awful prongs, fit to change the sex of horses, and then quickly remove the diseased tooth, nerve and all. Such men became, for young residents, as much a mark of the times as the circuses, the concerts, or the horse races.

Austin was not the site of major cultural events then, nor is it even now in the eyes of many residents newly arrived from the great cultural metropolises like New York and Boston. But every now and then major celebrities would make it through the town, to put on special performances and provide a small bit of enlightenment to those in the hinterlands. Carl Widen remembered the time when the "great Sarah Bernhardt" made her way to Austin, as part of a nationwide tour. Although old and "decrepit" by the time she first made the Austin cultural scene, in 1905, she left a definite impression on her audience. She performed in the role of Camille, heavily made up to appear as a young girl in her teens. She had to struggle vainly just to keep her body upright. But when the curtain rose, she reached out for the stagelights as plants turn to the sun. Her French, Morrison was sure, could not be understood by most of those in attendance. And yet she "held the audience so spellbound that no one left before it was over." [45]

Gamblers and horse traders also occupied the streets of Austin, as in Laredo and other towns in the West. They were testimony to the new land, and lawlessness, that grew up on the frontier. The horse traders trafficked in horses they had stolen from ranches near Austin. In 1962, Oswald Wolf recalled that the big business of the horse traders would take place in the fall, after the harvest. "I remember," he said, "how those horse traders would doctor those horses by filing their teeth, and also they would color their gray hair." [46] And in Austin there were several memorable gamblers in those times. There was John Allen, who got a reputation in the various bars and saloons in the city. And then there was the gambler Ben Thompson, perhaps the most memorable of all.

Thompson was unusual, or perhaps common, because before he became the renowned gambler in the community he was the city marshal. In this capacity, he left his mark on the city by driving out a group of cowboys who rode into town. Coming down Congress Avenue, just over the main bridge that ran over the Colorado and connected the city to the hills and trees on the other side, the cowboys began to shoot up the town and to scare the local residents. Like the mavericks so often and so well depicted in the great epic Westerns, like those who came after Gary Cooper in *High Noon*, these men rode roughshod along the main thoroughfare, shooting into businesses and destroying some of the globes covering the gaslights on the streets. Thompson heard of the ruckus and quickly went out to settle things down. Stopping the leaders of the band near the Congress Avenue Bridge, he asked them what they were doing. "We're playing Ben Thompson," Max Bickler reports their answer. "Thompson said, 'Well you can't play Ben Thompson. I'm Ben Thompson, hand over your guns and when they found out he really was Ben Thompson, they handed over their guns and he took them all up to city jail and locked them up over night, and the next morning he turned them loose and told them to get on back over the bridge and stay out of the city.[47]

When Thompson turned outlaw, he became infamous. He not only gambled in the local saloons, but he was given to frequent revelry himself. One day, Bickler recalled, Thompson had been gambling in the Iron Front Saloon, between Sixth and Seventh streets on Congress Avenue. (Incidentally, today at the same location there is a great skyscraper, known as One American Center, which houses gunslingers of a different type.) Thompson started to shoot his guns. We do not know whether he had lost or won the game. Fearing for their lives, people began to scatter, racing for shelter. Jacob Bickler heard the fuss, wondered what it was all about, and walked down to the Iron Front Saloon. Warned against doing so by others, he took the sidewalk by the front doors of the saloon, just as Thompson and friends were leaving. Thompson, Max Bickler remembered, said "howdy do" to his father and motioned to him to continue down the street. "Father walked on," Bickler recalled, "and Ben came on out and everything was quiet, and people wanted to know why Ben respected my father so, and Ben told them 'My boy goes to Professor Bickler's school, Ben Jr.'"[48] Later on, when Thompson got into trouble in San Antonio, he was sent to jail. From there he wrote to Jacob Bickler, apologizing for his misdeeds. "'Dear Professor,'" Max Bickler remembered the card to his father saying, "'I am very sorry that I'm in trouble again and I hope my Son Ben does not take after me. Please take care of Ben, and give him a good education. . . .'"[49]

Besides the traffic in purloined coins and stolen horses, there was traffic in Austin in the oldest profession of all. Not to be denied access to the lust of the frontier, a host of belles and madames came to line the streets of Austin, giving rise to a famous red light district, as memorable as anything else of the late nineteenth century. Carl Widen remembered something of these women and their wares, recalling that the "landladies" would make frequent trips to Kansas City to recruit new belles. With their fresh troops in tow, carriages of madames and young ladies would drive up and down Congress Avenue, outside the major business establishments and the saloons, "displaying the wares that had just arrived."

The women became the source of great pleasure and amusement for the students at the fledgling university as well. Long before panty raids and the fear of herpes, new students would be initiated to sexual pleasures, in special rooms called Llano or Marble Falls. The members of the University Glee Club often made forays down into the heart of the district, serenading the young ladies until they came out onto the balconies, dressed in their nighties and reveling in the attention of the young men. And, occasionally, new or enthusiastic members of the Glee Club received their first initiation into the perils of lust from these young women, through the trickery of their fellow students.[50]

Max Bickler, too, remembered well the red light district, and the famous ladies of the night. Georgia Frazer, Dixie Yarnell, Pearl Yoe, and Blanche Dumont were names that graced the lovely and bountiful features of these women. And Bickler, too, recalled the paths that the carriages of these ladies made as they ran up and down, back and forth, the dusty wheel tracks of Congress Avenue. The parades were a regular treat for the community, at least for the men, and many would gather to watch the parades, much as they assembled at other times, children in hand, to attend the circuses.

Bickler amusingly recalled that the carriages "usually had two seats, and had a driver, and they would go north on one of the back streets and then come down Congress Avenue with all their frills and furbelows on, and of course all of the men stood on the edge of the sidewalk, watching the parade and women would only look out of the corner of their eye and go on down the street, because they knew that that was the red light parade."[51] Other people who grew up in Austin in the late nineteenth and early twentieth centuries remembered even more impressive facts about these young women, among them the fact that some of the women married into the most notable and prominent families. But no one knew the family names, or, if they did, they managed to forget them.

There were other places, larger, older, and more civilized in other respects, in the nineteenth century where many of the same colorful events and episodes took place as in Austin. The difference perhaps is that in Austin these things stood out more vividly because the town was smaller and less well established. When the city marshal turns from lawman to outlaw, and becomes famous for it, you have to be in a frontier town. Laws had to be created, or at least a sense of lawfulness, where none had previously been. Business and government had not yet been fully established, at least to the extent of the host of regulations we know today. There was a tolerance for outlaws and for the ladies of the night, and a fascination, too. They provided relief when little other relief existed. And their very presence ultimately helped to define the nature of law; and, as in the case of the horse thieves, who stole horses from the ranges on which they still grazed, they brought into existence such notable institutions as the Texas Rangers. But Ben Thompson may well remain as the prototype of some of these early frontiersmen. He showed that the line between lawfulness and lawlessness was a very thin one, and yet to be clearly defined and sharply drawn, here on the border between civilization and wilderness.

There is one more thing to be told about Austin. And that is the story of business here, of what kept men and women and little children alive in the community. Already we know that farming in and around Austin was a common enterprise. Cotton, corn, and rice were among the principal crops grown by farmers. Cattle furnished a major source of livelihood, too, for some of the early residents. Many farms, if not most of them, were not designed to produce income, but simply to furnish the basis for everyday living and subsistence The early pioneers, according to some accounts, lived daily life, and survived with the aid of crops grown on small acreage, a few head of cattle, a dairy cow or two, and perhaps a couple of hogs or sheep. This way of life lasted a long time in and around Austin, so that the community retained its rural flavor. There even is a picture, taken in 1940, that shows a cow roaming fields in what now is known as Lamar Boulevard.

There were other occupations that furnished daily bread and butter for Austin residents. Then, as now, the legal career was a common one for many men. Frank Brown, in one of the last chapters of his *Annals*, covering the year 1874, notes that there were a large number of lawyers in town. There also were a large number of physicians, merchants, who dealt in dry goods and other such items, and dentists. There were barbers, and people who listed their occupations as "boots & shoes," one man Louis de Tejada, who classified himself as a translator, a ferryman, Mr. J. H. Tulk, who took people across the shores of the Colorado, and a notable number of bankers, too. A few people ran bars and saloons.[52] And then there were those men who operated the livery stables, and the wagon yards. Where the railroad tracks cross Congress Avenue, only a block from the Sheraton Crest and across the Colorado from the Hyatt Regency, there once lay wagon yards. Farmers and ranchers would come into town, park their wagons, and go off to shop. Nearby were the livery stables. Oswald Wolf recalled the existence of a livery stable on Fifth and Red River, as well as the fancy George Miller Livery Stable, which lay between the Driskill Hotel and the Capitol grounds.[53] The latter stable was the place where state politicians would rent handsome rigs and hacks, and where young men found princely carriages in which to woo young women.

By 1895, the character of occupations in and around Austin had not changed much. Two banks had been founded only five years earlier, the American National Bank, with George Littlefield as president, and the Austin National Bank, with Edward Wilmot as president. Both of these banks were to become major financial institutions of the community, and major instruments in the push for greater growth. Scarbrough and Hicks, later to become E. H. Scarbrough and Sons, the major department store in downtown Austin for many years until it closed its doors in 1983, was doing business in dry goods at Fifth and Congress Avenue. The Walter Tips Company, whose president, Walter Tips, was also a vice-president of Austin National Bank and would become a leading figure in Austin, was already selling hardware, tools, and wagon parts on Congress Avenue. And the Calcasieu Lumber Company, whose chief officer, William S. Drake, several decades later would serve as mayor of Austin, was providing the ranchers and farmers and homeowners with lumber for their places of residence and work.

Both state government and the university shaped the nature and extent of commerce in the community, though perhaps not so much as today. The discovery of black gold at the Santa Rita site, the key source of the university's economic prosperity, did not happen until 1923, and so the university, and the rest of the community, remained unaware of its riches. Of the two institutions, the state government in the late nineteenth century clearly was the more prominent force. It brought politicians to Austin every year who had to find temporary housing; in the case of many governors and other high officials, they might decide to settle in Austin permanently. The disproportionate number of lawyers among the professions was a fact of state government—many politicians either themselves were, or required the advice of, lawyers. Though nowhere near the number today, some Austin residents also found employment with state government, doing various sorts of clerical and other tasks. For young, and even older, Austin residents, the main benefits to the community of the state government were the regular inaugural balls. These, like circus days, stood out in the memories of early Austinites. Fireworks were shot off at the Capitol grounds, and young boys ran with torches and other paraphernalia.[54] Leading local figures of the community were chosen to arrange the balls; being chosen was a sign of their prominence in the town.

Austin was officially designated as the site for the state university in 1881. But the doors of the university did not open until 1883. A bare handful of 8 teachers made up the faculty, and 218 students entered the first year. The first classes were taught in the temporary Capitol building, erected in 1881 while the present Capitol was being constructed. In 1903, twenty years after it first opened, the university still remained small. Only a few hundred students were in attendance. Tuition then was free; now of course it is still low. Besides the main building, there was University Hall, the gift of George Brackenridge, a regent of the school. Board at the University Hall was $12 a month in 1903, and for an extra $1.50 a student could rent a room as well. The hall could accommodate 120 students, all men. A women's dormitory was nearing completion. It stood west of the Main Building, was four stories high, and cost a total of $75,000 to erect. Plans also were underway for a mechanical and electrical engineering building that would cost on the order of $150,000.[55]

What was absent in Austin, in the way of commerce and business, is as notable as what was present. There were no large manufacturing plants or enterprises, no great steel mills or iron works, no garment industry or woolen factories. There were the banks, the merchant stores, the bars and saloons. There was the Capitol and state business, and the fledgling university. There was the Walter Tips Company and the Calcasieu Lumber Yard. There was the Ice House, which would turn a small profit for Colonel Andrew Zilker later in the twentieth century. But there was no growing working class in Austin. This was an important fact of life here then, though unions would locate their statewide headquarters here. No great political movement could organize on the basis of the oppression of the workers because there were no workers, in the sense of the industrial heartlands of the country, of New York, of Philadelphia, of Chicago.

If there were overclasses in Austin, the rich, they were the bankers, but there were not many of them. There were, or there soon would be, those who dealt in commodities. Outside Austin, one could also find people who held large acreage in ranches, as in the case of S. M. Swenson, who owned over 100,000 acres of land in Travis County, on which he kept many head of cattle.[56] And if there were under-classes in Austin, or nearby, they consisted of the blacks who worked as cotton-pickers, or at some other tasks as slaves. They also included blacks and browns who worked as servants, helping around houses with yards, taking care of children, or carrying out the trash and doing other odd jobs for businesses in the community, or working as bootblacks or barbers' assistants. They lived in the same sections of town, in Clarksville and Wheatsville. But, for whatever reasons, they were then disinclined, except on rare occasions, to give vent to what-ever discontent they may have experienced. Besides, no one showed up to remind them they were unhappy, save for rare visits, like that of John Shillady, an official of the National Association for the Ad-vancement of Colored People. But he was driven out of town.

Austin, by the end of the nineteenth century, was a town just beginning to take shape as a small city. It numbered only something under 25,000 residents in 1900. It lay on the outskirts of American civilization. And it contained all those people and activities charac-teristic of the fringes – the rare visits of important personages, the circuses that were the main source of frolicking every year, the quack doctors who came to town to cure uncertain illnesses, and the gun-slingers who made their own law. It housed the state government, but that was no deterrent to the outlaws. In fact, that was sometimes an attraction. One favorite story tells of the time the state treasury was vanquished by robbers. The poor men unfortunately loaded the loot into their pants' legs. But the pants did not hold up, leaving telltale trails to the whereabouts of the robbers and leading to their eventual capture. Austin was not completely our image of a Western town, like Dodge City, because it also was home to that peculiar insti-tution called slavery. But for many of its residents, the world was open, a place to continue to explore and over which to emerge vic-torious. And it was the sense of conquest, of new worlds to explore, and of final victories to win, that would play a hand in shaping the vision of the community, a vision of growth and expansion, gained by thrift and industry.

2.

To Dream of
a Better Tomorrow

——

Where there is no vision, the people perish.

(Proverbs XXIX, 18)
Walter E. Long
Manager, Austin Chamber of Commerce
1915–1949

ON JANUARY 1, 1888, A LENGTHY NEWSPAPER AN-
nouncement appeared in the pages of the *Austin Statesman*, the leading newspaper in Austin. It urged the citizens of Austin to get behind
a project to build dams on the Colorado. Only with such construction, the announcement proclaimed, could the city of Austin hope
to become a better and more progressive community. Only with
dams could the vagaries of nature be halted, and the people gain control over their own destiny. The length and reasoning of this statement must have been unprecedented in the annals of the *Statesman*,
not to say Austin. At first glance, the declaration could have passed
as a founding document, as a vision for the future of Austin. And
that is precisely what the statement would become with the passage
of time. Those several paragraphs in the *Statesman* provided the direction and purpose that seemed to have been lacking in this small community astride the Colorado. The announcement called for a dam,
and within five years the first major dam in Austin would be built.
It called for growth and industry, developed through the capacity of
dams, and over the next fifty years, at least, growth and industry
would become the collective credo, the vision, and the goal of the
hamlet called Austin. The life and direction of few communities,

perhaps, can be as clearly and directly tied to a dream; in Austin a dream had as much to do with the making of the community as any human work, or the politics of the power-grabbers.

This chapter discusses the author of that statement, Alexander P. Wooldridge, his background and his great service on behalf of the community of Austin. The chapter then considers the details of the dream itself, of what Wooldridge hoped Austin could achieve if it were to implement his designs for a dam. The statement was, and became, a moral blueprint for lifting the community up and forward into the future: it was almost a utopian design and was conveyed with the same sort of moral conviction and religious fervor that passionate zealots routinely employ. Finally, the end of the chapter shows how the dream became a collective vision of and by the community. More than thirty, forty, even fifty years after it first was articulated, the very same themes appeared again and again in the printed pages of Austin papers: it truly had become a dream not only *for* Austin but *of* Austin.

To understand Alexander Wooldridge, and his dream for a better Austin, we must realize that his urban aspirations were part of a phenomenon that was sweeping many frontier towns in late nineteenth century America. Whatever the particular sources that inspired Wooldridge, there were other visions and visionaries across America whose ambitions rivaled those Wooldridge held for Austin. Writing of the frontier urban areas of nineteenth-century America, Howard Chudacoff, an urban historian, has noted the prominent booster spirit that pervaded the rhetoric of many such places.[1] Chudacoff, like historians such as Richard Wade, has found that such urban centers as Chicago and St. Louis, each of them latecomers to the metropolitan arena, were involved in intense and pitched struggles to become the biggest and best they could be. In Texas, the struggle was something like the one that took place between Galveston and Houston, which the latter city won hands down, once the river channel was completed.[2] Every urban town or village of the West, every center of some size that lay west of the Mississippi, wanted to be the next Athens, or the next Rome, or the next Paris. Each one strived to make itself a great center of civilization, its citizens seeking to emulate the riches and the long, storied past of those great metropolises in Europe. Moreover, in every one of these places there were certain citizens who took it upon themselves to help foster and create such a spirit. In Cincinnati, for instance, it was Dr. Daniel Drake who tried to do so, to make a great center of the area.[3] There were even prophets of the nineteenth century, something of a cross between an evangelist and a city planner, who made a name for themselves by spinning great prophesies of the future of America in terms of the growth of great civilization.

Thomas Gilpin was one such person. Gilpin grew up in Pennsylvania, then moved west to Missouri. In the mid-nineteenth century, he developed a theory about the location of the great cities of the world. Borrowing from the ideas of the German geographer Alexander von Humboldt, he claimed that great cities develop at the Axis of Intensity, a broad band that stretched, he said, across the midsection of the United States. He argued with great conviction that a place such as Independence, Missouri, would become a great center for civilization because of its location within this broad band and its other favorable characteristics.

> The peculiar configuration of the continent and its rivers and plains made these [Independence and St. Louis] *two* natural *focal* points. This will not be interfered with by the railroads or any other public works which may be constructed by the arts, as these latter are successful and permanent only when they conform with the water grades of nature and the natural laws which condense society.[4]

Of course, no such city ever arose. But Gilpin's was a compelling dream, no different from those of dreamers in other urban centers, save that it did not materialize.[5]

Many of the people who spun fantasies and urged growth in electric rhetoric stood to gain profit for themselves from the expansion of urban centers. With the growth of the city, with the creation of new trade routes or the enlargement of the industrial base of the center, some boosters believed there would come an inevitable expansion of business and profit. New markets, new consumers, greater profits were the watchword of the nineteenth-century urban developers. Yet, it would be a mistake, I believe, to hold fast to the notion that it was only markets and the pocketbook that drove the most vigorous of these promoters of an urban paradise. It was more than merely markets, at least for many of them. Chudacoff, for instance, writes of Ogden of Chicago and Drake of Cincinnati, noting that while good business was on their minds, their preoccupations seemed to be more than simply business *per se*.[6] There was something of a spirit, an aspiration, a dream, and a dedication to the place where they lived. It was for them more than land and water: it was their territory, their community, their home.

Austin, late in the nineteenth and early in the twentieth centuries, fostered much the same drive and ambition among people. Individuals in Austin sought to make it a great center, of education and of government. Designs were held in the mind's eye about what Austin would look like in the future. Moreover, because Austin lay at the edges of the world, its residents truly believed they could build a new empire, a new physical and social creation that would come to rival those of the great European capitals. This sense of being able to shape the world to one's own designs and plans was a large part of what stimulated early Austinites to remake the world. It is notable, for instance, that early in this century some people talked at length about how they wanted to make Austin a bigger and better place. At a Chamber of Commerce meeting, held on July 15, 1914, the minutes attest to the combative civic spirit flowering in Austin:

> [General Lightfoot] explained that perhaps few cities possess natural advantages as Austin did and he was of the opinion that this city had not progressed as fast as others which might be due largely to the fact that we were content to rest upon natural advantages. He spoke of the necessity for industrial development and for the heartiest support of the University of Texas. He dwelt upon mineral water that is bountiful in and around the city and also spoke of the contemplated development of the Bull Creek and Lake Austin property, and said if he got the people of Austin to cooperate in this movement he would be glad to do everything possible to develop it to its fullest extent. . . . [He] said . . . [it] was necessary . . . [to] *encourage home industries to get together and pull together and win*. . . . (my emphasis)[7]

After the speech of General Lightfoot, General W. H. Stacy arose and "said he was thoroughly imbued with the idea that Austin needed the boosters' spirit." "He felt," the minutes continue, "that this was necessary in order to insure success and he regarded the duty of all good loyal citizens of Austin to get behind any proposition that meant the up-building of the city."[8]

In Austin people wanted to make this place livable. This meant that a way had to be devised to prevent the great floods that overtook the community at regular intervals. And a way also had to be invented to make the land furnish people with a good and steady living. Water, land, and the accoutrements of a great urban center soon became the preoccupation of many residents of Austin; and a dream of growth became the driving force for many of those whose lives became intertwined with that of the community.

In late nineteenth century Austin, there were a number of prominent people and families. The names of Littlefield, Pease, Wroe, Goeth, Tips, and Scarbrough, among others, remind one of the leading figures, the bankers, and the few merchants who left their mark on Austin. The most prominent of these men and women was the lawyer and banker Alexander Penn Wooldridge. Today in Austin there is a park, a square in the downtown area, bordered on one side by the public library and on the other by the Travis County Courthouse, that is named for Wooldridge. There is also a Wooldridge Drive in Austin. And there is a Wooldridge School that serves as a further testimony to his residence, and activity, here.

Wooldridge was not a native of Austin. He had grown up in Kentucky and Louisiana, and for a short time was reared in New Haven, Connecticut, in preparation for attending Yale College. His father had been a minister as well as state engineer of Louisiana and was compelled by economic need to leave home for a time and to abandon the rearing of his six children to his wife. Young Wooldridge was taught to be a most conscientious and responsible lad and came to possess a stern and rigorous sense of moral rectitude, no doubt the result of his father's beliefs but also of his own education. He attended the University of Virginia, graduating with honors in moral philosophy and political economy. Afterwards he became a teacher of applied science at Bethel College in Kentucky. In 1872, he decided to move to Austin and after just one year's time was able to pass the state bar examination. For ten years, he served in the town as a lawyer, then turned to banking, which he pursued for a period of twenty years, until 1905. For the rest of his life, he remained very active in the social and civic affairs of Austin. In all these things he became extremely successful. As a banker, for instance, he not only acquired wealth, but also served for a time as president of the Texas Bankers Association.[9]

Wooldridge became the first of Austin's *urban entrepreneurs*. His life seemed to be given over to public service, and, in particular, to making Austin into a bigger and better place. He became inextricably bound to the fates and fortunes of Austin, and its success was very much his success. He pushed to have Austin take control of its own power plant, and in this regard he achieved victory. Austin, in fact, became the very first municipality in Texas to control the supply of its own electricity. Wooldridge led the effort to establish the first system of free public schools in Austin, and for a time he served as the president of the local school board. He spearheaded a drive to establish a public library in the community, and that project, too, came into being. And, from 1909, shortly after his retirement from business, to 1919, he served as the mayor of the community. During this time, a number of actions were taken that served to implement Wooldridge's ambitions for Austin. Congress Avenue was paved; the number of parks in the city increased; and to the great disappointment of many citizens, the red light district in downtown Austin was eliminated.

Wooldridge was important to the construction of modern Austin in the same sense that other heroic figures are important. He held a vision of what could be, and he worked steadily and hard on behalf of that vision. He saw himself as something of a self-chosen builder of a new world, here in the territory between wilderness and civilization. "I think it is not unbecoming to say that with me municipal administration is a profession," he once wrote, "as law, medicine, and teaching are professions to those who follow them, and I hope if continued in office, I shall continue to be increasingly useful to my people."[10] But in his role as an urban entrepreneur of Austin, Wooldridge was more than simply a builder of physical monuments. He became the standard-bearer in Austin of the curious mix of Christian morality and modern capitalism, what the distinguished anthropologist Anthony F. C. Wallace has termed "Christian capitalism."[11] He blended a stern sense of public morality and responsibility with a sense of good business. His drive to establish greater commerce and industry in Austin testified to his good head for business; his successful effort to outlaw prostitution is witness to victory in establishing a sense of strong public morality in the community. Like the crusaders of many centuries earlier, Wooldridge helped to convert a town in which lawlessness was common – and Ben Thompson stood as only one among many people on Congress Avenue to prove that – into a representative of the modern code of morality.

And like the earlier crusaders, too, Wooldridge's campaign made not only for good religion, but for good business, too. His greatest achievement, however, was to articulate the dream for Austin itself, a dream that many other people would work hard to fulfill.

What were the tenets of the Wooldridge dream, his vision of a better tomorrow? The reader will forgive me, I hope, but I want to go through some of the major points of Wooldridge's statement of January 1, 1888, and to highlight their features. What you will see, I believe, is not merely a statement about a dam, but a moral appeal to the citizens of Austin. Eventually it would be both the vision of a dam and the moral convictions of the dream that turned the vision from one of tomorrow into one of today.

First and foremost, the Wooldridge announcement in the *Statesman* speaks of the future, of planning for a better day tomorrow. This future is painted as superior to the past, and therefore it furnishes the incentive, the purpose, to doing certain things today, and thereby investing in a more prosperous tomorrow:

> . . . some will say this is all very pretty, but it reads of the
> future, and not the present; and what is wanted is something
> immediate, something now. Well, admitting this to be partly
> true, ought not every thoughtful and intelligent people to con-
> sider the future as well as the present? For after all, is it not
> the future of Austin, and that alone, which disturbs us? We
> could endure the darkness of the hour if we clearly say daylight
> ahead; and then, this is no more a matter of the future than
> would necessarily be the case with any other scheme for the
> public benefit.[12]

Notice how Wooldridge has cast the present as a time of darkness, and the future as a time of daylight. In the best tradition of moral zealots, he wants to make it seem that with industry and hard work in the future the citizens of Austin will be able to emerge from the Dark Ages into the modern era, into civilization—or, as in Plato's terms, out of the cave into the bright sunlight of the mountain peaks.

As with every good dream, this one goes on to detail the problems of the present, to show, in a fashion, what evil lurks in the hearts and minds of men. Almost as though he were a great Christian prophet coming among the infidels of the world, Wooldridge speaks of human weaknesses:

> . . . I assume that our community, as a whole, is a poor one, and, generally speaking, becoming poorer every day, and that, therefore, any large enterprise looking to the public good must and ought to be the accomplishment of the public, not of individuals. . . .[13]

Wooldridge becomes even more emphatic and critical of the mass of citizens toward the end of his argument:

> To all of the above, I can conceive many objections to be raised, such as the natural difficulty of the thing, owing to the topography of the country above Austin; the necessity of an amendment to the charter to bring the matter legally before the people; the costliness of the scheme, and last and most serious, the great indifference and lack of enterprise of our people. I have considered all of these objections, and all, except the last, are easily overcome; but the last is a serious difficulty, and there is no mistake about it, for with many of us parsimony goes by the name of prudence, and lack of public spirit is justified under the title of conservatism. Yes, to the weak and timid all things are truly impossible, and to them there is always a lion in the way; but I venture to believe that this lion must be scared from off the path if this town ever desires to advance to success and prosperity.[14]

The argument thus notes the failings of the people, but claims that they can be overcome, though to do so will cause considerable strain. To rid people of their natural sloth and indifference, obviously, will be a heavy task, but one well worth the final rewards.

The future will be ours, and happy, and full, Wooldridge goes on to claim, only so long as we, the citizens of Austin, get behind the construction of a dam on the Colorado. Wooldridge takes the notion of a dam—no specific one because nobody in the community had a sense of what one might look like—and makes it into the material symbol of the community's efforts. To erect a dam, just as to pray to a certain rock, or to conceive an individual as the representation of salvation, will provide for the glory and relief of Austin. Wooldridge goes on to suggest some of the details of the construction of the dam:

Have a complete survey made of the river and the adjacent country to such a proper point above the city as to afford the most suitable site for a dam. I believe such a site is to be found at Bull Creek Falls, or it may be at the Mormon Falls. After a site is selected, a careful estimate of expenses could be made for the dam and a canal leading to and below the city. . . . From this dam construct a ditch or canal to the upper sources of Shoal Creek. It will, I think, be found that such a construction is entirely practicable, and that the mountain's side, instead of being an obstacle, would be an advantage in affording the ready-made rock work out of which the Austin aqueduct, for most of its distance, could be cut. . . .[15]

At least partly because of the vigor with which he pursued his vision, and partly because of the evident dangers of the Colorado itself – it periodically ravaged portions of the community with damaging floods – an Austin dam would become the preoccupation of civic leaders over the next half century. Wooldridge's dream had linked future happiness to a dam, and only its erection would help to lift Austin from the depths of its indifference. Not only water power but community power obviously would spring forth from such a structure.

Every dream, it seems, is not only critical of the present moment, but also promises rewards just down the road. The Wooldridge dream promised wealth, in the form of manufacturing, capital aplenty, and other material promise for the public good:

[There will be] general public profit and advantage.

First, from irrigation. The immediate result of this would be the rapid and great enhancement of value of all land below the city suited to the purpose, and the large and certain increase of the crops grown therefrom. Next, the establishment of packeries, canning establishments for fruits and vegetables, and all the export business resulting from this line of trade. Next, the employment of labor, skilled and unskilled, in the various occupations growing out of irrigation, and the business thence resulting. Next, improved railway facilities for transporting our commodities.

Second, from manufactures. The offer of free water power for, say, ten years, to capitalists who would establish enterprises

of a given minimum capital, say \$100,000 — would bring manu-
factories — why? Simply because it has never failed to do so
elsewhere — when, as with us, the conditions of raw material,
labor, consumption, and transportation, are also present. . . .[16]

And now the document sets forth, in glowing terms, the pot that lies
at the end of the rainbow:

> Why, all the blessing and advantages — too manifold to mention
> — which just such a prostrated community as this requires, and
> which, and which alone, this community absolutely must have
> to enjoy any permanent and great prosperity; and from irriga-
> tion and manufactories combined, what? Why, increased and
> great wealth — general and individual — increased revenue for
> other public duties as you choose, such as street and park
> improvements, sewerage, etc., for, to my mind, the ornamental
> and luxurious should follow, and not precede, the practical and
> the necessary.[17]

In brief, Austin, Wooldridge avers, can move from wilderness to
civilization, from the Dark Ages into the Industrial Age, by creating
a dam. Such a dam will furnish to citizens all the wealth and happiness one presumes they will ever want, or need.

No dream ever comes true without its costs: salvation is never free
of some kind of sacrifice. And the Wooldridge dream for Austin
proves no exception here. What the declaration asks of people is not
simply to stir themselves from their lethargy, but also to be prepared
to pay a price to do so. Austin citizens ultimately would have to bear
at least part of the burden for the cost of the dam, would have to give
up some of their present well-being for greater well-being, happiness,
and, not so incidentally, wealth in the future. Wooldridge thus goes
on to observe that there would be expense involved, but, he insists,
it would be "an amount so inconsiderable that no individual taxpayer's share would equal the present loss of a month's rent upon any
vacant store or dwelling eligibly located in our city."[18] In other
words: citizens, be prepared to sacrifice today for greatness tomorrow!

The Wooldridge dream, finally, is a dream of growth and of prosperity for Austin. With a set of neat phrases, it sets forth the terms
of salvation, and these are the terms of growth and of prosperity.
Consider just these remarks, which capture the flavor of the entire
argument:

But is it [my plan for a dam] feasible? I think it is. I know it would be in some communities, of less conservatism and of more energy and enterprise than seems to characterize us. In any event, we will never know whether it is a practicable thing or not unless we earnestly take hold and examine into its merits and demerits, and then, and not before, decide. The cost of the project would probably be the greatest objection against it. That is simply so, because we have been used to small and not large, ideas, and to little and not to big undertakings. There are dozens of towns in the country that would consider such a canal as I suggest cheap and at twice the price named, and towns no larger and no richer than ours. Experience has taught them that it is wise and a profitable investment which returns five or tenfold the original outlay, and our people will have to learn to calculate in the same way if they desire to grow and prosper. Experience will teach us it is as bad to die from dry rot as it is from taxation.[19]

Eighteen months later, after little had been done in response to his urgings, Wooldridge felt once again compelled to declare his dreams to the public:

Let us establish factories in our midst and loyally sustain them when we get them, and let Austin as a city inaugurate and carry out a liberal system of public improvements, and our city will grow and prosper as the most hopeful amongst us have never hoped.[20]

The pot at the end of the rainbow, the rainbow cast in the sky above the dam, is a pot filled with golden coins, of growth and of prosperity.

The *Statesman's* pronouncement of Alexander Wooldridge's vision represents as clear a statement of a dream for a better Austin as any that would come to be voiced in the long history of the community. It echoed themes that were playing across American soil in the late nineteenth century, but it put the dream in terms that were suitable to Austin alone. And it provided a framework within which people could think about Austin. This framework, its general outlines and its particular elements, would time and again be voiced in the private councils of Austin and, most significantly, in the public forum, the Austin news media.

The Wooldridge dream turned into a collective vision for Austin. We know that for a fact because in the decade after its first publication the Austin papers time and again talked of a vision of the future, about the undertakings necessary to turn Austin into a more prosperous setting. The papers furnished the device through which the symbols of the Wooldridge dream were intermittently splashed across the consciousness of the citizens.

Consider, for example, the *Austin American-Statesman* of July 9, 1933.[21] Here the Wooldridge dream is made tangible. On the front page of this edition, there is a picture of a lake that would be created by a low water dam straddling the Colorado. There is an article, written by Raymond Brooks, a longtime staff member of the *American-Statesman* who was to become a member of the first Board of Directors of the Colorado River Authority, which speaks of the great beautification that will come to Austin with the development of a dam. The article, like the Wooldridge claim decades earlier, combines the practical with the recreational and notes that the municipal power plant would benefit from a low water dam by harnessing power for cheaper electricity. Growth and progress for the future appear once more as the dominant motifs in an advertisement in the New Year's edition only two years later.[22] Signed by the major business enterprises and firms in Austin, including the Chamber of Commerce and the Capital National Bank, the advertisement proclaims that 1935 "dawns with great hope." Further, it tells of the importance of added growth in the future, noting that "Austin has enjoyed marked expansion of territorial patronage during 1934, for which we are grateful. However, there is still room for still further expansion of our trade into surrounding territory."[23] And it encourages citizens to collaborate in the great tasks of growth and progress ahead: "Better understanding and closer co-operation will assure for Austin in 1935 the greatest growth in history. May not each of us do his or her part in this great family job of united progress."[24]

Six months later, in the pages of the *Austin American*, there appears an editorial that could have been written by Alexander Wooldridge, had he not died five years earlier. Entitled "Why Not Development of Manufactures?" the editorial speaks of an effort on the part of the Austin Chamber of Commerce and Joe Koen to encourage industry, and the harnessing of water power in Austin. "Men of vision," the article claims, "with the backing of brains and money have built cities in deserts. Texas is an agricultural state. There are many agricultural states, but the fact remains that the industrial states of America are the wealthy states, and powerful. Growers of things and developers of mineral wealth are in evidence in Texas. Austin could be made a wonderful industrial city."[25]

Within two years' time, the citizens of Austin and all central Texas were to see the Wooldridge dream come true. In the summer of 1937, dedication ceremonies were held at the Hamilton Dam site, north of Austin, near Burnet. The dam under construction would be named in honor of Congressman James Buchanan, a figure who had done much to see funds procured on behalf of dams over the Colorado. Raymond Brooks once more searches the collective memory of the community for the words to commemorate this day, and he comes up with the symbols straight out the Wooldridge dream: "Vision of the dreamers of half a century ago has come true. Vision of builders has been wrought in steel and concrete. Magnificent Buchanan Dam stands completed, the labor of many hands. It stands, the symbol of man's purpose to harness destructive floods and to turn them [into] beneficial, productive purposes."[26]

But the dam's commemoration did not halt the recurring themes of the Wooldridge vision. Growth and prosperity, while linked to physical monuments, became desirable in and of themselves, a sign of the very movement and progress of the community. A special supplement to the *American-Statesman* of June 5, 1938, proclaims that once again "progress marches onward in Austin," and it displays numbers of pictures showing the building of various new structures.[27] One advertisement in the section pictures the new City Hall, and briefly portrays Austin as "in step with progress," as a "friendly city, a growing city," possessed of a "city government and community marching forward."[28] Echoing the sentiments of decades earlier, when the dreams had first been published, another advertisement declares: "Nothing could have been done to give Austin people greater benefit, individually and collectively, than the completion of this dam. To those whose vision pictured the beauty and usefulness of this project in the long ago, and who never flagged in their zeal for its ultimate completion, Austin owes a debt of gratitude that can never be extinguished."[29] But while the dam would stand as the principal material symbol of the dream, as the cornerstone of the victory of Austin over the elements of nature, other pieces of the vision were extracted and used to plot out additional futures for the community. Thus, the Steck Company, a local office furniture and equipment firm, advertises that "since its growth and progress has been outstanding, we are proud of our city and the part we have had in serving its progress."[30]

At the inception of the next decade, Raymond Brooks looks back over the preceding year and reiterates all the themes of the Wooldridge dream. Beneath a picture of a soldier in military posture, and of two people gazing out over what purports to be modern Austin, a banner reads "then looking into the Future."[31] Brooks' article reads something like a less polished version of the claims made in 1888. He writes, for example, of the marvelous growth of the city: "Austin claims the 1940 United States Census as harbinger of its destiny: a census that recorded its growth from 53,210 to 87,878 in a decade—the fastest growing capital city in the American nation."[32] He goes on to load growth with all the positive attributes accorded it by Wooldridge: "It was gain by inherent strength, a gain which accelerated throughout the period and gave Central Texas the momentum for clear and assured advancement through this 1941 and on into the years of the new decade so auspiciously opened."[33] All the recurrent elements of the dream are here: a bright future; more industry; more population; growth as a symbol of prosperity, advancement, and happiness. Growth, in effect, for growth's sake, and for the material rewards that just so happen to accompany it. Only months later, an advertisement for the Austin National Bank reminds citizens that good banking is also good for the health and the wealth of the community. "Your banks," it reports, "marching forward with the growth of Austin. Marching toward a better Austin . . . they must be in step with the city's progress. Austin banks have records of which they are proud, and their records tell of Austin's growth as well as their own growth."[34] Throughout the decade, the advertisements and the announcements, the proclamations of the dream, continue, albeit at a less rapid rate and with lower frequency than in the previous decade.[35]

Finally, just at the close of the 1940s, the citizens of Austin are reminded that to have a great city requires a great vision. Charles Green, then editor of the *Austin American*, tells readers on November 21, 1948, of the visit by Paul Bagwell, national president of the Junior Chamber of Commerce of the United States. Quoting Bagwell's speech, Green informs his audience that "communities are great, not because of natural resources but because of people with a dynamic point of view."[36] And Green goes on to point to the essentials of the speech, and to the implications they hold for Austin: "It is obvious to Texans who more and more are thinking upon a heritage for the future which could be within the reach of attainment, that the dynamics of prosperous achievement is not a one-man affair for any state or community. It must be a composite, a general spirit, a response of many to the vision and leadership and purpose of those out front; but after all, such a response as to create a general and prevailing spirit."[37]

Six decades after Alexander Wooldridge spoke to his fellow Austinites of a dream for a better future, important public figures were still rallying the citizens to aspire, to dream on, to achieve greatness. People in Austin had dreamt of victories over nature, and with the dams they had achieved them. Today the Colorado—what of tomorrow?

How can we explain the growth of Austin to ourselves? There are so many forms of explanation in vogue today that it becomes next to impossible to figure out which is right. Maybe it is simply new industry, as the economists like to contend—jobs for people. Maybe it is just new forms of investment, as the bankers would like us to believe—money for industry. Maybe it is just more people that constitute growth, as demographers want us to think—higher birth rates, lower death rates. Maybe it is all of them; and yet maybe none of these arguments is quite right. My explanation here in this chapter is quite simple, and different from conventional wisdom. Austin grew in the twentieth century, beginning to expand noticeably by the 1920s, because someone had a dream to make it into a better, not to say bigger, place. If this dream had been that of only a single individual, if it had fallen on blind eyes, the dream would not have become a collective fact—or, as anthropologists like to say, a piece of Austin's culture. But the dream did strike a most responsive chord among the citizens, so much so that its author would become mayor from 1909 to 1919. The dream really enveloped the residents and was reflected in the way they thought of their common life. Perhaps the vision become collective because it was harnessed to a single major project for the community, the creation of a system of dams; still, even with the dams completed, the elements of the dream continued to be publicized, the future of a bigger and more prosperous Austin. And they were sometimes pressed with a zeal that would have embarrassed Elmer Gantry.

A dream of growth for Austin in 1888 was as pure as the driven snow—almost. Today who could or would offer such a dream—what reasonable person? Careful study of the *Austin American-Statesman* today, for instance, will quickly show that there frequently, if not always, is as much sentiment against growth, industry, and prosperity as on their behalf. People seem to have grown weary of such collective visions of prosperity and success over nature, finding the realities they create almost as disagreeable as those they seek to replace. Still, if we who now look back at Austin wish to know why it has grown, then we must remember the dream and how it came to prevail among Austin residents. We need to know that in the midst of the daily drudgery of their lives, toiling away, sometimes at places along the dusty Congress Avenue thoroughfare, some men and women thought about the future, and they decided to rest their hopes on it.

The common dream of a better Austin is only a piece of our story of why Austin grew in the twentieth century. The next one has to do with the prophets of boom, those who helped to implement the dream of modern Austin. And, after that, we shall turn to details of the politics of dam-building, of how the dream became transformed into a reality.

THE
DREAM UNFOLDS

———

3.

The Orchard Planters

—

. . . the admiration of the present and succeeding ages will be ours, since we have not left our power without witness, but have shown it by mighty proofs; and far from needing a Homer for our panegyrist, or others of his craft whose verse might charm for the moment only for the impression which they gave to melt at the touch of fact, we have forced every sea and land to be the highway of our daring, and everywhere, whether for evil or for good, have left imperishable monuments behind us.

Pericles funeral oration
(Thucydides, The Peloponnesian War)

IN EVERY PLACE, IT SEEMS THERE ARE A FEW PEOPLE who give something more to the construction of their community than others do. In the absence of such devotion, it is more than likely that the community itself would never take form, never come alive. I do not intend to suggest that places grow simply on the strength of such figures alone. They do not. History shows that it takes hundreds, thousands, sometimes millions, of people to give birth to new social or communal creations, to give breath to new social worlds. But everywhere, in every case, there are some few individuals on whose shoulders the burdens of new worlds fall. They stand out, perhaps, because of their uncharacteristic strength of purpose and energy, and no less because they also seem to match the needs of the people at the moment. Some such figures appear to lead because they impose their wishes upon an unwilling population. But more often it seems the case, as the great political analyst Antonio Gramsci has found, such figures, even small clusters of people like parties, exercise a voice and a will that effortlessly appears to be the will of the people.[1] Leaders lead, in brief, because they symbolize the people.[2]

In Austin, there were several people who in the early part of this century, but particularly during the 1920s, 1930s, and 1940s, played a central role in the making of this community. Although different in many respects, the essential characteristic they held in common was this: they projected their energies, their *élan vital*, into the community as though the community were but a simple extension of themselves. They are described routinely, in the newspapers, in personal correspondence, and in personal interviews I have conducted, as having had a love affair with the city of Austin. Austin became for them something like a love object, something to which they could turn and give their affection and which, in return, would console, soothe, respect, and coddle them, as they required. About Tom Miller, former mayor of Austin and someone described here, it is said that he seemed to live and to breathe Austin, to be absorbed fully and completely in the life of this place.[3] Miller himself once even commented that "she [Miller's wife, Nellie] claims I've always put the city first. She says with me it's Austin first, then my grandchildren, then the children and her."[4] And of Walter Long, former manager of the Chamber of Commerce for many years, his daughter, Janett L. Fish, told me: "But his [Long's] main interest, his terrific interest, was the future and in development, and he loved Austin."[5] These men and others saw the success of Austin as their own personal success. Austin's progress was their progress. By virtue of their own actions, and its results—the various edifices, the parks, the playgrounds, the new university buildings, the dams and the lakes created therefrom—they came to believe that the movement forward, the dream, was their own, their leap forward. Each of these people was described, furthermore, as possessing a vision, or as being a visionary. Mrs. Jim Tatum, the housekeeper and hostess for Edgar H. Perry, Sr., or Commodore Perry as he often was called, said of him that he seemed to possess a "long vision," and thus that he was a person often consulted by politicians and businesspeople alike.[6] The same also has been said of Long. It would seem that these men came to hold a certain picture in their minds of the future of Austin, and that picture also was a vision of their own future, and what they intended the world to look like after their deaths. *L'état, c'est moi; la cité, c'est moi.*

This chapter, then, depicts several of these figures who played a prominent role in the advancement and expansion of Austin during the first half of the twentieth century. Like their Athenian forbears whom, one must say, they sought to emulate in more than one respect, they hoped by their actions to have left standing monuments to their lives. And they did, in Tom Miller Dam, in the Perry-Brooks Building, in Highland Park, in City Park, in Robert Mueller Airport, and in many other sites. There also are a number of people whose lives played a part in the development of modern Austin that I shall not try to describe here. Men such as Dr. Goodall Wooten, a much beloved and admired physician in the community; Henry and Morris Hirschfeld, described in this Southern town regularly as "the Jewish bankers"; Malcolm H. and Dave Reed, very wealthy business-men, the latter a close associate of Commodore Perry; Colonel Andrew Zilker, a kingpin for several decades; and women such as Mrs. Wooten, wife of Dr. Wooten, a person of considerable grace and charm—all these people were important as well, but not quite in the same fashion or to the same degree. They were prominent in the sense of being admired, or standing high in the hierarchy of local society: they held parties, or were among the most privileged guests on special occasions. But they did not see themselves as the builders, the creators, and, it must be said, the rulers of this place. There were also other figures, such as State Senator Alvin J. Wirtz, Herman Brown, and, of course, Lyndon Baines Johnson. Again, these people, too, were different, in the sense that while their own considerable ambitions for fame and power and fortune often redounded to the benefit of Austin, it was the other figures discussed here who gave of their time and energy, who genuinely through their persistence and dedication helped to make this place, Austin, come alive, and move from its anomalous position, between wilderness and civilization, into something approaching a metropolitan center. Long before the dams were even a gleam in the eye of Herman Brown, or Lyndon Johnson, the men of the Colorado River Association—A. J. Eilers, Long, and others—and, before that, of course, Alexander Penn Wooldridge were busying themselves to determine how to conquer nature, and to control the river and the weather in this part of God's country.

In describing these people, I want to emphasize, I have two purposes in mind. First, in the very act of description of who these men were and what they did, I shall be furnishing a part of the explanation of the growth and change that have come to Austin over the

past half century or so of its development. These men were instrumental in producing those changes, in the manner of their own
work, in their own personal styles and energies. But second, by
describing them, with some detail and attention to their character,
it will be seen, I hope, how they stand out in comparison to those
men and women of Austin, or any other community like it, today.
For what we find out, on close study, is that these people of the past,
whether capitalists or idealists, gave a good deal of their "blood, sweat
and tears" to the life of Austin, making their lives into its life. Often,
in the interviews I have done, I have heard it said, for example, that
Mayor Miller was the best mayor this town has ever had; or if they
only had someone around today like Commodore Perry, someone
who could act as a benefactor for the growth of Austin. I do not
believe such thoughts are mere nostalgia on the part of people who
yearn for a happier and a simpler time. No. The sense of loyalty, of
devotion, of serving in the role of urban entrepreneur, has, it seems,
pretty much disappeared from today's landscape of Austin in the
1980s. Why, it is not clear. But surely it is no longer so visibly with us.

I would very much like to have met Walter E. Long, more so than
many other people. He was a very interesting person, full of opinions
and complex ideas, and driven by an enormous energy and vitality.
You probably have met people like him. They seem to be the sort
whose bodies barely can survive the assaults of their vigorous minds
and personalities, whose skins can barely contain their energy, whose
brains seem to bubble over constantly with fresh ideas and thoughts.
Two or three days before he died at the age of eighty-seven in 1972,
his son, Walter K., vividly recalls, Long was up in bed, still talking
about things he wanted to do and outlining five or six projects he had
in mind to complete.[7] A bright and energetic man, Walter Long
gave much of this vitality to his vision, and to the growth of modern
Austin.
    Like a number of other figures who helped to construct this com-
munity, Long grew up on a farm, in Ladonia, Texas. He did not come
from wealthy financial circumstances, but it appears to have been a
setting in which he learned to work hard, and in which work garnered considerable respect. In one of several autobiographies he
wrote, Long remembers the hours he spent working on the farm, and
the small amount of money both he and his father secured for their
efforts. The eggs they collected on the farm sold for 5¢ to 8¢ a dozen,

the frying chickens sold at seven for $1.00, and his father managed to sell cotton bales at 4¢ to 5¢ a pound.[8] With the aid of money given him by his father, he managed to attend Austin College in Sherman, Texas, where he gained a master's degree in economics, and then came to the city of Austin to attend law school at the university.

During his first few years here, he kept himself alive by serving as a statistician for the State Department of Agriculture.[9] He graduated in the class of 1914, among a group of men who went on to achieve considerable wealth and fame, among them some top corporate lawyers for oil companies such as Humble Oil. His daughter, Janett L. Fish, has told me that if her father had decided to go into private law practice, rather than to devote his energies to the development of Austin, it is likely he would have become a wealthy man.[10] As it was, Long did achieve a very comfortable standard of living. He began the Texas Legislative Service in 1925, and continued to run it until he was eighty years old. At that time, he turned its operation over to his son-in-law, Russell Fish, in 1965. This is a business that keeps a record of the bills that come before the State Legislature and that daily sends out a newsletter to its thousands of subscribers, keeping them abreast of the prospects of bills and their course through the legislative process. But Walter Long reserved the greatest of his energies and commitments for Austin.

The story of Long is as much the story of the Austin Chamber of Commerce as it is of his own life. For many people, he and the Chamber of Commerce were one and the same being, one and the same institution. In 1914, the chamber, formerly the Board of Trade, was looking for a person who would assume the task of serving as its manager, someone who would run the chamber on a daily basis, serve as its secretary, and take an active and overall role in charting its direction. There was some concern voiced at the time that Austin was going nowhere, at least in terms of its business prospects. Mayor Wooldridge was one among many people who articulated this worry in public. Statistics on the size of the population bear this out. In 1910, the population of Austin was 29,860; and by 1920, it had increased little more, to 34,876. Clearly the community needed some sort of injection of vigor and fresh juices. And the chamber was seen as one, if not the principal, vehicle through which Austin might move forward. Three men were interviewed for its position as manager. Each man left a very favorable impression on his audience.

But Walter Long, who was serving as the assistant manager of the San Antonio Chamber of Commerce at the time, was selected unanimously to serve as the new manager of the group. He would retain this position for the next thirty-five years.

The chamber always seems to have played a leading role in the growth of Austin, and it continues to do so today. Its industrial bureau, for instance, has served as a publicist, sometimes a very aggressive one, for the community, and it has gone out of its way to secure new industry. In the early decades of this century, the chamber was the organization through which cooperation was sought among the bankers, the cotton brokers, and the other merchants, the way of achieving some agreement on how to create greater business prosperity. It helped to get people to pick cotton, in and around Austin, working to bring pickers from south Texas to these parts. It took an active interest, too, in the public cotton market, and its directors were much pleased with the success of the new technology for handling cotton, such as the public scales.[11] The chamber served as the forum for a discussion in 1928 about the prospects of securing a cotton mill in Austin, an idea originally proposed by Wooldridge.

Toward the end of the 1920s, the chamber also promoted a campaign in Austin for the patronage of locally owned stores rather than the new chain stores that were sprouting up across the country. There was, in fact, a good deal of concern among the businesspeople of the community that the chain stores posed a serious and dangerous threat to local business. At its meeting of March 6, 1928, the directors spoke at length about how to increase buying at local businesses. The machinations of the chamber are revealed through this discussion: its directors discussed the amount of money needed on behalf of a campaign to encourage patronage of local stores and insisted that a word-of-mouth campaign occur through the efforts of "a woman – perhaps Mrs. Bonner Pennybacker – to do the work with the women's clubs and the civic clubs."[12] Leading merchants in the community stressed the importance of the campaign at this particular meeting. So desperate was the situation thought to have been that Mr. A. T. McKean commented that "we are not going to have a town here in ten years unless this problem is worked out."[13] Over the years, the chamber also has carried out vigorous campaigns to secure ever greater membership among the businesspeople and merchants in Austin. And, while attendance at its meetings normally has consisted only of its directors, or invited guests, it has been seen as the representative governing body, the voice of business, in the community.

Throughout its history, too, the major business and professional figures of Austin have served as its presidents. One year Malcolm Reed, a wealthy businessman, was president. Another year, Dr. Goodall Wooten was its head. Its directors have come from among the mayors of Austin, such as Tom Miller, or future mayors, such as William Drake, whose family owned the very prominent and profitable Calcasieu Lumber Company. They also have come from among the leading lawyers, such as Alvin Wirtz, or industrialists, like Herman Brown.

Because of its prominence as the voice of business in the community, and because of the distinction many of its members held, the Roosevelt administration used the Austin chamber, as it did many other chambers throughout the United States, to promote its own programs. There is no little irony in the fact that, in seeking to gain widespread acceptance for its package of new federal programs, the New Deal turned to the chamber for help. In the summer and fall of 1933, with the creation of the National Recovery Act, federal administrators asked the members of the Austin Chamber of Commerce to urge cooperation with the new guidelines on wages and prices to be adopted by local merchants. Fred Barge, then president of the Austin chamber, wrote to his members, urging support of the NRA codes.

> Just at this time we cannot refrain from calling your attention to the fact that in every big emergency which has faced our nation the past twenty years, the government has unloaded a very considerable part of the burden on the commercial organizations of the country. . . . On July 21st, 12,000 Chambers of Commerce throughout the nation were requested to call together the heads of various named groups in their sections and organize advising committees to carry out the educational work of the National Recovery Act. Within less than 24 hours the National Administration had its answer that the nation was ready to go. . . . Desiring to serve to the limit, the Board of Directors of the Austin Chamber of Commerce offered the use of the building, equipment, and all facilities in this work.[14]

Just a few years later, the honeymoon between the New Deal and business would end, and the chamber would stand as the most vigorous opponent of Roosevelt.

Walter Long labored hard during his tenure to represent the Chamber of Commerce of Austin, and to help secure new industry and business for the community. During his tenure as manager, he was credited with helping to bring in new airlines and to establish a large airport in Austin.[15] The chamber also cooperated with the city government in drawing up various plans for the development and growth of the community. Long, as manager, aided in securing the establishment of Camp Mabry, a local headquarters for the National Guard. In 1921, he accompanied Robert Vinson, president of the University of Texas, to Washington where they spoke with federal officials about securing some funds to help construct the Austin Dam.[16] Long also served as one of the founders of the Colorado River Improvement Association, a group organized in 1915 to help further the efforts to develop a sound and viable dam for the city. Long often remained in the background on these efforts; and he is described by Edward Clark as someone who was "apolitical" and "too smart for politics."[17] Nonetheless, he was very instrumental in bringing about many of the improvements in Austin, and in fulfilling his own particular dreams for it.

That effort to work cooperatively with the federal government, initiated at various points through Long's reign as manager and actively fostered by the Roosevelt administration, in particular, was fraught with tension and conflict. And it, too, is an important part of the story of Walter Long, the chamber, and Austin politics. Long, his daughter said, came in time to believe that the federal government was working against, rather than on behalf of, the best interests of the public, and of Austin.[18] That program to implement a scheme whereby the federal government would actively help to underwrite so many programs across the country came to be seen as anathema by Walter Long and his associates in the chamber. The members of the chamber viewed with suspicion any government effort to interfere with the easy workings of free entreprise. Long and the chamber cooperated with the federal government, but they often did so as unwilling participants.

Consider, for example a resolution endorsed by the attending directors of the Austin Chamber of Commerce meeting in 1927:

February 2, 1927

Mr. M. H. Reed, Pres.,
Austin Chamber of Commerce
Austin, Texas

Dear Sirs:

This committee, as representing the Directors of the Austin Chamber of Commerce, go on record as opposing any action of the Federal Government at this time toward increasing cotton and farm products; also opposed to federal ownership and operation of any purely local enterprise; especially that set out in H.B. 9826, known as the Swing-Johnson Bill, which contemplates the construction and operation of an electric and irrigation project as Boulder Canyon.

We ask that our action in this matter be conveyed to our representatives in Congress by proper letter from the president of our organization.

Respectfully yours,

A. T. Knies
Sidney P. Smith
G. W. Murray[19]

This document and the position it endorses are symptomatic of a deep philosophical division that ultimately came to divide the business community of Austin, with the chamber figures and merchants on the one side, and the proponents of the New Deal—among them, Tom Miller and Lyndon Johnson—on the other side. It was a controversy, furthermore, that would be fueled by personal attacks and jealousies as well.

This division of merchant against merchant in Austin was deepened by the policies and rhetoric of the national Chamber of Commerce, too. Bryan Spires, a former president of the Austin chamber, and head of the Goodyear Tire Company in town, attended the national Convention of the Chambers of Commerce in America in New York City in 1943 and returned with a report that outlined the package of the meeting's resolutions. Among them, there was a resolution that said, "The Chamber deplores, and will actively oppose, any effort, whether direct or indirect, to substitute for our tried and proved American system of free enterprise either new or old theories of economics, regardless of the source of the effort of its Utopian objective." The resolution continues: "Every consideration of the public interest suggests that government measures taken during the depression should be re-examined by Congress in light of experience and of the problems expected in the postwar period. . . . The Chamber should continue its advocacy of the advantages of the private-enterprise system, and seek wide support for restoration of the rights of private enterprise surrendered during the war."[20]

The same claims were made, but with the force of Old Dixie behind them, at an earlier national convention, attended by Walter Long in 1940. He returned with a synopsis of important dialogue there, including the following memorable passage—which conjures up an image of a pinstripe-suited Senator Bilbo of Mississippi. Porter Carswell, president of the Waynesboro Junior Chamber of Commerce, argued heatedly against the efforts of the federal government to supplant industry in this section of the country, particularly farming. Long records of Carswell's speech that "he wondered sometimes how the new deal supporters expected the American business man to get on his feet when the Government has got him by the heels trying to shake more money out of him." "You industrialists," he goes on, "are not the only ones that have been called names. While they were calling you Corporate Earls, pawnbroker bankers, etc. they were referring to us down there as the feudal land lords of the old South. . . . There seems to be a determined effort in one way or another by taking away our labor and other various and sundry means to break up the old plantation system under which out [sic] people have lived, and lived happily for generations. Even the tennants [sic] are opposed to it."[21]

Still, despite this opposition of Long and the chamber to the social and economic measures of the New Deal, the chamber did accommodate itself to the New Deal programs in Austin. No doubt, it did so because those programs were believed to hold greater material promise for the building of the community. The chamber, for example, helped to entertain federal officials when they came to Austin in 1941 to inspect it as a site for the public housing projects. They did labor hard to secure the dam in Austin. In his "Autobiography of a Fool," Long makes it a point to note "In February of 1934—A. C. Bull, President—the Chamber made its major project for that year, *completion of the Hamilton Dam* [later to be known as Buchanan Dam]. The help of Congressman James P. Buchanan was again enlisted and by June of that year he had secured $4,500,000 in a loan and grant to complete this dam as a flood control structure. In the fall of that same year the LCRA was created by Legislative action, fathered and pushed by these same hard working citizens through the Colorado River Improvement Association."[22] It does not take a sharp reader, I believe, to discover, lingering between the lines of this declaration, signs of the Chamber–New Deal tension in Austin.

The conclusion of Walter Long's tenure as manager of the Austin Chamber of Commerce, but certainly not his active life, came at the close of the decade of the forties, when Austin was beginning to change in very dramatic ways. This was a period when people were becoming aware of the injustices done to blacks–and the federal government was taking an active part in making such injustices visible–when the labor movement had reached the peak of its popularity, and when the great growth in housing after the war had just begun. Walter Long, it appears, had begun to feel challenges to his reign as manager of the Chamber of Commerce. He seemed to feel that the many years during which he and other people had worked so hard to help establish such monuments as the Tom Miller Dam were much too quickly forgotten. And that other people had come to take the praise for these things. He had come to believe, his daughter said, that the world was divided into two kinds of people–the orchard planters and the apple-pickers. Those with whom he worked so long and hard as part of the Chamber of Commerce, he thought, were the orchard planters. Their work was being supplanted, he further believed, by those who came after them, toward the end of that decade, the apple-pickers. "He often felt," Janett Fish said, "a lot of the work that many men had done before had been forgotten. The city was growing so fast people couldn't remember who Dr. Wooten was, or who Bryan Spires was. . . ."[23]

The resistance to the regime of Long took several forms. In 1948, a special group was created in Austin, the Austin Area Economic Development Foundation. Its officers were prominent businesspeople in the community, and serving on its Board of Directors were many of the same people who had served as director of the Chamber of Commerce. With a large amount of funds of its own, $150,000, obtained through public subscription, the Development Foundation sought to secure new industry for Austin—but to do so independently of Walter Long and the Austin Chamber of Commerce. Long felt this was a serious blow to his position and reputation. He writes in his books of the friction between the chamber and this new group on the block. And he also relates other criticisms that he began to sense, and to take very personally and deeply. C. B. Smith, for example, was the president of the Austin Area Economic Development Foundation. Long writes in his "Autobiography": "This conversation was reported to me on July 20, 1948. C. B. Smith said to W. W. Heath, 'Walter Long and the Chamber of Commerce are not interested in getting industries for Austin. He will not do anything to get industries for Austin.'"[24]

Similar criticisms, from other people who served on the board of the foundation, also are reported by Long. It is evident that he believed his hard work no longer was appreciated, that he no longer was much loved by the community: "I was tired, almost exhausted, but it was not time yet to quit."[25] Yet quit he did, submitting his resignation to the president and board of directors on May 9, 1949. Whether it was coincident in some deep fashion or not, this turned out to be the very same year that Tom Miller decided not to run again for mayor. Apparently there was a feeling alive in the community that the old guard would have to step aside, to make room for the young Turks. To make Tom Miller move aside, however, would prove to be a most demanding task.

For many people, especially the old-timers, Tom Miller was, and remains, Austin, Texas. Tom Miller, too, I think, believed he was Austin personified. Time and again, people describe him as the finest and most capable mayor ever to have ruled Austin. And rule he did. Time and again, too, people describe him as he was characterized by his enemies, of whom there came to be a goodly number, as a benevolent dictator.[26] Edward Clark, a good friend and close political ally of the mayor's, tells of remarks made by a friend as well as the mayor that lend color to this characterization. "I had a good friend," Clark says, "and he'd say, Tom, old boy, you're a dictator, but, by God, I'm glad of one thing, you're a benevolent dictator."[27] To which the mayor would reply, according to Clark: "Well, I hope I'm benevolent. I don't want to plead guilty to being any kind of dictator." And then, in words that would have warmed the heart of the great conservative Edmund Burke, Miller went on to say: "I'm a representative of the public. I don't claim to be a public servant. I never liked the word, servant. I prefer to be a representative of the people. But I get my authority from them. And they're the boss, it's up to them to decide."[28]

Tom Miller was the only native resident of Austin among those people I have identified here as Austin's urban entrepreneurs. He was born in the Tenth Ward in Austin, at the corner of First Street and San Jacinto, in 1893. He grew up in modest circumstances—some say poor—directly across from the residence of Colonel Andrew Zilker, one of the kingpins of Austin during the heyday of Wooldridge.[29] Colonel Zilker was in some ways as much a benefactor and shaper of Austin at the turn of the century as Wooldridge. The park of over 300 acres that today bears his name, on the southern side of the Colorado, was given to the city by him, with the provision that the city devote $300,000 over a period of years to public school instruction in manual training and home economics.[30] Contrary to the newspaper disclaimers at the time, when he ran for the City Council positions in 1931 and 1933, Tom Miller received the support of Colonel Zilker; in fact, Miller was only one of several people who were backed by the Colonel in their efforts to occupy positions on the City Council.

Oswald Wolf, in 1962, recalled that when he ran for office in 1933, it was at the urging of Zilker. "My reason for being on the Council was that Colonel Zilker called me to come to his home, and said he knew my Daddy well and that my Dad had helped him to be elected as Alderman in Tenth Ward and he wanted to return the favor to his son. He said he wanted me to run for the Council with Tom Miller and Simon Gillis and [C. F.] Alford and [Hillaire] Nitschke. Colonel Zilker said he would foot all the bills. Mr. Miller, Mr. Gillis, Mr. Alford, Mr. Bartholomew, and myself were elected."[31]

But Miller played a hand in sponsoring his own ticket in 1931. Only two members on it were elected to the council, Mssrs. Simon Gillis and C. F. Alford. It was not until 1933, when he ran on "The People's Ticket" along with Gillis, Alford Nitschke, and Wolf, that Miller's campaign to get himself elected was a successful one. And then he was not unseated until he decided not to run in 1949.

To get a full sense of the role of Miller in Austin politics during his reign from 1933 to 1949, and then again from 1955 to 1961, one must compare him to other dominant politicians in the cities of America. He was a most colorful person, given to quotes and filibustering and language replete with vivid imagery. He was also an enormous man, standing about 6 feet 2 inches tall, and weighing, it is claimed, anywhere from 270 to 300 pounds. In light of his physically impressive stature, one thinks immediately of other politicians of enormous bulk—and, incidentally, reputations—people like Richard Daley of Chicago, or Boss Tweed of Tammany Hall. Dave Shanks, a former Austin journalist, has said that "you might compare him [Miller] to Mayor Daley of Chicago, except that Daley's long-time control depended on patronage, whereas this was not at all true with Mayor Miller."[32] Tom Miller was as physically imposing as Daley and Tweed, and as politically powerful as well. He was a master politician. Yet, unlike Daley or Tweed, or others who ran the machines in the various locales scattered across urban America, Tom Miller did not have to rely exclusively on patronage to secure his continuation in office. Nor did he appear to be in need of filling his own coffers through his political offices.

Miller was a very successful businessman in Austin by the time he first elected to run for mayor in 1931. He had entered his father's produce and cotton business, along with his brother, James; and after his father's death in 1916, the two brothers together with Freeman Taylor continued the operation, making it a very prosperous one. The work involved the buying and selling of pecans, cotton, wool, turkeys, and hides. It was the last that mattered most. Many an Austinite alive at the time remembers, with a certain vivid sense of both the mayor and their own nasal passages, Mayor Miller's hide plant downtown, at 301 West Fourth Street. When the wind was right, meaning when it was blowing from the north, a smell would be driven from the bowels of the firm that drifted across the river and left people in South Austin wondering who, or what, had died downtown.[33] There also were those who said that, had Miller not remained on the council, the hide plant might have been moved earlier from its downtown quarters, though this slap at the mayor is one of the few to be forthcoming, from either friend or foe.

Miller engaged in a number of other business pursuits as well, land deals and other such things that were the trade of successful businesspeople in Austin during these times. He was a frequent business associate of Edgar Perry's in various deals as well as being a close friend. Perry, in fact, got him started in the cotton business with a loan of $750. And he did have his hand in any number of business operations. He was elected as a director of the American National Bank in Austin and remained on the board until his death in 1961. He was viewed not merely as a supremely good politician, but also as a good businessman. And the latter quality was of key significance to the prevailing business interests in Austin, to the bankers and the leading merchants. From at least the reign of Mayor Wooldridge, good government in Austin meant good business; and there is little question that, had Miller not possessed such an excellent head for business, he would not have served so long as mayor.

Miller was, by all accounts, a most scrupulous and honest politician. Trueman O'Quinn, who served as an assistant city attorney, and later city attorney during the reign of Miller, recalls the following episode:

> He [Miller] didn't want to do anything that seemed to reflect badly on a public official. . . . He owned ten acres over here on the east side of town, that had a beautiful pear orchard. . . . He said one day he believed he was going to sell that ten acres of land. It's good rich soil over in. . . . Govalle. . . . And I said, 'Mayor, what do you want for it,' and he said, 'I've got to get $250 an acre.' 'Well,' I said, 'I'll buy it,' and he said, 'No, you won't,' and I said, 'Why not?' And he said, 'The Mayor cannot sell the City Attorney anything.' And he refused to sell me that ten acres. . . . He was very strict about things of that sort. He never wanted his personal affairs to be in any way mixed up with the city.[34]

But to claim that Miller was an honest politician is not to argue that he did not know the nitty-gritty of dealing and trading in power. He knew it; and he did it well. He much enjoyed his period of rulership over Austin, relished it in fact. But he did not live off politics so much as he lived for it.[35] In the period of his tenure on the council, the people who served, including the mayor, were not paid for their services. Thus, those people who came to sit on the council had to be self-supporting or to have some kind of wealthy benefactor. As such, benefactors were few and far between in Austin—save for Colonel Zilker, who, it seems, only assisted with the nominal expenses for campaigns. The men who sat on the council in the 1930s and 1940s were people like the Bartholomews, Eugene C. and Carlos M., father and son bankers, employees of the Austin National Bank; or people like Simon Gillis, a retired contractor; or Oswald Wolf, a retail grocer and scion of an old Austin family that controlled a good deal of property in Austin.[36]

But while scrupulous and honest, Miller loved political battle, and he relished the privileges of power. Much like a feudal lord, Austin became his fiefdom, his estate, his source and his inspiration for power. Miller was a shrewd negotiator and bargainer in office, which also helps to account for his long tenure as a member of the council and as mayor. (Let me note that it was not until 1971 that candidates ran for a separate position as mayor on the city council in Austin. Until that time, the mayor was elected by his or her fellow council members. Miller achieved the unprecedented distinction of having been elected to the post as mayor on nine successive occasions by his council colleagues.) Miller knew how to trade, and he knew what was involved in the nature of political bargaining. Edward Clark describes Miller as being constantly on top of the political situation, even of his audience at a particular political meeting. He could persuade even his most stubborn political foes, such as Emma Long, Clark claims, and bring them over to his side.[37] One illustration Clark uses to capture the hard political sense of the mayor is the way Miller handled an audience. If there were forty people in his audience whom he was seeking to convince of a position, whether it be to join the Roosevelt forces at a Democratic Convention or to work on behalf of a project in Austin, and thirty-eight of them came up afterward to shake his hand and congratulate him, Miller knew where the other two people stood. He had, in Clark's words, "checked up on them." Miller was, it appears, a born persuader, someone who knew how to get people to come around to his point of view without their being the least conscious of having done so.[38]

Miller was a politician, according to Clark, who sought to persuade people by praising them, to convince them of his side of the case not by ridicule, but by gentle, subtle, and powerful persuasion. "He [Miller] did not tell people this is what the city is going to do," Clark relates. "He would say, 'I'm thinking about this, and I want to get your point of view, what do you think about this?' And he would lay out a problem. . . . And he would get to talking, and then he'd finally come back and say, 'Well, it's like you said, I *agree* with *you.* . . .'"[39] Then, Clark further recalls, Miller would recapitulate the discussion, and draw out the favorable remarks of the other person, and say, "'I agree with you, I'm going with you on that.'"[40] Miller's fine qualities as a bargainer and negotiator perhaps may best be summed up with Clark's remembrance that Miller would say, any number of times,

" 'You catch more flies with sugar than you can with vinegar.' "[41]

Those people who remember Miller, and the articles about him, also tell of his great fondness for words, for poetry, and particularly for Shakespeare. There is, it seems, a certain quality to be found among some politicians, most notably those from the South but also a rare bird from the North, such as the late Senator Everett Dirksen, that encourages them to be invincible warriors with words. If politics is the art of oratory, then Tom Miller may have been one of the finest politicians around. At council sessions, he would go on for hours using his knowledge of Shakespeare to drag out the discussion of an issue. Much of this verbosity was tactical. Miller assumed that if you talked long enough you would eventually wear your opponent down. Newspapers report the times that Miller would extend council meetings until the wee hours of the morning; and many of those I interviewed recall much the same thing.[42] When people came before the council to plead for certain favors, particularly when the utilities made their pleas, the mayor often threw them off guard with various quotes.

One of the more famous and memorable of these was the time some utility officials appeared before the council, to insist as usual on a rate hike for their firm. Miller turned to his fellow council members, having observed the solemn faces of the officials, and quoted from Julius Caesar, "If you have tears, prepare to shed them now."[43] Not only the master of the art of oratory and suasion, he also was a most shrewd businessman, and sought to run the city as a good piece of business. Another quote attributed to Miller, on his return to city office in 1955, was addressed to city department heads. "We're not trying to massacre anybody," he is reported to have said, "but we have to stabilize [the city budget]. We must run our business as cheaply and efficiently as any business in town. You must be careful with the dollars entrusted to you."[44] His own business operations were conducted regularly from his office in City Hall. He was the only council member to have such an office; and his desk was across from that of the city manager, a man with whom he worked very closely, Guiton Morgan.

Mayor Miller sustained himself in power through an adroit use of the resources he had at his disposal. Above all, he was someone who could be enormously persuasive if he had to be; in this regard, he was like each and every effective politician. He paid his debts and secured his power in many ways. For instance, after the funds for the construction of the Austin Dam had been obtained from the federal government, Miller wrote over one hundred letters on behalf of applicants for positions in the construction of the dam.[45] Miller could trade and bargain with the very best of them. Black and white Austinites alike remember that the mayor went out of his way to sustain his electoral hold over the black community in Austin by cutting various deals with politicians. Working hand-in-hand with Dr. Everett H. Givens, a dentist and the self-selected "bronze mayor of East Austin," in words of Ada Simond, and with Arthur DeWitty, the publisher of a newspaper for the black community, Miller sought to give black men and women things they wanted in return for their support.[46] He helped to insure they had good facilities and a fine public park, Rosewood Park. He would sit down with Givens and DeWitty and try to figure out which roads would have to be paved in East Austin. He helped, but with some reservations on his own part as well as considerable resistance among businesspeople in Austin, to secure the first low-income housing projects in Austin. This was a political plum that Lyndon Johnson obviously thought appropriate to secure his own power in Austin. Tom Miller knew how to deal and to bargain in the realm of politics in a way matched by few other people in the local community, save perhaps someone like Johnson himself or Alvin Wirtz.

Besides all else, Tom Miller also seemed to be a deep and loyal supporter of Franklin Roosevelt and the New Deal. Here, in the effort to make sense of Miller, I must necessarily tread on some uncertain ground. For as a politician, Miller desired as much as anything else to be on the winning team, and to maintain his own base of power in Austin. That is the simple nature of politics, as it is of sports. In fact, in Austin, it just so happens that politics is as popular a local sport as football at the university. And, if you have ever been to a game at Memorial Stadium on a Saturday afternoon, with 80,000 folks pummeling your ears—or one in Ann Arbor, or Columbus, or a soccer match in Rome—you get a sense of just how popular that is. To many people living in the midst of the Great Depression, the winning side in the 1930s was the New Deal.

But did Tom Miller only join the New Deal forces to secure his own power? On that matter, it is impossible to decide clearly. To hear Edward Clark, his close friend, tell the story, it seems as though the mayor did, indeed, feel himself a friend of the "blind, the lame, and the poor," but at the same time, Miller was much concerned with cultivating and sustaining his power and influence in Austin, as in the Democratic party throughout Texas and the nation.[47] To hear his enemies tell it, Tom Miller was simply concerned with his own name and power. Regardless, after a time Miller and the New Deal became as intertwined as Miller and Austin: the destiny of both the New Deal and Austin, Miller felt, rested largely on his own shoulders. Miller took up the cause for Roosevelt, and did everything he could to promote that cause, even in the face of considerable opposition from such quarters as the Austin Chamber of Commerce. His colorful and persuasive and electric approach to politics served Roosevelt well here as it served all of Tom Miller's other causes. There is a famous scene, etched in the memory of Guiton Morgan, of the time in 1934 when Roosevelt came through Austin and gave a talk from the back end of a train—a Pullman car down on what was then East Avenue: "he [Miller] had a big flashing sign made, and hooked up which he turned on. When the President's car came across East Avenue [the sign flashed] 'Prosperity blooms again with Roosevelt.' "[48] There was a boyish quality to Tom Miller, it has been said; and perhaps no incident reveals it so well.

To maintain and ever enlarge his power in Austin, Miller went to great lengths. He came to believe it necessary to cultivate important persons, much as his good friend and associate Edgar Perry thought.[49] He worked the streets of Austin, particularly Congress Avenue, as a good politician works any crowd. More than one person remembers Miller walking up and down Congress Avenue, shortly after it was no longer simply a dusty street leading up to the Capitol.[50] And Miller would be out there, breathing and thinking and talking Austin.

Miller also had a very firm hand on the newspaper, and what it printed.[51] He knew Charles Marsh, publisher of the *Austin American*, well. And he kept after Charles Green, editor of the paper, to sponsor and to promote his various projects for the city. Emmett Shelton, Sr., reports that Miller spent much of his time at the offices of the paper, after council meetings, making sure that the editor, and the reporters, described the meetings to Miller's own liking. In 1935, when the whole council ran unopposed for office, the *American* came out with a front-page editorial, endorsing the entire body.[52] And in 1939, just days before the council election, the *American* had another front-page story, telling how successful Austin had been in securing federal funds for its development.[53] Tom Miller wanted Austin to grow; as a practical businessman, he also held a vision of this growth, so the paper became a vehicle for getting the notion of growth to be accepted by the public, and to be implemented as though it were through their will. When Miller and others began to labor on behalf of some sort of flood control and dams, the papers, Charles Green, and reporter Raymond Brooks also became sponsors of these projects. So close did the ties become, in fact, that William Weeg, one of the reporters for the *American*, often would sit in as an unofficial member of the council when a member was absent.[54] If Miller loved Roosevelt, so must the paper. And it did, proclaiming in front-page articles and in lengthy editorials the importance of the New Deal to Austin, and to the nation.

Miller maintained his support of Roosevelt everywhere. He was extremely active in Democratic party politics. When he and his good friend Edgar Perry were delegates in 1940 to the Democratic Convention in Chicago, he had served the same year as state campaign manager for Roosevelt. He had come out in fierce opposition to the attempt to nominate John Nance Garner for president, thus dividing himself from a number of other Democrats in the state. In this effort, he aligned himself with such other notable figures and friends as Alvin Wirtz, Herman Brown, Lyndon Johnson, and Edward Clark. In the 1944 State Democratic Convention, he was again on the side of the New Deal forces, along with his usual friends and allies. And, at the 1948 state convention, at which various Southern states insisted on a "states' rights" platform, Miller steadfastly stood behind Harry Truman. He also served as finance director during that campaign for Truman.[55] Here he found himself in deep trouble. In fact, he was removed from the Travis County delegation by the more conservative forces of Governor Beauford Jester. Emma Long, a foe of Miller's on many occasions, still recalls that Miller stood with her, Stuart, and other very liberal Democrats during the 1948 convention.[56] And, given the opposition they faced here in Texas, from Jester, Allan Shivers, and the Chamber of Commerce group among many others, this stand perhaps as well as anything else fully illustrates Miller's deep conviction about New Deal principles.

Miller was one of those fairly numerous anomalies in the South — the good businessman, the deep Southerner, who also stood strong on behalf of much of Roosevelt's New Deal, and Truman's Fair Deal, civil rights, and the like. Politics, we have heard it said many times, makes strange bedfellows; but the fellows lying with Tom Miller must

have seemed positively out of this world! A lot of Miller's own concern grew from his effort to maintain his power, to be sure. Fellow
council members recall, for instance, that while Miller was in favor
of equal privileges and rights for blacks and browns, he was personally opposed to having them mix together.[57] He found something dis-
tasteful about the fact that blacks and browns might bathe together
with whites at Barton Springs; or that they might study together,
white girls with black boys, at the downtown library. Give them good
facilities, he seemed to say, but let them stay apart. The paradoxes
and contradictions of Tom Miller, however, are not his alone, but
those of a whole breed of people, raised in the late nineteenth and
early twentieth century, in this part of the world.

Throughout his reign as mayor, Miller succeeded through his political acumen and skills. He was so effective that in 1937 he was touted
by some Austinites as a possible replacement for Congressman
Buchanan.[58] And Johnson seemed for a long while to feel a certain
threat from Miller, from his popularity and political adroitness.[59]
Miller usually only had nominal opposition at election times, as
did the rest of the council, for that matter. The sort of campaigning
we have heard about in the Chicagos of this century, the heavy
patronage in the wards, or the sort we presently see – the gobs of cash
spent to gain name recognition – simply were not facts of political life
in Austin in the 1930s, 1940s, and 1950s.

As an astute businessman, Tom Miller pleased the business community in Austin. His enemies came about not because of any sort
of corruption, but chiefly because of the New Deal, the very liberal
policies he endorsed, and, of course, the power he exercised. At the
time of the federal housing project in Austin, Miller received a good
deal of criticism from those who felt the government-owned housing
would threaten the enterprise of the realtors.[60] There were a number of public meetings held at the time, with Miller, Johnson, Clark,
and others assembled on the side of public housing. This was a true
and deep confrontation, as I hope to have underscored in my discussion of Walter Long, and it must have caused no little enmity among
the businesspeople of the community. It was a symptom of the division among the merchants, and it served to accentuate that split. But
throughout his reign as mayor, Miller constantly encountered this
sort of opposition, from those who believed that a more conservative
fiscal and social platform was to be preferred to the so-called give-
away programs of the New Deal. A large part of that opposition did

come from people like Walter Long and the Chamber of Commerce. But Long and the chamber were not nearly so effective as politicians as Miller; thus, Miller was able to remain in office as long as he did, and the New Deal continued to be *the* deal in Austin for a long time.

In fact, Tom Miller went out of his way to bring Walter Long and the directors of the Chamber of Commerce over to his side. He served for a long period of time as a director of the chamber—he was first elected as a director in 1936, and then re-elected each of the next three years—he sought to lobby the chamber on behalf of his projects for the community. Miller informed the chamber directors of the Austin Dam, and of the need for various community projects, like the paving of streets. He was sensitive to their opposition, at least their opposition based upon the possible sources of funds for these projects. He did tend to get their hackles up because he was possessive about Austin and the projects; jealousies no doubt developed, particularly with Walter Long, because each man sought to sustain the affections of the community. Miller sought to soften such jealousy, and to dampen the chamber's opposition. Consider, for instance, the persuasive, colorful, and loquacious Mr. Miller as he delivered the following comments at the chamber meeting honoring Bryan Spires. Walter Long, who also served as chamber secretary, records:

> In his usual appropriate manner and style, [Mayor Miller] discussed the splendid spirit of cooperation which had existed over the years between the City Commission and the Chamber of Commerce. Mayor Miller reviewed the work of the city and the Chamber of Commerce had kept itself in the background when results were accomplished, choosing rather to get results than credit. He spoke of the many things on which the city and the Chamber of Commerce had cooperated in a most happy way, among these being the fish hatchery, hospital, dams, recreation, parks, cotton stamps and other projects too numerous to mention. . . . At the conclusion of his remarks, the Mayor paid special tribute to the large number of Austin citizens who not only give their time but their services through the Chamber of Commerce upbuilding in this community.[61]

This was the master politician at work. His accounting, I suspect, probably comes as close to the truth of how Austin grew in the 1930s and 1940s as any such account could. That he put it into words, and thereby corrected the impression left by Marsh, Green, and the

American, was testimony to his magnanimity. Or perhaps he simply wanted the chamber crowd on his side for the next vote.

Miller had threatened to leave office on any number of occasions. These threats repeatedly were met by large outcries from members of the community. Almost with clockwork regularity, the prominent business leaders would assemble, shortly before the upcoming election, and show their approval of the mayor and his administration. For instance, in 1939, Miller announced that he did not intend to run again for the council. After returning from a trip to Washington, in February, he indicated a change of heart—he would run after all. Nonetheless, a meeting had already been called, and more than 500 citizens showed up for it at the Driskill Hotel. At the meeting, Miller was openly moved by this display. He said to the assembled mass of citizens: "we try to carry out your wishes and commands, although we sometimes fail in that effort, but we invite you to visit the city hall and your criticisms, whether they are constructive or not, although we prefer constructive criticism."[62] Yet, finally, the opposition got the best of him, as it did of Walter Long, too. Although Miller served again as mayor from 1955 to 1961, he seemed to have lost the affection and support of the community, especially the businesspeople. Emma Long recalls that Mayor Miller was urged by the leading businesspeople of the community to take on the post as president of the Chamber of Commerce.[63] This was perceived by them, and by him, as something of a sop, like the promotion of someone who no longer does his job well. Perhaps the years of combating the forces on his right, in the form of the Jesters, Shivers, and Chamber of Commerce crowd, coupled now with the burgeoning liberal forces on his left, in the form of Emma and Stuart Long and their troops, just wore Miller out. He was, Emma Long further recalls, "deeply hurt, very hurt" by these events. Miller returned to office in 1955, but by this time his physical condition had begun to deteriorate, due to a serious diabetic illness. Pictures shown of him at the end of the 1950s portray a man whose physical powers had been drained. And so, too, were his political powers. He died in 1962; like that of so many other politicians, his death was not seen by the public as that of a hero, but as that of someone whose time had come, and gone.

If Tom Miller was something like Austin's Richard Daley, then Edgar Perry, Sr., or Commodore Perry as he often was called, was something like its Averell Harriman, its Bernard Baruch. There is a letter from Lyndon Johnson in the testimonial to Austin and Perry, in which Johnson says the following: "I have often thought of Commodore Perry as the Barney Baruch of Austin. He is always in the forefront of every effort to foster the further cultural and civic development of that beautiful city. . . . He is, in short, that dependable Rock of Gibralter type every city needs to insure its progress."[64] And Perry played precisely that part in Austin politics, especially during the 1930s and 1940s. He was viewed by both friends and enemies—and he appears not to have possessed too many of the latter—as the aristocrat of the Austin social and political scene. Before a person considered making any serious move in Austin politics, at least in the Establishment circles, the imprimatur of Perry was one of those necessary to success. Perry, for instance, was one of two men—the other being A. J. Eilers, a prominent businessman and, among other things, co-founder of the Colorado River Improvement Association—whose endorsement and financial aid Lyndon Johnson sought in the course of his campaign to fill Congressman Buchanan's post.[65]

Edgar Perry was a man of somewhat diminutive stature. In the famous picture in which he is arrayed with the select group of his most important friends—Edward Clark, Herman Brown, Lyndon Johnson, and Tom Miller—Perry quite obviously stands a good deal smaller than the others. By his sixties, he displayed a crisp and tidy appearance, projecting an aura of wealth and influence. And wealthy he was. His grandson tells the story, relayed to him by his grandfather's bookkeeper, Miss Ruby Lee Ransom, that in 1913, before the federal government instituted income tax, Perry had earned about $750,000 from his various business investments. By the late 1920s, Perry stood as one of Austin's wealthiest citizens. There were few to rival him in this respect. His partner in the cotton, oil, and ranching business, Dave Reed, was another wealthy figure, perhaps even richer than Perry. But, in contrast to Reed, Perry was considerably more interested in the public arena, and in fashioning a bigger and better Austin. It is not those who possess considerable riches that make a difference, but those who with their wealth decide that a life's project, an ambition, will be the development of an empire, in this instance, an urban empire. Like Wooldridge, Long, and Miller, Edgar Perry represented one of Austin's urban entrepreneurs.

Perry was not born and bred in Austin. He was a self-made man, born in 1876 in Caldwell, Texas, and raised on a farm. During his youth, he tells, he had to work hard, tending to various animals, the goats and the cows, and he was taught the importance of savings and thrift.[66] At the age of eighteen, he became involved in the cotton business, working in Texas as a cotton grader, buyer, and clerk for the Philadelphia firm of George H. McFaddin and Brothers. He moved to Austin in 1904, and in 1910 began his own cotton firm, called Edgar Perry and Company. Perry's sense of grand style, which led him to build a great and stately home in Austin, probably was developed in the course of his frequent visits to Europe for his cotton business. In his memoirs, he remembers his very first trip to Europe. He went to Liverpool, England, to learn the craft of dealing in cotton and was taught the various tricks of the trade by experts there. On the same trip he became the traveling companion of two men—William Clayton and Sheppard King—who also dealt in cotton and who became very wealthy in the business. Perry was most impressed with them, and with their later successes.[67]

If there is one quality that Edgar Perry grew to appreciate over the course of his life, that was a person's success. And importance. His grandson, Edgar Perry III, who himself later would become engaged in Austin politics for a time, remembers that Perry, Sr., urged him to cultivate important people. That was perhaps the key lesson one should know in life.[68] Perry's scrapbooks certainly attest to this trait. Various letters and other memorabilia of important persons adorn the books.[69] It is as though Perry viewed himself as a meticulous stamp collector; but, in this instance, the stamps were men and women who had, or would, leave their mark on the world. Among other recollections, Perry, Sr., recalled that he and his wife, Lutie, were the very last people to have seen Will Rogers alive before the flight that took Rogers to his death.[70] And Perry's housekeeper, Mrs. Jim Tatum, like Perry himself, could not forget that great evening in the Perry penthouse, atop the Driskill Hotel, when Perry entertained Governor William and Mrs. Oveta Culp Hobby, former Governor and Mrs. Dan Moody, Senator and Mrs. Lyndon Johnson, Senator and Mrs. Richard Russell, and Cornelia Otis Skinner.[71] Perry's penchant for prominent people was well known. A pamphlet of the Democratic party of Texas in 1946 relates that Edgar Perry "led a comparatively blameless life until he moved to Austin where he has been majoring in governors. . . ."[72]

In view of Perry's preeminence in Austin during the first half of this century, it is not in the least surprising that Lyndon Johnson would

turn to him for sponsorship when he ran for Congress. Their relationship eventually became a very warm and close one, as close as
father and son. Perry had one child, Edgar, Jr., who went on to
achieve considerable financial success, as head of the Southwest
Tablet Manufacturing Company in Dallas. But father and son never
achieved much rapport, as much the fault of father as of son; nor did
the son get on well with anyone else. Eventually the younger man
turned to alcohol, and died at the age of fifty-six.[73] But Perry and
Lyndon did achieve the warmth absent from the blood relationship.
In his reminiscences, Perry writes:

> I am looking now at a portrait of him [Johnson] taken in the
> headquarters of General Douglas MacArthur in Australia. He
> was in a Naval Commander's uniform and beneath it is in-
> scribed, 'To my other Dad, with love from Lyndon.' I love the
> picture; not long ago—before the slight attack [Johnson's heart
> attack in 1956] I wrote him that my great ambition was to ring
> the White House door some day and say to the person who
> answered, 'I want to see Lyndon.'[74]

Mrs. Jim Tatum and Miss Ransom both recall that Johnson gave
evidence of a very strong filial feeling for Perry. Mrs. Tatum says that
"Lyndon used to, well he'd tell me that Mr. Perry was the same as
his father"; and Miss Ransom adds "Yes . . . I've heard him say that
many times."[75] Perry served as Johnson's chief financial supporter
during the latter's congressional campaign in 1937, and subsequently
served as his close advisor, someone always available when Lyndon
needed political and economic advice. Even Lady Bird recognized the
significance of Perry, writing him in 1942, when Johnson was in the
navy, to ask for information about happenings in Austin.[76] Perry
offered Johnson advice on any number of topics. And he also, Tatum
remembers, was responsible for Johnson's move of the headquarters
of his radio-television operation, KTBC, from the Driskill Hotel to
its present location, at Tenth and Brazos streets. Perry owned the
property; according to the recollections of Tatum, one day he awoke
from a nap, demanded to see Lyndon, and then arranged to sell the
property to him and the station. Perry also became connected to
Johnson in other ways. His first cousin, Arthur Perry, was one of
Johnson's first acquaintances in Washington and subsequently became an aide.[77]

How close and deep this relationship truly was, at least on Johnson's part, remains open to question. Johnson himself seemed to cultivate important persons as well; and he seemed to cultivate mentors as often as rabbits mate. Besides his relationship with Perry, for example, at the same time Johnson had a warm, intimate relationship with Alvin Wirtz and Sam Rayburn.[78] In fact, the relationship between Perry and Tom Miller appears to have been far more genuine, affectionate, and strong than that between Perry and Johnson. Perry served as close counselor to the mayor on many occasions and for many different things. Perry and Miller seem to have thought pretty much alike about the world, from city projects to the New Deal. The mayor worked hard on behalf of the dam, and Perry was chosen to serve as head of the citizens' advisory committee for the dam. He also was first head of the Austin Housing Authority, and with Miller successfully argued on behalf of low-income housing, at government expense, in Austin. Perry and Miller, moreover, also engaged in numerous business ventures together.[79]

Despite being the friend and counselor of politicians, Perry himself disliked the ruckus and nastiness of politics. After all, he had seen his good friend Tom Miller, and also Johnson, exposed to the criticisms that come with holding office and wielding power. When his grandson decided to embark on a political career, in 1959, Perry, Sr., remarked to him, his grandson remembers, "you're aching for a bruise."[80] Still, Perry did engage actively in Democratic party politics for a time, attending and working with his several close allies. All were very active in the Roosevelt effort at the state convention in 1940. Perry, as noted earlier, served as the host for the 1,000 people who attended the "harmony banquet," intended to bring togther the Garner and Roosevelt factions. But Perry seemed to think politics was a dirty business; and in Texas politics he probably was right.

Edgar Perry owned and developed a great deal of property in Austin. While never himself a candidate for office, or a negotiator in politics in the same way as Miller, he did help to reconstruct a section of downtown Austin he owned. Thus, when he wanted a hotel for himself he built the Commodore Perry Hotel, at Eighth and Brazos streets, in which he included a penthouse for himself. When he desired an office building, he built the Perry-Brooks building, designed by another protégé, Max Brooks. Brooks, incidentally, had first come to Austin in the 1940s, to attend the university, and Perry took him under his wing, as he had done with several others. Perry made available to Brooks a house on his estate, in which Brooks lived while a student. Brooks' eventual wife, Marietta, also received high marks from Perry. And in light of Perry's many political acquaintances, perhaps readers may not be too surprised to learn that Marietta Brooks was to become a leader in the Texas Democratic party in the 1950s.

But Perry, while owning a large amount of real estate in downtown Austin, and developing these properties, also helped to develop other sections of the community. He owned a large amount of acreage west of downtown and in the 1950s transformed what had been gravel pits into a new development, Highland Park and Highland Park West. He sold lots in these sections to a number of friends, among them, Tom Miller and his wife, and Miller's son, Tom, Jr. Edgar Perry III recalls that his grandfather seemed to have that special knack for knowing when and how to develop such property.[81] Long before anyone else ever realized the land would be valuable, Perry had bought it. Like the other people in this story of Austin growth, Perry was possessed of some kind of sense of what the future would be like, a business and political prescience. "Somebody called," Mrs. Tatum has told me, "and made an appointment, you know, and you had to screen the best you could. And this one person wanted to ask Mr. Perry how he happened to make his money, and Mr. Perry said, 'You tell 'em, by my long vision' . . . that's what he said, his vision, his long vision."[82]

A picture of Edgar Perry is not complete without noting that, in addition to all his other riches, he was possessed of a wry sense of humor. Unlike Alexander Wooldridge, or Walter Long, Perry seemed able to make fun of himself, and of ambition, success, and wealth, as his most intimate acquaintances and relatives recall.[83] Miss Ransom recollects that "Mrs. Tatum did a lot of work and tried to keep Mr. Perry entertained and one of her methods of entertainment, when she first came in, was about once a month she'd tell him it was her birthday. So he took that for three or four months"; and Mrs. Tatum continues, "I was putting his shoes on him . . . and I just looked up and he wasn't in a too good humor, and I said, 'Mr. Perry, today is my birthday.' He had a crooked smile like he didn't wanna smile but it kinda slipped, and he smiled. And he said, Miz Tatum, you've been with me six months, and you've had seven birthdays. . . ."[84] And, in his unpublished memoirs, Perry writes of the oilmen of Houston. "So, they stop at nothing because of cost that adds comfort to existence," he observes. He goes on to note that there are two possible places where men and women, it is claimed, go after death. One is the place where all are happy, and the other "has been pictured as a blaze of brimstone, and all consuming and unendurable heat." One man in conversation is reported to have said that unless the oilmen changed their ways, and became more ethical, they would be condemned to spend eternity in that other place. "The other is reported to have remarked," Perry continues, " 'You haven't heard the latest. Now that several of those Houston oilmen have died and gone there they have air-conditioned the place.' " [85]

If Walter Long was the idealist of Austin politics, given to a vision of what he hoped the community would become, but without the political fortitude or savvy of Tom Miller, then Perry was its practical businessman who thought that good politics was good business. His own life, he wrote in his later years, was guided much by those precepts of thrift and industry so common among the successful men and women of this place, still lying on the edge of civilization well into the twentieth century. Like his fellow urban entrepreneurs, he believed that Austin could become a great center of civilization, a great city. So he brought to his own estate in Austin treasures and riches from Europe, in an effort to emulate, maybe even draw upon, the magic inspiration of that earlier seat of civilization.

Perry was in his daily life guided by certain precepts that smack of religious zeal and energy; yet he himself was guided every day more by pragmatic considerations than by any others. He writes in his unpublished memoirs like the good businessman, and with some of that same Puritan vigor that Max Weber, the great historian and sociologist, years earlier had identified with Benjamin Franklin. [86] Weber would have felt his theories much confirmed by reading Edgar Perry's words: "I have always wanted to work. I have always found Sunday am's and holidays the longest of the year. I am happiest when I feel I am going somewhere – and not waiting until next week to attend to passing matters needing immediate attention. I seem to always be in a hurry." [87] And further, he was driven by an ambition to achieve ever greater things, and to leave his mark on the world. His ambition, in effect, may have been his vision. "We are born equal and the sky is the limit – and only with an ambition to make the most of our advantages can we hope to make ourselves known and appreciated. Better to aspire to things unobtainable than to be satisfied with mediocre things of life." [88]

Once more we find in Edgar Perry one of those strange anomalies

in Austin, a keen businessman who stood as a strong and loyal supporter of the policies of the Roosevelt administration, long after such
a position was fashionable. It is not entirely easy to explain such a
personal point of view, especially if we are given to looking for logical
coherence in the midst of the various ideas and attitudes one professes. But history and individuals are sufficiently complex to under-
mine the claim to ultimate truth on behalf of formal logic. Perhaps
Perry thought that to get behind the Roosevelt banner was simply to
align himself on the side of victory and to benefit from the federal
coffers that would thus be opened to build modern Austin. A prag-
matist in business or politics would behave in such a fashion, harnessing his wagon to successful ventures, under any title. Whatever
we might decide about this matter, Edgar Perry, and the monuments
he helped to build and to sponsor, remains one of the important
figures in the collage of people and events that have become modern
Austin. He died in 1961, one year before his friend Tom Miller, and
just two years before his friend Lyndon Johnson assumed the
presidency. He always believed Johnson would be president, from the
day he first met him, in 1937. He may have regretted then that he
never saw that particular dream materialize. But many other dreams,
dreams of Austin, did.

Alexander Penn Wooldridge and, somewhat later, Walter Long,
Tom Miller and Edgar Perry were key figures in the construction of
modern Austin. They helped to change Austin from a small, frontier
settlement into something that approached a civilized urban dwelling. There were other people, too. But even their contemporaries
agreed that these particular men were significant to the growth of
Austin, and to its vision. Each of them, for instance, was at one time
or other voted the Most Worthy Citizen of the community. Consider
the recommendations for Most Worthy Citizen that found their way
into the Austin newspaper in 1939:

Miss Louise Haynie, insurance, 2420 Jarratt.

E. H. Perry, who has given so much time and energy to the
housing authority, and for all the things he has done in the
past—things that many people don't know he has done for
them. The housing program is certainly helping the people who
need it most.

C. F. Gibson, attorney, Govalle.

I would nominate Mayor Tom Miller for the honor of Austin's Most Worthy Citizen of 1939 because he has consistently worked constructively for Austin and has often spent his own money in behalf of the city.

R. Pearson, linotype operator, 1208 Baylor.

I think that for many years Walter Long, manager of the Chamber of Commerce, has been doing a lot for Austin. It is true that he gets paid for being manager of the Chamber of Commerce, but he does many things he doesn't get paid for. And he always wants someone else to be given the credit.[89]

Each of these men lived for Austin, more than they lived off it. Each dedicated a large amount of his time and energy, indeed his life, to make Austin a bigger and better place in which to live. This is not to say they gained nothing from their involvements. Walter Long did get paid for his efforts; but it was not a large sum. He supported himself mainly from the Texas Legislative Service, and, as he recalls, he often returned monies to the chamber when he thought he had been paid too much, or paid for purchases out of his own pocket.[90] Yet the motivation of Long, Miller, and Perry does not appear to have been in terms of the financial profits to be secured through the course of their involvements. Many other men and women who did not become involved in the public life of Austin made very handsome salaries and developed very healthy business enterprises; such were their lives. But for Long, Miller, and Perry, Austin became a projection of themselves. They loved the place; and they bathed in its affection for them.

Besides the self-chosen role of urban entrepreneur, there were other common threads among these men. Long, Perry, and Miller did not work independently of one another, even though they often seemed to work at odds. Tom Miller and Edgar Perry were among the best of friends. The degree of this friendship went so far that Miller moved to a house one block down from the estate of Perry, in 1934, to live at 714 Park Boulevard. A few years later, just to stay in touch, he moved even closer, to 813 Park Boulevard, and became Perry's backyard neighbor. They helped to host dinners together for leading political and business figures, at the Country Club just across the street from the Perry estate at Forty-first and Red River. And when Perry moved to the Driskill Hotel, Mayor Miller became his constant companion there, joining him on the balcony, where they would discuss city affairs and watch the city grow.[91] Walter Long traveled in somewhat different circles. But he, too, was a constant visitor of Perry's, seeking his wisdom on city affairs that also involved the chamber.[92]

Of the three men, Walter Long was by far the most possessed of religious idealism. Not only did he hold high ideals for the city, and for what it would become, but he also actively engaged in church activities. For a long time, for instance, beginning in 1924, he taught a Sunday School class at the University Presbyterian Church, the Century Class, where students of different ages would come to learn how to apply precepts from the Bible to their daily lives. Ambition, hard work, and dreams were the virtues Long held up to the students. He chose the following as a poem with which to embellish and introduce his write-up about the Century Class:

As wider skies break on man's view
God greatens in his growing mind.
Each age he dreams his God anew
And leaves his older God behind.
He sees the wondrous scheme dilate
In sky and flower, star and cloud,
And as his universe grow great
He dreams for it a greater God.
                              Anon.[93]

But Tom Miller was himself something of the same kind of person, though not to the same extent as Long, or perhaps even Perry. He is claimed to have often quoted the saying "the past makes the present, and the present makes the future."[94] The Shakespeare-quoting mayor had, it seems, his own special set of ideals, his own grasp on history, to guide him.

Edgar Perry was the financier of the three. He made his wealth early, and was therefore able to retire from active business life in 1929, at the age of fifty-three. He retired just before the Great Depression broke out, robbing many other men of their wealth and their lives. Perry sought new horizons to conquer, new monuments to erect; and he sought to build them in and around Austin. Miller was the master politician, who used both his good business sense and his great political skills to further the growth, the progress, the vitality of Austin. The actual visions of these men may have differed—we can never fully know the private fantasies they entertained—but their public vision, the one they shared, despite ideological differences, was, in the language of the time, the "upbuilding" of Austin.

There were many Austinites, thousands of them, who went about their daily lives, during the reign of these figures, grateful for the jobs that came by virtue of federal monies, or who taught at the university, or who served in state government. The principal and distinguishing feature of those men I have depicted in this chapter is their long record of service on behalf of the community. Among their other lifetime goals was the personal and public project, a greater Austin, an urban kingdom over which they could rule, in one way or another to serve as a mark of success of their own lives.

4.

Taming the River

Boiling, steaming, charging, assaulting
the mighty river runs.
Like a fox let loose on unsuspecting sheep,
its blood churns, its fury unleashed.
It snarls and stalks, it whips itself until,
foaming and dripping, its breath expelled in mighty swells,
it rests; its anger released, its hunger satisfied.

A. Orum
June 1982

All of my life I had heard of walls of water coming down rivers. . . . but I
didn't really think of it as real walls, i.e. a solid 5 or 6 foot wall come down
without warning until I personally experienced one of them, while fishing on
the Llano. . . . The ranchman, whose land we were camping on, rode up
rather briskly and told me to get out of the river on to the bank, that a big
rise was closely approaching. Of course I did as advised and started back to
camp when to my astonishment there came this actual wall of water, it looked
to me to be a straight up and down wall about five feet high. It was approaching with speed; it was swirling and muddy, filled with all manner of
debris, and before long actually was carrying with it . . . a cow and again a
pig. . . . It then became understandable to me how incidents we read of in the
papers, where vehicles such as horse-drawn [carriages] and autos are often
reported swept off low bridges, washed down stream frequently with loss of
life and property. It is a sight once seen will not ever be forgotten.

E. H. Perry, Sr.
Unpublished autobiography

SATURDAY, APRIL 6, 1940. NOON. ABOUT THREE HUN-
dred spectators were assembled at the Austin Dam. The day was cold
and rainy. A mild blue norther had settled on Austin, chilling the
air. Throughout the region, the rains came, after a dry spell of inter-
minable length. Despite the weather, it was a grand occasion. Just
one day short of that Saturday, forty years earlier, when the first
Austin dam had been destroyed by a heavy flood, a new dam was
being dedicated. Dedicated in the name of Tom Miller, but also dedicated to the many men and women who had worked so hard to
ensure the reconstruction of the first dam. Edgar Perry, the Commodore, was on hand to serve as the master of ceremonies. Two years
earlier, his friend Tom Miller had chosen him to serve as the chairman of the Citizens Advisory Committee, a group of prominent
Austinites who worked in Austin and Washington to secure the
dam. A. B. Spires, president of the Chamber of Commerce was there
too, and soon would make a speech praising the men and women
who helped to build the new dam. Naturally Walter Long, ever the
circumspect but guiding figure, was there, but, as his custom, he
would remain in the background, letting others make speeches and
raise the hoopla. Alvin Wirtz, undersecretary of the interior, was on
hand, but his close friend, Congressman Lyndon Johnson, was not,
having been unable to attend the ceremonies. And Tom Miller, the
large, ebullient mayor was there, beaming with pride in another ac-
complishment for this city on the Colorado he loved so much.

Commodore Perry introduced the various people one by one.
Maury Maverick, former congressman from Texas and now mayor of
San Antonio, was on the platform, seated next to Ralph Yarborough. Maverick watched with interest as the people were introduced, and was particulary taken with the splendid way in which
the city of Austin had decided to honor itself, and its mayor. Ever
envious and contentious with his sometime friend, sometime foe,
Tom Miller, he leaned over to Yarborough and inquired about a
group of young men, attired in naval uniforms and standing ramrod
straight. Why, that's Tom Miller's navy, Yarborough replied, leaving
Maverick to wonder why he could not have a navy of his own down
in San Antonio.[1] Maverick soon rose and provided a short New
Deal speech, saying that "this is no time for a political speech, and
I'm not making one but if I were I'd say vote for Roosevelt."[2]

One by one the speakers stood and lavished praise upon the people, alive and dead, who had helped construct the dam. Most were

especially appreciative of the active help of the federal government. Wirtz remarked: "it was only when a real New Deal placed a man of wisdom and courage in the White House that we were able to see our way to accomplish what had been in the minds of so many people for so long. His ability, and the ability of his assistants – like secretary Ickes and Administrator Carmody – was manifest in their willingness to understand what the people wanted and to set about translating these wants into accomplishments."[3] Congressman Johnson, in a message sent to Miller, praised the federal government, too, and commended the collective effort of many individuals that resulted in the dam. And Tom Miller rose, and with uncustomary brevity – thank heavens for that, they all must have thought! – particularly complimented the efforts of Lyndon Johnson. He was a man, Miller said, who played a major role in making the system of dams on the Colorado a reality instead of a vision.[4]

This was not the final act in the creation of dams on the Colorado, for more would be built and more would be dedicated. But it was a vitally significant one in the history of Austin. The vision, indeed, had become a reality: growth and industry, so long ago imagined by Alexander Woolridge, had come so close people could feel them. Years of hard labor had made it so. The dream had inspired men and women as different as the extraordinarily ambitious Lyndon Johnson and the self-effacing Walter Long. Flooding waters, of the sort encountered on the Llano by Perry, could now be controlled. Water, that precious fluid, now could halt the thirst and wash the body in times of drought. And power, hydroelectric power, was now available, at incomparably low rates, to drive the engines, turn the machines, and transmit light here, in the wilds of central Texas.

This chapter tells the tale of the Tom Miller Dam and of the other dams on the Colorado. It tells the saga of the almost endless failures that led finally to the completion of the dams. It tells of the role of the federal government, of the New Deal, and of battles waged between public power and private industry. It tells of the work of our orchard planters, and of many more men and women like them, who helped insure the vision of growth would materialize in Austin. And, finally, it tells of those men who used public power to secure their own private gain.

To understand the story of Tom Miller Dam, we must first take ourselves beyond the city limits of Austin. We must consider the troubles faced by people all up and down the Colorado River, troubles that eventually produced a common awareness and a common determination to harness the turbulent Colorado.

Far downstream from Austin, where the mouth of the Colorado yawns wide into the Gulf of Mexico, there was as much worry over the river as in Austin. But it was of a different sort. In Austin people for years had been deeply concerned with holding back the water, with preventing it from so often ravaging the streets and homes and businesses that decorated the state capital. Downstream, near Bay City, in Matagorda and Wharton counties, people were worried about floods, too, but for different reasons. Here there were numerous farmers who had planted their farms with many acres of rice. When the water washed down from above, hundreds of miles away, their crops and land would be swept off with a fury that took lives and ruined livelihoods. Farmers here could not count on regular harvests if they did not know whether the rice would be there, if the soil had been washed out to the Gulf. Flood after angry flood had come through, and year after year left behind material devastation and spiritual despair. Urged by local citizens to attempt to repair the situation, the United States Army Corps of Engineers conducted various studies of the river and of the floods. One of their reports revealed that between 1900 and 1913 seventeen floods had caused a total damage in this region of $61,400,000 and had claimed the lives of sixty-one residents during this time.[5]

There also was concern with navigation among downstream residents, although this was chiefly an obsession of the late nineteenth and early twentieth centuries. A few boats over the years had managed to make their way up the Colorado to Austin. In the 1840s, the Kate Ward managed to make its way up to Austin, covering over 200 miles.[6] Soon afterward, the Colorado also managed to find its way to Austin's shores. Eventually, however, the river became useless for navigation. Because the waters of the Colorado often would move ever so slowly, owing to the occasional dry spells, numbers of logs, all manner of plants, and even the silt that washed into the mouth of the river from upstream grew into a massive tangle of mud and wood, an immovable object. This material, known as raft, collected to such an extent downstream, around the towns of Bay City and Matagorda, that it clogged the flow of the entire river. Besides making navigation impossible, during times of heavy rains the raft actually forced the river to renegotiate its course, and made flooding all the worse over lands directly adjacent to the river.[7]

Upstream from Austin, the residents had other worries. True, there were people who had planted crops, like corn and wheat, who wished to make sure that their fields would not be inundated whenever the skies opened up. And true, too, here there was some loss of life as well. But the main concern upstream from Austin was harnessing the river, making the water available directly for power, through water wheels, and later, well into the 1920s, for hydroelectric power. Tom Ferguson, a member of the first Board of Directors of the Lower Colorado River Authority (LCRA), relates that the people in Burnet, a small town that lies north of Austin, lived in a very simple style, without the benefits of many of the trappings of modern civilization.[8] Even today, a visit to Burnet reveals a modest assortment of houses and businesses, a town that the modern age of high technology and Texas Tudor seems to have overlooked. In the 1930s, Austin at least possessed some semblance of progress, in the form of a dam that, however poorly it worked, still managed to furnish brief moments of power. But, in Burnet and in nearby Llano, and elsewhere upstream, the picture was far more dreary. Ferguson remembers:

> Of course, the development of the river, up here in this area, was really motivated by a different motivation than that below in Austin. . . . Up here, we, of course, wanted the dams, the lakes. We wanted the irrigation. But the recreational feature of it was an attractive angle, too. And the power was also an attractive angle because . . . in 1927, the town of Burnet had electricity . . . and Marble Falls had some, and Bertram at night, just a small local plant, and that was the only power in the country. Very inadequate for anything except just for lighting. The other counties around here were very much the same way.[9]

Worry, concern, and interest took place all along the shores of the Colorado, from the headstreams to the mouth, over how it would be controlled and used for human purposes. And it became a matter of channeling this, like the waters themselves, that eventually would bring about the reconstruction of the Austin dam.

The builders of Austin fashioned the first genuine success on the

Colorado. Soon after the public pronouncement of Alexander Wooldridge in 1888, the one that urged a vision of industry and progress on the community, citizens more or less eagerly responded. John McDonald served as mayor of Austin during the years of the construction of the first dam, in the early 1890s; in fact, he had won office running on a single plank—that a dam should be constructed in Austin.[10] Various problems beset the construction of that dam, among them leakages and difficulties in the construction of the power house. Nevertheless, the work finally was completed on May 2, 1893.

The dams had been fashioned from large blocks of red granite from nearby Granite Mountain, and with an interior created from limestone rubble. Even today, many of those red granite blocks can be seen in the small islands that surface just below the site of the modern dam, and they are so large and strong that one wonders how they ever gave way. But crumble they did. Problems with leakages in the dam and troubles with the foundations continued to plague the first structure, even after repairs had been made. In 1897, G. H. Palm, member of one of the first Swedish families to live in Austin, discovered that the material under the toe of the dam gradually had been eaten away.[11] Whether because of this erosion, the gradual leakages that continually had to be plugged, or other such faults, the dam was made useless only seven years after its completion. A flood in early April 1900 brought unmatched destruction to the city and nearby areas. With the crest of the floodwaters fully eleven feet above the height of the dam, on April 7 a large, central portion gave way. Eventually it was carried several feet downstream by the floodwaters. Although it remained standing for a time, the force of the water broke the section apart, leaving it to disintegrate completely within days.[12]

The next fifteen years were a time of great expectations and unfulfilled dreams for Austin residents, as for all those people who wished to harness the river. Efforts were undertaken almost at once to repair the dam. Numbers of studies were made of the dam site, and investigators were brought in to assess stability of the remaining sections of the structure. One new fact came to light. Austin is the site of many springs, and of caverns carved out of limestone. These waters throughout the years have been one of the great attractions of the community, particularly the cool and handsome springs that run into the Colorado a couple of miles south of the present dam site, which are known as Barton Springs. Interspersed with this array of

beautiful waters and rocks are an equal amount of dangers, in particular the fault line that traverses Austin, the Balcones Fault. Engineers, such as Daniel Mead, who undertook studies of the dam site,
recognized rather quickly that fault lines probably had something to
do with why the first dam gave way so quickly. As Mead observed
in his 1917 report, "it is obvious that these fault lines must extend
through the dam foundation and to hundreds of feet in depth. . . .
There appear to be numerous lines of weakness subsidary to the principal fault line under the structure of the dam."[13]

Even in the face of these and other problems, citizens were willing
to persist in the effort to complete the dam, knowing that its completion meant hydroelectric power, industry, and a victory over the
vagaries of nature. An agreement thus was reached in 1911 with William Johnson for the reconstruction of the dam as well as the power
station. Instead of trying to build and pay for the dam through direct
taxation of the residents, the city committed itself to pay Johnson
$100,000 outright, and to continue with payments of $32,400 annually for a period of twenty-five years.[14] Bonds eventually were sold
to the William P. Carmichael Company by the City Water Works to
finance the plans. Much of the expanse in this effort went toward
profit and the cost of promoting the bonds. Of about $1,000,000 to
be spent over time for the reconstruction of the dam, less than half
this amount, or $453,000, actually would go for the construction it-
self.[15] The effort to reconstruct the dam ended in faliure. The Carmichael Company went bankrupt before finishing the dam, leaving
the city with an incomplete structure and no source of further funding. That proved to be only a minor failure. Flooding again occurred
in the spring of 1915, the highest floodwaters to reach Austin since
those of 1900. Reaching to the crest of the dam, the waters began to
seep through the sluice gates, revealing unsuspected weaknesses.
Only months later, in September 1915, new floods arrived in Austin,
and this time they absolutely ravaged the structure. Damage was unbelievable, stirring S. S. Posey, the inspection engineer, to conclude
that the main workings of the dam simply no longer were usable.[16]

Would central Texans ever manage to overcome the waters? Would
they be condemned to live on the outskirts of civilization for ever,
far removed from the benefits of progress? The year 1915 proved to
be a turning point.

The social sciences have important things to say about people, and about the way communities are created. One of the most important is this: worlds are not built by single individuals alone, though they will act as leaders. Rather, worlds are constructed by collaborative architecture, by individuals who join together to fight some imminent danger, to drive off some constant foe. Such a collaborative venture was born in Austin on May 28, 1915. On that day forty-seven men descended on the community, intent to work the magic of human design. They came from up and down the shores of the Colorado, from those many communities that, like Austin, were prey to the floods[17] – from Bay City, Wharton, Columbus, La Grange, Smithville, and Bastrop. They included people who were to be prominent later in the story of the dams. Congressman James P. Buchanan was there, representative of the Tenth Congressional District, which included Austin. Earlier in the month, he attended a meeting of the Austin Chamber of Commerce at which he expressed great interest in enhancing navigation of the waters of the Colorado, and in ridding the downstream river of the raft. There was also J. J. Mansfield, from Columbus. Two years earlier, he had served as head of an organization known as the Colorado River Association, made up of downstream residents from Matagorda, Wharton, and Colorado counties, those near the mouth of the river. In 1917, he would be elected to the Congress of the United States from the Ninth Congressional District.

The meeting, originally intended to convene at the Chamber of Commerce headquarters in the Scarbrough Building, was so packed it had to move across the street, to the Driskill Hotel. The main purpose of the meeting, it was announced, was to consider how navigation of the Colorado could be implemented. Congressman Buchanan spoke at great length. He noted that the studies were to be made of how navigation could be improved. Representing the Army Corps of Engineers, Colonel C. S. Riche devoted his talk to methods that could be used to remove the raft from the mouth of the river, noting the merits of cutting rather than blasting it out. He also pointed out that for the army and navy, navigation was the most important issue, and reclamation of lands only incidental. Later speakers spoke to the matter of the reclamation of lands, particularly those men who represented the rice growers from downstream. While navigation offered some attractive features, they were far more concerned with relieving the burden of living in a place that alternated between the extremes of severe drought and heavy flooding. Mr. S. J. Cleveland, for instance remarked that " 'the lower Colorado River Valley must be irrigated. . . . I am sure that, if the proper levees are built on this river and proper means provided whereby this irrigation can be carried on, the value of this country as a farming district will be immensely increased.' "[18] At the conclusion of the meeting, the Colorado River Improvement Association was formed, under the guiding hand of Walter Long and the Austin Chamber of Commerce. It numbered among its directors people from the various counties up and down the river, including Mansfield from Colorado County, and Fritz Engelhard, a farmer and businessman from Eagle Lake. Twenty years later, he would become chairman of the first Board of Directors of the Colorado River Authority. Political pieces gradually were being laid in place for the dams.

Once the Colorado River Improvement Association was formed, it began to alert people to the need for improving sections of the river. Meetings were held in June in La Grange, and in August in Bastrop, to draw attention to what the association hoped to accomplish. Various speakers with expert knowledge about the river addressed citizens on the dangers and told them of ways the river could be controlled. And the citizens appeared to be very interested. At the Bastrop meeting, Walter Long reports, there were over two hundred people in attendance. Rice growers who attended the meeting publicly thanked Austin for enabling them to have water from the still unfinished Austin Dam, water that had saved their crops from complete destruction. And Congressman Buchanan spoke of several reasons for improving the river, noting that "the three prime objects for improving the Colorado River are reclamation, irrigation and navigation."[19]

In the course of these and subsequent meetings, knowledge was shared among participants, awareness heightened of the dangers and of the benefits to be achieved from reclamation, and social relations established among people from different sections of the river. It was the latter that were of considerable significance and would help to shape later political efforts.

The Colorado River Improvement Association harnessed the energies of many people and was singularly effective in keeping interest alive on behalf of the dams. Efforts would be made to reconstruct the Austin dam as well. Elsewhere there were other plans afoot to develop other dams on the Colorado, dams whose effect could

prove more significant than a single dam at Austin. In the late
nineteenth century, General Adam R. Johnson had settled in the
region of Burnet. Friend to Alexander Wooldridge, he may have
been the first person ever to envision dams on the Colorado, but his
designs were intended to be practised far above Austin. His idea was
to put up a structure at Shirley Shoals, only a few miles from Burnet,
where the red granite formed a firm bottom for the dam, and a basin
seemed to occur naturally above the site. Despite his dreams, Johnson was unable to prosecute the dam to completion. But he was successful in interesting another man, Colonel C. H. Alexander, in
continuing the project.

Alexander was wealthy, a person who already had one transportation success under his belt, the interurban railway in Dallas–Fort
Worth.[20] He became interested in the project for the same reason
that other developers would – it would provide hydroelectric power
and add no little amount of money to his already full pockets. In
1909, he began construction on a dam at Marble Falls, just below
Burnet. He even managed to complete part of the dam. Over the next
fifteen years or so, he carried out surveys of the Colorado, trying to
assess other points on the river where it seemed advisable to build
dams. During this same period, he acquired the water rights for
various sites, including those at Shirley Shoals.[21] Throughout, he
was interested in creating structures that would generate hydroelectric power. But he also knew of the interests of the downstream residents, and hoped to help them, too. Yet, like so many whose lives
had been tied to the fortunes of the Colorado, Alexander's luck
turned sour. His millions vanished. Tom Ferguson relates that one
of Alexander's problems came about because of simple carelessness.
His contractor left large quantities of concrete, intended to erect the
dams, open and vulnerable to the rains when they fell. Hence, the
material became useless for construction.[22]

Once more, it seemed, the river had been victorious. Like Moby
Dick, the river continued to elude human efforts to control it, pursuing a relentless journey of its own. But never fear – where profit
lurks, can big capital be far behind? Martin Insull, brother of Sam
Insull, was the president of Middle West Utilities. He knew of the
concern of downstream farmers, particularly those who grew crops of
rice, and recognized the benefits to be achieved from the dams upstream. Also, he realized that a good deal of easy money could be
made from building sources of hydroelectric power in central Texas.

If anyone could take over from Alexander and rescue the construction of the dams, it appeared it would be Insull. He, too, ran into difficulties, however. A number of citizens of west Texas, represented by the West Texas Chamber of Commerce, were concerned about their water rights on the Colorado.[23] Here, where the headstreams of the Colorado lay, drought was as much a problem as elsewhere in Texas, indeed, even more so. This area would soon become victim to the great Dust Bowl of the 1930s, and, perhaps with a certain degree of prescience, the people here realized how vital water would be to them. Thus, they undertook to keep a hold on the water rights of the Colorado, and, feeling their interests might well be threatened, stirred up a political controversy that would not abate for many years. Insull, sensing the political difficulties of obtaining water rights, and securing control over use of the Colorado, ultimately lost interest in building dams and, on July 24, 1928, he informed the West Texas Chamber of Commerce that he would pursue the project no further.[24]

Now there enters the picture of this morass of tangled human interests and downstream riffraff a figure who would prove absolutely decisive to the construction of dams, Alvin J. Wirtz. Wirtz, indeed, stands to the Colorado dams as Ahab did to Moby Dick, a man obsessed with pursuing a vision, and one who pursued this effort in spite of overwhelming odds. So far as one can tell, he was a brilliant lawyer and had an absolute genius for handling the tactics and strategies of politics, both within and outside legislatures. "The smartest man I ever knew," says Beverly Randolph, his secretary for many years. Wirtz seemed the type that probably played a fine game of poker, never giving evidence of a first-class hand, but projecting the power of a first class mind.[25] He always played life close to the vest, had few, if any, confidants, and in the end proved to be at least one of the guiding forces for the dams. Our fine poet, the mayor of Austin, said of Wirtz at the dedication of the Alvin Wirtz Dam in 1952 that "he was the architect, the legal adviser, the contractor of the building of these man-made lakes and dams. He constantly gave his mind, his body and soul in the creation of the [Colorado River] Authority, the carrying out of the plans and its successful consummation."[26]

Wirtz had grown up in Columbus, Texas, received a law degree from the university in 1910, and began his practice of law in Eagle Lake. He moved to Seguin in 1917, where he became a law partner of Rudolph A. Weinert. Like himself, Weinert would serve in the

State Legislature as a senator from Guadalupe County. Throughout his years of maturation, Wirtz resided in exactly those places along the Colorado most subject to devastation by the river. And, though no biography exists to tell us of his own concerns, we can have little doubt that his knowledge of this destructive force must have been a memory that drove him to continue his tireless work on behalf of dams. Naturally, he had his own pocketbook in mind, too. In the late 1920s, he was serving in Seguin as counsel for the Garwood Irrigation Company, a firm that had been interested in securing Martin Insull's work on behalf of the dams on the Colorado. Wirtz also served at the time as legal representative for Emery, Peck and Rockwood Corporation, the development company that was building dams on the Guadalupe River, near Seguin. Writing of his effort, Wirtz would later inform an acquaintance that there "are six dams on the Guadalupe River in the vicinity of Seguin, and I think any citizen of Guadalupe County will tell you that I was the local citizen who had most to do with constructing those dams. . . . I was a director of those companies until I accepted this job [as undersecretary of the interior] and until I left Seguin I was active in their management and operation. In fact, during their beginning period I had practically sole responsibility."[27]

Wirtz's work on behalf of dams on the Guadalupe, and particularly his association with Emery, Peck and Rockwood Corporation, produced the next episode in the saga. Once Martin Insull lost interest, it appeared as though the dams might never be built. The floods never would be controlled, the rice crops would continue to be assaulted, life on the Colorado, in short, would remain miserable. But Wirtz managed to interest George Peck in the Colorado River project. Peck already had the experience of developing dams on the Guadalupe and knew how much similar construction on the Colorado would mean to the people. In 1929, therefore, Emery, Peck and Rockwood managed to secure the several water right permits to Colorado properties from the Alexander estate, and from Jay Alexander.[28] Shortly thereafter, Peck had Wirtz open offices for his firm in Austin. Most of the early work was simply devoted to securing property in and around the site of Shirley Shoals. It was decided that a dam at this site would be the major project. The dam, soon to become known as the Hamilton Dam, seemed to offer excellent prospects for both hydroelectric power and for irrigation.

The employees of the company, Jay Alexander, Ward Arnold, and

Beverly Randolph, the latter of whom had begun to work for Wirtz while he served in the Senate, toiled long and hard to develop land rights in the area of the dam. Days were spent in a car, traveling across dirt roads, and speaking to various farmers and ranchers who owned property in the vicinity of the dam. So enterprising were these young developers that early in the days of air travel they relied upon a plane to take them to the dam site from Austin. Always the conscientious worker, Randolph, who once was praised to the heavens as the "finest typewriter around," carried her massive machine with her constantly, drafting memos to the senator and keeping accurate records for Peck. Emery, Peck and Rockwood put in a great deal of time and money in the development of surveys, acquisition of land sites, and related tasks. Altogether, they spent over $1 million on their work.[29] Part of the money was required to hire an engineering firm, Fargo Engineering Company, to draw up plans for a whole series of dams.[30] At this point, the company was ready for the construction of the first dam, that at Shirley Shoals, or the Hamilton Dam. They let a contract to a reputable firm, the Fegles Construction Company, Ltd., of Minneapolis, and the estimated cost of construction of the dam was expected to be $3 million.[31] It seemed at last that the hope of taming the Colorado would come true. Headlines ran in the *Austin American*, announcing the event as though it were some great victory. Of course, in a sense it was.

One more event still had to be played out, however, and this reintroduced the interests of Martin and Sam Insull. It was arranged that a new company, the Central Texas Hydro-Electric Company, would be organized and would operate the Hamilton Dam. This company then took over the assets of Emery, Peck and Rockwood. In turn, Central Texas Hydro-Electric Company funded the purchase by the sale of $3,714,500 worth of six percent bonds, of which $2,873,000 was bought by Mississippi Valley Utilities Company, and the other $841,500 by the Central and Southwest Utilities Company.[32] Moreover, the power of the yet incomplete Hamilton Dam had already been purchased from Central Texas Hydro-Electric. Fifty percent of the power generated by Hamilton Dam had been bought by West Texas Utilities Company and the Central Power and Light Company, each with thirty-year contracts.[33] Now, do not be confused by the number of bit players, for behind them stood but a single corporate giant, the Insull empire. The Insulls had reintroduced themselves into the project for building the dams, and in a very grand manner. As Randolph recalls of the time, the fact that the Insulls now would be involved in the Hamilton Dam project seemed to everyone to assure its success.[34]

Construction finally started on the dam in 1931. Central Texas Hydro-Electric employed the very same staff in Austin as Emery, Peck and Rockwood had, and Alvin Wirtz served in an important capacity, as one of the vice-presidents of the new company. Business offices were moved to the Hamilton Dam site. In these days, the area was thoroughly isolated, with few homes and people nearby. Randolph now recalls being out there by herself at night, with animals howling. She is a most unusual person, however, and found the isolation not in the least disturbing. She worked round the clock, keeping Wirtz and other company officials informed of how the construction was progressing. This was a great period for people connected with the dam, as for many central Texans. The Great Depression had hit the region hard, as it had everywhere else. While men and women in New York were standing in food lines, or even throwing themselves out of skyscrapers, here at least 1,000 people had jobs, working to build the dam. Again, as Randolph recalls of this period, the awarding of the contract itself was seen as a great boon:

> All the newspapers in the area headlined the news and told of the effect the construction program would have on the unemployed. This was during the Depression and the project would give work to hundreds of people. . . . The announcement caused widespread excitement, not only for those who looked forward to employment, but also the people along the river who would benefit from the project.[35]

History should have taught them otherwise.

The house of cards the Insulls built collapsed in early 1932, and on April 20, work on the Hamilton Dam was called to a halt. The workers fully believed they would return to their jobs soon, after the troubles were ironed out. Still, it was a very sad day, etched deeply in the memory of Randolph. Now eighty-six, she remembers, as though yesterday, that it "was a desolate thing . . . I tell you when they had the wire . . . to cease working you saw hundreds and hundreds of old work gloves. . . . a thousand people working on the dam at that time. It was the saddest thing. Every time I see a work glove, I think of where they threw those gloves down."[36] Another chapter came to a close.

With work brought to a halt, the dam languished. And so did peoples' hopes. What next transpired is a major turning point not in central Texas history alone, but in the history of America over the last half century. Central Texans found themselves in their recurring predicament, how to tame the Colorado with no funds. Until then private financial investors had tried to build and operate the dams. The exception had been in Austin. What better source to turn to than the federal government. Empires like that of the Insulls were falling everywhere, the product of intemperate greed built on shaky foundations. The only hope seemed to lie in getting the boys in Washington to finance what no one else could. Or would.

When the Insull empire collapsed, Central Texas Hydro-Electric went into receivership. The receiver was Alvin Wirtz. Ralph Morrison, a resident of San Antonio and holder of a large number of investments, hoped to secure control over the Hamilton Dam. He offered a deal to Eugene Thayer, receiver for the Mississippi Valley Utilities Company, an Insull organization that had contracted to purchase power from Central Texas Hydro-Electric. Morrison would form a company to finance and complete the dam, he informed Thayer, so long as Thayer was willing to trade his bonds, worth more than $2½ million, for forty-nine percent of the common stock. In other words, Morrison would get controlling interest in the new company, to be called the Colorado River Company. Thayer, hoping somehow to avoid considerable financial loss, agreed to the deal. Legal problems remained, but eventually were cleared up.[37]

There were many rumors about the wealth and influence of Ralph Morrison, some obviously intended to halt his attempt to secure control over the dam. What is clear is that Morrison had contributed a substantial sum of money to the Roosevelt election campaign of 1932, and just on the eve of Roosevelt's New Deal he sought repayment.[38] He approached Jesse Jones and the Reconstruction Finance Corporation, erected to help the nation recover from the Depression, for purposes of securing a loan. With the loan, he intended to complete the Hamilton Dam. He was refused. The New Dealers in Washington, particularly men like Harold Ickes, wanted nothing to do with private corporations of the sort proposed by Morrison. Instead, they wanted to create a whole array of public agencies and institutions, federal and state organizations that would finance and regulate many of the operations of the economy, especially those of public lands and riverways. Obviously, Hamilton Dam, like the entire set of designs for the Colorado, furnished a prime example of the kind of thing they wished to bring under public control. Not to be denied, Morrison continued to entreat the federal government, this time turning to the Public Works Administration (PWA), run by Ickes. His hope now was the federal government would provide a loan to his fledgling company, based upon the emergency relief measures that were dispensed by the PWA. Once more, he was refused. It must have seemed to him that he couldn't make an offer that wouldn't be refused.

Now Congressman James Buchanan reappeared, to try to get Hamilton Dam finished. In the preceding years, since his first efforts to get studies made of the navigability of the Colorado, Buchanan and the Colorado River Improvement Association had persisted in their efforts to get dams built on the Colorado. The association had kept up a steady stream of correspondence with Martin Insull and Middle West Utilities to sustain their interest. Both Buchanan and the association sought in the 1920s to press for ways to rid the river of the raft, none of which proved successful.[39] In 1933 however, it appeared to Buchanan that the prospects for securing dams at last were very bright. Together with Senators Tom Connally and Morris Sheppard, and his friend, Congressman J. J. Mansfield, Buchanan approached Roosevelt to get funds.

By then, both Buchanan and Mansfield had attained positions of considerable prominence in the national government. Buchanan served as the chairman of the House Appropriations Committee, thus standing just under the Speaker of the House in importance, while Mansfield headed up the Rivers and Harbors Committee. Buchanan, especially, carried a great deal of influence, characteristically wielding it, as people remember, as though it were a gentle wand rather than a heavy bludgeon.[40] In dealing with Roosevelt, they were aided in no little measure by Charles Marsh, the part owner of Marsh-Fentress Newspapers, which ran various newspapers in Texas, among them, the *Austin American* and *Austin Statesman*. Marsh was a key supporter and friend of the president. After a number of unsuccessful efforts, they finally were able to convince Roosevelt to provide a loan that would permit Hamilton Dam to be completed. But he would only furnish a loan, of $4½ million, so long as an agency were created in Texas that would control the operations of the dams. No such agency existed. One more bridge thus had to be crossed.

All attention now turned back to Texas, and to the State Legislature. If the legislators could be persuaded to create a new state agency that would control the Colorado, then Roosevelt and the federal government were prepared to furnish funds to finish construction of Hamilton Dam. A precedent already existed in Texas for such a venture.[41] Alvin Wirtz, ever the visible presence on behalf of the dams, used his considerable skill and knowledge to draft the bill to establish a Colorado River Authority. The bill defined the boundaries of a river district. It included the ten counties bordering the Colorado that would most benefit from dams and other projects: Blanco, Burnet, Llano, Travis, Bastrop, Fayette, Colorado, Wharton, San Saba, and Matagorda. The bill also described officers of the new authority, outlined its obligations and duties, and spoke of the ties between itself and the state. And it established limits on the extent to which the authority could go into debt in securing revenue bonds (later this would be adjusted upward).

There were two major provisions of the bill that were absolutely essential to its success. The first outlined powers of the authority in the matter of conservation and reclamation of the waters of the Colorado, the flood control purposes on which almost everyone could agree. One function of the authority, the bill stated, is "to control, store and preserve, within the boundaries of the District, the waters of the Colorado River and its tributaries for any useful purpose, and to use, distribute and sell the same, within the boundaries of the District, for any such purpose."[42] A second principal function, it stated, is "to develop and generate water power and electric energy within the boundaries of the District and to distribute and sell water power and electric energy, within or without the boundaries of the District."[43] This second provision turned out to be exceedingly controversial. If a loan were to be secured from the federal government to the state agency, then it had to be repaid in some manner. The state of Texas itself was not prepared to furnish the funds to the proposed agency in order to repay the loan; rather, those funds would have to come out of the agency's own revenues. Of course, such revenues were nonexistent. To the architect and sponsors of the bill, it seemed, the main source of those revenues must be the generation and sale of hydroelectric power. Such a feature, of course, was very attractive to a number of residents along the Colorado, particularly those who lived in and around Burnet. Yet there was a problem. If the project involved the sale of hydroelectric power as the major source of revenue, could a loan to the authority be justified on the grounds of flood control and reclamation benefits? More to the point,

the federal government had no constitutional right to enter into competition with private utility companies, an issue that later would have
to be settled by the Supreme Court. Federal officials were especially
sensitive to this matter. Later, as the drama unfolded, Henry Hunt,
legal counsel to Harold Ickes, assessed the legality of federal funding
to the Colorado River Authority by highlighting irrigation benefits
of dams on the Colorado, but downplaying the sale of hydroelectric
power.[44] There was another reason for downplaying hydroelectric
power. Texas Power and Light Company.

There were two private utility companies in Central Texas that
sold electricity to consumers, Central Power and Light and Texas
Power and Light (TP & L). The latter was the dominant firm. It
sold power both to private customers and to municipalities. For
a time, in fact, negotiations took place with the City of Austin
over the reconstruction and operation of Austin Dam. These negotiations proved fruitless.[45] The president of TP & L was John W.
Carpenter. Carpenter was a very aggressive man and went to considerable lengths to maintain and enlarge the hold of his company
over the marketplace. TP & L lobbied hard, using personnel and
money whenever and wherever it seemed necessary. Beverly Randolph today remembers when Mr. Head, the principal lobbyist for
TP & L, went out with her to the Hamilton Dam site. Together they
walked the suspension bridge overlooking the dam, and he said to
her, " 'Beverly, no water will ever flow over this dam.' "[46] Thus,
when Carpenter learned of the possibility that the federal government would embark on a program to produce and sell hydroelectric
power, he became absolutely incensed. While he, like many businesspeople in the region, yet had to be shown the benefits of the New
Deal philosophy, his real concern was profits. How could he possibly
compete with the federal government in the sale of hydroelectric
power, particularly when the government intended to provide cheap
power? The issue had already been raised in the case of the Tennessee
Valley Authority, and was much on people's minds.[47]

When the bill to establish the Colorado River Authority was introduced in the State Legislature, for the first time in 1933, TP & L,
as well-equipped with lobbyists as any firm around, vigorously sought
to block its passage. They were helped by citizens from west Texas,
from the areas in and around Abilene and Brownwood, who themselves continued to fear that their water rights at the headstreams of
the Colorado would be abrogated if the authority were established.

The concern of the west Texans had lingered since the late 1920s, and was especially forceful now because of terrible drought and dust storms. Together both TP & L and the west Texans managed to prevent the bill from getting beyond committee discussion in the House. It never even reached the floor of the House for a vote.

During the course of the 43rd Legislature, there were, all told, four called sessions. This was during the reign of Miriam "Ma" Ferguson, who ostensibly occupied the position of governor, even though most people knew her husband was in control. True to the character of Texas politics, the most notable thing I have learned of Ma Ferguson is that, besides being the first woman ever elected as govenor, she may have been the most antifeminist of all Texas women at the time. That there were four called sessions is not in the least surprising in light of her other problems. In any case, the bill to establish the Colorado River Authority came up again in the second and third called sessions, each time being defeated by the failure of the House to approve it. All the while, people in Washington were considerably anxious about its fate, particularly Buchanan and Mansfield, each of whom knew how much its passage would mean for the construction of central Texas dams. Buchanan carried on a fast and furious correspondence with different people in the state, seeking to impress on them the urgency of the bill's passage. In a most memorable remark, Buchanan wrote to Wirtz to inform him of the delay in the president's signature to the allocation for Texas. "Nothing should be left undone to hasten the consummation of this loan," he writes. "There are several billion dollars in application for loans pending in P.W.A. and only about one billion dollars to loan. The early birds will get the worms."[48]

Finally, the bill came up in the fourth called session. This session, according to knowledgeable informants, was intended to deal only with two outstanding matters, the Colorado River Authority and the site of the Texas Centennial.[49] Now the barrage of criticism against the proposed authority became intense and almost merciless. Parties on both sides of the issue were fighting over potential profits, but also on ideological programs on how best to resurrect the American economy, and with it, of course, the American spirit. A number of people in central Texas were hell-bent against federal intervention. Many of them were members of the Austin Chamber of Commerce, people who still believed that only private industry could help the nation overcome its hardships. Walter Long remained in the background.

He hoped not to antagonize his constituents and friends, but he also hoped, more than anything else, to see the dams materialize. Growth in Austin, after all, was a vision he hoped to inspire and sustain. Without dams, he knew, growth would be a virtual impossibility.[50] The main criticisms were leveled at Ralph Morrison, and the profits he stood to gain if the dams were built. Morrison became the target of considerable publicity. An editorial in the *Chicago Tribune* of November 4, 1934, entitled "Mystery in Texas" claimed:

> At the last special session, a month or so ago, the enabling bill for the Colorado river project failed of passage. That bill was calculated to pave the way for a grant of $4,500,000 of federal easy money for the construction of the Buchanan dam [Hamilton Dam had by this time been renamed in honor of the congressman]. The grant was to include more than a million dollars as an outright gift.
>
> It has been repeatedly asserted, and not denied, that the control of the property is to pass from the receiver for the Mississippi Valley company, an Insull subsidiary, to Ralph Morrison, a wealthy Texan who was an original supporter of Mr. Roosevelt and has remained on intimate terms with many of the New Dealers. Mr. Morrison recently took Prof. Moley on a trip into Mexico. Prof. Moley was the original brain truster [of the New Deal]. . . .
>
> Knowing no more than has here been recited, anyone could have predicted with considerable confidence that further efforts would be made to pass the Colorado river enabling act. The prediction is being fulfilled. What could be less mysterious?[51]

There were several leaders of the resistance to the bill, the principal one being Sarah Hughes, a representative from Dallas. Many years later, on November 22, 1963, it was Mrs. Hughes, federal district judge, who administered the presidential oath of office to Lyndon Johnson aboard Air Force One. Hughes decried the Colorado bill, arguing that it was a device designed to enable a wealthy Texan to profit from the New Deal. Her tone carried the conviction of a moralist bent on ridding the political arena of filthy lucre and influence-peddling. Later, it was learned that Mrs. Hughes' husband had been employed at the time by the TP & L.[52] What price glory!

Two amendments were offered to the bill in the course of the fourth session. One was the Dean Amendment. It intended to ensure that west Texas did not relinquish its water rights with the establishment of the new authority. There were various claims and counterclaims about the sponsorship of this new amendment. Tom Ferguson, an active combatant in the struggles, recalls that the West Texas Chamber of Commerce was a strong backer of the Dean Amendment, and believes that the chamber was dominated by people on the payroll of TP & L.[53] Years later, John Babcock, a longtime employee of the authority, learned that, in fact, Dean was on the TP & L payroll.[54] The second amendment was the Moore and Kayton Amendment. Its purpose was to prevent Ralph Morrison from gaining any money whatsoever from the sale of the properties he now owned, through his contract with Thayer of Mississippi Valley Utilities. So determined were Moore and Kayton to stop Morrison from gaining any benefits that their amendment would have made it a felony if either Morrison or Wirtz got any compensation.

Congressman Buchanan now was working at both ends of the proposed bargain, seeking to secure passage of the bill in Texas and to secure the massive funds from Washington. He and Mansfield spent many days in Austin, speaking on behalf of the bill to legislators. Federal officials, especially Ickes, were growing reluctant to provide PWA funds. The grounds for Ickes' resistance are unclear. Ferguson claims that Ickes simply thought that all Texans were crooks—and the man didn't even know of J. R. Ewing—whereas Walter Woodward, good friend of Buchanan and president pro tempore of the Texas Senate, speculated that Mrs. Hughes had gotten to Ickes.[55] Whatever the grounds, Buchanan was finding Ickes increasingly uncooperative. Thus, on November 8, he wired to Woodward:

> I conferred at length with Hunt and Burke of PWA on the Colorado River Authority now pending in the Legislature of Texas. Stop. As you know I favor the development of Texas and every section thereof therefore I want the Colorado Authority Bill to deal fairly and justly with the people throughout its Watershed. Stop. Believing as I do that there is abundant flood waters go [sic] down this river which if conserved will meet every demand of municipalities irrigation and production of hydro-electric power and further believing that I can procure the allotment of the necessary funds to complete the Buchanan Dam as well as the three of four other dams on other good dam sites immediately below the Buchanan Dam

with the Dean or Public Policy Amendment in the bill. Neither Public Works or myself deem it fatal to the project. Stop. The Moore Amendment dealing with compensation commission etc. arising out of a contract entered into between Sayer [sic] and Morrison about two and one half years ago, making it a felony for the Court Receiver and Morrison to carry out this contract etc. is fatal to the project. Stop. It will render impossible for the public authority to procure title and possession of the dam site and other property now vested in the Colorado Rover [sic] Company. . . . If the Legislature will pass this bill with the amendments above mntioned [sic] eliminated I feel reasonably sure that the Federal Government will ultimately allot ten to fifteen million to complete the entire project. . . .[56]

One day later, the Conference Committee decided to drop the Moore and Kayton Amendment. Now Buchanan urged Woodward to expedite the passage of the enabling act, and the creation of the authority, for otherwise "if the Bill does not take effect for ninety days there is danger of PWA funds being allotted to other projects in other states."[57] Buchanan further underscored the precedence that this act, and authority, would have for Texas: "Remember . . . the Colorado River Authority will constitute the first precedent in the development of intra state rivers for any purposes other than navigation by the Federal Government in the entire Southwest. Stop. With the recent trend and activity of the Federal Government in aiding states and public authority therein this pred [sic] will prove to be of great importance to our entire state."[58] Little did the gentle congressman from Brenham, Texas, fully imagine how very revolutionary this act would prove!

On November 13, 1934, Governor Miriam "Ma" Ferguson signed the bill to permit the creation of the Colorado River Authority.[59] In the end, it was a bargain struck between contending parties, one that would permit Dallas representatives to get the Centennial exposition in return for their support of the Colorado River Authority bill, that produced agreement.[60] Among others on hand to witness the event was Walter Long, to whom the governor gave the pen.[61] With the enabling act in place, the final ends had to be secured in Washington. Buchanan had been concerned because of the delay in getting the act finalized. Now he had to fret even more. The original $4,500,000 set aside by the president for Buchanan Dam in the meantime had been spent, and it appeared there would be no federal funds at all. Irony of ironies, in view of the fact that it was at federal insistence that a Colorado River Authority had been created in the first instance! The pressure on Buchanan increased. An effort was orchestrated in Austin to convince the congressman of the need to acquire federal funds. Letters poured in to him from A. C. Bull, president of the Austin Chamber of Commerce, from Capital National Bank, from the law firm of Oatman and Oatman in Llano, as well as from various citizens in Burnet.[62] The telegram from Ray Lee, managing editor of the *Austin American*, reflected the sentiments of many people: "As you know, our newspapers fought for the Colorado Valley Authority Legislation on premise project would afford great direct work relief for unemployed this winter. Now is the time this work is needed and we hope sincerely you will be able to persuade all parties to bring this promise into fact."[63]

The opposition was not dead yet. TP & L as well as Mrs. Hughes, the latter of whom had refused to endorse the enabling act, continued to try to scuttle the plans. Buchanan got wind of the fact that Hughes had pleaded with Ickes not to fund the project, and in a letter to Ickes sought to defuse the criticisms, particularly accusations about Morrison's potential gains. Though himself a fiscal conservative, Buchanan also sought to persuade Ickes of the victory this battle promised for the federal government:

> I hope Mr. Secretary that I am not being too insistent but my heart and soul are in this project and I am determined if within my power, to see this project prosecuted to a successful conclusion, not only for the benefit to the unemployed, to prevent floods and provide cheap electrical energy to the people but to demonstrate to the Utility Companies that they cannot defeat the President, the people and the PWA in carrying out the Administration's policy that natural resources shall be used in the public interest and not for the aggrandizement of private interests.[64]

Ickes continued to be suspicious. He had his general counsel, Henry Hunt, prepare reports on the financial status of Buchanan Dam. He also sought an independent and impartial outside assessment of the legality of the Colorado River Authority.[65] Ickes wanted the federal government to take over the waterways and rivers throughout the land, but he also insisted that any such actions be defended on constitutional grounds.

Ickes finally satisfied himself on all counts of the propriety of the project, and on April 11, 1935, he announced that the Colorado River Authority would probably be the recipient of anywhere from $17 to $20 million of federal funds. After final approval by the president, and by other PWA officials, Ickes announced on May 16 that the PWA would provide $20 million in funds to complete dams on the Colorado. After so many years, and after so many people had devoted such extensive effort to getting dams built, one can imagine the excitement this announcement brought to Austin, and to the rest of central Texas. The *Austin American* proclaimed the great event in a lead story published on May 17.[66] Normally in these times lead stories were reserved only for kidnappings, the divorces of Hollywood stars, or the murder of archdukes; surely, the River Authority could be proud to stand in such a class. The article spoke at length of how these monies would assure the construction of the dams, and how such dams would solve the age-old problems of floods and of power up and down the Colorado. Fish hatcheries, land reclamation, and hydroelectric power were to be the principal benefits of the construction of the dams, the article said. And, besides all this, the Buchanan Dam would create a large lake, suitable for recreational purposes but to be used primarily to control the flow of water, to increase it when the rice fields downstream required, or to hold it back during times of heavy rains. At last, it seemed to everyone, the river would be tamed.

The creation of the Colorado River Authority and the provision of funds to the authority by the PWA tell us of two important historic acts—one to create the dams to control the Colorado; the other to permit the federal government to finance this control. Both acts were decisive to saving, indeed, to building this part of the United States, and to the development of our little community on the Colorado. We cannot and should not deny their importance in this regard. But with the provision of funds to build the dams, another event occurred, one that many people would claim simply is part of human nature. Twenty million dollars, whether it be private or federal, is nothing to sneeze at; and in the spring, when it takes next to nothing to tweak the nose in Austin, people certainly were not sneezing at these funds. Many poor men, previously unemployed and living by the skin of their teeth, ravaged by the hardships of the Depression and the un-availability of work, now could look forward to jobs. But some saw in the federal funds, and the dams, and the authority, something more. They saw a way to great personal gain, to help lift themselves above the crowds, to be more than another face. And some of these people made their appearance in this saga quite early.

One such person, it appears, was C. G. Malott. Malott was the president of the Colorado River Company, the last of the many pri-vate firms to be involved with the Buchanan Dam. Control of the Colorado River Company was in the hands of Ralph Morrison, Malott's father-in-law. Once the authority had been created, Malott believed that he should take over as its general manager. Why he should have thought himself entitled to do so is uncertain, in light of the fact that the state had created a public agency to operate the dams. In retrospect, it now seems likely that Sarah Hughes' concern over the operation and control of the dams may have been well founded, that, indeed Morrison was to get repayment on his check to FDR. Alvin Wirtz was willing to endorse Malott's appointment not, it seems, because he wanted Malott and Morrison to have con-trol of the authority, but rather because he believed that Malott pos-sessed a good deal of relevant experience and knowledge, particularly with the Buchanan site. In a letter on August 17, 1935, to Congress-man Buchanan, Wirtz advised that he had been the person to insist on Malott's appointment, not "as a personal favor to Malott," but "because I thought his selection would be to the interests of the project, on account of his ability and familiarity with the details of the project."[67] Buchanan himself believed that knowledge and familiarity with the project were essential to its successful completion, so even he favored the appointment of Malott.

Malott was a most dislikable, somewhat odd person, so Beverly Randolph remembers, and he did not impress members of the Board of Directors of the new authority with his goodwill and diplomacy.[68] He did intend to take over control of the project, and to run it pretty much as he saw fit. He showed little respect or friendship for mem-bers of the board, many of whom, like Tom Ferguson and Fritz Engelhard, had helped to shepherd the enabling act through the State Legislature, and had been involved in efforts to tame the river for many years.

In late August 1935, this issue came to a head. In seeking to resolve the matter, once more the aid of Charles Marsh, publisher of the

Austin American, was sought. The board members simply were unwilling to accept Malott and his efforts to control the project. They rejected Buchanan's endorsement of Mallot, and even threatened to resign *en masse* rather than to accept Malott as general manager. Raymond Brooks, member of the board and employee of Marsh on the *Austin American*, sent a telegram to Marsh on August 16, stating that the "Board unanimously declined to elect him [Malott] for political intriguing comma efforts to discredit the Board and dominating attempt to control project. . . . My opinion is board would resign rather than select Malott after what has occurred."[69] The situation obviously had gotten out of hand, and, at the time, it must have appeared that the river project was on the verge of yet another collapse. The directors, however, indicated that they were more than willing to cooperate with Buchanan and Ickes. They simply would not accept Malott as general manager. A bargain soon was struck, at the initiation of the board, to accept any general manager who was recommended by Ickes. Very quickly thereafter, the issue was resolved. Ickes recommended Clarence McDonough, who was the director of engineering of the PWA, and who already had considerable experience in the construction of dams.[70] The board quickly complied, and Malott was left out in the cold. But others soon would fill his shoes more than adequately.

In the course of his early years in Congress, Lyndon Johnson made it seem that he was the single driving force behind the Colorado River Authority, and the taming of the Colorado. Neither friend nor foe, I believe, can disagree with this assessment of Johnson's actions; certainly, the *Austin American* issues of the late 1930s and early 1940s would not disagree. To be sure, Johnson deserves considerable credit for his work. Without it, there is some chance the dams might not have been finished. Not much of one, in the light of the many people who already figured in the story—but some chance. Johnson made his entrance into this drama in early 1937.

Over the course of 1935 and 1936, the work on the construction of the dams proceeded. The properties at the Buchanan Dam site were purchased by the Colorado River Authority from the Colorado River Company and Malott. Funds still owed to the companies that had undertaken some early construction work, Fargo Engineering and Fegles Construction, also were paid off. It is not clear whether Ralph Morrison actually made a substantial profit from his investments in the Colorado River Company, but some participants, such as Beverly Randolph, claim he did.[71] Even Alvin Wirtz seems to have cleared a handsome sum.[72] Once these transactions were completed, the actual work at the dam site began. Among other contractors hired to do work were the Brown and Root Construction firm, owned by Herman and George Brown, of Austin and Houston, respectively. They received a contract to clear 26,000 acres of land that would eventually constitute Buchanan Lake.[73] The relief funds were put to good use: over 1,000 men were employed in the construction. Work also proceeded on the site just below Buchanan, the Roy Inks Dam, which would furnish additional hydroelectric power and be one of the several dams envisioned to straddle the Colorado above Austin. Altogether things were moving smoothly. Until Monday, February 22, 1937.

On that day Congressman James Buchanan died of a heart attack. His death was most unexpected. He was a mild man, and a powerful figure on Capitol Hill. People everywhere were fond of him. Tom Miller eulogized him as a man of "infinite patience; gentle yet having a balancing force which in a quiet way overcame every obstacle in his path."[74] More than anything else, the death of Buchanan portended a blow of potentially deadly force to the consummation of the dams. Miller, Long, Wirtz, the Colorado River Association, all had been of signal importance in creating the social and political architecture for the dams. But it was Buchanan who had carried the ball with Roosevelt, the PWA, even the Texas Legislature during the crucial period in late 1934. Miller gave voice to these fears when he said that "we in Austin are going to feel his loss to a greater degree perhaps than any other part of the country. He was responsible for the Colorado River Authority being created and for erection of Buchanan dam, Inks dam, and Marshall Ford dam which was dedicated last Friday."[75]

With Buchanan gone, the race was on to fill his seat. On February 28, Lyndon Johnson became the first person to announce for the position. Already the young man from Johnson City had built up a fine reputation in Washington, where for a time he served as secretary to Congressman Richard Kleberg, scion of the King Ranch family. While aide to Kleberg, Johnson had learned much about how things were done on the Hill, and, in the words of Creekmore Fath, "ran a beautiful office."[76] In the winter of 1937, Johnson was back in Austin, serving as state director of the National Youth Administration. Other people besides Johnson flocked to the race. Some suggested that Buchanan's wife run for the seat, but she declined. Others suggested Tom Miller. But Miller, beloved though he was, was perceived by many people as having qualities unsuitable for Washington. As Edward Clark remembers it, people thought that Miller simply was better at oratory, and handling the local politics in Austin, than he would be in the complex vagaries of the Washington scene.[77] State Senator Houghton Brownlee threw his hat in the ring, too. And so did Polk Shelton, an Austin lawyer.

The campaign was a contest in which Franklin Roosevelt's policies were put to the test. The New Deal had suffered some setbacks in Washington, and it seemed that the Supreme Court was determined to scuttle the ship of state. Johnson decided to run his campaign on behalf of the New Deal and FDR. He supported the president's plan to enlarge the Supreme Court, a plan that had created controversy across the land and that many people in Austin and central Texas decried. In the course of the race, Shelton came out in strong opposition to the Roosevelt plan. When the votes finally were counted on April 10, Johnson had won a decisive victory. He tallied 8,068 votes compared to his nearest rival, Merton I. Harris, another supporter of the Roosevelt plan, who had won 200 votes short of 5,000. Polk Shelton came in third, with just over 4,000 votes. Johnson was on his way to Congress.

In Austin, the victory of Johnson was seen as a victory for Roosevelt. It was also seen as a victory for central Texas, insamuch as Roosevelt's influence seemed so crucial to the completion of the dams. On the day results were announced, Marsh's *Austin American*, ever the faithful supporter of the New Deal—and decried as such by Brownlee during the course of the campaign—wrote: "the voters' verdict was seen as a strong endorsement of the supreme court reform in this, the first expression by voters on the issue since it came up. The court issue was pressed as the main issue of the race with the completion of the $20,000,000 Colorado river program, a Roosevelt undertaking, at stake."[78] Johnson's key supporters included many of the people who were so actively pushing the completion of the dams, and who had worked so intimately with Buchanan. Even though he urged Johnson not to run, because of his youth, when Johnson did decide to enter the race Alvin Wirtz became a strong backer.[79] Indeed, Wirtz initially had approached Tom Ferguson about the position, but Ferguson declined.[80] E. H. Perry was another important backer of Johnson and provided some key financial help. And A. J. Eilers, a local businessman of some prominence and wealth in Austin, figured as a significant Johnson financier, too. All these men, of course, wanted to see the work on the Colorado completed, and all now hoped that Johnson would see to that task.

When Johnson arrived in Washington, he was besieged almost immediately by his Austin associates, friends, and connections with requests to get the funds necessary to complete the Austin Dam. Within six weeks of the election, Tom Miller had been to Washington, and was in touch with Johnson as well as PWA officials to see what could be done to complete the Austin Dam. That structure had stood unfinished for almost forty years, and people were beginning to wonder whether it ever would be rebuilt. Miller and other citizens hoped to prevail upon the freshman congressman and the Colorado River Authority to get federal funds. It was at this moment that Miller wrote Johnson the famous letter, which I earlier quoted, in which he professes his willingness to strike a bargain: "As I stated to you, I have no ambition to be congressman from the Tenth District, and I will support you next year if you use the ability I know you possess for your district."[81] But others prevailed on Johnson, too. Dr. Goodall Wooten, president of the Austin Chamber of Commerce, wrote on behalf of his organization, pleading that "since 1888 when plans first materialized for a dam at Austin this city has been very much interested in building this dam here at Austin."[82] And so, too, did Commodore Perry, who impressed on Johnson the need to negotiate an arrangement between the Colorado River Authority and Austin, one that would permit the city to retain its control over the Austin Dam even after its completion.[83]

In the next several months, Johnson displayed his political acumen and his ability to learn the rules of politics swiftly. Over the summer months, he was able to help negotiate a contract between the Colorado River Authority and Austin. Both came out winners. The authority required control of the Austin Dam because, in the words of its chairman, Fritz Engelhard, its revenues "are all pledged to PWA for the loan, and bonds are already issued against them."[84] In turn, the city and Tom Miller wanted to retain control of their own municipal power plant and flood control system, something they had kept in their hands since the turn of the century. The final agreement struck, the one that would trigger the events to culminate on April 6, 1940, permitted the authority to lease the dam from the city for a forty-year period, during which time it would receive a certain amount of power in return for no cost. The bargaining was intense and fierce, feelings of both parties were aroused, but ultimately an accord was reached. And Johnson, whatever his faults, had won supporters to his side in Austin. It would be the first of his many successes for Austin, and one for which he was fully prepared to take sole credit.

There were two more dramas to be played out before control of the river was complete. One has to do with the Marshall Ford Dam. Originally, it was thought, Buchanan Dam and Inks Dam, just below it on the Colorado, would prove sufficient for flood control purposes. Another major flood took place, however, in June 1935, one that made engineers reconsider their earlier estimates. The flood swept down the Colorado in its usual deadly manner, and left Austin, and many other areas, devastated. Floodwaters in Austin were particularly memorable. The river spread over its banks and moved with an almost relentless force into residential areas and the nearby business district. Residents alive at the time still remember the flood as historic because it spilled across Congress Avenue, reaching the interior of a famous restaurant on the south bank, the Night Hawk. In other places, too, along Fifth and Sixth streets, the flood brought terrible destruction, uprooting trees and homes and families as well. Pictures of the waters show that even whole houses were washed away. Sim Gideon, then a law partner of Alvin Wirtz, recalls that the water backed up the sewer systems, and the dissaray was so terrible that he had to send his wife packing, to San Antonio.[85] To these people who had created designs for a flood control system on the Colorado, this event meant one thing: the river had yet to be tamed. The most savage and turbulent waters had entered the Colorado below the site of the Buchanan Dam, from the Pedernales and Llano rivers, and thus Buchanan Dam would obviously do nothing to halt such floods in the future. More dams, more kinds of controls would have to be erected on the Colorado.

As a result of the 1935 flood, and floods later in 1936, the Department of the Interior revised the plan for the dams, making a dam at the Marshall Ford site into the chief flood control device. These revised plans, it appears, first came to the attention of Congressman J. J. Mansfield in 1937 shortly after the death of Buchanan. In a letter to Mansfield, John Page, commissioner of the Bureau of Reclamation, notes that the revised plan for Marshall Ford led to two major alternations. The Bureau of Reclamation, he writes, would devote all the funds allocated to it by the PWA loan and the grant of $20 million to work on the Marshall Ford Dam. Of these funds, $5 million had been given to the bureau, another $4½ million had been given as an outright grant to the authority, and the remaining $10½ million was in the form of a loan to be repaid through revenues. Page also notes that full flood control of the river could only happen if a higher structure were to be erected at the Marshall Ford site, one fully seventy-five feet higher than the original low dam. He writes to Mansfield:

> The estimate by the Lower Colorado River Authority of the cost of constructing the project was given as $20,000,000 at the time the allotments were made in 1935. Studies by the Bureau of Reclamation have disclosed that works to provide flood control, in addition to irrigation and power development, cannot be constructed for this amount. The Marshall Ford dam, to provide adequate flood control benefits and also supply water for irrigation and power, should be built to a height of 265 feet, instead of 190 feet as now proposed. The low dam was chosen to be constructed, with provision for raising the dam at a later date, in order to more nearly stay within the $20,000,000 estimated cost of the project.
>
> Looking back upon the floods that have occurred in recent years [June 1935 and September 1936], it is found that with the low dam the floods could not have been reduced to any appreciable extent regardless of the need for such reduction in the heavily flooded river downstream. If the high dam had been in place, complete control would have been obtained. . . .[86]

Page goes on to say, further, that the estimated cost of the high dam would be a little over $20 million, whereas that of the low dam would be about $11½ million. In the spring of 1937, the government was eager to curb its spending on domestic projects, like that on the Colorado; while Page urged that an additional $5 million be secured for 1938, it also was known at the time that such a sum could be the last to be obtained for a while. In the light of government studies, it would obviously not be enough.

Mansfield and, to a much lesser extent, Johnson were effective in the summer of 1937 in procuring the additional $5 million necessary to complete the low Marshall Ford Dam. Johnson let his constituents know, too, of this success. On July 21, 1937, he wired Tom Miller that he had just secured Roosevelt's approval of an additional $5 million in PWA funds to complete Marshall Ford. The other person to whom he sent a wire was Herman Brown.[87] Herman and his brother, George, were the operators of a firm that built roads in Texas. Their business had been moderately successful, but nothing fancy. Not until the dams came along. Their first contract was for work on the Buchanan site. But their major financial gains came along with the first contract given for construction of the Marshall Ford Dam. Presumably through a system of open and competitive bids required by the federal government, Brown and Root, and McKenzie construction of San Antonio, had acquired a contract in the amount of $5,781,235 to begin work at Marshall Ford. They were fairly effective builders, it turned out, having completed the initial construction work six months later. In the summer of 1937, another allocation of $5 million to complete the low Marshall Ford Dam was available, and Johnson had very nicely decided to inform the firm, and Herman, of this fact.

There is little evidence to indicate what kind of relationship Johnson and Herman Brown had at this time. Within a year's time, they would become close friends, and by the time of the Democratic party's Harmony Barbecue, in the spring of 1940, Edward Clark could describe Brown, Johnson, Wirtz, Perry, and Miller as his "Number One" gang.[88] But in the summer and fall of 1937, their relationship was not yet on firm footing. In any event, just as Miller, Perry, and other people would try to exercise their influence over Johnson in order to get the Austin Dam reconstructed, so, too, did Herman Brown. Brown was for power, and he saw that the Marshall Ford Dam could become a great little plum for his pocketbook. Somehow—again the evidence is unclear—Brown and Root managed to secure the second $5 million allocation to Marshall Ford, but this proved not enough to satisfy the hungry Brown. In the fall of 1937, he began to manipulate Austin politics, as he would do time and again, in such a way as to create a public demand for the high Marshall Ford structure. A meeting was held at the Austin Rotary Club on November 30, 1937. The topic of discussion was the Marshall Ford Dam, and the featured speakers were Mr. Bunger, engineer for the Bureau of Reclamation, and Ross White, construction superintendent for Brown and Root. Ray Lee, former reporter on the

Austin American, and an associate of Johnson's from the National Youth Administration as well as the preceding spring congressional campaign, wrote to Johnson to inform him of the meeting:

> After the meeting I happened to meet Senator Wirtz at the hotel door. I told him about the matter, and he made the statement that there was considerable controversy about the matter, and that you were anxious no great public uproar arise for the bigger dam, since it seemed unlikely that favorable action would be had on the whole project. . . .
>
> Then I called Charlie Green [editor of the *American*]. . . . Charlie Green said: 'Don't you think we've got enough dams already? Herman Brown and McKenzie spend all their time cussing Roosevelt. Why, if it wasn't for Roosevelt where would we all be? . . .'
>
> It seems definitely that a carefully staged coup was pulled to get this thing into the public demand stage, and that a predicate was laid for a campaign. For the time being, the newspapers are on the negative side. what [sic] will happen when Mr. Brown begins to ride Mr. Marsh [Charles Marsh] about the matter is just a guess. Charlie guessed today that Mr. Marsh would turn him down.[89]

Brown had helped to stage this event, and he had obviously done so because he hoped to secure the additional millions of dollars for the dam. The idea was to pressure Johnson, and then Ickes and the Department of Interior, to fork over the money. Johnson ultimately succumbed to the pressure, and one can only guess why he did. (Today there still are all sorts of rumors rampant in Austin about the nature of the Johnson-Brown connection. Brown clearly supplied funds to Johnson's campaign in 1937, but what else did he provide to Johnson? Who knows? Tom Ferguson confided to me that one day, in the late 1930s, Johnson drove up to Burnet to visit him. Ferguson commented on the car Johnson was driving, and Johnson claimed it had been furnished him by Brown and Root.)[90]

Over the next several years, Johnson would work the federal government in order to secure funds to complete the Marshall Ford structure. Herman Brown pressured him to do this, but so, too, did Alvin Wirtz and others on behalf of the Colorado River Authority. At best, one must call what they did to secure the monies for construction cleverness; at worst, it often involved terrible lies. Thus, in early 1938, again with the government and Ickes determined to limit funds, Johnson, with the aid of Wirtz, sought to secure the passage of an amendment to a House Appropriations bill. The bill was intended to furnish an additional $2 million of funds for the dam but in the form of money that would not be reimbursable to the government.

This was the first time that such funds actually had to be approved by the Congress. Earlier allocations had come directly from relief, or PWA, monies, and thus had bypassed the congressional approval. Various people in Austin worked to influence the members of Congress, and they did so by telling damnable lies. Fritz Engelhard, chairman of the Lower Colorado River Authority board, wrote to senators Tom Connally and Morris Sheppard and urged them to support the passage of the amendment, noting that "I wish to state that this item will complete the Marshall Ford Dam, thus giving us two huge storage reservoirs on the Colorado River above Austin, as well as two operating dams below the reservoirs."[91] But, of course, this letter was written long after people, the Lower Colorado River Authority officials in particular, knew that a higher dam was envisioned, so Engelhard must have been well aware of the falsehood. Regardless of the moral implications, Johnson and others ultimately were successful in getting the funds, and so continuing the effort to build the high dam at Marshall Ford. Of course, they also kept the Brown brothers in business.

Other times, different stratagems were used to procure the funds. In the fall of 1940, the world situation changed dramatically. World War II had broken out. Germany was engaged in combat with the European allied nations. America had not yet entered the war, but the federal government was preparing the economy so that it could do so, quickly and easily. Funds now were diverted from relief programs, fashioned during the miseries of the Depression years, to defense industries and the military. A large military base, Randolph Air Force Base, was housed in San Antonio, less than one hundred miles from Austin, on the border of the hill country. Sensing that an argument on behalf of national defense would pry Roosevelt's fingers loose from additional money, Johnson wrote him on September 3 that the "completion [of Marshall Ford Dam] is further desirable in order to provide supply of power, all of which will be immediately consumed, and a part of which will be distributed in connection with the national defense program in the San Antonio area. . . ."[92] The president, who much admired Johnson and only one year earlier had offered him the position of administrator of the Rural Electrification Administration, acceded to his wishes, and clever politics once again had won out.

Ultimately, the high Marshall Ford Dam, as it was called, was finished at a cost of nearly $30 million. There were cost overruns, delays, and other such things, all of which worked to the financial benefit of Brown and Root. Johnson had become their boy in Washington, and he worked hard on behalf of their financial gain. Early in 1940, the Brown brothers were worried about continuing work on the dam, inasmuch as costs were higher than anticipated, or so they made it seem. Johnson kept them informed about his own work, and in a most revealing letter, of February 3, 1940, tells George of his work—and us of his relationship to George:

> Imagine my surprise when I called you in Houston and learned that you had taken the train to Mayo's.
>
> Besides not having fully recovered from the shock, I am pleased with your decision. For a long time I have realized that you should slow down some and quit taking life so seriously because I want to live and play with you and love you for a long time yet.
>
> . . . I am on my way now to see the Director of the Budget on a little five million dollar item involving a dam down in central Texas with which you have had some little connections.
>
> Affectionately,
Lyndon B. Johnson[93]

Throughout the history of the construction, an observer must wonder, how was it that Brown and Root, which occasionally appeared to show a degree of incompetence in being able to complete work on time and in other matters, was able to continue to secure contracts from the federal government? Bidding for the government funds was an open and competitive process, although Lyndon Johnson was doing his best to make sure to keep the brothers in business. How did all of this work? How did Brown and Root secure such a favorable position? What kind of hanky-panky was going on in Austin? Or in Washington?

There exists no single document to show us the inner workings of this process, to show us how the details of politics worked here. There are, however, two documents that inform us how people in Austin, and fellow contractors, perceived Brown and Root and the millions they seemed so easily to secure. One letter is from Carl White, a member of the Board of Directors of the Lower Colorado River Authority, and a friend of Johnson. The letter concerns a discussion White had with Robert, or Bob, Alsop, who was the construction superintendent for the authority, and who had supervised the rebuilding of the Austin Dam. By all accounts, I have learned, Alsop was a person of considerable integrity and honesty, as well as being a fine engineer.[94]

January 10, 1940

Dear Lyndon:

. . . about ten days ago I got a call from Bob Alsop asking me to come to Austin as soon as possible. I dropped everything and took out that night and was in Bob's office the next morning. He had a set of specifications for Marshall Ford power house on his desk, and he asked me what I knew about the situation in regard to this proposed contract. I told him I knew nothing whatever. He then told me that he was interested in it for two reasons—because it was to become an integral part of a project he had put his heart and soul into building, and because under certain circumstances it could prolong for a few months the employment of many of the men who now constitute his crew at Austin dam. For the purpose of helping these men get jobs he had consulted with several reputable contractors and had offered his services to help at least one of these estimate the job and prepare a bid with the understanding that if he was successful that the contractor would give jobs to men in his crew. He explained that if Brown and Root got the job that none of his men could expect to get a day's work out of it. That seemed to me to be a perfectly legitimate and laudable interest. Bob knew that I had been battling with Max Starcke [operating manager of the Lower Colorado River Authority] to select as many of his permanent operation employees as possible from the ranks of our own construction forces, and he knew that I was interested in anything that would help or benefit workers who had proven their loyalty to us and their ability to do good work.

He said that in all his experience in the contracting and

building business that he had never seen a poorer or more inadequate set of specifications. He said it was extremely difficult
for any legitimate contractor to prepare an intelligent bid from
any such specifications. He said contractors did not mind bidding in the face of the physical advantages enjoyed by Brown
and Root if they could have any assurance that the cards had
not been previously marked and cut for Brown and Root. He
said that in many places in the specifications there was evidence that we were using every means at our command to
make certain that Brown and Root got the job. He pointed out
the bonus feature of the contract as a flagrant example of such
effort.

He assured me that if we could give contractors some assurance that they would get a square deal that there could be
plenty of legitimate competition in the bidding. All of this was
news to me. I told him I would get with Fritz [Engelhard] and
some of the other board members and see what we could do to
correct the situation. We sent out letters to all board members
asking them to protest this bonus feature of the contract, and
Bill wired Senator Wirtz in Washington, asking him to get
P.W.A. to remove this feature. I talked to George Harley, and
he told me that several changes, including this one, had been
made in the specs after they had been sent to Washington. He
said Brown and Root had a physical advantage, but not an impossible one. He thought a good contractor could overcome
this advantage and make a legitimate profit out of the job. I
soon found that I was treading on hallowed ground. I got
plenty of, "Shu.!, better lay off this. It's hot." kind of talk.
"Well, what do we care, just so we get a good job and it is
under our estimate." I asked for and got our estimate, and Bob
gave me his estimate. I found that letters had been sent to
fifteen contractors and that three had taken out specifications.
Two of these had been brought back. At that time it looked
like there was going to be one bid. Two days before the bids
were to be opened, a San Antonio contractor whom Bill clas-
sifies as a first class house mover, came in and got a set of
specs. He turned in a bid which Brown and Root beat by
about $100,000. When the bids were presented to the board for
approval I made a motion that all bids be rejected and the job
re-advertised, because it was my conviction that we had not

received competitive bids. The motion was seconded by Bill
Arnold. I asked George Harley and Mac [McDonough, general
manager of the Lower Colorado River Authority] if they
thought a contractor could figure a job of this kind in two
days and make an intelligent bid. Harley said he thought it
would take any good contractor at least a week to estimate the
job. Practically everyone on the board admitted that there was
much evidence of a frame-up. We then had this line of thought
advanced. Loss of revenue because of delay, and probability of
collusion and higher bidding in the second go. The vote to
give the contract to Brown and Root was five positive, two
negative, one present and not voting, and one absent. . . .

I am budening [sic] you with this detail for two reasons. One
of these is because you are the key-stone of the whole project,
and you should know about everything that affects it, and the
other is that if there is collusion in the higher-ups you make
capital of it, and see that a good slice of the ill-gotten gains
goes into the campaign to elect a good democratic president in
1940. . . .

. . . Bill and I had a conference with Bob Alsop just before
we left Austin, and although he is mighty low over the recent
Brown and Root raid, we left him in improved spirits with the
assurance that he was going to be the last man on the construction force to go. Harley says Bob is the best construction
man he has ever met or known in his entire experience. He
said that if Bob could have been backed up by an engineering
department and a purchasing department that had properly cooperated that we could have saved thousands of dollars.

Mac admits that the Brown and Root bid on Marshall Ford
power house is little more than a system of unit costs to be
used in making up the final bill. He says the plans were of
necessity very incomplete, and that the job is liable to cost
much more than the amount specified in the bid. So it looks
like you and the Senator had better get set to pull some more
rabbits out of the hat. . . .

It is trite to say I love you and miss seeing you a lot. . . .[95]

Two months later, Johnson indeed had pulled more rabbits out of
the hat, and had secured passage of an additional $3 million ap-
propriation for the Marshall Ford Dam. Poor Carl White, who was

so fond of Johnson, was, it seems, little aware of Johnson's own close relationship to the Brown brothers, and that the shenanigans of the higher-ups most certainly implicated Johnson himself. The controversy over this particular appropriation by no means died down. In July 1940, the Al Johnson Construction Company, which had submitted a bid and lost to Brown and Root, smelled something fishy, and asked the comptroller general of the United States to rule on the recent award. They were concerned that Brown and Root had linked bids on two separate contracts together, so that if the first contract were to be awarded to them, the second would be, too. The comptroller general ruled that the Brown and Root bid for only the first contract could be accepted; eventually they got the second one, too.[96]

Hard work by many folks built the dams on the Colorado. And helped the vision of growth to materialize. But ambition, greed, and personal relations did so, too. However much we seek to make sense of the world in terms of the notion that visions can indeed become realities, the lesson of the Marshall Ford Dam also must be that these other elements underlie the process as well. Upon its completion, incidentally, Johnson saw to it that Brown and Root also got a nice little naval station to build at Corpus Christi.[97]

Sleeping dogs should be left to lie. And so, too, should the construction of dams. Unfortunately, neither nature nor people ever easily comply with our wishes. In the summer of 1938, the last and final great act in the taming of the Colorado happened. A great flood had occurred on the river in late July. Once again, devastation of land and crops was enormous. Over $4 million in damage, it was estimated, had been inflicted on the area. Particularly downstream from Austin, thousands of acres of rice and cotton were lost to the waters of the flood, washed out into the Gulf. Entire farms were destroyed as the land was denuded one more time, and farmers were left to hope for one more miracle.

Many genuinely honest citizens asked themselves a simple question: if the completed Buchanan Dam was all the Lower Colorado River Authority proclaimed it to be, why had the floods taken place? Wasn't the dam, they asked, intended to prevent such floods? Of course, these citizens were unaware of the studies by the Department of the Interior that only two years earlier had revealed that the Marshall Ford Dam would be the key flood control structure. At the moment, their question certainly seemed reasonable. Yet there were a number of other people who raised the same inquiry, and who worked to create a great public outcry over the floods and the failure of the Buchanan Dam to stop them. The nature of their concern resurrected an issue thought to be long dead by everyone—whether the dams on the Colorado were to be flood control devices or structures to generate hydroelectric power. The battle between the federal government and the private utilities was not yet over.

The uproar reached great proportions. As in 1934, when the passage of the Colorado River Authority bill was at issue in the Texas Legislature, even national publications became involved. The *Saturday Evening Post*, no friend to Roosevelt and the New Deal, declared in its editorial of September 10, 1938:

> The fundamental dishonesty of the New Deal's power and flood-control program had, in July, a dramatic demonstration in the flooded lower Colorado River Valley of Texas.
>
> . . . the Lower Colorado River Authority, a little TVA, was formed for the stated purpose of controlling these disasters, with the incidental purpose of irrigation and electric power. . . .
>
> High water has recurred so often in the lower valley that the lowlands of the five counties below Austin had largely ceased to be cultivated, though they are rich land as may be found in Texas. This year, under the promise of Buchanan Dam's protection, the farmers planted the bottom lands in cotton, turned their uplands to non-revenue-producing legume crops, under the Department of the Agriculture's soil-building program.
>
> The July floods destroyed all their three-quarters-bale and bale-to-the-acre cotton when the crop was virtually made. . . .
>
> Constitutionally, the Government can produce power only incidentally to flood control, irrigation and navigation. In its determination to produce power primarily, Constitution or no Constitution, the New Deal approved high dams on the Colorado. . . .[98]

The facts as reported by the *Post* and reprinted in the *Austin American* basically were correct. Later, in their editorial, the writers noted what proved to be the most controversial point, that "even with its inadequate flood-storage capacity, had the Buchanan Dam's flood gates been opened promptly, the flood could have been held to a maximum of nineteen feet, instead of thirty-four feet, the local Weather

Bureau is quoted as saying."[99] Investigations commenced at Austin soon after the flood, with the first one chaired by Governor James Allred. The exchanges between residents from the affected downstream counties, which included Matagorda and Colorado, and the proponents of the authority were heated and intemperate. Later in August, an investigating committee of the Texas Legislature was impaneled, with powers to determine the cause of the flood, and whether, in fact, the Lower Colorado River Authority was culpable.

The great debate over the flood represents one of those instances in politics where two different matters are at stake, and where the debate over one fuels controversy over the other. The great devastation to the lives and fortunes of farmers who lived below Austin was a real issue. Many people had lost great sums of money, in some instances whole livelihoods, to this flood. Because the federal government had provided assurances that there would be no further floods to expect, people like Charles Hackett, history professor at the University of Texas, genuinely believed the government should compensate them for their losses.[100] But the other matter, the one that truly worried officials of the federal government and the Lower Colorado River Authority, was the old debate between the government and private utilities and whether the purpose of the dams was mainly, or only incidentally, the generation of hydroelectric power. (In Washington, the matter was being discussed by the Supreme Court.) Representative Sam Arnhim, a county judge from Fayette County, where millions of dollars of damage had been visited upon crops, was most concerned about this question and sought to reprimand the Lower Colorado River Authority officials. There was considerable concern in Smithville as well. The *Smithville Times* in its editorial of August 11, 1938, relied on various authorities, including the renowned Dean T. U. Taylor of the University of Texas, who actively consulted on the Austin Dam, to argue that flood control and hydroelectric power worked at cross-purposes.[101] Leading citizens of Smithville caught in the midst of the flooding waters had on July 28 telegrammed Congressman Johnson to say: "we are vitally concerned to know as to whether or not these dam projects are to be primarily for flood control or for the generation of power and amusement, it is unanimously agreed that they should be used for flood control even though the power consideration be sacrificed."[102]

The proponents of the dams—Johnson, Wirtz, (who served as general counsel for the authority), Tom Miller, and others—grew con-

vinced that the real opposition they faced came from the Texas Power
and Light Company. Years later, in fact, John Babcock learned,
Judge Arnhim was on a retainer at the time from TP & L.[103] The
real worry of the dam supporters now was not whether the dams
would be completed or not. They believed that funds probably would
be forthcoming—though this was no certainty—and especially that,
once Marshall Ford Dam was finished, the major problems of flood
control would be solved. No, their real worry was with securing consumers for all the hydroelectric power to be generated by Buchanan
and the other dams. Without the sale of that power, the federal
government's argument on behalf of cheap power, the one used here
on the Colorado as well as in Tennessee, was just empty words, sig-
nifying nothing. Moreover, without the sale of that power, the dams
never would pay for themselves, and the authority would remain sub-
stantially indebted to the federal government.

To understand, then, why the public battle over the flood was so
heated and even at times vicious, it is important to know that at the
time of the flood Johnson and his associates in the authority were in
the midst of battling TP & L for the sale of electricity in central
Texas. During Buchanan's term in Congress, there had been little
pressure to repay the federal loan of $10½ million. But, once Johnson
reached Washington, federal officials began to pressure him to see
that such monies were repaid, in part to show how effective New
Deal programs like cheap electricity were.[104] Johnson himself gave
some evidence of his own personal conviction on behalf of the program. In a letter to Clarence McDonough on March 16, 1938, he
wrote:

> You and I both realize there are plenty of rural communities
> throughout the whole area, where smokey lanterns are the
> chief means of lighting and elbow-grease is still the main
> motive power, although this is the Twentieth Century and not
> the Middle Ages. We know there are many towns in the Tenth
> District either entirely without electric light and power or strug-
> gling with inadequate, expensive, wasteful and cumbersome
> plants of their own, which supply light and power of most un-
> satisfactory kind at rates nothing less than blushful. There is
> no reason why either of these conditions should longer exist in
> the whole 40,000 square mile area the Colorado River is getting
> ready to serve.

There is no program of more interest to me personally and officially than that upon which you and your associates have been working the last few years, and I want you to know that we must see to it that it is made entirely effective. I shall be happy to assist in spreading information on the organization of rural electrification cooperatives and corporations and to give these projects my full attention when they reach the Washington office for final approval. . . .[105]

A massive campaign had been initiated in the spring of 1938 throughout the central Texas region to develop customers for the power. It was directed by Johnson, and further orchestrated by the authority. Max Starcke, mayor of Seguin and friend of Alvin Wirtz, was hired as the operating manager of the authority specifically to help with the political work necessary to recruiting electrical customers.[106] Among other things, he symbolized the success that Seguin had had in running its own municipal power facility. During the spring, Johnson constantly was after the officials of the authority to convince municipal officials throughout the region to take control of their own power plant and utility operations.[107] Many, if not most of them, presently were controlled and operated by TP & L. Obviously, TP & L was reluctant to give them up.

During the course of the campaign, federal officials made TP & L appear to be an ogre taking unfair advantage of the consumer. The federal government, the New Deal, would act as the knight in shining armor, coming to rescue the fair maiden, the People, to save her from the clutches of the evil dragon, TP & L. Johnson, ever the tireless campaigner and effective crusader, captured the flavor of this battle with a speech he delivered at a mass rally in Austin on August 16, in the midst of the public debate over the flood:

> Yes, we are going to have four dams. They are going to hold back flood water and they are going to pay for themselves with some electric power which doesn't have to run through the cash register of a New York power and light company before it gets to our lamps. . . .
> The time has come for all citizens of Austin and for every citizen of this part of Texas to get a hold of his representative in the Legislature and to say to that representative:
> We are going to have dams on the Colorado River to control floods. We are going to complete the four dams we are building

now, and we are going to build some more dams if we find
they are needed to do the job.

We are going to keep building these dams in a business way.
When we store up flood waters we are going to release them
through hydroelectric turbines and we are going to sell the
electricity those turbines make to the people. It will be the people's electricity and the people are going to get it at cost—for a
small fraction of what they have been paying the power
monopoly for twenty years. . . .

. . . as far as I am concerned we are going to say to the Dallas News and the TP & L, 'We are going to build our dams
and we are going to keep our men at work,' and that is what I
want you to join me in saying tonight. . . .[108]

Obviously, nature, it must have appeared to the New Dealers, was
an active combatant on the side of TP & L; or, given the widespread
lobbying efforts of the company, nature might even have been on its
dole!

Whatever the source of the flood, whether by divine intervention
or money from TP & L, this battle ultimately was won by the
authority and the dams. Over the next several months, the authority
was able to secure the cooperation of citizens across central Texas, as
municipality after municipality voted almost unanimously to take
control of its own power plants. For a while, it looked as though the
cities would build their own plants, thus making the TP & L structures redundant and useless. Ultimately, a contract was hammered
out between the two parties whereby the authority actually agreed to
purchase the facilities. With this agreement in place, and with the
electric cooperatives established later for rural districts, such as the
Pedernales Electric Cooperative, whose headquarters not so coinci-
dentally were founded in Johnson City, Lyndon's hometown, the
authority at last had found a way to sell electric power cheaply.
TP & L, like the great, muddy Colorado, had finally succumbed to
the work of the New Deal.

Two years after the dedication of the Austin Dam, Marshall Ford
Dam was finished, and on August 25, 1942, it was dedicated. Re-
named Mansfield Dam in February, 1941, to honor the congressman
who had helped lead the effort to construct dams on the Colorado,
its completion did signal the final step in taming the river. Austin

residents, like all of those along the shores of the Colorado, now could rest easy that the years of trials with turbulent and unmanageable forces of nature were over. Yet this did not mean the end of struggle and conflict at all. As so often seems to happen, the creation of such great physical monuments as the dams masked some old problems and bred some new ones. Years later, the river, the streams, and the lakes once again would become the source of great concern; and once more they would stir people to battle not only with nature, but also with one another.

5.

Of Ancient Regimes

———

"Prosperity blooms again with Roosevelt."

Tom Miller, 1934

FOR MORE THAN FIFTEEN YEARS, FROM 1933 THROUGH 1949, Tom Miller, Lyndon Johnson, a few bankers, and the federal government shaped the growth of Austin. It happened not simply because of the dams, though they represented a major part of the plan. It took place, too, because Miller and Johnson were so much a part of the New Deal crowd, so caught up in the rhetoric and the plans of the New Deal, that whatever big money poured into Austin came from federal coffers. There were the millions and millions of dollars spent on taming the Colorado, but there were additional funds spent on other projects. There was the fish hatchery, developed in the early 1940s, the development of Bergstrom Air Force Base, near Austin, and numbers of other projects. There was also the magnesium plant that Lyndon arranged to have built in Austin. The plant, which later would become the site of the university's Balcones Research Center, was put in Austin to buy up much of the unused electricity generated by Tom Miller Dam. The plant was operated on behalf of the Department of Defense; payments for the electricity went for retiring the federal funds that were used to construct the Miller Dam. A nice boondoggle Lyndon had arranged—the government, in effect, was repaying itself for building the dam.[1] But Lyndon and Tom knew where their bread was buttered and were good at getting their hands on federal dough. The resentment from the chamber crowd, from people like Walter Long, usually could be quieted because they, too, liked money, and how the money helped Austin to grow. Still, there were episodes that rent the community, ones that ultimately would topple the Miller regime.

Long before anyone called it urban renewal, the federal government had furnished hundreds of thousands of dollars to Austin to build public housing projects. With the passage of the Wagner-Stegall bill in 1937, the federal government got into the business of building low-cost housing for the poor. And Lyndon jumped on this bandwagon quickly.

On January 13, 1938, the *Austin American* announced to its readers that Lyndon Johnson had secured $450,000 in federal monies to finance the construction of low-cost public housing in Austin.[2] Just a few days later, on January 23, Johnson went on public radio station KNOW to deliver an address to citizens of central Texas on the deplorable housing conditions. He noted that there were terrible living conditions in Austin, ones that rivaled those in the tenement sections of many large American cities:

> I found one family that might almost be called typical. Living within one dreary room, where no single window let in the beneficent sunlight and where not even the smallest vagrant breeze brought them relief in the hot summer — here they slept, here they cooked and ate, here they washed themselves in a leaky tin tub after carrying the water for 100 yards. Here they brought up their children ill-nourished and amid sordid surroundings.[3]

Johnson went on to remark that such conditions in other communities bred crime and delinquency, and were a blight on the whole community. To remove them, he claimed, would prove beneficial to everyone. Public housing in Austin would rid the town of shacks and shanties, provide for the improved health of residents, and also furnish jobs to those people who were hired to build the housing.

Many people did not believe there were slums in Austin. Some of them, like Walter Long and the chamber, had worked hard to prevent slums, not so much by furnishing aid to the poor as by discouraging heavy industry from coming to Austin. They reasoned that heavy industry promoted poverty, and poverty promoted slums. If there was no heavy industry in Austin, how could there be slums?

Johnson addressed this concern in his speech. He told his listeners that of the 14,407 dwellings in Austin at the time, 3,798 of them were overcrowded – that is, there were two, three, even four people living in a single room.[4]

However persuasive Johnson tried to be, there were sharp differences of opinion about whether slums existed in Austin or not. The *Austin American-Statesman* even sent out a reporter, Lorraine Barnes, to do a special story on the matter. She returned from her assignment and told readers of the many deplorable conditions she had found throughout Austin.[5] Just west of Congress Avenue, in beautiful downtown Austin, she found there were people living in pup tents, including an eighty-year-old man living on his old-age pension and surrounded mornings by his "teeming brood." In the northeastern sections of the city, she also discovered, there were people living in tarpaper shacks, with outdoor plumbing facilities, and in the midst of a mess of garbage. So much were citizens divided over the issue that the *American-Statesman*, in a rare show of openness, published two different points of view about the slums and public housing in its issue of January 23, 1938, out on the streets the same day that Johnson addressed the citizens.[6] The argument on behalf of public housing was pretty much along the lines of Johnson's, claiming that public housing would help to rid the city of crime and improve the health of citizens. But the argument against it took up the issue that continued to bother many people – that the federal government had captured the Austin economy lock, stock, and barrel. The writer of the article declared at the conclusion of his piece that probably "the next move under way will be agitation to canalize the Colorado river with federal money and make Austin a seaport."[7]

To supporters, the rejection of the federal funds would be like looking a gift horse in the mouth. After all, almost half a million dollars would come the way of Austin. The money would take the form of interest-free bonds that eventually must be paid back, and the city itself would be required to come up with another $50,000 of its own money. But proponents fully believed the investment would be a wise one, and that underwriting the bonds would be a fairly easy matter. Even the banker C. M. Bartholomew, who sat on the council, thought the banks would be more than willing to underwrite the bonds; he himself, he said, was willing to put up $3,000 of his own funds to purchase bonds.[8] Still, there were numbers of citizens who genuinely disapproved of any further effort by the federal govern-

ment to become linked to the Austin economy. Some, like Long, disapproved because they were concerned about things like the federal
debt.[9] Others were unhappy because they simply did not want the
New Deal in Austin.

At the council meeting on Thursday, January 27, the controversy
broke out in the open. The meeting, it was reported by the *American*,
was one of the most heated in many years.[10] The chief opponent of
the public housing was Simon Gillis, a retired contractor who had
first been elected, along with fellow council members Miller, Bartholomew, C. F. Alford, and Oswald Wolf, in 1933. Gillis voiced the
sentiments of many when he claimed the housing was a "socialistic"
step. His chief complaint, he said, was that the plan did not furnish
housing for the very poorest members of the community, but that
funds would be provided only to those people with a certain minimal
level of income. Edgar Perry, who had been selected by Tom Miller
to serve as the head of the new Austin Housing Authority, spoke to
Gillis' concerns. The plan, Perry argued, was to provide housing for
families who could help themselves; thus, to qualify for an apartment
a family must have a certain minimum monthly income. But Gillis
pressed forward with his questions and was particularly upset that
the public property would not be taxable. Other concerns were
voiced by people in the audience. Some wondered about the legality
of condemning private property in order to construct public housing.
Miller himself took particular offense at charges of socialism and communism. "I think it is the patriotic duty of this city," he charged,
"which has been helped a lot by the Roosevelt administration to
cooperate in this program. This is the answer to communism, to Hit-
lerism and to Mussolini-ism."[11]

This debate was a profound one, one that would linger for years
and surface in a variety of different guises, sometimes as fights between the conservative Democrats and their liberal counterparts at
Democratic conventions, other times simply as battles between the
ins and the outs in local politics. Could the federal government step
in and provide welfare that would permit at least some poor people
in Austin to live better? Could it do so when such a step actually
threatened the interests of private property, of those men and
women, it was claimed, who paid the largest share of tax monies to
the federal government? This was not Sherwood Forest after all, so
could the government really take from the rich to give to the poor?
It was here, at the juncture of private property versus federal author-

ity, that the issue was joined. At the January 27 meeting of the council, the whole body, including Gillis, voted to accept the slum clearing program of the federal government. But the passage of the motion was secured through the intense and heavy-handed efforts of the mayor, who, among other things, publicly scolded Bartholomew and Gillis for not attending a public hearing on the matter the previous Monday.

The furor did not abate easily, however. When loose ends were being tied up one year later, federal officials came to town to explain the nature of the housing in much greater detail. At the council meeting of Thursday, March 9, 1939, tempers flared once again.[12] Simon Gillis wondered how rents would be collected, whether the federal government would be required to buy the electric appliances locally, and once more restated his concern that the housing did not truly provide for the poorest Austin citizens. He claimed that Lyndon Johnson had not been at all forthright in his explanations of the nature of the housing, and that Commodore Perry acted as a "dictator" on behalf of public housing in Austin. Miller rose to the bait. He accused Gillis of disrespect for Perry and Johnson, and of reneging on his support of the program. The next day, the *Austin American* reported the meeting in full detail. Moreover, in defense of its fair-haired boy, Johnson, it provided him an opportunity to respond to Gillis' attacks. Johnson praised Perry as a fine public servant, voiced his support for the mayor, and claimed to quote Gillis verbatim when he observed that Simon "told me he was for the housing project if it did not compete with his rent houses and affect the rents on his tenant houses."[13]

Eventually the New Deal came to Austin and built public housing. Three separate projects were constructed—one for blacks, one for Mexican Americans, and one for whites. Still, the underlying issue remained. Years later, two leading members of the community who had been active in its politics in the 1930s, 1940s, and 1950s, Edward Clark and Taylor Glass, would recall the troubles over public housing.[14] And both wondered whether it had been a good idea for the federal government to get into the business in the first place. Clark and Glass seemed deeply troubled by the decision. The federal government may have won the round, and poor people did get cheap housing. But to Clark and Glass, the disrepair of the housing projects meant that the whole notion of government housing was a bad one. "The doors get holes in 'em," Glass observed in 1982, "there's no paint on 'em, the yards are not kept, there's papers scattered everywhere, rubbish. . . ."[15] Glass believed that some other plan might have been better at the time, something like long-term loans to tenants. Then the tenants, he claimed, would have felt the property was theirs and would have tried to maintain it. Yet, Glass remembers, Austin had very little to say about getting the funds. "The only decision we had," he notes, was 'do you want it, or don't you want it?' But they made the decision in Washington, D.C., and that was probably one of the first mistakes . . . they simply can't make decisions in Washington, D.C."[16] But they did.

The effort to get New Deal money for Austin began almost from the very day Tom Miller entered office. In June 1933, just three months after Roosevelt took over the presidency, Miller was off to Washington with his family. The trip, it was reported, was intended by Miller to combine pleasure with business.[17] Miller's main hope, however, was to get together with the Roosevelt people and figure out how to lift Austin from the muck of the Depression. What Miller wanted was funds for public utility and building construction in Austin, and he had drawn up plans to get those funds with the help of Guiton Morgan, the city manager. Both men hoped they could get federal monies to put up new buildings, to improve the city water plant, to redo the power plant, and to rehabilitate Lake Austin.[18] In the preceding months, the public groundwork for the effort had been well established. Charles Marsh's *American*, for instance, had run a series of articles on the importance of rehabilitating the sewage system in Austin, of improving the power plant, and of getting more funds for road improvements.[19] The articles, all written by Raymond Brooks, strongly urged the citizens to get behind these programs. Indeed, in one piece Brooks wrote of the great need for citizens to rally behind these efforts; to fail to do so, he argued, was a sign of lack of patriotism.

The original package drawn up by Miller and Morgan called for the federal government to provide $2 million to Austin in loans and grants. Austin did not succeed in getting all of these monies, but it did generate a good deal of funds. In that first large arrangement between the New Deal and Austin, the city obtained some funds in the form of a loan, others in the form of a direct grant from the Public Works Administration. The citizens were required to vote on the bonds to finance the construction. And they did so, readily. On June

13, 1934, a bond election was held, and a package of $857,000 in loans from the Public Works Administration was approved by voters, by a nearly three to one margin.[20] The bonds thus approved were to be used to construct a new sewage disposal plant, new sewer lines, new water lines, and a new service building. As a result of that first large request, other federal funds came into Austin as well, ones that provided the community with a new public market, just north of the river, at First Street.

Tom Miller continued to work the Washington programs. If nothing else, he labored extraordinarily hard on behalf of Austin. Once again, in July 1935, he was off to the federal government to explore some new avenues for acquiring federal funds. And once more his work paid off. He returned days later to announce additional funds for the public market project.[21] By the end of 1935, in fact, the city had managed to secure a considerable amount of federal funds. A report in the *American-Statesman* of July 19, 1936, said that the city had obtained over half a million dollars in outright grants from the federal government for different construction projects, including more than one-quarter of a million dollars to improve the Austin schools. Other, smaller programs had been undertaken by the Works Progress Administration of the New Deal, at a cost of just over $115,000. These included the construction of a bath house at Deep Eddy pool, a playground project, a sewing room, and other things.[22] On and on the monies flowed, and the city continued to profit. By March 1939, Austin had been the recipient of over $1½ million in outright grants for public projects from the Public Works Administration. Schools, sewers, playgrounds, University of Texas buildings, parks, new roads, and a host of other developments took place in Austin because of the federal monies.[23] And because Miller and Morgan sought to get these monies with a good deal of energy and flair. But they also got the funds because Austin was truly a New Deal town.

From the very beginning, Austin and many of its citizens had put itself at the forefront of the New Deal effort. Miller displayed some of his well-known enthusiasm before Roosevelt had yet discovered he was president, and Charles Marsh, good friend of FDR, had helped, too. The town went crazy, in fact. On June 12, 1933, just before Tom went off to Washington, Austin held a Roosevelt celebration. On

Congress Avenue, the normally staid and subdued buildings, including the American National and Austin National banks, overnight gave way to large posters and banners on behalf of Roosevelt. Pictures of Roosevelt beamed from the faces of dusty windows. In the evening a special program was held at Wooldridge Park, and Miller and other members of the City Council were in attendance. Fireworks lit up the sky, and the mayor, who had given birth to the idea, was delightfully happy.[24] Bands marched down Congress Avenue, and people lined the streets to watch them and other participants. For many Austin folks, it must have been a great relief, and helped them escape some of the obvious misery of the days.

But this was just the first of the New Deal celebrations in Austin. On March 4, 1934, another party was held to honor Roosevelt in Wooldridge Park. This one was advertised in full-page announcements in the *Austin American*. Intended to commemorate the first anniversary of the Roosevelt administration, the praise of FDR verged on the beatific. Beneath a picture of the president, ringed by a "Hail to the Chief," was a statement that Roosevelt "gave the American people the New Deal Administration. He has been carrying on ever since. He blazed new trails for all concerned. He dragged the nation out of the ditch of despond. He placed the farmers on their feet. He placed stagnant industry on the road to recovery."[25]

Naturally, it should come as no surprise to learn how much Marsh's *American* supported the New Deal. Throughout the 1930s, Austin residents were treated to a variety of editorials that sought to foster faith in the New Deal. Federal monies would come to Austin, but only so long as Austin was willing to display its appreciation. Early in the New Deal era, the *American* urged citizens to get behind the president, to show their full and dedicated support on his behalf. "Well, there is a New Deal on," it declared. "It is for those who believe in a government of and for and by the people regardless of past political affiliation, to get in behind the president and back him to a fighting finish. He is a conservative liberal. He does not believe in a government of the few. He is not a Stalin, a Mussolini, or a Hitler. He believes in a people's government, and laws for all of the people, and not some of them."[26] But it was not only the *American* that tried to corral Austin residents on behalf of the New Deal and FDR. Others were doing so, too, particularly in the mid-1930s.

Many people in Austin, and Travis County, committed themselves to the Roosevelt programs. For example, in the election of 1932,

Roosevelt won Travis County, with eighty-five percent of the vote, and in 1936, he garnered fully ninety-one percent of it.[27] But he attracted more than simply marks on paper ballots from Austin citizens. He won the hearts of people, their minds, even the souls of some. He made people like Tom Miller engage in outrageous feats of emotional display. To others he appeared Christlike. In 1933, Matt Gallagher, a resident of Austin, published a little booklet entitled *Our Friend, the President.*[28] Somehow the booklet made its way into the files of the Austin Chamber of Commerce. Gallagher speaks of Roosevelt and the New Deal as though he were witness to the Second Coming. "His firmness, is his gentleness," Gallagher writes, "his power, is his mercy and kindness. . . . His faith, is the power—for our progress. . . . His purpose, is great; and his achievement shall be greater. His motives, are to be governed by the greatest good; and he is sure to win." And Gallagher goes on, in evangelistic manner, to urge his readers to "go to sleep praying; wake up smiling; start out with the sun, and 'do something!'"[29] Plainly Roosevelt became something like a savior to people like Matt Gallagher. His New Deal meant to such men and women not merely a political program to achieve specific benefits, but it meant hope. Surely, in some way, if Austin grew in the 1930s it was because, in part at least, the vision of growth, of progress, of prosperity came to be connected to the New Deal. And the New Deal came to mean salvation in a very profound and significant fashion.

Charles Marsh, Tom Miller, and Guiton Morgan were among the strong believers in this way out of misery. And Miller on occasion would do more than simply arrange another celebration on Congress Avenue, or in Wooldridge Park. There is, for instance, the time he spoke at the vespers service of his church, the First Presbyterian Church of Austin. On Sunday, January 27, 1934, Tom spoke to his fellow congregants not about some esoteric theological matter, not to present a new interpretation of the Scriptures, but, fittingly, about the relationship of the church to good citizenship.[30] Sadly, there is no report available of what he said. But it is not too far wrong to guess that he tried to show how goodly religious action was also important for goodly political action. And it would be nice, in the event, to help support the New Deal. In Austin, the New Deal paraded as the religious faith of the 1930s and 1940s.

"Dictator" was a word people liked to use in Austin in the 1930s, almost as much as they liked the word "democracy." Not only was Hitler a dictator, or Stalin, but so was Roosevelt, some people believed. A dictator, it seemed, was someone whose views you did not appreciate, and sometimes someone whose views you did not appreciate and who also held office too long. Tom Miller, it was claimed, was such a dictator. But if this were true of Tom, then it must have been true of his fellow council members, like C. M. Bartholomew, for they, like he, were regularly and routinely returned to public office.

The election of Miller and the other council members often was an interesting affair, a showcase for apparent community harmony. In the 1935 election, for example, the first to occur after the People's Ticket had been victorious in 1933, support was so overwhelming that no one opposed the council members. The *Austin American* urged in its editorial of March 31 that the accomplishments of the full council be endorsed, and all members returned.[31] "The council will conclude this month a happy, peaceful and constructive two years in office," the editorial proclaimed. "Truly, it's a privilege to live in Austin."[32] All the council members chose to stand for re-election, and all were returned to office. But the community harmony may only have been superficial—a small turnout, just over 1,200 voters, was recorded. The election of 1937 was equally routine, and all the members were returned to office without a contest.

But by 1939, some resistance had developed, particularly to Miller. Miller had waged his battles over the housing authority, and he still had not yet gotten a dam to grow in Austin. He was on the verge of deciding to withdraw from the race, and in Washington to round up more federal funds, when a group of hundreds of Austin businesspeople gathered on his behalf and that of his fellow council members. Among the more than 600 people in attendance were the standardbearers of Austin respectability, people like Dr. Goodall Wooten, Mr. L. J. Schneider, who then was president of the Chamber of Commerce, and numbers of other key men and women. The mayor, openly touched by the public display, thanked his audience profusely, and then told them that "we try to carry out your wishes and your commands."[33]

But the race became a very heated one, and the five incumbents were challenged by an antiadministration slate, headed by Emmett Shelton, an Austin attorney. Shelton, among other things, accused the council of inefficiency and corruption and took out after the *American* and the *Statesman* for reckless bias in favor of the current administration.[34] Both papers, he claimed, had lied when they reported some of his stands, and they had hidden his own political advertisements out of sight of the reader, on the back page of the paper.[35] The incumbents indeed were forced to make a battle of it, and for the first time in recent memory various community citizens came forth with public support of the current council, including Dr. Everett Givens and other members of the black community.[36] The voting in the election on Monday, April 3, was unusually heavy. Simon Gillis, the big vote-getter, received 7,315 votes, trailed by C. M. Bartholomew's 6,349, and Miller's 6,177.[37] All the incumbents won, but they realized that community support for their policies could no longer easily be taken for granted.

The same council members were re-elected in a much less hotly contested election in 1941. Only two people, Ben White and O. R. Stephens, chose to oppose the incumbents. The highest vote-getter was E. C. Bartholomew, who replaced his father on the council when the latter died in 1940.[38] Bartholomew, however, drew only 2,797 votes, far fewer than had been cast in the 1939 race. Six years later, the composition of the council had changed somewhat. Simon Gillis and C. F. Alford no longer were members, replaced in 1945 by Taylor Glass and Homer Thornberry. Once again, Tom Miller threatened not to run. He and his regime continued to be the targets of different political attacks, for corruption, inefficiency, and the like. Taylor Glass, who was elected to the post of mayor just two years later, remembers in fact that he spent the first six months in office trying to uncover evidence of Miller's corruption.[39] Miller began to tire of the assaults. He and Morgan had let themselves in for much of the trouble just months earlier when they had proposed a plan to re-assess property taxes for downtown real estate, hoping thereby to boost the city's revenues. Miller was still reeling from this battle when Brown Robbins, a local businessman, assembled several hundred people in a draft-Miller move at the Stephen F. Austin Hotel on Congress Avenue. The mayor and his fellow council members showed up, and were treated like the governors of ancient Rome. Speakers like E. H. Perry got up to praise the mayor and the council for their good work. Responding to the character of some of the attacks on Miller, Will Caswell, a leading citizen, declared: "I don't believe in a person staying in office forever, but right now we are facing a critical time. With a bond program and the property reevaluation plan confronting the city, we should ask the present council to run for another term."[40] Various others lauded the mayor, including the editor of the *American-Statesman*, Charles Green. Green, in particular, spoke of the great progress and growth to come to the city during the previous fourteen years, and of the way that Miller himself had grown in stature during this time.

Miller, Bartholomew, Glass, and Thornberry were the incumbents returned to office on Monday, April 7; only Oswald Wolf lost his seat, to Will T. Johnson. The race had drawn eight candidates and sparked the interest of the voters. Glass received the highest total, almost 8,000 votes. But this election was in some respects the last hurrah for Mayor Miller. He chose not to run again in 1949. Things were happening to Austin. New social forces had begun to emerge. Blacks and their battles with the university, the state, and the city had come to occupy ever more prominent and frequent space in the *American* and the *Statesman*. A black mailman, Harry Lott, even chose to enter the council race in 1949. Labor was becoming much more outspoken in Austin and elsewhere. The division between the Texas regulars and liberals was becoming more pronounced, heightened especially by the failure of the Democratic party in Texas to support Truman in 1948. Miller had aligned himself with the liberal wing of the party from the outset, and he remained with it to the end. When he decided not to enter the race in 1949, the floodgates opened up. Seventeen men and women ran for the City Council in March 1949, more than had ever done so before.

By the late 1940s, the tides of fortune had shifted in Austin. A great deal of growth had taken place in the 1930s and 1940s under the regime of Miller and his fellow council members. Business was good, so good, in fact, that in May 1937, the tiny friendly, sleepy town of Austin was reported to rank seventeenth in home building in the entire country. Much of the good business had been spawned, of course, by the federal government. The university continued to be a stable employer; though it did not grow enormously, it did provide some new positions for faculty and staff. The state government also furnished a steady means of employment. But growth now took on heightened emphasis in the postwar years, almost a frenzied one. Soldiers were returning from war, demands were being put on the city to take a definite role in shaping its growth for the future, and other citizens, especially the poor, were knocking at the doors asking to be let in. The time of the people had come to Austin, Texas.

The
People Awake

6.

The Dawn of Democracy

——

Orum: Did you see yourselves as reformers, even as revolutionaries, in Austin in the late forties and early fifties?
Informant: I suppose so. We wanted things to be better than they were.
Orum: Better for whom?
Informant: Better for ordinary people.

LATE IN THE 1940S, THE PEOPLE REVOLTED IN AUSTIN. It was not a large-scale revolt, nothing to compared to the revolution in Russia earlier in the century. But it was a rather sizable uprising against the Establishment in Austin politics, against the rich and powerful. The revolt took place on several fronts, not all of them of a piece. There were battles and skirmishes fought between black and white Austinites, the former fighting hard to gain rights and privileges so long denied them. The next chapter discusses at length the dimensions and the sources of the black uprising. Another set of battles took place directly in the political arena, and in the chambers of the City Council. Until the late 1940s, no genuine populist had ever been elected to a position on the council. There were some men, such as Simon Gillis, who often dissented from the majority conservative opinion on the council. There also was Tom Miller, who pushed hard for his New Deal desires. But there had been no true voice for the masses, no genuine interest in pushing ahead the interests of the large majority of citizens. That was to change in 1948, with the election of Emma Long to the council, and to be reinforced in 1951, with the election of Ben White, who was to become her lifelong ally in council decisions. The story of Emma Long and some of the wars she waged against the Establishment is so intriguing that I have set aside a separate chapter for it (chapter 8).

The rise of black resistance as well as the emergence of Emma Long as a major advocate on behalf of the people in Austin have to be seen as set against an atmosphere ripe for popular revolt. This atmosphere had been developing over a period of years. The fact that Austin was home to the Capitol and that it brought in such a wealth of talent and diversity of interest no doubt helped to create this climate. But there were more important factors at work in Austin, conditions that genuinely made the community into a Mecca of liberalism in Texas. The University of Texas stands as the important force in this regard. Over a period of several decades, there were certain quarters in the university, specific academic departments, but also university-affiliated religious bodies, that bred an enlightened, progressive out-look on the world, an outlook that would soon become implanted in the minds of a sizable and vocal segment of the Austin community.

This chapter traces a few of the developments that took place at the university in the 1940s and somewhat earlier as well. It begins with a very brief sketch of campus life as seen, in part, through the eyes of two graduates who would later become active Austin Demo-crats, Venola Schmidt and Creekmore Fath. The chapter also traces some of the furor surrounding the firing of Homer Rainey in the 1940s. The role of the union movement in Austin, and how the unions proved to be a vital factor in the birth of the people's revolt in the late 1940s, is examined as well. And finally, the chapter traces the rise and describes the inner workings of possibly the most crucial element in the creation of a viable and sustained liberal voice in Austin, the Travis County Social and Legislative Conference. The conference was fashioned in Austin late in the 1940s, and it came to be the major vehicle through which many of the populist ideals and goals were introduced to the community. It also helped to furnish the campaign machinery that kept Emma Long in office.

The university, the union movement, and the Social and Legisla-tive Conference, in brief, created and sustained the climate so neces-sary to the people's movement in Austin in the late 1940s. We turn first to the university, and its impact on the coming-to-adulthood of Schmidt and Fath.

Venola Schmidt, neé Morgan, was just a junior when she enrolled at the University of Texas in 1938.[1] She had grown up in north

Texas, outside Dallas, and had come to display all the prejudices as well as the strengths of being raised there. It was a region of farmers, and a land in which cotton still was king. Schmidt's father had been a farmer for a while. Like many others, he and her mother—indeed, everyone she knew as a child—were segregationists. Her father was a strong supporter of Franklin Delano Roosevelt and the New Deal, but he also was a member of the Ku Klux Klan during its heyday in the 1920s. Near her home were towns such as Greenville and Terrell, Texas where blacks could work but never feel at peace. For example, until recently Greenville paraded a large metal sign over the highway that led into it. The sign read: "The Blackest Land and the Whitest People." Terrell posed a similar greeting: "Nigger don't let the sun go down on you here." Where Schmidt grew up, the division between the races was taken as a common fact of life, as irrevocable as the daily rise of the sun in the east, its dip in the west.

Somehow Schmidt broke out of the mold. She involved herself in debating in high school, started to read books on topics in anthropology and other similar topics having to do with different peoples. Debate proved to be a powerful stimulus to her thought. She was forced to think things over in an entirely new light simply because she was required in the course of debating to take stands opposed to her own. Many other people like herself, she recalls, students at the university, became liberals because their worlds, too, were opened up by the rigors of debate. But reading also helped. Learning about the various peoples of the world, understanding there were horizons reaching beyond the plains of north Texas, all this and more prompted questions in her mind about the nature of life and about life's customs. "When I began to do a lot of reading," she told me, "I began to realize . . . that [things like] segregation were wrong."

At the University of Texas, Schmidt's outlook was stretched even further. In the 1930s, the university was, by many accounts, a most provincial educational setting. It numbered on the order of ten thousand students, most of them residents of the state. At the time, only about four to five percent came from out of state, contributing to an incestuous educational climate. Nevertheless, every now and then novel ideas and novel solutions to the world's ills would crop up on campus. Schmidt remembers, for instance, that a few students in the late 1930s belonged to groups like the Young Communist League, the Young Socialist League, and the Workers Labor party. There also were many people, some who would later become extremely prominent in state and national politics, who made up the Young Democrats on campus and the Social Problems Council, a free-ranging discussion group. Memorable political activities also took place in university quarters in the 1930s. There were visits of people such as Oscar Aneringer, who ran a paper in Oklahoma and came to the university to spread socialist and populist ideals. There was even a Peace Strike in 1939. It attracted large numbers of supporters who were concerned about an impending world war. And when Hitler marched into the Sudetenland in 1939, a major rally occurred at the Physics Building. There the leaders declared the building off-limits, and sought to prevent faculty and students from entering it. Led by Bob Eckhardt, a vigorous young man who would go on to become a famed United States congressman from Houston, the demonstrators decried war and the growing appetite of the forces of the Third Reich.

Courses and university departments fostered a good deal of intellectual activity among students in the thirties. For example, there was a large lecture course in geology that drew students in by the droves to hear of the novel and radical materials on human evolution. A course in anthropology, which examined the origins of varieties of human societies in the world, also proved to be extremely popular with students. But the courses with the broadest appeal in the thirties, according to Schmidt's recollections, were in economics.

The Department of Economics at the University of Texas, from the late twenties through the early fifties, excited and interested thousands upon thousands of students. At the same time, it was anathema to administrators, the State Legislature, and the Board of Regents, to cite but a handful of the groups it antagonized. The department was composed of a distinguished group of men and one woman, yet they were people who tended to stray from the teachings of mainstream economics. Thus, they came to be viewed with considerable suspicion by many of their academic colleagues across the country. Clarence Ayers, for example, was a former editor of the progressive periodical the New Republic.[2] He had a fine reputation as a scholar but encouraged skepticism among colleagues because he did not adhere to the growing emphasis on price and income theory. Then there was Edward Everett Hale, Jr. He served as chairman of the department throughout most of the period from the 1920s to the 1950s. He probably also was the most radical of the entire staff, an avowed Marxist, though he never identified himself as such to his classes.[3]

The most influential of all members of the department, however, was Robert Montgomery, or Dr. Bob, as the faithful called him. Someday Montgomery will have a book all to himself. A native Texan, he was a radical populist who hated big corporations with a vengeance that bordered on fanaticism. He harangued his students about the evils of corporations, leaving many with a lifelong distrust of the corporate giants of America. And he wrote a witty and entertaining little pamphlet, *The Brimstone Game*, in which he took the corporation to task.[4] Early in this story of the history of corporate monopolies, Montgomery relates the case of Allen *v.* Darcy in England in 1602. Darcy, Montgomery notes, had been given a special royal grant to control the manufacture, importation, and pricing of playing cards. He tried to prevent Allen from entering into competition with him. The court eventually ruled in Allen's favor, and against the special royal privilege. Darcy is the whipping boy of Montgomery's assaults on corporations in *The Brimstone Game*. "If we want a system of free business enterprise," Montgomery writes, "and a democratic government, we cannot allow the Darcys to monopolize our most important industries. . . . Unless prices are free to move, our community cannot direct men and money and machines into the production of those things the community wants. Unless prices are free to move, our system of competitive business enterprise is at an end. And it may carry democracy down with it."[5] Montgomery's claims in this passage, with their emphasis particularly on democracy and free enterprise, could almost serve as the banner under which the people's forces assembled in Austin late in the 1940s.

Besides Montgomery, Ayers, and Hale, Clarence Wylie and Ruth Allen also were on the staff of the economics faculty. Venola Schmidt was particularly drawn to Allen, the only woman in the department. Allen was a labor economist who, among other things, wrote about how labor unions in Texas had been handcuffed in their efforts to secure better wages and working conditions for the labor force. She also taught courses at Tillotson College in Austin, a school attended primarily by black students (see also chapter 7 on Tillotson). Other scholars joined the department at various points in the 1940s, one of whom, Wendell Gordon, soon would become the focal point of a major controversy on the campus.

But it was not simply the curriculum that excited students in the 1930s and 1940s. Schmidt and her classmates often were enrolled in very small classes, enabling them to get involved in vigorous discussions. For many upperclassmen the courses numbered on the order of ten to twenty people. Students became absorbed in deep intellectual debate over important issues and ideas. Professors such as Ayers labored hard to draw them out, and to open their minds to the stimulation of novel thoughts. Church organizations on campus also provided eye-opening kinds of experiences. The local YMCA, as well as campus ministries such as that at the University Methodist Church, frequently assembled students of different ethnic and racial backgrounds, and encouraged them to reflect on topics like racial injustice, or even their religious principles.[6] After some of these experiences, Schmidt informed me, she came to realize if one took the Christian faith seriously it would be impossible to justify the harsh treatment blacks received from whites. "Most Protestant kids," she recalls, "[wondered] how could it be that people who had never been introduced to the Christian faith [could possibly] be damned."[7]

Just as it had in downtown Austin, the New Deal left its own impact on the university campus. Many young men and women were furnished jobs by New Deal programs, such as the National Youth Administration. The cost of tuition at the university was only $30.00 a semester, yet for many students it was still out of reach. In return for their labor – Schmidt, for example, worked in the Dean of Women's office – the federal government provided compensation at the rate of 30¢ an hour. Some students worked as receptionists on campus, while others served as administrative clerks and secretaries. Altogether, Schmidt believes, the great majority of her friends engaged in some kind of National Youth Administration job. The effect, of course, was obvious: young men and women, thankful for a meal and an education, soon were to become the loyal troops of FDR and the New Deal.

Creekmore Fath was a contemporary of Venola Schmidt's at the university in the late 1930s.[8] Fath went on to become a lawyer, and during the war years served on the staff of Roosevelt's White House. Like Schmidt, Fath was especially impressed by Bob Montgomery, and became a favorite of his. Montgomery took Fath to Washington, introduced him to key figures at the Brookings Institution such as Abe Fortas and Tex Goldschmidt – who became cornerstone intellectuals of the New Deal – and whetted his appetite for politics. Even in Austin, Fath remembers, Montgomery would provide important political stimulation to university students. Many were the times he took a handful of people with him to visit Governor Jimmy Allred at the State Capitol. Allred would chat informally with the students, tell them about the intricacies of Texas state politics, and provide counsel on what the good liberal programs of the 1930s were.

There were other professors, besides Montgomery, who helped to set the intellectual tone of the university for Fath. Three of them had major reputations as scholars and teachers on the campus. They were Walter Prescott Webb, historian of the Great Plains and later president of the American Historical Association; Roy Bedichek, an inveterate naturalist and sometime thorn in the side of the University Regents; and, the most beloved of all, J. Frank Dobie, historian, storyteller, novelist, and purveyor of all manner of Texiana. The three were something of a team. Almost weekly they would invite handfuls of students to their homes to sit and chat, talking about the world in general or some topic that was of special importance at the time. Sometimes these visits took place at Webb's estate on Friday Mountain. At other times, Bedichek would take the students on tours of the various natural wonders in and around Austin, and on still different occasions people would just assemble to hear Dobie spin some special kind of yarn about Texas, and the West.

The memories of Schmidt and Fath, of course, are but a small part of what took place at the university in the late 1930s and the early 1940s. What makes these remembrances so special is that they provide a sense of what took hold in the minds of two liberal activists, of what was really impressive about the courses and the teachers. And it was these specific events and personages that came to affect hundreds of students during this time and would provide seeds for the populist movement that came to blossom in Austin late in the 1940s.

The university not only sparked the minds of students. It stung the good sense of many people. Texans not at the university possessed almost a congenital distrust of education and of educators, a distrust that lingers today in debates over such matters as the adoption of textbooks by the State Board of Education. To many Texans the faculty were nothing but communists, Reds, spies—in brief, they were the enemy.[9] A number of people remember the times that Bob Montgomery was called before the State Legislature to testify and to prove that he was not, among other things, a communist.[10] Asked once whether he believed in private property, he replied that everyone should have some private property.[11] Another time he was asked how he could recommend policies to govern corporations when he had never run one himself. "I can scramble eggs better than the hen that laid them," he responded.[12] David Miller, a contemporary of Montgomery's in the Department of Philosophy, echoes the memories of many when he observes that the political climate was such that Texans could not understand, much less tolerate, academic freedom.[13] Homer Thornberry, who later would become a federal judge and who grew up in Austin, furnishes similar observations, noting the time he "heard a senator saying he had heard they had copies of *Mein Kampf* in the library and the next time they had any Regents up [for confirmation by the Legislature] before he'd vote to confirm him they would have to take [the books] out. . . ."[14]

Historians speak of the rifle shot at Lexington in 1776 as the shot heard round the world. In Austin there was a similar shot. It took place in 1944, and resulted in the firing of Homer Rainey as president of the University of Texas. Rainey had been hired in 1939. He came from the presidency of Bucknell University, a small school in upstate New York. Years later, when the time came to reconsider his dismissal, a rumor spread that Rainey had been in some trouble with the Bucknell administration. It turned out that the rumors came from Judge Albert W. Johnson, a man soon to be removed from the federal bench in Pennsylvania for improper conduct.[15] Rainey, it appears, was a most enlightened person, someone who believed deeply in education and liberal democracy. He said often and forcefully that education helped to improve society and to create better minds for its citizens. He generally was very loyal to his faculty and stood strongly for academic freedom. In other words, he was not the kind of educator apt to endear himself to the Legislature or the Regents. Why he ever was hired is not at all evident. But soon after his administration began, Rainey fell into disfavor with the Regents.

A number of incidents precipitated his firing. There was the episode of the proposed dismissal of Bob Montgomery. At a meeting of the Regents in June 1940, Fred Branson made a motion to eliminate Montgomery's position and salary from the budget.[16] J. R. Parten, then chairman of the Regents, overruled Bransons' motion on the grounds that it would constitute a violation of tenure. Although the dismissal never happened, the proposal itself contributed to a split over academic policy between Rainey and the Regents. Later, at a meeting in June 1942, the Regents declined to approve several research grants that had been passed on to them with approval by

Rainey and the Research Council of the faculty. One was a project conceived by Dr. G. Louis Joughlin, an assistant professor of English. It dealt with the effects of the Sacco-Vanzetti case on American literature.[17]

Sacco and Vanzetti were two Italian immigrants from Boston, both of whom professed an active faith in anarchism. In April 1927, they were convicted in a Boston court of a 1920 payroll robbery and murder. They were put to death only months later. Many people came to believe Sacco and Vanzetti were convicted not because of the murder and robbery, but because of their belief in anarchism. Soon the pair became heroes to many Americans, particularly those people sympathetic to the plight of immigrants and underdogs. The Texas Regents, displaying a phobia of anything that smacked of anti-Americanism, used the character and background of the two men as the grounds for refusing Joughlin's request. Orville Bullington, speaking for the board, remarked that "Sacco and Vanzetti will be recalled as two immigrant Communists who were convicted of murder in Massachusetts several years ago and executed. The Board could not see how the study of literature could be advanced or society benefited by the expenditure of the taxpayer's money on such a study."[18]

One year later, in January 1943, academic freedom met its match at the university. In the fall of 1942, an English course had used *The Big Money*, the third novel in the John Dos Passos trilogy *U.S.A.*, as a required text. The Regents, learning of the use of the book, were outraged. Bullington later said before the Senate Committee convened to investigate the grounds for firing Dr. Rainey: "about 1400 or 1500 pages of that book are filled with filth and obscenity. . . .No teacher who would put that book in for a sophomore to read is fit to teach in a penitentiary or reform school—let alone the university. . . . As long as I'm a Regent I'm going to repress that book and put out any teacher who teaches it."[19] Rainey once referred to the book as one of the best American novels written in the previous twenty years, noting its selection in a poll taken by the *Saturday Review of Literature*. This obviously did little to endear him to Bullington and the board. The 1943 session took an even more serious turn, however. The Regents embarked on what can only be described as an inquisition. They undertook a long questioning of each member of the English department who used that book. The questions dealt with such unrelated matters as where the person was born and whether he was married. As this inquiry progressed, one of the

Regents, Frank Strickland, became increasingly upset and blurted out that he wanted to fire someone from the university.[20]

None of these things compared to the removal of several young professors from the Department of Economics. Despite their continuous efforts to dismantle the department by getting rid of people like Ayers or Montgomery, the Regents had been unable to do so. Instead, they went after three young men, each of whom was without tenure. The story of this episode goes something like this. On March 17, 1942, an advertisement appeared in the *Dallas Morning News*. It told of a mass patriotic rally upcoming in Dallas at Fair Park on Sunday, March 22.[21] The rally had to do with the Fair Labor Standards Act. The advertisement clearly suggested that the act was improper. It included the claim: "Factories which can turn out 1000 instruments of war a week are only turning out 500! Why? Because there is a law which says a man should work only 40 hours a week! A law indeed! 40 hours of work! *Is there a law which says our sons must fight only 40 hours a week or die?*"[22] After learning of the rally, several young university economists decided to attend. They were W. N. Peach, an instructor; C. Wendell Gordon, also an instructor; Fagg Foster, a graduate student and part-time instructor; and Dr. Valdemar Carlson, a visiting assistant professor of economics from Antioch College. The men, Gordon recalls, hoped to inform the audience that the Fair Labor Standards Act did not prohibit people from working more than forty hours a week. Rather, it enjoined employers to pay workers time and one-half for any labor beyond the forty-hour limit.[23] The four men also were convinced the rally was designed as part of a nationwide effort to repeal the act.[24]

The group drove to Dallas. Once they arrived at the meeting, they asked the chairman, Karl Hoblitzelle, for permission to address the audience for two minutes. Their request was denied. Rebuffed and tired, they started the five-hour return trip to Austin, stopping at a small restaurant for supper. The restaurant, it just so happened, was located across the street from the *News*.[25] On the spur of the moment, they decided to write a letter to the *News*, protesting, among other things, the refusal to allow them to speak as well as the bias against organized labor voiced at the rally.[26] Their letter to the *News* said, in effect, that the patriotic rally was nothing but a fraud. Days later, an article appeared in the *News* and paraphrased their letter. The paraphrase proved enough to ignite the tempers of a number of Dallas citizens, prompting them to send letters directly to the

Texas Board of Regents. A few demanded the professors be fired. It was not in the least a coincidence that Karl Hoblitzelle owned the Interstate Theatres of Dallas and employed Frank Strickland, member of the Board of Regents, as a lobbyist. The fat was in the fire, and Rainey and the Department of Economics were called on to justify the actions of the young men.[27]

The Regents elected to take matters into their own hands. On June 27 and 28, 1942, they held another one of their "inquiries." They grilled the young men one by one. Rainey sat in the room while the questioning took place. Rainey, Gordon remembers, helped to defend the men under the fire of questions, but he did not take a stand on the proper course of action.[28] Some of the questions addressed to Gordon were pretty outlandish. Bullington, for instance, asked Gordon whether he had ever picked cotton.[29] Gordon found the session an ordeal. After it was over, the Regents convened and decided not to rehire the economists. The grounds for the Regents' action were that the activities of the young men at the Fair Park Rally violated the rules of the university. In effect, the men were dismissed because they were unpatriotic. Gordon took it hard. To be fired because one is unpatriotic is "a pretty big cross to bear during wartime," he recently remarked.

The various incidents contributed to a growing tension between Rainey and the Regents. Then, in the fall of 1944, the matter came to a head. On October 1, Frank Strickland called Alton Burdine, vice-president of the university, to complain that Rainey was making too many out-of-state speeches that did not pertain to university business. The *Austin American* described the incident at great length, including the text of a speech Rainey presented at Christ Church in New York on the topic "Fulfilling the Commitment of Science, Democracy and Christianity."[30] This talk provoked the wrath of Strickland. And it was the last straw for both sides. On October 12, Rainey convened a meeting of the faculty. He informed his audience of sixteen instances of improper action by the Regents, including those I have described above.[31] And he told in detail how the Regents were trying to abridge the rights of academic freedom. The assembled faculty gave warm and broad approval to Rainey's position.[32]

The shot came not long afterward. The Regents met in Houston in late October, and on November 1 they announced they had decided to fire Rainey. Even they believed this action to be extraordinary. Three members of the Board—Chairman John L. Bickett, H. H. Weinert, and Dan J. Harrison—announced their resignations, and three others—W. Scott Schreiner, Strickland, and Bullington—said they soon would tender letters of resignation.[33] The concern in Austin was immediate, the outrage unprecedented. Gordon Fulcher, writing in the *Austin American* on November 2, began his article by stating, "The multi-millionaire corporate-dominated board of Regents at the University of Texas Wednesday night levelled at that institution what is probably the severest blow ever to have been given it."[34] It seemed evident to many people that the big Texas corporations finally had succeeded in bringing the university to its knees. Sam Hall, writing in the *Texas Spectator*, suggested that something resembling a cabal had been formed among the Regents, a cabal that grew out of their common corporate interests and ties to the Texas Regulars, a group of splinter-Democrats who failed to support Roosevelt at the 1944 Democratic Convention. All six of the Regents who voted in favor of ousting Rainey, Hall noted, had amassed large corporate wealth or, like Strickland, served on the payroll of corporations. And all also were active participants in the Texas Regulars.

The anger of students and faculty flared at once. Immediately after the firing, virtually the entire student body went on strike.[35] On the following Thursday, Reverend Blake Smith, pastor of the University Baptist Church, spoke to a student rally at Gregory Gymnasium, and was strongly critical of the Regents.[36] On Friday, masses of students assembled at the university and, several thousand strong, marched on the State Capitol, assembled behind a coffin carrying the corpse of academic freedom.[37] Hundreds of students went to the local YMCA and wrote letters home to their parents, urging them to support Rainey. Then, in mid-November, while the campus was still abuzz, Senator Penrose Metcalfe, chairman of the Senate Committee on Education, convened a hearing of his members at which various principals in the case were invited to present their views. The hearings lasted eight days. They furnished a thorough, but often unpleasant, airing of the dispute between Rainey and the Regents. The issues that prompted his dismissal were made public, including incidents such as the Dos Passos controversy. The Regents voiced their concern about the issue of immorality at the university. They noted their displeasure with Rainey over the hiring of several faculty they believed unworthy for appointment. One such complaint concerned Arthur Billings. He had been an instructor in economics at the university. During the war, he had received classification as a conscientious objector. Regent Strickland spoke of his concern with materials on communism taught at the university. And the Regents also expressed some concern that Rainey was far too liberal on the issue of race, particularly for anyone who served as the president of a Southern university.

The Metcalfe hearings finally made public what many in the university community already knew: the university was on the hit-list of large corporate interests. One can imagine the atmosphere. Although there were a few exceptions, the campus community stood squarely in the corner of Rainey and his allies. Bob Montgomery had a large and devoted following among the students. Many of them took the dismissal of Rainey as though it were a blow to Montgomery and all he stood for. Academic freedom became the watchword of the university reaction to the Regents. To save the university was to protect free speech. Soon university affairs came under the scrutiny of the American Association of University Professors (AAUP). In an interim report, it found: "The evidence in the University of Texas situation indicates that what is happening in Texas with reference to the University is a reappearance of an old phenomenon, namely, *an effort on the part of certain special interest groups to control education* [my emphasis]."[38] Eventually the AAUP censured the university for its actions. And the Southern Association of College and Secondary Schools, which provided accreditation to the school's programs, put the university on probation because of the Regents' action.[39]

The dismissal of Rainey took a terrible toll on the university community, leaving people stunned and dispirited. Walter Firey, distinguished university sociologist, remembers that when he arrived on campus in 1946 there was pronounced distrust of the Regents, and a lingering worry over academic freedom. There were certain topics he was told not to discuss in his classes, especially those of race and sex. A questionnaire on sexual matters administered to students had been the downfall of a fellow sociologist, Rex Hopper, who had been dismissed months before Firey arrived.[40] David Miller, in philosophy, also recalls the years after the Rainey firing as a period of great disquiet at the university. Clarence Ayers, he remembers, often would get up in the faculty meetings and accuse the Regents of being a bunch of "liars."[41] The so-called Era of Tranquility, as the new chairman of the Board of Regents, Dudley Woodward, called it in early 1945 with the selection of T. S. Painter as acting president, was anything but tranquil. When Painter was signed on by the Regents as permanent president, in what many faculty members saw as a further usurpation of their power, Horace Busby, editor of the *Daily Texan*, the campus newspaper, wrote a stinging editorial against the decision. It was entitled "Era of Hostility."[42] Painter had not even been on the faculty's list of men recommended to the Regents as candidates for president. Moreover, he had gone so far as to inform the faculty that he would only serve as acting president. Thus, for several years he served without the support of many colleagues. A few faculty even resigned over his hiring. Another blow came in the fall of 1947, when one of the most admired men on the faculty, J. Frank Dobie, a key supporter of Rainey, was fired.[43] Indeed, until Logan Wilson took over as president in 1952, the University of Texas resembled nothing so much as an armed battleground, with constant faculty meetings devoted to discussing yet another willful act by the Regents or by university administrators.[44]

The removal of Homer Rainey gave notice to everyone of the profound split between the university community and much of the rest of Texas. A more liberal atmosphere, a greater tolerance of opinion, paraded in the halls of the university than in the anterooms of the State Capitol or the boardrooms of Texas corporations. But still the university community was not nearly so radical as the Regents and their allies claimed it to be. What the Regents' reaction did was highlight and emphasize the liberal ideals of a university—the importance of free speech and free thought, the importance of upholding individual rights, and the current effort to wage a war on behalf of democracy at home, like that which had been victorious overseas. Men and women, returning home from war to attend the university, fought hard on behalf of those ideals. And many of them soon turned their energies to Austin affairs in order to secure the rights of the people. The university finally began to promote, as Homer Thornberry has put it, "a more progressive atmosphere in Austin."[45]

The last word on the university in this era falls to Wendell Gordon. Gordon returned home from military service in the fall of 1945. He had served in counterintelligence operations. Vice-President J. C. Dolley wrote him at his home in Houston, requesting that he reapply for a position. Gordon believed the university was seeking some way out of its controversial position by trying, among other things, to rehire someone it fired. He expressed his interest in returning, and soon was called to a meeting in Dallas with Dudley Woodward. Woodward asked Gordon to sign a letter, in effect saying that Gordon had never intended to malign the motives of the Fair Park Rally participants: "I should like to state that I have at no time and do not now intend to impugn the patriotism of anyone who participated in the Dallas mass meeting of 1942. I regret the notoriety which has resulted from the incident and that the notoriety has been injurious to the University."[46]

Gordon signed the letter, and was rehired. When the faculty learned of this, a number protested. They grilled Gordon at length about why he signed the letter. Not long ago he confessed to me that he might have been naive in committing himself to a retraction of his earlier actions.[47] But, he informed me, he was young after all, and had been subject to an afternoon of persuasion by Woodward. In view of all the questions raised about his patriotism, I asked him whether his wartime service had not made it evident that he was a patriot. Tears welled up in his eyes and, for a few brief moments, he was speechless. The Regents' action did exact a terrible price on the University of Texas—and on a number of decent human beings, too.

While the university served as a major pipeline for much of the dissent on behalf of the people in Austin, a second one involved unions. But it did not come about in the usual way. Since there was no heavy industry, owing in part to the efforts of Walter Long and the chamber, there was no large group of workers that could be assembled to fight for labor ideals. Yet there were individuals who were sympathetic and active in union work in Austin—in fact, a number of them. This happened because Austin was the state capital, and, therefore, the headquarters for many unions and trades councils. The union movement drew into the city a number of people who were well educated and who had been active in the labor movement for years. And many of them were willing to join hands with the hardy band of populists coming forth on other fronts.

In Austin as well as elsewhere in Texas, the unions were a force that was feared. The close of the 1940s was a high point in union activity. Men like Walter Reuther, who served as the head of the United Auto Workers, and John L. Lewis, his counterpart in the United Mine Workers, were trying to carry forward certain of the principles of the New Deal, as of the earlier labor causes in America. Business and government fought back, securing, among other things, the passage of the Taft-Hartley Bill in 1947, which prohibited workers from going on strike. Still, many businesspeople felt threatened by the power of the unions, believing they would seriously damage their profits and their control over employees. In Texas, at about the same time that the Taft-Hartley Bill succeeded in Congress, a right-to-work law was passed in the State Legislature. It prevented the unions from securing control over hiring policies on jobs. The 50th Legislature, which carried through this legislation, passed a number of other measures that scuttled the union movement in Texas. They included several bills that prohibited workers from picketing against their employers as well as a bill that prevented the unions from collecting dues from members without the consent of the employer.[48]

Ed Clark, close friend of Lyndon Johnson and Tom Miller, helped to shepherd much of this legislation through the State House.[49] And just behind Clark stood the Brown brothers, ever active in Texas politics. Once their firm got off the ground, with the construction of the dams, they became millionaires overnight. They used some of their gains to finance an antiunion lobby in the Legislature. Why they did so is not clear.[50] Homer Thornberry claims it happened simply because the Browns were ornery and indepedent Texas folk; Creekmore Fath speculates that it might simply have had to do with the Browns' desire to keep wages down, and profits up.[51] Regardless, the Browns were longtime opponents of the unions, and had on several occasions been involved in labor trouble at the Mansfield Dam, trouble that Lyndon Johnson helped them overcome.[52] But the Browns carried on a continuing war with the unions and frequently were in court, seeking to get an injunction to forestall strikes or picketing carried on by unions against their firm. Their actions, however, often seemed to boomerang. While they succeeded in undercutting the union effort, they also rekindled a few fires on behalf of the people as well.

The intensity of the struggle between unions and their opponents in Texas often was fierce. Many times it involved vicious attacks, particularly by the antilabor groups. The minimum-wage legislation, which was passed in the 1940s to guarantee American workers a fair wage on the job, was seen as a threat to the roots of the free enterprise system. Many Austin businesspeople, sometimes the very same as those who so opposed the federal government on other grounds, were dead-set against the whole notion of a minimum wage.[53] The group included such renowned figures as the men who operated Scarbroughs, the leading Congress Avenue department store.[54] Various activists, moreover, often fell victim to the same kind of ridicule as university professors. To be a union organizer in Austin was little better than being an intellectual. There may have been a grain of truth to the charge that some union efforts were communist, as Venola Schmidt noted to me in conversation. But, for the most part, the union movement in Austin was served by people who were committed simply to improving the condition of the working classes in America, not beholden to a radical notion of the overthrow of American democracy.[55] At the height of one particularly bitter battle over unions in Austin, Emma Long, populist champion, even felt it necessary to separate herself from communists and their fellow travelers. She commented to a reporter for the *Statesman:* "By coming out for good things which would improve the American way of life in Austin these party-liners try to turn us against good things. They want to keep up [sic] from making democracy work."[56]

Some of the attacks on the unions in Texas are recalled with bitter clarity, such as the time Allan Shivers publicized the so-called Port Arthur story during the course of his 1952 gubernatorial campaign. The Port Arthur story claimed to show how the unions had destroyed the coast town of Port Arthur, Texas, leaving it empty and destitute, no more than a ghost town. The advertisement, used by Shivers in his campaign against Ralph Yarborough, was composed early in the day when the docks were totally deserted. The story, in other words, was a nicely composed fraud, intended to smear the unions. Numbers of people active in the union effort at this time with whom I spoke each independently volunteered memories of this campaign, and how it was symptomatic of the viciousness of antilabor sentiments in Texas.[57] And they further recalled that the advertisement had been created by Jake Pickle's agency. Pickle now occupies the seat in the Tenth Congressional District once held by Lyndon Johnson.

Now and then the war between the unions and their opponents produced moments of decisive resentment and pitched struggle in Austin. Perhaps the most memorable of them was the one in the spring of 1950, when Brown and Root secured a small contract to construct new boilers for the power plant of Austin. Brown and Root employed exclusively nonunion workers on the job. Other workers, not employed by them, many members of the Austin Building and Trades Councils, threatened not to work alongside laborers they considered scabs. Months before any battles erupted, the City Council had been warned by the representatives of the Austin Building and Trades Councils that problems could arise. Emma Long, then seated on the council, even cast the single vote against awarding the contract to Brown and Root, an act she would come to regret.

When the construction began in mid-March, Brown and Root and the union members were quickly at one another's throats. The union workers almost immediately went on strike, and picketed the site of the construction. Creekmore Fath was called on a Monday evening by two representatives of the Austin Building and Trades Councils and asked whether he would serve as the lawyer on behalf of the unions. He agreed. The next morning his friend Tom Miller called him up and asked him to work on behalf of the Brown and Root subcontractor, Jaime Odom. By this time, it was too late, and Miller and Odom sadly regretted their failure to call Fath earlier.[58] Brown and Root eventually used Alvin Wirtz, their longtime friend, as counsel. The case wound up in court, argued before Judge Charles O. Betts. Neither side was victorious. The unions were prevented from picketing. But, in order to get the work done, a fence was erected to divide Brown and Root construction from that of the union laborers. Clearly, a nice job of fence-sitting by the judge. (See chapter 8 for further details on this incident.)

Despite the half-victory, the unions and trades councils, their chief officials in Austin, and people in sympathy with them carried on battle after battle with the antilabor forces. Often they failed to win. Indeed, theirs was an uphill struggle most of the time, outfinanced as they were. But they helped to promote the people's cause in Austin, and to act as yet another thorn in the side of their enemies, the Establishment.

Homer Rainey decided to run for governor of Texas in 1946. He ran on a platform of liberal democratic ideals. At a meeting of the Travis County League of Active Democrats in March 1946, he outlined his program. He argued that Texas politics should be opened up so that all citizens, not only those who paid the poll tax, could participate. He spoke of the need to make Texas a two-party state rather than to continue the rule of the Democrats. He urged that the quality of political leadership be improved in Texas, drawing on people of high intelligence and impeccable character. And he demanded that the Texas Regulars, including Wright Morrow and George Butler, be purged from the Democratic party of Texas for having "tried to rob a whole people of their democratic rights."[59]

Some of the corporate and oil-rich members of the Texas Regulars had helped to get Rainey fired in November 1944. To liberal Texans like Rainey, the Texas Regulars were traitors to the cause of the people. At the 1944 Democratic Convention in Chicago, two delegations had been seated. One was composed of the Texas Regulars, led by Governor Coke Stevenson and former Governor Dan Moody. The other was led by the so-called true Democrats. The Regulars, consisting of many people who, in other circumstances, would have supported the Republicans, had the previous spring decided not to support FDR for another term. After the national convention produced a ticket consisting of Roosevelt and Truman, the Texas Regulars returned to Texas, bolted the party, and put themselves on the November ballot, beside the national Democratic and national Republican nominees. They were badly defeated, and some sought to regain control of the party apparatus in Texas. Ever afterward, they would be seen by the true Democrats, the FDR supporters, as little better than scum. It was the Texas Regulars that Rainey fought in his effort to become governor in 1946.

Rainey embarked on the spring Democratic primary trail against seven other candidates. Eventually he found himself in a runoff with Beauford Jester. The Texas Regulars supported several candidates in the primary. When they lost, they shifted their support to Jester. The quarrels and arguments from Rainey's days at the university were resurrected. Rainey was attacked for his view of liberal education, for his belief in academic freedom, and for that most sensitive of all issues, his stand on racial matters. The last attack became the most vicious. It was the hope of Rainey's opponents to play on the racial prejudice and hatred common to many Texans. Among the rumors let out in the campaign was the claim that Rainey's daughters worked as prostitutes in whorehouses in downtown Austin.[60] Rainey's campaign against this viciousness failed, and in the end he was defeated for office. Months later, he left the state for good, assuming a post as president of Stephens College in Missouri.

But while Rainey was defeated, the cause of the people in Texas was not. In the fall of 1946, a small group of Rainey supporters gathered in Austin to continue a broader and more intense struggle on behalf of the people's cause. They were led by a woman who is a beloved legend to Texas liberals and despised by Texas conservatives, Minnie Fisher Cunningham. Minnie Fish, as she was called, was a woman in her seventies who, throughout her life, had fought for every important liberal endeavor in Texas. Just two years before, she had run for governor against Coke Stevenson, mainly so she could attack his policies. But decades earlier, she had been a vigorous advocate of women's suffrage in Texas, and had helped to get the Nineteenth Amendment through Congress. Not only a political activist, Minnie Fish lived in New Waverly, Texas, and maintained a small farm. Her true genius, it is claimed, lay in political organization, and in this post-Rainey effort it was this genius that she turned to the liberal cause. Another key figure was Bob Eckhardt, a young Austin lawyer, cousin of the Klebergs of King Ranch fame, and contemporary of Venola Schmidt and Creekmore Fath at the university. A third central figure was Marion Storm. Before her tragic and premature death in an automobile accident in 1950, Mrs. Storm was one of the prime movers of people's democracy in Texas, and was the central force in the group that held its first Austin meeting on December 7, 1946.[61]

The individuals who assembled in Austin, described by *Texas Week* as "Texas' first 'people's political organization' since the Populist Party," hoped to pursue all those ideals in bloom at the university, in the minds of people like Rainey, and evident in the work of union people in Texas. At the original organizational gathering, held in Waco, they declared themselves to

> work for government which will tolerate no monopoly, but will guarantee the equality of economic opportunity implied in the phrase 'free enterprise' to all its citizens; government which will not discriminate against any person because of race, creed, or national origin, but will provide equality before the law for all peoples; government which will be a competently functioning democracy in political and economic fields in our modern age.[62]

The group called themselves the People's Legislative Conference. Later they would name themselves the Texas Social and Legislative Conference. And in Austin they would become known as the Travis County Social and Legislative Conference. Those who composed the group were determined to carry forth many of the New Deal programs, especially the spirit of the New Deal in Texas. Not ones to ignore the importance of some degree of diplomacy in politics, they decided in the fall of 1946 to help with the legislative passage of programs proposed by Beauford Jester, among them a package to raise the salaries of schoolteachers in Texas.

In time the group grew into a very active and influential force in Texas politics. It organized branches in key cities and counties of the state, and its members were very active in state conventions. It sought reforms on issues such as education, and worked hand in hand with labor organizations such as the Congress of Industrial Organizations to prevent the large corporate and oil influences from gaining too much control in Texas. In Austin and Travis County it became a particularly central element in liberal circles, serving as the cohesive and organizational device through which various policies were pursued. There were perhaps thirty or forty people in Austin who served as the core. Among them were Venola and Fred Schmidt, Wally and Ruth Ellinger, Creekmore and Adelle Fath, Henry and Mary Holman, Helen and Irwin Spear, John and Mary McCully, and Emma and Stuart Long. The group was composed in general of people active in union politics, members of the university community, a few black and brown residents of Austin, such as Arthur DeWitty and Roy Velasquez, and a handful of New Dealers who had moved from Washington to Austin after the war.

The key to the work in Austin was Jean Lee. Along with her husband, Russell, a world-renowned photographer, she had left the frenetic pace of Washington to settle in Austin. The two had been part of the small circle of people, numbering on the order of fifty or sixty, who had composed the New Dealers. They were friends of people like Creekmore and Adelle Fath, themselves longtime Washington New Dealers. Lee, like Minnie Fish, turned out to have a genius for political organization. Under her leadership, the Travis County Social and Legislative Conference eventually established a large and complex network of people throughout the area who could be called on for electoral work. There were precinct organizers in each of the precincts of the county who would make contact with the voters and keep a rough tally of the political composition of their areas. A filing system was developed in the headquarters that contained a complete history of all registered voters in the county. If someone moved out, or someone moved in, Lee soon would know the identity of that person and how he or she was apt to vote. When particularly tough elections were coming up, the precinct captains would be phoned to round up the vote. Big city political machines had nothing over the Travis County Social and Legislative Conference.

Electoral successes did not come often for the group, however. People worked hard for the election of Ralph Yarborough, but often lost.

The great successes in Travis County came mainly on behalf of Emma Long in her races for the City Council, although there were a few others, such as the capture of the Travis County delegation to the state and national Democratic conventions. There were other important activities carried on by the group that helped to get important legislation passed in the state. For example, the group sometimes had its members attend City Council meetings in Austin, or hearings at the State House on important pieces of legislation. Helen Spear recalls that she would often do such tasks, and then return to report on the meetings or hearings to the conference.[63] These kinds of activities proved indispensable to the legislative and lobbying campaigns carried out by the group, and also to keeping members informed of the important legislation pending before city or state officials.

The conference kept active in Austin politics from the moment it was formed in 1946 until the end of the 1950s. During this period, it provided an indispensable service to the cause of the people. Speakers would come to the weekly meetings and talk to the group about such matters as medical care for the elderly, new labor bills, measures designed to improve, or sometimes impede, education in Texas. So informed, the men and women who constituted the conference easily could mobilize and get their members to lobby legislators. The group was vital, too, simply because it furnished a forum for a number of like-minded, but otherwise very different, individuals. It brought together a few East Austin blacks with a number of Austin whites and Mexican Americans, and thus was among the first devices in Austin for insuring a racially integrated setting. In fact, its very integration forced it to vacate its regular meeting place in the basement of the public library, which did not at the time permit blacks or browns in its quarters, and to move to Johnnie Crow's restaurant on South Congress Avenue.[64]

It may sound like a cliché, but it is one of those truisms of politics that no cause, no movement, ever succeeds in the absence of organization. In Austin that vehicle in the late forties was the Legislative Conference. It became the means for the coalescence of various and sundry liberal groups. Without it, in all likelihood, the fight on behalf of liberal democracy and against the Establishment of bankers and businesspeople would have run aground.

The atmosphere was ripe in Austin, then, at mid-century for

various kinds of reforms and changes to take place. The essence of all of them was to pry open the gates to the political arena a little more, to let in people who previously had been denied access to the various privileges and rewards of American society. And no group stood to benefit more than the black community.

7.

We the People

———

Keep in mind we live in a structure. . . . If you don't operate in that structure, you are lost. . . . How many years it's gonna take us to learn that, I don't know. But your whole life is structure, and the higher up you go, the more structure, not the less of it. . . . And the further down you are, the less of the structure touches you. Now the structure touches people down there because they get it at the bitter end. So you need to keep all this in mind. This is the structure within which people live.[1]

ALEXANDER WOOLDRIDGE HAD A VISION OF GROWTH. It served as the cornerstone, the guiding light, of Austin for a period of more than fifty years. Then in 1940 it was consummated with the completion of the Austin dam. Now growth had become a material factor in Austin, something that came to touch every sector, every niche and corner, of the community. The post–World War II boom brought even more growth. And now the expansion began to impinge in new ways on the state capital. The backwaters of Austin were touched, the alleys and byways that had not seen the full benefits of the Wooldridge dream came to stand out, in deep contrast to the growth elsewhere. And the one part that came to stand out in greater, in more glaring, contrast to the rest was the black community. There it stood, poverty in the midst of increasing plenty, scarcity in the center of abundance.

On August 18, 1949, the Austin Housing Authority, first formed and chaired by Commodore Edgar Perry, announced that it was about to develop plans for more public housing in Austin.[2] The dwellings would house blacks, who represented thirteen percent of the community, as well as Mexican Americans and poor whites.[3] Shortly afterward, there was another announcement, also concerning housing for the poor. St. John's Regular Baptist Association, which ran an orphanage for black children in northeast Austin, declared that it had plans to sell its property, of almost three hundred acres, to establish a low-cost housing project for blacks.[4] While the Austin Housing Authority project was greeted with mild dissent, St. John's announcement produced a deafening roar of disapproval. The St. John's tract of land, located where Highland Mall is now, stood on the northern outskirts of Austin. Since the early teens, blacks had been settling in East Austin. To create a low-cost public housing project in the northeast would destroy the established pattern of racial segregation and thereby greatly upset many people. Petitions were quickly circulated, urging the city to purchase the land and build such vital additions as a new football stadium.[5] Black leaders were divided over the matter. The longtime spokesman of the black community, Dr. Everett Givens, demanded that St. John's not develop the tract for low-cost housing, noting that "[racial] understanding will be seriously hurt if we try to go to [sic] fast."[6] But W. Astor Kirk, speaking on behalf of the Austin chapter of the National Association for the Advancement of Colored People (NAACP), argued that the owners of the property had the right to use the land as they wished.[7] City government, he added, could not go around willfully choosing when and where it wished to condemn property so it could be used only for public purposes. The city, he further observed, had not condemned a separate ten-acre parcel of land in the same vicinity, implying that it was the black low-income housing that really was at issue in the debate. And Arthur DeWitty, correspondent in Austin for the *Houston Informer*, stated that the Federal Housing Authority was unprepared to approve land in East Austin for low-cost public housing, while the St. John's tract could easily acquire such approval.[8]

But this was not the end of the housing discussion. City officials decided to undertake a study of living conditions for the Austin poor. They hired a consulting firm from Madison, Wisconsin, and they directed the firm to survey the quality of dwellings among Austin's poor residents. On April 1, 1950, the agency reported back to the Austin Housing Authority with its findings.[9] Yes, the report declared, there were many instances of poor, or dilapidated, housing in Austin. A large number of homes were without hot and cold running water inside, and many residents had to use toilet facilities outside the house. The authors of the report believed that their survey results would assist the city in making some kind of decision on housing for many members of the black community as well as for their Mexican American and poor white counterparts. The city government, under the leadership of Taylor Glass, abided by the spirit of the report and, on May 4, 1950, the council voted to go ahead with a large-scale public housing program in East Austin.[10] The decision brought to a close the discussion over whether to locate public housing on the St. John's parcel of land; no low-cost housing for blacks ever went up on the site.

The growth of Austin affected blacks, and in a rather strange way. Comfortable white Austinites could not rid themselves of their fellow residents, nor did they truly hope to. Instead they claimed that the living conditions of black residents were so poor as to be publicly inappropriate for a progressive community. How can you show yourself off to the world, be a first-class place to live, be the dream of Northerners who wish to come South, if you have poor people? So the city officials did what they had done in the past. They declared the area of East Austin to be one of slum housing, and thus the object of slum clearance. And the way to improve these circumstances was to introduce low-cost public housing. Just so long as it did not arise in an unexpected area, one of anticipated white expansion, Northeast Austin. Black residents were bewildered by the strange sophistry of the "structure." Ada Simond vividly recalls that "when they said slum clearance, people got the impression the thing they were building was gonna be the slum. They didn't see it as clearing up the places where they had been living. . . . I remember . . . hearing this woman talking and she says, No, I'm not gonna live in those slums."[11] This was not the first time that the expansion, even the vision of a better future, had brought forth public condemnation of the living conditions of blacks in Austin. Earlier in the century, in the mid-teens, another report had been commissioned. This report, too, had found evidence of dilapidated housing among Austin's black and brown poor, on the east side of town.[12] Twenty-five years later, when Austin was engaged in another period of boom late in the 1930s, Lyndon Johnson, Commodore Perry, and Tom Miller had discovered evidence of slum conditions in Austin.[13] And this provided the basis for bringing the first public housing into the community.

What one must wonder about all this commotion over growth and housing for the poor is why the larger white community failed to take itself to task about the deeper circumstances that underlay the poor housing. Of course, sometimes its view was clouded by other concerns. When the federal government wished to push its housing program in the late 1930s, it proved essential for city officials to identify the housing in East Austin as slum housing. In that way the city got funds from the New Deal. The same was partly true in the late 1940s. A new federal housing program had been enacted in 1949. So the city officials had to label certain housing as slum housing in order to qualify for public funds. Public monies from the federal government helped everyone in Austin, including the banks, the lumberyards, the construction business, just about everyone.

But surely there were some people out there wondering about the root cause of the poverty of their black and brown brethren. The Progressive party, a radical political group, did so in 1949, and it spoke about the real estate interests in town, and why such interests did not want public housing to be built in the heart of Northeast Austin.[14] But were there no citizens among the longtime residents, people like Tom Miller, who wanted to get at the roots of poverty, of so-called dilapidated housing—who wanted to rid Austin of the continuing problem? Were there no white people who wondered deeply about the plight of the black poor?

This chapter describes in some depth the character and quality of the black community of Austin. Until the 1960s, this community represented the principal minority segment of East Austin, the one that demanded greater public attention, the one that white politicians like Tom Miller would court in order to capture public office. The chapter tells of the evolution of this community, from its changing patterns of residence to the growing and emerging sense of self-confidence on the part of its inhabitants. The chapter also tells how segregation came to fall apart in Austin, how the little practices that had come to be established early in the twentieth century soon came to be a burden for blacks as well as whites. And, in the course of this story, the chapter informs readers of some individuals who left important marks on the history of the black community and its relations with white Austin. Through their ingenuity, through their tireless efforts, through their devotion to the life of black people in Austin, these men and women came to demonstrate that change could happen even if it was neither swift nor of revolutionary proportions.

Today most black Austin residents live just east of Interstate 35, in the area known locally as East Austin. Black people have not always been concentrated in this section. At the turn of the century, black families could be found interspersed throughout the community, living in housing near the Capitol, clustered in dwelling units on the west side of town, residing in the small community as though they were no different from anyone else. Several separate enclaves of black families actually arose in Austin late in the nineteenth century, at least one of which, Clarksville, remains semi-intact today – although urban development is about to wipe it from the face of the earth as though it were enemy territory.

One part of town, which today houses dwelling units along with fraternities and sororities for University of Texas students, came to be known as Wheatsville. It was an area of several acres, bordered by Twenty-fourth Street on the south, and Twenty-sixth Street on the north, by Rio Grande Street on the east, and Shoal Creek Boulevard on the west. The area was named for James Wheat, a black freedman who just after Emancipation purchased the first plot of land there, at 2409 San Gabriel Street.[15] At one time there were a large number of black families living in Wheatsville. Even today, it is claimed there are more than two hundred former residents who still call Austin their home.[16] The heart of Wheatsville began to be eaten away as the twentieth century progressed and, in particular, as the university sought to expand its quarters westward from the center of the Forty Acres. The movement accelerated in the 1930s, and families were forced to flee to East Austin to find a side of town that would welcome blacks. At present all that remains of the former Wheatsville black neighborhood is an old building, here and there, and the Wheatsville Co-op at Thirty-first Street and Guadalupe. But the Wheatsville Co-op is one of those late twentieth century inventions that enshrines history in name only. It is white-owned, and run for the benefit of a primarily white clientele who appreciate the idea of a cooperative market.

A second important location of black residents was the area known as Clarksville. Parts of Clarksville remain standing today, such as historic Sweet Home Baptist Church, originally founded in 1877 by the Reverend Jacob Fontaine and several others.[17] Clarksville at one time was a very lively place, the center of which was the church. Like Wheatsville, Clarksville was a rather small but self-contained community. Even today some longtime residents keep chickens and other creatures fit for a meal milling about their backyards. Located in West Austin, once on the very outskirts of town, it is situated between Waterston and Tenth Streets, with its eastern and western boundaries at West Lynn Street and the Mo-Pac Freeway. Charles Clark, former black slave, purchased two acres on Tenth Street here in 1871, and built a home at what is today 1618 West Tenth.[18] The number of black families living here grew very slowly and, because there was no great push from a university or a business, it took longer for the residents to disperse. Streets were not even paved, and sewers not installed until 1979.

Today there are still a handful of early dwellers living in the Clarksville area, including the Carringtons and the Hales, both descendents of some of the original settlers. Sweet Home Baptist Church, a lovely building erected at its present site in 1935, beautiful in its simplicity, has been selected as a historic landmark by the Travis County Historical Survey Committee, and will remain standing until the property becomes so valuable that someone will want to take a killing on it. But elsewhere in Clarksville, where there are no small shacks, shotgun houses as Ada Simond calls them, or two- and three-room dwellings that serve as home to university students, stand the gentrified houses of the 1980s.[19] They are painted, of course, in pastel browns, pastel blues, pastel greys, and pastel pinks, all signs of the great progress of urban development. And decorators, potters, real estate developers, and beauty salons straddle the land where once stood shacks, and where black men and women relived the horrors of slavery.

A third major site of black residences in Austin was in an area now somewhat less well remembered than Wheatsville and Clarksville. It was called Masontown, and was found in the heart of Austin. Settled by two brothers, Sam Mason, Jr., and Raiford Mason, it was the first community of blacks in Austin. The two men lived in the 1500 block of East Fourteenth Street.[20] The borders of the community were Third and Sixth streets, Waller Street on the west, Chicon Street on the east. Masontown continues to be home to numbers of black residents, though many of them are unaware of the historic roots of the area.

These three small enclaves, plus a small site on South Mary, just south of the Colorado River, and another one in the northeast section of Austin, at the site of St. John's orphanage, began to fade sometime in the 1920s. At the same time, more and more black people took up residence in East Austin, just on the other side of what then was known as East Avenue—where the Interstate lies today. The precise dates of this *urban resettlement program* are not cetain. A study done for the city in 1977 shows that as early as 1910 blacks began to be concentrated in the East Austin sector, leaving the black enclaves to stagnate.[21] And by 1940, the study shows, it was clear that a minority section of town had developed, the one that would become known to everyone as East Austin. Still, there is a good deal of mystery, even controversy, about how the resettlement of blacks happened, and even why it came about.

At the request of the City Council, a city plan was drawn up by the firm of Koch and Fowler in 1928, and it soon received the official approval of the council.[22] Its recommendations are worth our attention. It proposed a number of specific policies for a new and growing Austin. Of special significance to black Austinites, even to whites, was a design for the deliberate segregation of the city. The matter appears to have been much on the minds of many public officials at the time. Walter Long, and the Austin Chamber of Commerce, had recently been the recipients of a pamphlet from the city planning engineer of Dallas, a Major E. A. Wood. Major Wood had urged Long and other public figures in Texas to take heed of those plans now abroad in America to segregate the cities. Major Wood observed that any "plan that is prepared should provide districts for negroes and Mexicans, giving them the same facilities as whites, that is, wide paved streets, standard size lots, and all of the public utilities. In this way, there will be no slums or blighted districts, and the only question is how to define such areas so that the boundaries will be hard and fast, will be supported by the courts and be mutually agreeable to all."[23] Koch and Fowler echoed the Woods recommendations, but they did even more. "There has been considerable talk in Austin," their report states:

> as well as in other cities, in regard to the race segregation problem. This problem cannot be solved legally under any zoning law known to us at present. Practically all attempts of such have been proven unconstitutional. In our studies of Austin we have found that the negroes are present in small numbers, in practically all sections of the city, excepting the area just east of East Avenue, and south of the City Cemetery. This area seems to be all negro population. It is our recommendation that the

nearest approach to the solution of the race segregation problem will be the recommendation of this district as a negro district; and that *all the facilities and conveniences be provided the negroes in this district, as an incentive to draw the negro population to this area.* This will eliminate the necessity of duplication of white and black schools, white and black parks, and other duplicate facilities for this area. We are recommending that sufficient area be acquired adjoining the negro high school to provide adequate space for a complete negro play-field in connection with the negro high scool. We further recommend that the negro schools in this area be provided with ample and adequate play ground space and facilities similar to the white schools of the city.[24]

The plan was adopted by the council. Yet it is unclear that it was implemented to an exact degree and with conscious, almost conspiratorial, forethought by city officials. The minutes of the council, for instance, never once tell of implementing proposals, but perhaps their unconstitutionality—which Wood and Koch and Fowler alike observed—prevented them from doing so.

The urban resettlement of Austin blacks to the East Austin area may well have begun long before the Koch and Fowler report ever saw the light of day. Until the Austin schools finally were integrated in 1979, after at least a decade of tortured inaction, there was but a single high school in Austin serving the black community. Named Anderson High School after its longtime principal, the major quarters for the school had been erected in East Austin at 1607 Pennsylvania Avenue in 1913, a full fifteen years before Koch and Fowler came up with their recommendations. Black Austinites with a marvelous penchant for history, chief among them Ada Simond, today assert that the Anderson High School was built at its East Austin site so that it would force blacks to resettle there.[25] Simond and other reason that if a black family wished its children to attend high school, the trek across town, from South Mary or Wheatsville, would be so long the family would be forced to moved to be nearer the school. There is no concrete evidence whatsoever that city officials acted in this manner. Nevertheless, whether intentional or not, the long-term effect of locating Anderson High on Pennsylvania Avenue was to draw more and more black families into East Austin, thereby encouraging the urban relocation of blacks.

Within several decades of the Anderson High decision, East Austin had come into existence as the place where black people resided. The 1940 census, for example, shows that of the 14,861 blacks tallied, fully seventy-five percent lived in the two major census tracts of East Austin, tracts 8 and 9.[26] Parks and playground facilities gradually were constructed in this area, as was the public housing project in the early 1940s. Rosewood Park, the principal recreational site in East Austin for blacks, was developed during the 1930s, and other sites, such as Givens Park and Dorie Miller Auditorium, were not long off. Even today, great sums of federal and private funds are put into the area, the apparent motive being to keep East Austin blacks and browns happy. And keep them there.

The year is 1907.[27] We are in downtown Austin, on Sixth Street. Picture to yourself some Lower East Side street in New York City, perhaps a little less crowded but equally overgrown with small shops and businesses. There is a lot of ethnic traffic and business here, some of it operated by black proprietors, some of it run by Austin's newly arrived Jewish immigrants. These are people who cannot find spaces on Congress Avenue, or who cannot afford them. Jonas Silberstein, for example, runs a small dry goods and clothing store there on the south side of the street, at 305 East Sixth. Silberstein will remain at this location for many years, buy other property up and down the street, and father sons who will take up the clothing business as well. Herman Becker, one of the German immigrants, has a combination restaurant, fruit stand, and confectionary store just down from Silberstein's at 315 East Sixth. All along the dusty byway, a visitor will discover scores of tiny shops lining the walks, many of them offering drink for refreshment. In the same block as Silberstein's and Becker's, there is the Silver King bar, the Little Casino Saloon, and, just one block east, the Bowery Saloon and the Favorite Saloon. Fish markets and meat markets also straddle the street, offering the passerby a little something to take home. Saad Ferris, an importer of Oriental goods, runs a store here on East Sixth, and lives above the premises. In the 600 block lies the Joseph Nalle Lumber Company, one of the prominent enterprises of early twentieth century Austin. The Nalle family, among the fairly early settlers, is one of Austin's more wealthy and influential families, and its lumberyard occupies almost an entire city block.

As one moves farther down the street, closer to where East Austin lies, businesses operated by black and Mexican American owners appear. William Tears runs a major enterprise in the 600 block, on the south side, at 615. Tears is one of the more prominent and industrious figures of the black business community, and he operates an undertaking and embalming establishment, one of only two available to black Austinites. In the next block from Tears the visitor will discover a grocery and feed business owned by Isaac Joseph, a restaurant at 716 East Sixth run by E. D. Morales, and, at the end of the block, the "66" Saloon.

If you should visit here on a Saturday, you will observe small congregations of families along the walks, visiting and shopping in the various stores. This is the heart of Austin for its black and brown residents, the place that will remain etched in their memories forever. The East Sixth Street shops, such as Silberstein's, are among the few stores in Austin where black residents can freely shop. Few stores, if any, on the fancy thoroughfare, Congress Avenue, would dare permit blacks to shop in them, reserving their wares instead for the so-called higher class of people, whites. But the East Sixth Street establishments welcome, nay thrive on, the traffic of black and brown Austinites. And they cater to the tastes and incomes of the poor, most of the clothing stores, for example, dealing only in used clothing. Over the next two decades, the crowds of minority shoppers and sightseers, the adults as well as the children, will expand even more. By 1927, some of the names and faces have changed, but the diversity and multitude of small businesses continue. Three blocks east of Congress Avenue, one now finds the Frank Brothers Clothing Store and, just on the opposite side of the street, the Lincoln Theatre. R. L. Gilbert operates a small barbershop at 303, on the south side, and John Joseph runs a dry goods store at 307. Herman Becker still has a thriving business of edible goods in the same block. Down in the next block there have been some changes. A hardware company now is housed at 401 East Sixth under the name W. H. Richardson, while two recent immigrants from the Middle East, Mssrs. Karambelas and Fayad, sell fruit from a tiny space at number 405. Louis Silberstein, who had been a clerk for his father twenty years earlier, now has his own business, a store merchandising used clothing, at 410 East Sixth. Many of his clients, like his father's, are black men and women.

One of the most prominent and successful black residents of Austin in the twentieth century, Dr. Everett H. Givens, has by now returned to his hometown and opened a dental practice at 419½ East

Sixth, in the upstairs quarters.[28] Dr. Givens attended Tillotson College in East Austin, left the community for a time, and has come back, to spend the remainder of his life doing good things on behalf of black people. He is a giant of a man with a booming voice. Like many another public figure, he loves power, and will enjoy using it, engaging in wheeling-dealing with white Austinites. Soon he will strike up a lifelong friendship with Tom Miller, who, like himself, has grown up in Austin and who, it just so happens, also stands a good deal taller, and certainly rounder, than other men. By the 1930s, Givens will be referred to by his fellow black Austinites, even by many white residents, as the "bronze mayor of Austin," a title assumed without election to office. Givens' dental practice will expand; he will in time make a handsome income, drive a fancy Cadillac, wear a large silver belt buckle, and strike many a good bargain between East and West Austin, getting school funds here, more money for a park there. For the present, he is simply happy to serve his black patients at his East Sixth Street quarters. Just down the street, on the same side, is a fellow black physician, Dr. C. R. Yerwood. Yerwood's offices are located in the same building as some important institutions that have developed in black Austin. The *Herald*, a newspaper for black residents, is to be found adjacent to Yerwood's quarters, as are the offices of the Ideal Colored Mutual Aid Association, the Negro Missionary Baptist General Convention of Texas, and the Peoples' Ideal Colored Local Mutual Aid Association.

There is a new assortment of business enterprises as well. Included among them is the grocery store operated by L. D. Lyons, Louis or Colonel, to his close friends. Colonel Lyons, somewhat senior to Dr. Givens in age and experience, has already become one of the great men of the black community. He helps out in various public undertakings that will better serve black Austin, and takes the initiative to raise matters of concern before the City Council. Saad Ferris still runs his Oriental dry goods store on this block, which now has expanded into a rather massive establishment that stretches from 503 to 507 East Sixth Street. Simon Weintraub, a fairly recent Jewish arrival in Austin, sells clothing out of a small shop across the street from Ferris, at 502. There still are a whole host of barbers, grocers, and shoemakers on East Sixth Street, enough to service the growing black and brown population.

Joseph Nalle and Company continues to deal in lumber materials out of its quarters in the 600 block of East Sixth Street, though by now Mr. Nalle himself is gone. William Tears, the prominent undertaker, still prospers, and his business is now graced with a more magnificent appellation, the National Burial Association for Colored People. Grocers and druggists crowd against one another in the 700 block. H. M. Daywood markets groceries in the large space between 700 and 704 East Sixt Street, on the north side of the thoroughfare. Just opposite his shop there now stand three new markets—Garza's, a Mexican American establishment, at 701, Kamp Market at 703, and the Alamo Market at 705 East Sixth Street. The Joseph family runs its grocery store at number 723. Adjacent to their quarters is the store of yet another immigrant, John Nassour, which dispenses fresh pears, peaches, and other fruit to hungry customers.

Over the next ten years, few noticeable changes will occur in the composition of East Sixth Street. There are occasional alterations, such as the commencement of a dry goods business at 419 East Sixth by Abraham Schwartz.[29] But the small grocers and restaurants remain, and the prominent black businesspeople, such as Louis Lyons, still ply their trade. Everett Givens, who is housed above the Schwartz enterprise, still works on peoples' teeth, and William Tears embalms. The black residents of Austin have expanded by a few thousand, so more as well as larger families now traffic the area. It will not be until much later in the century, well into the 1970s, that some of this property will change hands, and the street will begin to achieve the crafted historic and genteel look it now bears. In the intervening years, bars and saloons will come and go, some of the shops will decline or fail to keep pace with change, all this and more will provide spurious cause for the City Council occasionally to voice its concern over the supposed blight on East Sixth Street. As time passes, black men and women will continue to patronize stores on the street. And a demimyth will soon arise, a belief that falls into the zone somewhere between the vigorous sinews of culture and the mistaken perceptions of the world, a demimyth that will seem to be as real for many as the name of the street itself. It will hold that the culprits for the plight of Austin black people, the source of much of their misery and a good deal of their poverty, are the Jewish shopkeepers on East Sixth Street.[30] Black children, who will grow up to inform me of their lives and fortunes, will claim that the men and women such as the Silbersteins, or Simon Weintraub, or Abraham Schwartz, hold all the property on East Sixth, if not the world. It is worth our time, as temporary visitors to this past, to dwell on this claim, for it seems to lie deep in black consciousness in Austin, and often elsewhere, too.

Who, in fact, held the property of East Sixth Street? We know that certain Jewish families ran businesses here, and we know that most of their clients were black Austinites. But did these men and women actually control all the property up and down the street? Let us just examine property ownership at two separate times, 1917 and 1937.[31] In 1917, there were several Jewish families, including the Silbersteins, who owned East Sixth Street property. For instance, Jonas Silberstein held one piece of property, valued at $5,500, in the 300 block, another piece, valued at $4,500, in the 400 block, while Louis Silberstein, his son, owned a store at 408 East Sixth. Mary and Sarah Levi were the proprietors of land and building in the same block as Louis Silberstein. But there were a good many other property owners on East Sixth, so many as to make false any claim that most of the coins from black pocketbooks lined the bank accounts of Austin's Jews. The Henry Robinson estate, for example, held a major piece of property in the 300 block, valued at $13,770. The estate of Charles Wolf, father of Oswald and scion of a wealthy Austin family, held a piece of property, valued at $8,000, in the 400 block. Colonel Andrew Zilker and his wife jointly held property, valued at $3,400, in the 500 block block of East Sixth Street, while the prominent Austin banker E. C. Bartholomew, a major figure in banking and on the City Council, owned two pieces of property, in the 400 block of East Sixth. The largest property owner in 1917, however, was Mrs. Sallie Nalle, widow of Joseph, whose lumberyard was valued at $25,000, exclusive of inventory. Some of the people who ran businesses on the street also owned the buildings and land on which they sat. These included Saad Ferris, whose property in the 500 block of East Sixth was appraised at $7,500, and the black undertaker William Tears, who owned his building and land in the 600 block. In 1917, in other words, it is evident that while the Silbersteins and the Levis owned property and ran businesses on East Sixth Street, they were far outnumbered in holdings, and, one must suppose, daily business, by the combined numbers of many other persons, some of them, like Bartholomew and Wolf, among the most visible and influential residents of Austin.

The pattern of ownership was little different twenty years later. The Levis and the Silberstein family now had increased their holdings, but not markedly so. Mrs. Jonas Silberstein, for example, was listed as the owner of property in the 300 block, valued at $7,000, while Max Silberstein, son of Jonas, held two pieces of property in the same block, valued together at $8,500. The Sarah Levi estate also owned one piece of property in this same block, appraised at $5,250. Down the street, in the 400 block, Samuel Hirschfeld is listed as the owner of land and a building, valued at $9,500, and Mrs. Jonas Silberstein as the owner of one parcel on the books for $4,500. Directly across the street, the Sarah Levi estate owned a piece of property, valued at $5,200, and another one valued at $4,660, while Louis Silberstein and his wife owned one piece appraised at $2,500. The largest property owners on the street at this time, however, were not the Jewish clothiers. M. K. Hage, who ran a booming five and ten cent store on the south side of 300 East Sixth Street, had property that was assessed at $14,000. Ada Zilker Robinson, daughter of the late Colonel, continued to own the property in the 500 block, now valued at $10,000. Louis Lyons held the property on which his grocery was located, but its value was listed as only $1,000. By far the biggest property owner on the whole of the street was Saad Ferris. He held the land and building that housed his dry goods store at 501 to 503 East Sixth Street, valued at $30,000; and just opposite, across the street, he held more property, assessed on the books at a value of $18,000. His holdings, in short, represented a greater sum total of valued property than that of the Jewish clothiers and families on the street. There also were many small property owners, such as the barber P. C. Rhambo and his wife, who held property not only on East Sixth Street but elsewhere in Austin as well.

None of this evidence is definitive, of course. We cannot easily determine the volume of retail traffic carried on by the Jewish clothiers with their predominantly black clientele in these years. In all likelihood it was sizable. Still, there were numerous places of business along the thoroughfare, meat markets, food stores, and even other clothiers, so many and of such ethnic diversity that the notion of a cabal of Jewish pecuniary predators does not easily fit the reality of this marketplace. But that may not be the point. That black Austinites came to believe they were hapless victims to the Jewish merchants on East Sixth seems to have been as much a part of the life here over the years as the shops themselves.

Beyond the East Sixth Street area, life in black Austin was much like that in other black communities of America. Children were raised in homes where mothers and fathers, sometimes grandparents, occasionally even an uncle or aunt, would dote on them. Black men and women have sometimes informed me of a parent or grandparent

who was of special importance in their lives, of someone who provided comfort and wisdom and solace. Some black men and women
were raised to think the white man was the devil because that was
the lesson repeatedly hammered home by a parent over the burning
embers of fires late on cold nights.[32] Others have spoken of the
strength of their kinfolk, of those relatives who provided so clear an
example of what it meant to be a human being—that difficult times
in life could be met, a white adversary overcome. John Q. Taylor
King, currently president of Huston-Tillotson College, speaks that
way of his grandmother, as does W. Astor Kirk—Bill to his
friends.[33] Kirk was raised in Marshall, Texas, but his memories of
his grandmother seem to duplicate the experiences of many a black
Austinite. His grandmother, Kirk, told me, was possessed of a special
mother-wit that seemed to help him over the hard times and gave
him a sense of what black and white folks were all about. She taught
him that the individual was good even though the system might not
be, and that he had to learn how to dislike sin without hating the
sinner. Her wisdom, this folk sense in a woman who had the benefits
of only minimal formal education, led Kirk to be ever optimistic
about life, and made him deeply certain that solutions could be developed to any problems that arose between whites and blacks. At his
grandmother's knee, he truly came to realize that people are people,
and that the proper approach to take to the white person is not one
of thoughtless violence, or deep anger, but of pragmatism, of seeking
solutions, of effecting small but perceptible changes, of having
dialogue.

    If ties between young and old blacks were powerful, there were also
strong bonds knit between white families and their black help. These
bonds, which seemed to dampen the harsh antagonisms and deep injustices felt elsewhere in the "structure," left as permanent a mark on
black adults as did their own home lives. Why, I asked several informants, was there no sharp racial conflict in Austin, no serious political division between the races that mirrored the division of East
Austin from the rest of the community? Always, I learned, it was the
strong and resilient ties between the white families who employed
them and the black servants who were employed that helped to
diminish the intensity of black anger. Ada Simond, for example,
spoke of the food that blacks would receive from families for whom
a woman worked as housekeeper, or a man as groundskeeper.[34] No
one today writes long volumes about the piece of meat left over from

dinner in the parlor that could serve a black family for days. But that small piece of meat helped out. Even from a white employer's point of view, in a home or business, black people sometimes came to be cherished and trusted as good family friends, as people who were as important to daily life and to the family unit as the white relatives— perhaps even more important. Gifts would be given at the special times, at Christmas or other holidays, to provide a sign of good feelings.[35] The gift might not be large or expensive, maybe a trinket or two, some money, or some other small item. But it would be offered in friendship, in trust, even as a sign of love, to make the receiver feel a part of the family, and to provide the giver a sense that everything would be all right. Across the races, between a white employer and a black servant, the little things would be given, feelings exchanged, forming the ties that kept any potentially revolutionary anger in check. Perhaps it was the growth of the labor force, and the movement of blacks out of white households into the large, impersonal marketplace, this rending of the personal bond, that helped make possible the historic demands of the late 1940s. Perhaps.

Many of the black men and women who lived in East Austin, or earlier in the century, in Clarksville, or Wheatsville, or in the South Mary district, lived as routine and regular a life as any white. Up early, maybe at five in the morning, off to a home in West Austin, perhaps one of those newly arisen on West Enfield, or maybe to the downtown district in the area north of the Capitol around Nineteenth Street, a black man would trudge off to work, a black woman go to care for some white children, or to take charge of the housecleaning of some state legislator, or some important Austin citizen, like Dr. Goodall Wooten. After a day spent taking in the wash, caring for the children, perhaps cutting a lawn, or even just serving as the janitor in a downtown department store like J. C. Penney's, or the fashionable women's store T. H. Williams, or the large department store E. H. Scarbroughs, then it was home to East Austin. In the days of the streetcars, there was a break on Congress Avenue. The car would deposit black riders at the intersection of East Sixth and Congress, and there a new car would take them back home, into the depths of the black ghetto. Groups of black people would gather here on the corner to await the streetcar, waifs to a world that refused to recognize their existence after late afternoon. Sometimes they would be compelled to urinate, even defecate, on the walk, in the gutter, or by the side of a building, because no business on Congress

Avenue dared to let them use the restrooms. They would be tired. And when they arrived home, after supper, it was rest for the next day.

Did they ever think about lashing out, about taking to the streets, in the teens or the twenties, to right the imbalances? I have asked. No, because all black people could do was to survive.[36] *Survive.* If you just make a small amount of money, if that money puts just a tiny portion of food on the table, if you must work from day to day just to get by, with no savings in sight, if you live in a rented dwelling barely maintained by an absentee white landlord, all you can hope for is survival. Moment-to-moment. Day-by-day, as Eva Marie Mosby has said.[37] Year-to-year.

For many black men and women in Austin what kept them alive, what gave them hope, was the church. It is nothing new to learn of the significance of the church as of the minister in black Austin. Volumes have been written about these things by many observers of black life in America. The religious experiences of black Austin were no different. In Clarksville, as I have noted, the Sweet Home Baptist Church was center to many collective gatherings. Elsewhere in Austin there were other important churches that became the focus of the joy as well as the sadness of life. The Reverend Jacob Fontaine, who had helped to establish Sweet Home, also founded the First Baptist Church for blacks in Austin in 1864. In 1881, it was relocated in quarters at the site of the current Austin Public Library on Guadalupe Street and remained there until mid-twentieth century, when it was moved to the corner of Red River and Fourteenth streets. Other churches also sprouted up to serve blacks, including the Ebenezer Baptist Church, the St. John's Baptist Association, the Mt. Zion Baptist Church, the Metropolitan AME Church.

Surely one of the more interesting important churches founded within the black community was the Holy Cross Church. Father Francis Webber, a white priest from Detroit, came to Austin in 1935 to serve the parish, located at 1604 East Eleventh, in the heart of East Austin.[38] The Catholic population among blacks was not especially sizable, but Holy Cross took care of more than merely its own worshipers. Father Webber reached out and created bonds of fellowship within black Austin, and people, parishioners but also others, would do things like entrust him with their savings, fearing for the safety of these things in their homes. Owing to the kindness of such residents as Mrs. Louis Novy, wife of the head of the Interstate

Theatres in Austin, and of Simon Gillis, City Council member, Holy Cross also established the first hospital in Austin where black as well as brown residents could be treated by physicians of their own race.

Life was full and rich for the black inhabitants of Austin. There was some jealousy, even some internal rivalries among blacks, particularly between those on the way up and those on the way down the ladder of success. It was this quality that sometimes upset the goodly Father Webber, and drew the attention of even some white Austinites who wondered why black leaders so often provoked the enmity of their black brethren.[39] Several of my black informants also remembered the differences within the black community, especially early in the twentieth century. Clarksville was a place thought to house somewhat poorer residents, while East Austin, even South Mary, was home to a more affluent segment of the population.[40] If you had a lawn, for example, or a living room, if you did not have to traipse outside in the dead of winter to use an outhouse, then you were presumed to be living in better circumstances. Many black men and women professed great pride that they had gotten the funds to build their own place, people like Eva Marie and James Mosby, among the most generous and loving of any people I have met.[41] The Mosbys were able to secure a bank loan to build their home in 1952. The two see themselves as successful, maybe even more so than many other blacks. But they are also wise and charitable enough to recognize that the failure of blacks to rise above the impoverished circumstances of many people in East Austin rested at the doorsteps of the Austin National Bank, and the American National Bank, the major banking institutions that flatly refused to provide housing loans to blacks.

Just as there is a demimyth about the ownership of property along East Sixth Street, so, too, similar kinds of myths prevail about the ownership of property in predominantly black and brown East Austin, as in Clarksville. Some of my black informants were certain that Austin Jews were the leading slum landlords. Others were convinced that the leading bankers and public officials, such as the Bartholomews, or their descendents, even a figure such as Commodore Perry, held much of the property of East Austin. Then there was Lyndon Johnson's famous tirade in 1938, when he viciously accused Simon Gillis of being a slum landlord in East Austin and therefore unwilling to entertain low-cost public housing there.[42] Which, if any, of these claims is accurate? Let us begin with Johnson's accusation. A careful study done of the tax records of Austin at several different points in time – 1907, 1917, 1927, 1937, and 1941 – shows that Gillis did not hold a single piece of property in East Austin.[43] So much for Johnson's claim. The same research reveals that none of the major public figures in Austin, men like the Bartholomews, Commodore Perry, Tom Miller, Goodall Wooten, Walter Long, or others who figured in the growth of Austin, held property in East Austin. Further, it is true that several of the Jewish clothiers and landlords on East Sixth Street did hold parcels of property, people like Jonas Silberstein, Max Silberstein, and the Levi family. And yet they possessed no more property than some black merchants and businesspeople, such as P. C. Rhambo, who owned a number of lots in the East Austin area.

Over this period during which the examination was made of the city tax records and values of Austin property, only two families and figures, in fact, stand out as the dominant landowners in East Austin. One was the F. W. Sternenberg family, and the lumber company they owned, Kuntz-Sternenberg. The lumber company held a number of lots that may, or may not, have furnished timber. The family itself also owned some lots. Sometime in the 1930s or 1940s, they began to sell off this property at a rather small price, just a few dollars an acre, and blacks bought them up rather quickly.[44] The other dominant landlord of East Austin as well as Clarksville was a man who seems to have done little to push the growth of Austin in the public arena. His name was Edmund J. Hofheinz, and he is listed in the city directories as an expert public accountant as well as real estate dealer. He and his wife of many years, Stella, held many pieces of property in East Austin, so-called slum housing, which remained in their possession until husband and wife were divorced. Even then the property was jointly divided. The Hofheinz dwellings were easily identifiable in the community, bearing a customary black trim over grey wood, and often showing little visible upkeep.[45]

There is one last, very startling fact to reveal about the ownership of property in East Austin. Once again it is a rather common claim among both black and white Austinites that most black residents here have been the easy prey of slum landlords, such as Hofheinz, who maintained only the most minimal standards of housing. Kind-hearted people like the Mosbys rue the conditions of their black neighbors who, because of their low incomes, have been forced over the years to rent from an indifferent and often negligent white landlord. The great surprise is that a study of the city tax records suggests that the majority of property in East Austin was in the hands of individual homeowners, husbands and wives who held their own property. The impression actually is confirmed by the study of Austin housing commissioned by the council in 1949. That study, which included an unprecedented survey of thousands of homes in the East Austin area, shows that of 3,562 dwelling units occupied by blacks, fully fifty-five percent of them were owned by their residents, and only forty-five percent were rented.[46] Only among the white and Mexican American inhabitants of this area were there a majority of renters.

At just about the moment that blacks began to move from West to East Austin to be nearer the high school, the complex tangle of law and custom known as Jim Crow, or more commonly as segregation, began to evolve. Janie Harrison claims that many of the policies in Austin took hold about 1906.[47] Whatever the exact date, much of what was done came about informally, without the sanction of law. Bill Kirk, who helped to undertake the first broad attack on segregation in Austin late in the·1940s, found there were only three legal statutes in Texas and Austin regulating the separation of the races. The statutes required that blacks and whites be segregated on public conveyances such as streetcars; in public educational systems, such as schools; and in coal mines.[48] The reason for the last is something of a mystery. Nonetheless, the separation of blacks and whites took hold in many, many other respects. And a number of these practices proved extremely hurtful to black men and women, often leading to tears, as was the case of a plaintive black woman who poured out her heart to Father Webber because she was refused permission to shop in a Congress Avenue store.[49] Sometimes the hurt was deeper, the harm far more prolonged.

The separation, the division, was bad in Austin, as bad and as deeply rooted as anywhere else in the South. Blacks not only did not and could not live alongside whites in Austin, they could not dine with them, shop with them, or mingle with them in any way. The Ritz Theatre on East Sixth Street, which remains standing, was the only place where black children could watch a movie, but often it was only a second- or third-run show. Even then, the black youngsters had to trek to the balcony upstairs, from which the view was difficult, while white children were permitted to view the movie from ground level.[50] Black children who attended Anderson High School had the benefit of a high school education. But their books were always hand-me-downs from the white Austin High School, and not until college would they have the benefit of brand-new textbooks.[51] Black students, too, would sometimes wonder about the advertised field trips for their white counterparts at Austin High, curious about the places those tours visited.[52]

If you were a black woman who wanted to buy a hat, you usually had to confine yourself to a shop on East Sixth Street. White women could shop at Scarbroughs or at T. H. Williams on Congress Avenue, but black women rarely were permitted this privilege. Even if you were, the only way you could try on a hat would be to slip paper over your head, sometimes a plastic bag.[53] White women were never subjected to such indignities. If a black woman wished to buy a dress from Scarbroughs, she could take it home, but not don it in a dressing room.[54] A handful of black women might be permitted to try on an article of clothing in the Scarbroughs store, but they would be the privileged few, the special servants, not the common man or woman. If you were black and wished to drink water from a fountain in downtown Austin, you had to steer clear of White's Pharmacy at Sixth and Congress.[55] You would be lucky to find a "colored only" fountain on Congress Avenue. Eva Marie Mosby once risked tasting the "white only" water downtown to discover if it differed from that for "coloreds." Tasted pretty good, she remembers.[56]

Jim Crow ranged far and wide across Austin. If you were black and you had to take a streetcar across town, then you would be compelled to sit at the rear of the car.[57] One time, John King recalls, a lovely old black woman boarded a streetcar he was riding. King may have been only six or seven years old. The woman sat down momentarily at the front so she could count her change and give it to the conductor. The conductor screamed at her to go to the back, startling and embarrassing a number of riders and deeply affecting young King with the shame of it all. King never again boarded an Austin street-car.[58] Of course, there were no public places on Congress Avenue where black people could feed themselves, stop for a bite to eat on the way back into the heart of East Austin. White's Pharmacy would not feed blacks. But, as Volma Overton remembers, you could purchase a peanut patty, or some other candy, there. And even though Sam Wah's Chinese Restaurant would not allow black people to eat in its main quarters, a few, such as Dr. B. E. Conner, were occasionally given the privilege of some food just so long as they ate in the back room.[59]

The worst of the indignities of Jim Crow, it seems, happened with medical care in Austin. Blacks, of course, could not easily provide funds for white physicians. Thus, black physicians such as Dr. Conner would charge them only small amounts, something on the order of $5.00 an office visit.[60] He did not alter his charge over a period of several decades. Brackenridge Hospital, the large public hospital, had separate facilities for the two races, relegating the care of black patients to the basement and the quarters behind the main hospital. When a black physician had a patient sent to Brackenridge, the physician could not treat her there because he was not a member of the local medical society. The society did not allow black doctors to belong. Black patients also received worse care at Brackenridge than whites.

This particular injustice came to a head sometime in the early 1950s with the death of Dr. Carl Downs, president of Samuel Huston College, a local school in Austin established in 1880 by the Methodist-Episcopal Church principally for black students.[61] Dr. Downs today is recalled as a large and vigorous figure who worked hard on behalf of the members of his race. One day he was diagnosed as having appendicitis and rushed to Brackenridge. When the operation was over, he had to be wheeled through the cold, damp air into the black quarters back of the main hospital. His condition worsened, and within hours of the operation he was dead. His family was shaken by his death, so sudden and seemingly so unnecessary. His mother arrived in Austin from Chicago, convinced her son had been killed by the poor facilities. Physicians such as Dr. Conner believe Downs could have been saved with the emergency room resources set aside exclusively for white patients, while white nurses such as Mary Holman are equally certain that segregation had once more taken a black life in Austin.[62] Downs' death angered many Austin residents and soon helped lead to action that would eventually desegregate Brackenridge. But how many others like Downs had died over the years from similar neglect and poor facilities?

Jim Crow began to fall in Austin in the late 1940s, the result of activities on many fronts. It was an outworn institution created out of fear as much as anything else. And it had hurt blacks, cut them savagely, made them feel worthless.

Black residents of Austin never took segregation lying down. Well before the major assaults in the late 1940s, there were small skirmishes, evidence perhaps that both the black and white communities here were somewhat more enlightened and receptive to change than those elsewhere. The battles began late in the teens as the City Council displayed a willingness to listen to pleas for improved conditions on behalf of black Austinites.

In 1918, there was a march along Congress Avenue by the Ku Klux Klan. The Klan was in a period of revival in America, and the main thoroughfare of the state capital was as good a place as any to attract a lot of publicity. Like many whites, the Klan was not entirely of one mind about its aims. While it marched on Congress Avenue to condemn the existence of "colored people," some of its leaders were in the rotunda of the Capitol presenting a gift of several hundreds of dollars to aid the orphans at the all-black St. John's orphanage in northeast Austin.

The Klan's arrival appears to have stirred up feelings in the black community, for at the council meeting on March 21st, Mayor Alexander Wooldridge read a letter than detailed a number of concerns about conditions in Austin for blacks.[63] The letter came from Dr. W. H. Crawford, a black physician. Crawford shared quarters with Everett Givens at 419½ East Sixth Street. His letter spoke about the indignities to which blacks were subject in Austin, and it asked the council to take some immediate steps to improve things. Wooldridge and the council, giving evidence they were not indifferent to their fellow residents, sought to pacify Dr. Crawford. The council agreed that a "Welfare Board and an Advisory Board, both to be comprised of negro citizens of this city [be created], whose function it shall be to keep in intimate touch with the varied interests of the colored people of Austin. . . ."[64] Within months such a board had been established. At the meeting of May 2, the duties of the board were outlined.[65] It was proposed that the board act to cooperate with the council, and especially with the Police and Charity Departments of the city, to insure that "social, political, moral and physical progress" be worked out for the "negro race" of Austin. The black citizens named to the board sounded like an elite of East Sixth Street merchants and professionals. They included Dr. Crawford, as chairman, William Tears, who ran the funeral home on East Sixth Street, N. W. Rhambo, who operated another funeral parlor in Austin for blacks, and the recently returned Everett Givens.

However well-meaning the action by the council might have been, it did not produce much in the way of improved circumstances for Austin's blacks. The council ordered at its May 2 meeting that the new Welfare Board furnish monthly reports, which would presumably alert the council to problems and provide the basis for remedies. The first report was filed on June 6, one month after the board's creation. No details were described in council minutes. So far as one can tell, no other report was filed with the council – or, at least, it was not so registered in the minutes. Surely this did not signal the end to the suffering of blacks in Austin. Yet it was not until eight years later, in 1927, that we again learn of the needs of black citizens through the council records.[66] On February 24 of that year, the Colored Knights of Pythias asked the council's permission to use Wooldridge Park, lying adjacent to the public library on Guadalupe, for its June 6 Jubilee Concert. The council agreed to the request without complaint, and shortly thereafter it provided the sum of $150 to pay for summer concerts for the "colored people" of Austin.

By 1928, steps to upgrade the conditions for black Austinites had increased appreciably. Much of the credit for the talk and some of the ensuing action was due to the efforts of Dr. Givens. The council decided to set aside a sizable amount of money, $14,000, on behalf of parks for the black community of East Austin. The funds helped to establish the center of recreational activity for black residents, what would come to be known as Rosewood Park.[67] Only four years later, the man who soon would come to rule over Austin politics, the good friend of Givens, Tom Miller, stood before the council to urge that the city officials take steps to create a library for the black community.[68] It was a courageous and certainly political act by Miller. Few other white men or women in Austin could have taken to the public forum for the black underclass. But Tom was the boy from downtown, Colonel Zilker's protégé, who had run one year earlier and lost. By now he had come to realize that the support of black citizens could help his council campaigns.

The issue of a library for black Austinites soon became one of the hot topics of debate of the early 1930s, so far as blacks were concerned. Miller's advocacy of it probably had something to do with this, but there were other features of Austin's black community that helped, too. Few other black communities in America, save for Atlanta and possibly one or two others, were home to two predominantly black institutions of higher learning. Samuel Huston

College sat at the intersection of Twelfth Street and East Avenue where a large Safeway store is now found. The Collegiate and Normal Institution bearing his name had been founded by the Reverend George Jeffrey Tillotson, a member of the American Missionary Association, in the late nineteenth century. Both schools had been established by whites and were designed to fill the religious and educational needs of the entire population.[69] In time they came to serve an almost exclusively black clientele.

The presence of the schools in Austin, coupled with the emphasis on some kind of education in many black households, made black residents sharply aware of the importance of books and libraries. Thus, soon after Miller's address elicited a response from the council that it was "deeply interested in the matter of a library for the colored people of Austin," the attempt to secure such quarters expanded into a full-fledged political campaign. A mass rally was held on the east side within a month of Miller's appearance. The audience was questioned about its desires, and tallies made of responses to the various options for a library, a site, the building, and the resources for it.[70] Mary E. Branch, the president of Tillotson College, attended the February 23 meeting of the City Council. There she informed the officials of the details of the rally and noted that, while there were differences of opinion, everyone agreed that East Austin must have its own library.[71] She noted, moreover, that the library was essential because black residents were not permitted to use the facilities of the Austin Public Library. If a black person wanted a book, the only option would be to use the resource at Huston or Tillotson. But these quarters were privately owned, and thus not easily available to every black citizen.

The debate over the library for East Austin dragged on. More meetings were held in the black community, more rallies took place, and the City Council invited its own library commission to consider the status of a black library for Austin. Then, on May 18, 1933, Givens and Louis Lyons, the East Sixth Street grocer with premises just one block east of Dr. Givens, showed up in the council chambers.[72] They spoke about the possible location for a library, as well as about a building that could be used to house books. After a lengthy discussion, it was agreed that a library should be erected at the corner of Angelina and Hackberry streets in East Austin, and that the available lot be purchased out of city funds for the price of $1,800. One month later, a small sum of money, $945, was set aside to purchase books for the new library.[73] The facility became known as the George Washington Carver Branch, and it grew into a repository not only for books but also for many artifacts relevant to the history of black Austin.

This success seemed to quiet the public demands of black residents for a time. But still, throughout the 1930s, Givens, Lyons, and a few other black Austinites pressed ahead with some simple requests. They asked that a "colored" public health nurse be provided the black community to help treat the sick and elderly residents who could not afford a doctor. Givens also demanded that improvements be made to the streets of Austin, that lights be furnished for Rosewood Park, and that other resources be provided to the community. He never raised his voice in favor of integration of black and white Austin, only pushing for comparable public facilities in the black community, much as Koch and Fowler had. East Austin, however, continued to be inferior to West Austin by the early 1940s, so Givens pressed ahead with more demands, sometimes taking up large amounts of council time with his requests. On the eve of the new decade, he appeared with a shopping list of needs.[74] He asked that the black community be given a share of the proposed increases in school revenues, that a youth center be built in Rosewood Park, that there be better hospital resources for blacks, and that the streets of East Austin, unpaved and littered, be improved. Some of these requests were met, some were not. Much depended not only on Givens' powerful rhetorical style, which often was as colorful as that of his friend the mayor, but also on the kind of bargain Givens and Miller managed to strike.

Gradually, the circumstances of black Austin improved. New problems would arise, such as the wartime arrival in Austin of black servicemen who were stationed at nearby Camp Swift. Their arrival occasioned several council appearances by Givens as well as by Mary Branch, who urged that new resources, such as separate USO quarters, be set aside for black servicemen. The war did bring its own special problems to East Austin, unleashing the lust of the soldiers going overseas, so the council was urged at its meeting of August 20, 1942, to make improvements to a "Negro Prophylactic Station" in the city.[75] Major changes were still to come, alterations in the fabric of race relations in Austin, that would have significance far beyond the borders of East Sixth and Congress Avenue. They happened in 1946, and they had nothing to do with Everett Givens, Louis Lyons, or

Tom Miller. They had to do with a shy, retiring postman by the name of Hemann Marion Sweatt.

In 1946, Hemann Sweatt was a letter carrier in Houston. He decided to advance his career, so he took a civil service examination open to everyone. On the basis of his high score, he learned, he was entitled to become a postal clerk. The job paid more money and provided him the greater prestige he longed for. However, because he was black and despite his merit, he was not allowed to take the position. Like many other black men and women, the denial of his rights prompted him to wonder about segregation, about the legal and extralegal means used to keep black people as the underclass of American society. His wonder soon turned to concrete action. He decided to apply to the University of Texas Law School, where, he hoped, he could earn a law degree, learn about the intricacies of the Jim Crow laws, and eventually serve his fellow black Americans. On March 14, 1946, the officers of the University of Texas Law School turned down Sweatt's application, using Jim Crow statutes to support their decision. They informed Sweatt that since there were comparable legal facilities to train blacks elsewhere in the state, he should obtain his legal education at one of them.[76]

Whatever his personal style, which was diffident at best, Sweatt decided to press forward with his plan to enter the University of Texas. He brought suit against the university on the grounds that his constitutional rights as a citizen had been abridged. Amidst great commotion, the case went to trial in Austin. Quickly Austin and Sweatt became household words in many cities across the country, particularly among educated black families. Already the site of considerable turmoil owing to the firing of Homer Rainey, the university soon had another revolt on their hands. The Austin chapter of the NAACP went to the campus to solicit support for Sweatt from university organizations.[77] University administrators—T. S. Painter, acting president, in particular—tried to thwart the NAACP campaign. But many campus organizations rallied behind Sweatt, including the American Veterans Committee, the Wesley Foundation Council, and the Baptist Student Union. Members of these groups, plus many other students, some dressed in their war uniforms, daily attended the Sweatt trial at the Travis County Courthouse downtown. And a few went so far as to solicit funds for Sweatt's defense on the courthouse steps, causing no end of commotion.

Jim Crow was not about to die an easy death in Austin, even in the supposedly progressive quarters of the university. Some university denizens, including teachers and the student editor of the *Daily Texan*, argued strongly against any popular support for Sweatt. They claimed, almost in a single voice, that any further evidence of campus disruption would unsettle an already delicate situation. The Legislature, some claimed, might even be tempted to reduce the size of the university's appropriation. The *Dallas News*, a university protagonist already well known in campus circles for its role in the Fair Park Rally debacle, got into the act, too. The *News* wrote of the limited size of student support on Sweatt's behalf, noting that the campus rally led by the Austin NAACP and various campus groups drew something on the order of sixty students.[78] Surely, the *News* argued, that was a tiny crowd compared to the many thousands who attended the university. Only days later, Hart Stilwell, an aspiring writer living in Austin, wrote amusingly of the *News* editorial that since

> it is the general opinion on the campus that a majority of students would actually vote for the admission of Sweatt this means that the *Dallas News*, in stating 'only sixty students' favored the case, has a margin of error of around 12,500 percent. This is considered good for the *Dallas News*, its margin of error in the reporting of news dealing with labor and race discrimination ranging, ordinarily, between 14,000 and 15,000 percent. In that editorial the *Dallas News* suggested a poll on the University of Texas campus to 'determine the extent of infiltration of liberalism.' This came as quite a surprise to those people who did not know that it is against the law to be a liberal.[79]

Stilwell's comments probably were the only light touch to the serious battle brewing between Sweatt and his supporters and the multitude of their antagonists in Austin and elsewhere in Texas. Many black residents got wrapped up in the case; on the night before the final ruling by Travis County Judge Roy Archer, they gathered in Dorie Miller Auditorium in East Austin to hear J. Frank Dobie proclaim that "I know keeping one's fellow man, no matter of what color, down in ignorance is evil and undemocratic, and that such injustice results in evil to the oppressors as well as to the oppressed."[80]

Hemann Sweatt's legal defense bordered on the historic and spectacular. The national offices of the NAACP provided an associate counsel to help argue the case. His name was Thurgood Marshall, and he had gone to Howard Law School, where he became practiced in how to attack Jim Crow laws at their weakest points. He and Sweatt's chief counsel, W. D. Durham of Dallas, proceeded to argue at the trial that Sweatt was entitled to an education the equal to that of white Americans in every respect.[81] The Constitution of the United States, they noted, provided that every man, woman, and child was the equal of every other and was therefore entitled to enjoy equal rights and opportunities. This was one of the first trials in American history where the lawyers had pressed forward the notion of equal opportunity and treatment for blacks in America. Their attack on the University of Texas did not dwell on breaking down the tangle of segregated practices and customs so much as it did on providing equal facilities to blacks. The difference in emphasis was key, and it would not be until 1954, eight years hence, that the same Thurgood Marshall would appear before the Supreme Court of the United States to attack segregation head-on.

The Texas judicial system proved unsympathetic to the pleas, however brilliant, of Marshall and Durham. At first Judge Archer postponed a decision so as to permit the university time to provide equal educational facilities for the training of Sweatt. After the university was unable to do so, Judge Archer was pressed to rule on Sweatt's behalf. Now it was learned that Texas A&M College, in nearby College Station, would be willing to provide legal facilities in Houston for Sweatt, ones comparable, it was claimed, to those at the all-black Prairie View A&M. Judge Archer, believing those resources to be the equal of those at the University of Texas, ruled against Sweatt once more. During the whole course of pleas and appeals, the lengths to which the university was willing to go in order to prevent Sweatt's entrance approached the ridiculous. After the Travis County Court ruled on one occasion against Sweatt, his attorneys took the case to the Court of Civil Appeals. In the meantime, Texas had furnished Sweatt with his own private law school in downtown Austin, in a building on Thirteenth Street. There, in the basement, three rooms had been set aside for the legal education of Hemann Sweatt. But they had been leased only for a six-month period, from March 1 to August 31, 1947, had no standing faculty, and provided only a handful of books.[82] The university obviously had a most perverse sense of what constituted a legal education for black Americans.

Sweatt and his attorneys pressed ahead with their suit. And at every level of the Texas judicial system, including the Texas Supreme Court, Sweatt was turned down for admission to the Texas Law School. Finally the case was taken by Marshall and Durham to the United States Supreme Court. There, on June 5, 1950 Chief Justice Fred Vinson delivered a unanimous opinion in favor of the plaintiff, Hemann Sweatt. The opinion read, in part, that Sweatt should be permitted to enter the University of Texas Law School since "in terms of number of faculty, variety of courses and opportunity for specialization, size of the student body, scope of the library, availability of law review and similar activities, the University of Texas Law School is superior to other schools in Texas."[83] Thus, Sweatt was finally admitted to the Law School. But, while Marshall would go on to help overthrow the entire doctrine of "separate but equal" facilities in Washington, Sweatt never finished his degree in Austin. Like much that seems to have happened in the racial affairs of the community, the trial exacted a serious price from Sweatt, producing a divorce and his further withdrawal into himself. He died in 1982, the victor over the system but still without his law degree.

The Sweatt trial helped to stir up the black community of Austin, and promoted an ambition for freedom the community had never experienced, not even under the leadership of Everett Givens. The late 1940s, in fact, signaled the end to the unquestioned rule of Givens over public matters concerning Austin's blacks. And it produced a whole new wave of efforts that no longer asked for piecemeal handouts from whites but, once and for all, to be allowed full and complete entry into the system.

Half a decade before the bus boycotts in Montgomery, Alabama, and more than a full decade before four youths sat in at a Woolworth's store in downtown Greensboro, North Carolina, people were chewing away at Jim Crow in Austin, Texas. The Sweatt trial had something to do with this. So did the rather enlightened views of many blacks and white citizens, and the presence in Austin of Huston and Tillotson colleges. Several people figured very prominently in the attacks on the Jim Crow practices, among them, the Reverend Bob Bryan at the University of Texas, Professor Joe Witherspoon of the University Law School, and, of course, many of the liberals who were members of the Travis County Social and Legislative Conference. But two black men seem to have been absolutely essential to the new progressive atmosphere.

One of the men was Arthur DeWitty. Like his more conservative counterpart, Everett Givens, DeWitty was tall and strikingly hand-some.[84] As he aged, his hair turned silver grey but his physical bearing remained unstooped, and his presence was overpowering. DeWitty had been a cook at Scarbroughs in downtown Austin. At some time in the 1940s, he retired and devoted himself full-time to the business of politics. He became a self-taught newspaperman, and wrote the Austin columns for the black newspaper out of Houston, the *Houston Informer*. He regularly harangued readers about the liberal way, about getting rid of the oppressive poll tax that prevented thousands of blacks from being citizens, about the need to improve the quality of housing and thoroughfares in East Austin, and about the importance of electing liberal people to the City Council, figures like Emma Long, for example. "Arthur DeWitty," the Reverend Bryan has said, "had a vision. He kept hammering away at that vision in his slow, persistent fashion."[85] A vision different from the guiding scheme for Austin, DeWitty's view held out hope for all people to participate in the benefits of growth, and, in the late 1940s, black and brown people especially. He regularly attended the Travis County Social and Legislative Conference meetings downtown in the Public Library, later at Johnnie Crow's restaurant in South Austin, and used the information he gained there to help enlighten his Austin readership. His columns eventually became read outside the black community. Politicians like Emma Long used them as a means of learning about the needs and the longings of black Austinites.[86] DeWitty's skills and energies grew, and with them his appetite for success on behalf of blacks. He eventually became the head of the Austin chapter of the NAACP, and narrowly missed being the first black person elected to the City Council in 1951.

The other figure to exercise considerable influence over Austin race relations at mid-century was Bill Kirk.[87] Kirk arrived in Austin in September 1947, fresh from completing a master's degree in government at Howard University in Washington, D.C. He remained in Austin on and off until 1961, his residence interrupted by periodic Ford and Fulbright fellowships to study abroad as well as by dissertation work in Washington. Extremely intelligent and personable, Kirk's impact on Austin was as marked as that of the Sweatt case and Arthur DeWitty. Kirk took a position as a teacher of government at Tillotson. Once in Austin, he came to realize how Jim Crow laws and various customs enveloped the community, separating the races from one another. While he had experienced the agony of segregation in the North, it never matched the restrictiveness practiced in the South, even in places such as Austin, which, Kirk felt, was mildly oppressive as compared to other Texas cities like Waco, Houston, or Dallas. Kirk had experienced the same renaissance of spirit on the Howard campus that had infected the likes of lawyers such as Thurgood Marshall, so when he arrived in Austin he was primed to take up the cudgel on behalf of racial emancipation.

Sometime after his arrival, about 1948 or 1949, Kirk decided that he would have one of his Tillotson government classes study the background of racial segregation in Austin. His hope was to discover which of the various Jim Crow practices, such as separate water fountains or racial restrictions on streetcars, were founded on legal statutes and which were not. He found only three legal codes in the state of Texas. As I noted earlier, they held that the races must be segregated in schools, in public conveyances, and in coal mines. He also had the class investigate the city ordinances of Austin to learn which city codes covered the various restrictive practices. His class worked on the project intensively for a full year. As a result of its effort, Kirk and the students found that many of the activities in Austin failed to have the support of law. Kirk now decided to attack the "structure," to use Janie Harrison's vivid notion, at those points at which no legal foundation existed for segregation. He thought of them as the "points of pliability," that is, he believed the system of racial segregation could be broken apart at these points so long as city officials and other authorities could be shown that custom, not law, upheld Jim Crow.

Kirk's attacks at the "points of pliability" quickly became a major part of the story of how racial segregation was fought in Austin during the late 1940s and early 1950s. On his own, Kirk decided to break down the barriers at the Austin Public Library. Ever since the city provided separate library quarters in East Austin in the 1930s, city officials had assumed that these facilities were sufficient for the black population. Of course, they were not. The small building was hardly larger than one of the shotgun houses that was home to many black families and the collection of books was meager by comparison to that in the Colorado Street offices of the main library. Kirk believed that the "separate but equal" doctrine with regard to public library facilities was a sham, and therefore that he had to do something to open up the downtown library to the black community.

What he did do was to "overload the system," in his words. He began by going to the Carver Library at Angelina and Hackberry, and asking for the *Harvard Classics*. Of course, Carver did not possess these books, so it had to request them from the main branch down-town. Eventually they were shipped over, but not without some dis-gruntlement among the staff. That was precisely the point of the Kirk strategy. Inconvenience the staff, demonstrate that separate facilities were inefficient. Attack the system not as immoral, but as impracti-cal. Soon after he requested the *Harvard Classics*, Kirk had another request sent over, asking for the whole set of the *Encyclopedia Britan-nica*, another collection unavailable at Carver. And then he asked for the entire collection of the *Great Books*, published under the editor-ship of Morton Adler. Within a short space of time, the librarians at the downtown library became exasperated.

Kirk continued this treatment over the course of a year. Then he went before the City Council to ask that the downtown library facili-ties be opened to the minority population of Austin. He made his first appearance before the council in the summer of 1951, and another in mid-August of that year. At both sessions he voiced his concerns, noting that he "could find no ordinance or other support for the city's refusal to admit Negroes to the main library."[88] The council, of course, did not know what to do. By this time, Emma Long and Ben White, close liberal allies, sat on the council. They both were predisposed to support Kirk's request. But other council members, like W. T. Johnson, were not. The debate continued for a period of several months. DeWitty got into the act through his column in the *Houston Informer*. He wrote that the council found itself in a dilemma, and notified his readers of Emma's characteristic tactic in these situations. She had urged, he wrote, that if the council did not wish to open up the downtown library to the black citizens of Austin, all it had to do would be appropriate $250,000, and duplicate the downtown branch in East Austin.[89] Finally, through the persis-tence of Kirk, and the consent of Long, White, and the University of Texas government professor Stuart MacCorkle, the council agreed on December 27, 1951, to permit blacks and other minorities to use the downtown library facilities.[90] Kirk had been victorious.

This victory convinced Kirk that his strategy of overloading the system at its points of pliability could work. He next turned to the Austin Fire Department. There were no black firemen on the staff, another one of the city provinces affected by racial segregation. Kirk instructed some of his Tillotson students to take the civil service examination necessary to become a member of the fire department; several did, and a few passed. Since the city could not refuse to train and eventually hire successful examinees, it reluctantly agreed to train some black men to become firefighters. One went on to become a longtime member of the department. Kirk thus had broken the "structure" at yet another point.

A third point of pliability he chose to attack was the segregated swimming facilities at Barton Springs. Long the delight of white Austin residents, this historic site west of downtown and just south of the Colorado had not allowed blacks to swim in it, although a few, such as Eva Marie Mosby, occasionally did so without creating too much fuss. Kirk went to R. D. Thorp, chief of police, and asked that blacks be permitted to swim in the pool. Thorp refused, of course. When Kirk informed him there was no legal ordinance requiring the pool to be segregated, Thorp replied, "Well, that's just the way we do things here." Eventually Kirk did get blacks into the pool. But, in the meantime, the council protected itself by building a swimming pool in Givens Park in East Austin. The new facility there soon deterred masses of black Austinites from traveling the distance to Barton Springs. And yet, Bill Kirk had made his point.

Throughout the 1950s, more and more racial barriers were overturned in Austin, the result of efforts by people besides Kirk and DeWitty. Numbers of the liberal white community helped out, including some of the populists like Creekmore Fath. The story of some of these events becomes even more interesting, as various powerful figures from the larger community debated and argued about the issues. Eventually theatres, restaurants, and other public institutions fell to the assaults. We shall save some of this intrigue for our later chapter on the case of the Fair Housing Ordinance in Austin. It is sufficient here to note that the mid-century efforts of Kirk and his allies, on and off the council, were almost as historic as the Sweatt case. And, surely, they demonstrated that Austin citizens marched to the beat of an earlier, if not different, drummer than many of their fellow citizens across America.

The system of the enslavement of black men and women in America has sometimes been depicted as that "peculiar institution." Certainly the practices of segregation were just as peculiar. The Constitution of the United States declares equality for all, yet some, including women, are far less equal than others. The picture held as true in Austin as anywhere else. The treatment of blacks probably has been a little better here than in many other places, for reasons I have noted. Still, the practices of segregation took a heavy toll. For blacks they meant being treated as part of the white household, or the white-owned business, for a greater part of the day, but then being denied the full privileges of humanness after dark.

Whites, too, suffered under the "structure." And perhaps no one suffered so much as the famed Judge David Pickle. Judge Pickle, you might recall, admitted to Walter Long in a 1961 oral interview that he had been involved in the scuffle in 1919 with John Shillady, the NAACP representative who had come to Austin looking for support.[91] As a result of this assault, Shillady quickly departed Austin. He returned to his home in the North, where he died from the injuries soon afterward. Seven years later, in 1926, Judge Pickle sold a parcel of land to the City of Austin for $5,500. It lay along what has become known as Airport Boulevard. Honoring the Judge's request, the land was used as the only cemetery in Austin for black people.[92]

8.

Emma Long: *Vox Populi*

———

Dear Mrs. Long:
To the average Austin family you have become their Joan of Arc. Please keep
helping to keep the big ones from devouring the little ones.[1]

EMMA AND I ARE SEATED IN HER DEN. IT IS A COM-
fortable room. There is nothing garish here. The pieces of furniture,
the bric-a-brac, the vases, the ornaments, all of them seem appropriate to the tasteful but modest homes of the 1950s and 1960s. This
was the heyday of Emma's career in Austin politics. We talk over
these times. I try to get a sense of what she was all about, what moved
her. She mentions the struggles in 1948 between the liberal
Democrats and the others, the Texas Regulars and the anti–civil
rights contingent. Her allies, the liberals, wanted to help the poor
folks. They worked hard. They were even victorious in the 1948 campaign in Texas when everyone expected them to lose. Then she
decided to take on the Establishment, here in Austin. It was the
bankers who ran things, she says. They used Mayor Miller, they
worked through him, she claims. Yes, she wanted to clean out the
Establishment . . .[2]

We are at the Lyndon Baines Johnson Library in Austin. I have
come along as Emma's escort. Virginia Durr is here to discuss how
she and other New Dealers helped to defeat the poll tax in Alabama.
Emma informs me of the fights in Austin over the poll tax, how she
and other liberals, like Creekmore Fath, who also is here, tried to get
blacks to pay the poll tax. They did what they could; often it was not
enough. A lot of the people at the talk somehow look familiar. They

are, or were, famous public figures. Afterward Emma and I go over
to the tables where the food and drink are being served. Fancy silver
trays with delicate hors d'oeurves and large, ornate silver bowls full
of punch contend for our thirst and appetites. Emma introduces me
to Liz Carpenter and informs her that I am writing a book about
Austin's history. Ms. Carpenter looks at me rather suspiciously, then
backs off. Robert Caro's book on LBJ has just been published, I
remember. He did not treat the former president at all kindly. Lady
Bird Johnson and Lucy Baines Johnson are here as well, and Emma
asks me to escort her over to them. They greet, Lucy gives Emma a
big hug and calls her "Miss Emma." They exchange war stories of
Texas and Austin politics. Lucy talks about what a legend Emma was
in Austin and how much she adored her . . .[3]

Emma and Stuart Long have gone out with the McCullys to dine
in an Austin restaurant. It is some time after she left the council in
1969. Dinner has not yet been served, and they are chatting about
harmless little things. As they converse a couple of black women
come over to the table. They introduce themselves to Emma, and
give her a body-deflating hug. "Miss Emma," they say, "we sure do
love and miss you, Miss Emma" . . .[4]

It is sometime in March, and some March, I am not sure which.
I have just served Emma a big Chinese dinner, to return the favors
she has given me, the many hours in which she sat and redid Austin's
past. Somehow we get onto taxes. They are not my forte. She mentions that I should be real smart with my investments, look for deduc-
tions here and there. I don't grasp much of what she says. She speaks
of the money she has saved, her rental properties, her wealth. A certain fire comes into her eyes as she talks, and her hair takes on a brilliant, glowing red lustre beneath the lights. Definitely feisty, I think
to myself. And just like she must have been in the council chambers
when she railed on about the city budgets . . .[5]

Mary Holman recalls the time they opened a new restaurant in
Austin. Emma still sat on the council. On the menu they had a salad
named just for her, the "Emma Long" salad. It was a concoction of
cucumbers and vinegar . . .[6]

"Mrs. Emma Long," the letter reads, "ask you plase mam send a
doctor out here to look at my fut. i slept in a hold up on chicon st.
and had a hard fall—that got me down all most past walking. i sure
need a doctor and havent got money to get one i tryed to work but
had hoble home. plase mam help me i have a parlise girl to car
for" . . .[7]

Creekmore Fath and Judge Joseph Hart have gone before the City Council to learn whether it will rezone some property the two men own in the university area of Austin. Fath and Hart want the land to remain Class "A," or residential land. Emma speaks up. "Creek," she says, "what we're going to do is make the land Class "C"—like lawyers' and doctors' offices." Hart and Fath respond simultaneously. "We don't want it," they say. "But," Emma replies, "you don't understand. It will make your property twice as valuable." "You *don't* understand, Emma," they respond, "we don't want the land to be twice as valuable" . . . [8]

Emma and some close women companions are gathered in a friend's living room. The talk is about their husbands. Do you ever quarrel with your husband? someone asks. Each woman discloses an intimate detail. It is Emma's turn. Stuart and I never argue, Emma says. I simply will *not* allow it . . . [9]

"Dear Council Lady," a writer begins, "as you seem to be the only one that has the nerve to go for the People in the Way. You should visit the Jail on Sunday morning after Saturday Night Early. Small towns have better food than Austin" . . . [10]

Pampa is west Texas ranchland. There on her grandfather's ranch Emma was born to Bob and Lillie Mae "Dot" Jackson on February 29, 1912. Unusual even at birth, Emma emerged in a leap year. Her father was primarily a rancher and a farmer throughout his life, but held assorted jobs at different times. A coal miner, a laborer in a flour mill, he did anything to keep life and limb together. At the time of Emma's birth, the family lived on a section of land that was given to Bob by his father. After a series of moves, which took them from Raton, New Mexico, to Wichita Falls, Texas, they finally settled in Hereford, Texas, in Deaf Smith County. Sometime in the 1920s, good fortune befell the Jacksons. Oil was discovered on the Pampa ranch. Almost overnight, it was transformed from scrub brush and mealy dirt to oil riggers and wooden scaffolding. Today the entire property is covered with loads of pumps, churning up and down, dredging out the gobs and gobs of oil. The wells brought a handsome income to Emma's grandparents, and they shared the largesse with their children. Soon after the great discovery, Emma and her family moved a couple of miles from Hereford, where they set up a farm for themselves. The family decided to settle there for good. Today a brother and sister of Emma's still live in Hereford.

Charity begins at home. And so it was with the Jackson parents and their children. The unexpected wealth made it possible for the Jacksons to live better than most of their friends and neighbors. Always good, Bible-reading Baptists, the Jacksons shared their gains with different people during the years of the Great Depression. "There was one widow with eight children," Edith Hicks, one of Emma's sisters, recalls, "and she had nothing. My parents gave her a home."[11] There were lots of similar stories about the Jacksons at this time, about the families they would help. O. J. Bean, an orphan, who hung around with Emma's brother, had an aunt and grand-mother who were homeless. The Jacksons gave him an apartment in a store of theirs in Hereford, and told him to use it for himself and his kinfolk. "My parents were helping people," Hicks remembers. "If somebody needed help, then you helped them."[12] Years later, much the same thing would be said about Emma. And about Emma's hus-band, Stuart.

Emma grew up as the second of six children born to the Jacksons. Like many families, they were very close. The children and adults would daily gather around the dinner table to eat. In the evenings, they would sit in the living room, listen to the radio, or to their mother as she read the Bible to the family. Emma always seemed to be the most outspoken one. She wasn't mean, but her father some-times had a difficult time keeping her in harness. "I remember the time when Emma came home from college. She said something to make daddy really angry," Hicks recalls. "He grabbed Emma by the arm but she kept running around and around so he couldn't hit her with his belt."[13] At the dinner table Emma would test her parents and sibs with her many opinions and attitudes about the world. Sometimes, just to show how smart she was, she would correct her brother's English, which did little to make him happy.[14]

All the Jackson children were bright and went to college. Emma attended the University of Texas in the 1930s, a fellow student of Creekmore Fath and Venola Morgan. She was not especially active in campus affairs, giving no indication of her later political energy. At the university she majored in history, minored in government, and took courses in the journalism department. And there she met Stuart Long, a young Texan from Abilene whose father was a phar-macist. Stuart was tall and bony, possessing an almost Lincolnesque bearing. The very opposite of Emma, Stuart was quiet and soft-spoken. When he talked, the words emerged in a long Texas drawl and seemed to be spaced fifty feet apart. Whereas Emma was known for her temper, Stuart never made much of a fuss about anything. Soon after Emma graduated from the university in 1936, the two married. Thereafter they formed as intimate and close a team in political life as any on record.

During the war years, Emma and Stuart lived in Atlanta, Georgia. After a couple of jobs, which included a stint as a reporter on the *Austin American-Statesman*, Emma became a housewife, raising a young child, Jeb, while Stuart served in the Marines. In 1945, they returned to Austin. Stuart took up a position as a news reporter at Lyndon Johnson's radio station, KTBC. The two had known one another since Johnson was director of the National Youth Administration in the thirties.[15] Stuart remained with KTBC for just a year, when he resigned to take up the post of news editor with a new radio station in Austin, KVET. The station had been organized by a group of ten returning war veterans—hence the name—the principal ones being Texas political pros Edward Clark and John Connally. Stuart also began to work in different newspaper ventures, including *Texas Week*, a magazine he published for a while with John McCully and Paul Bolton, and the *Texas State House Reporter*.

Now Stuart and Emma began to involve themselves in statewide and national politics. Both had been vigorous supporters of the New Deal and of Roosevelt, and they joined forces with such like-minded allies as Johnson and Tom Miller. The two attended the 1946 Democratic State Convenion in San Antonio at which the loyal Democrats bolted. Stuart and Emma naturally sided with the loyal Democrats. By the time of the 1948 campaign, the Longs were heavily involved in the effort to re-elect Harry Truman as president. The tensions between the two principal wings of the Texas Democratic party, the loyalists and the Texas Regulars, continued undiminished. The Texas Regulars had resecured some control in the councils of the State Democrats. Matters had become even more muddied as supporters of Governor Beauford Jester formed a new faction of the Democratic party. In Travis County, the liberal Democrats were able to gain a position of dominance. Over some opposition, and with the support of the Johnson troops, they managed to get Stuart and Marion Storm, head of the Texas Social and Legislative Conference, elected as the Tenth Congressional District delegates to the statewide convention.[16] Tom Miller, the happy warrior for the New Deal, had gained considerable support from various quarters to be the nominee for national committeeman from Texas. His principal opponent for the post was Wright Morrow, one of the original group of politicians who made up the Texas Regular wing of the party in Texas.

When the Democrats convened at Brownwood in May, the Jester factions and the Texas Regulars came out in opposition to Truman. They also were dead set against the inclusion of any civil rights plank in the 1948 platform. These were the very issues strongly favored by Storm, Long, and Miller, among the liberals. Of course, the liberal forces turned out to be too weak for the combined numbers of the Texas Regulars and the Jestercrats. The national delegate section committee at Brownwood rejected Storm and Long as Tenth District delegates. Not surprisingly, Miller lost to Morrow in the battle to become national committeeman from Texas.

The liberal forces from Travis County were not dead yet. In June, Homer Thornberry entered the race for representative from the Tenth Congressional District. Johnson had abandoned the seat earlier in order to make a run for the United States Senate. Creekmore Fath, by now one of the spearheads of the liberal effort in Austin and Travis County, also ran for the seat, and entered the primary campaign against Thornberry. For a while it looked as though Fath might indeed be victorious, even though Thornberry was backed by many members of the business community of Austin. But the strength of the liberal forces, even aided by Johnson and his supporters, was not enough to offset the more conservative strength that lay outside Austin. When the ballots were tallied, Fath had run third, behind the front-running Thornberry and another candidate. At this point, as Henry Holman recalls, fate played into the hands of the liberals. Homer Thornberry was a teetotaler. He vigorously opposed the sale of alcohol in Austin. The beer industry wanted him off the council and went to work on his behalf throughout the Tenth District.[17] In the runoff in August, Thornberry won out against his opponent. A seat on the City Council now was up for grabs.

In the summer of 1948, anything could happen. Much of it did. Fath and Tom Miller, supporters of Truman but condemned within the conservative ranks of the Texas Democratic party, had the last word. They were selected by the national Democrats to lead the Truman effort in Texas. Through some ingenious political strategies, such as the five-dollar Truman-Barkley club they organized in the state, they were able to secure more money on behalf of the national Truman campaign than any other statewide organization.[18] So much for the Jester supporters and the Texas Regulars. But something even more significant came out of the summer's heat. One evening, Creek and his wife, Adelle, were at dinner with several friends, including Emma, Stuart, and the Holmans. For some reason they started to discuss the City Council race. If the people's forces truly wanted to gain a secure foothold in Austin, someone said, they should send up a candidate for the council seat. Who would it be, one of them wondered. Adelle Fath suggested that Emma make the race, even though Emma had a six-week-old baby, Jeb. The idea quickly took root. Though no woman had ever run for a seat on the City Council, Emma seemed to be just the right person. She was knowledgeable and possessed most of the right values and instincts. And she was more outspoken than anyone else in the room, maybe even in Austin. They jointly weighed the pros and cons of the campaign. Could a housewife, especially one with a young infant, possibly make it? What about the reputation Stuart had developed in state and local politics, a reputation as too liberal for Texans? The pros of the friendly exchange soon came to outweigh the cons. Emma was off to the races.[19]

Emma's first campaign in the fall of 1948, was fashioned on her strengths and those of the Travis County liberal forces. The very equipment that had helped to get Marion Storm and Stuart selected as the district delegates to Brownwood was swiftly deployed, precinct organizers and all, to work on her behalf. Her weakness in the public eye was turned to her advantage. Bumper stickers appeared on the cars of her legions in Austin, proclaiming "Sweep City Hall Clean with a Long Broom."[20] Her ads played up her qualities as a housewife. One favorite ad read "The City Needs a Good Housekeeper," and went on to tell of Emma's support for better schools, better streets, and better sanitation.

Emma's task of getting elected to office was by no means easy. Not only did she have to suffer public skepticism that a housewife could handle a council job, but members of the business community were firmly against her. They feared her because they feared Stuart. So deep was their concern that an effort developed to bypass an election and to fill the post with an appointment by Mayor Miller. Some pressure, in fact, was even applied to the mayor, but he resisted.[21] After all, he was in the midst of fighting a common war with the Longs on behalf of Truman and the Fair Dealers. One resident of Austin went so far as to bring suit against the city, claiming that the election violated the city charter.[22] The suit failed. Local newspapers did not know what to make of Emma. For a while they could describe her only as Mrs. Stuart Long, wife of a local radio commentator. They wrote of her in quaint terms, informing readers that she had thrown her "bonnet" into the ring. The chamber crowd came up with their own favorite candidate, Ed St. John. He was a close friend of many businesspeople in Austin, among others, Taylor Glass, current council member and head of the Austin Junior Chamber of Commerce. Emma defeated St. John and two other candidates for office, and was sworn in as Austin's first female council member on October 14, 1948.

In her first couple of years on the council, Emma set about shaking up city government. If there were a clear ideological thread to her positions, it was not always entirely evident. She supported measures to benefit the entire community, not merely the poor. One of the major controversies on the council concerned utility rates. The phone company, in the years immediately after World War II, had a difficult time keeping pace with the rapid growth of Austin.[23] Often then, as now, it lagged far behind in providing services to new customers. The company went before the council to ask for large increases in the rates charged for service. As soon as she got on the council, Emma worked to keep the rates under control. The phone company came to the council to request an increase of eighty-two percent in the 1949 residential rates. Emma's fellow council members offered little resistance to the request. She felt the rate hike was outrageous. Her allies came from within the community, and particularly from the liberal forces assembled in Austin. Henry Holman was so angered by the request that he gathered a list of a couple of thousand petitioners who demanded the rate increase not be granted.[24] With this kind of broad support, Emma and the council were able to keep the actual increase to just over twenty percent.

Emma worked awfully hard to make the city government more receptive to people's demands on it. Always attentive to the needs of the poor, she and other council members were surprised to learn of the sometimes callous and indifferent treatment indigent citizens would receive at the hands of the Austin Welfare Department. A study done at Emma's insistence by an outside consultant in 1950 revealed that Miss Edna McDaniel, who headed the department, ruled her little fiefdom with an iron hand, occasionally condemning her clients for being lazy, or simply ignoring them. Emma took out after Miss McDaniel like a west Texas dust storm and kicked up just about as much dirt. Eventually she forced McDaniel to resign.

City employees also benefited from Emma's vigilant surveillance. She pressed hard in 1950 for raises for the city firemen and police-men, arguing they were underpaid. And she took her own campaign slogans very seriously, sweeping out incompetence where she thought it lay. In 1950 and 1951, she began a series of critical attacks on the chief of police, R. D. Thorp, accusing him of failing to keep the city of Austin free of crime. Austin, it so happened, had come under attack by various citizens for its "loose ways," and Emma attempted to link the casual morality to the chief's failings. She worked hard in these early days to help individual citizens save money. The city streets were badly in need of paving. Emma helped to develop a plan that would make it easier for citizens to bear the cost. As a result of her proposals, the city agreed to pay for one-third of the cost of paving residential areas, while neighbors on either side of the street would bear the other two-thirds. The residents were permitted to extend the payment over a seven-year-period. Much of Emma's work, particularly in the early years, was invisible to the public eye. Her style gained her attention as someone who could get things done. Even those who disliked her brash manner prevailed on her for little things, such as correcting a bill in error, having some broken city light repaired, or getting a leash law passed in order to corral way-ward dogs.[25]

Especially unrelenting were Emma's efforts on behalf of blacks and Mexican Americans in Austin. When Everett Givens, the prominent black dentist, came before the council in 1951 to ask that blacks be given a public golf course, he ran up against the historic intransigence of white Austin. Dr. Givens had been promised a golf course for the black community if he and other blacks would help to pass a much-needed bond package for Austin. After the bonds passed, Givens came before the council and reminded Mayor Miller of his assurance. At this point Emma stepped in. She claimed it was ridiculous to build a separate golf course for blacks. Why not allow blacks to use the present public links? she asked. To the dollar-minded members of the council like Bill Drake, who owned Calcasieu Lumber Company and was a leading member of the chamber crowd, building a golf course for blacks was out of the question. Eventually the council gave in to Emma's demand, preferring integration to spending public funds.[26]

About the same time she worked together with W. Astor Kirk to get the main public library opened to minority residents. This battle took some months, but Emma and Kirk were victorious. He wrote to thank her for support, "to express my very deep appreciation of your statesmanlike decision with respect to the City Public Library issue. Your decision . . . clearly reflects your continuous concern for the public interest of this community."[27]

Although Emma continued to get re-elected to the council by large margins, such as the fifty-four percent she secured in the April 1949 race, or the top spot she carried in the 1951 election, she remained the lone wolf for the people's cause. The vote on many issues, including some of the utility rate increases, normally would be four to one, with Emma the single dissenter. Not until the election of Ben White to the council in 1951 did she manage to gain some kind of continuous friend for the effort to improve the city government on behalf of the public. By this time, however, she had developed an active opposition in the community, especially among the bankers, land developers, and the large businesspeople. She, and Stuart, suffered a critical blow to their efforts on behalf of the little people, particularly the blue-collar folks, in the Brown and Root shootout of 1950.

In the fall of 1949, the city of Austin decided to erect a new power plant on First Street, bordering the lake. The expansion of Austin's population in the post-war period had caught many people by surprise. It soon became imperative for the city to upgrade its facilities in order to keep pace with the exploding number of new residents. Several months after City Hall entertained bids for the power plant, separate bids were let on the city boilers for the plant. The lowest bid came from Herman Brown, and Brown and Root. Herman already was well known in the Austin area. Many people had him to thank for jobs during the Depression years. But the unions knew him well, too. Brown and Root was an open-shop employer. They hired both union and nonunion workers at job sites. When the union officials in Austin learned that the city was about to sign a contract with Brown and Root to erect the boilers, they became livid. At the council meeting held on January 24, 1950, a free-for-all of sorts broke out between union representatives and Herman Brown, with council members there almost as bystanders.[28] Paul Sparks, the secretary of the Texas Federation of Labor, prevailed upon Guiton Morgan, city manager, not to award the contract to Brown and Root. He noted that the company had not agreed to a nationwide fair labor practices agreement, and, further, that it treated Texas unions in a far shabbier manner than those in other states, like Louisiana. Moreover, he observed, Brown and Root had little familiarity with the construction of boilers, since much of their work involved the construction of roads. Brown rose and replied that his company had begun in the business of roadwork in 1919, but over the past decade and one-half had secured more than $1.25 billion in contracts from the federal government. The exchange unraveled, and so did the tempers of the two men. Emma took the side of Sparks and labor, but despite all her efforts the council decided to award the bid to the lowest bidder, Brown and Root. The union workers went on strike, and the case eventually wound up in the courtroom of Judge Charles O. Betts, who came up with a fence-sitting decision favorable to both sides.

Through it all, Emma made Herman madder and madder. Stuart continued with his nightly broadcasts on KVET. His own news reports, which had been praised for their candor and objectivity, had gotten him into hot water in the past, with people like Ed Clark and other luminaries in Texas politics. For example, in 1948, Stuart reported on a case in which Clark was an attorney for the Phillips Petroleum Company. The state had brought suit against Phillips for a million dollars. Eventually it was settled out of court by Attorney General Grover Seller and Ed Clark for something on the order of $100,000. The two assistant attorneys general who worked on the case with Seller resigned their positions rather than agreeing to the settlement. Stuart reported the matter on his broadcast. Soon Clark was after him. John Connally remained on the side of Stuart, however, and would not give in to the entreaties of fellow KVET owner Clark. Nor did he succumb to others who found Stuart's liberal views too radical for their tastes. The Brown and Root controversy proved the last straw. In an oral history made shortly before his death, Stuart told interviewer Chandler Davidson, "I don't know whether it was Clark or Brown who led Willard Deason to decide he ought to get rid of me."[29] But someone did. In the midst of the heat of the Brown and Root case, Stuart was let go. This was big news to little, humdrum Austin, and was reported in the *Statesman* in an article of several paragraphs.[30]

Stuart provided a memorable swan song on his February 23 broadcast. He did not give names, though a number of people were afraid he would. What he did was furnish a vivid portrait of the obvious struggle between the people's and the business forces in Austin. Its words described the course of the struggle in Austin, and how those in power sought to wield it:

The rest of this broadcast has been read beforehand by Bill Deason, the manager of KVET. This morning Charlie Herring, KVET's lawyer, called up and said that word was going around town that I was going to tell all tonight, and he thought that it might be a good idea for him to look over my script. This is the first time this has ever been done in the three years and five months I've been on KVET, but it isn't hard to understand why they would be a little curious and jumpy. . . .

There was a time when I used to peep out the alley door of KVET before I started home at 10:30 at night to make sure nobody was waiting for me. There have been times when friends on the police force would drop by Kayvet at 10 o'clock . . . just visiting of course.

Those campaigns [I made] against crime were interesting, and a lot of fun, and sometimes those campaigns led into strange places. Some of them even led into public offices, and those things were reported, too.

But in the course of three years of reporting, I stepped on some powerful toes. Most of the owners of those toes have forgiven me. Some have told me that it was the best thing that ever happened to them, although at the time they were pretty mad at me.

But some people can't forgive when their shortcomings are reported to the public. One in particular.

It seemed like I would run into this particular man everywhere I went for news. He has his hand in a lot of things.

A long, long time ago, he started to get me off the air. In case you ever want to get somebody off the air, here's the technique. You listen to him every night, even if it chokes you. If he mentions someone who's in a position of influence, you call that man up and assure him that what the reporter said was libelous. And you suggest that he phone the manager of the radio station and raise old billy about it.

Then, if you are fortunate enough to have quite a bit of money and to hold various directorships around town, you see to it that the firms with which you have influence cancel out their advertising on the radio station. Just keep it up long enough, and finally you'll get your man off the air.

It would have been a lot easier, and a lot nicer, for me to have resigned as news editor of Kayvet when I found out they didn't want me anymore. It meant personal hurt to me, and personal hurt to the management of Kayvet for us to announce that I had been fired. But let folks know what unbearable pressure can be applied to a small radio station. . . . It's no secret, of course, that some of Emma's votes on the City Council have resulted in more pressure on Kayvet to fire me. . . .[31]

The next week Stuart resumed his news broadcasts on another, smaller station in Austin, KTXN. He managed to sell the new show to various symphathetic sponsors. He remained there for three years until he elected to leave and work full-time for the Long News Service, a capitol news bureau.[32]

What the Brown and Root affair revealed about Austin, even about much of the nation, was how limited the freedom of speech had become. Such talk was the sort of stuff that Joe McCarthy was condemning with his lists of alleged communist agents who sat in various high offices in America. Businesspeople in Austin were no more indifferent to this climate than others. Some were able to have their opponents fired. But the firing of Stuart was only the first blow. Others soon followed in the fight over the city charter, the meanest, nastiest, and toughest battle to touch modern Austin politics.

At a meeting of the City Council on Thursday, October 19, 1950, Emma proposed to modernize the city charter. Ever diligent in her plans to make improvements on behalf of the public, Emma advised her fellow council members that the city charter, enacted in 1909, was desperately in need of revision. For instance, she informed them, the charter did not permit women to participate in city elections. That, of course, had since been overturned by the Nineteenth Amendment to the United States Constitution in 1920. The charter, she noted, prescribed that vacancies on the council should be filled by the council itself, but it failed to specify how this would happen. Only a few blocks away, in the federal courthouse, Emma and Stuart were the subject of another meeting. It was the court trial of the fight between the unions and Brown and Root over the construction of the Austin boilers. Paul Sparks was being questioned by Everett Looney, law partner and close friend of Ed Clark. Looney asked Sparks whether Stuart Long had ever done work for the unions. Looney's inquiry may have appeared irrelevant at the time, and Emma's effort to get changes made in the city charter may have seemed equally harmless. But within two years' time, these issues would be interwoven in the tapestry of hate.[33]

As a result of Emma's prodding, the council set itself the task of revising the city charter. Members finally reached a list of eleven possible amendments that they planned to submit to the voters in early 1952. At a meeting in late December 1951, however, the council decided that the revisions required more work and thought. In January 1952, the council agreed to select a group of fifteen citizens from the community who would draft a series of amendments. The charter revision committee, as it came to be known, was deliberately representative of the various segments of Austin, including the black and brown minorities and women. A young Austin attorney, Frank Erwin, a strapping man with the energy of at least a dozen longhorns, was named the chairman of the committee. In the course of the next year, the committee developed a set of far-reaching changes in the old charter. By late 1952, they had reached agreement on the revisions and were ready to submit them to the council for its review and approval.

The review session took place on December 8. What happened probably took many observers by surprise. Most of the proposed amendments, such as the decision to simplify the charter, seemed to be sensible. All but one. Proposition 5 required that a change be made in the system of city elections. The present system, in effect since 1926, required that voters choose among a group of candidates through an at-large method. A voter could select as many as five candidates; many just voted for their favorite. The people elected to the council were the highest vote-getters. The proposed change called for a place system. Five separate places would be designated, and a candidate could choose to run for whichever place he or she desired. The voters would be permitted to vote for a candidate in each of the five places. It was not entirely evident what benefits this would provide to the community. For example, it might have made more sense to create a district-system in order to furnish representation to the very diverse segments of the Austin population, particularly the East Austin poor. But such a step, of course, would not have received the endorsement of the bankers and other businesspeople who wished to retain their dominance over Austin politics.

Only a few people at the meeting probably were aware of the true intent of Proposition 5. People like Emma, Stuart, and Erwin. Ever since the Brown and Root shootout, the effort to get rid of Emma had intensified. Her support of the unions as well as her generally liberal stand on issues incensed the members of the business community, particularly the bankers. They did what they could to get her defeated; but, as her 1951 election victory showed, the efforts seemed increasingly fruitless. Proposition 5 was designed to get Emma off the council.[34] The thinking seemed to be that if Emma were forced to run against a single candidate who was supported by the concentrated numbers of the business community, she would lose her seat. Emma believed that to be the intent of Proposition 5. So did the four members of the revision committee, who did not endorse it. And so, too, did Frank Erwin. Sometime in the fall of 1952, prior to the December meeting, Erwin, it is reported, met Fagan Dickson, a highly respected Austin attorney and an ally of Emma and the liberal forces, on Congress Avenue. Erwin, it is said, informed Dickson, "I'll just tell you we'll get rid of Emma if we have to abolish the city charter and the whole city government." Dickson replied, "Boy, you better start abolishing tomorrow because you're not going to get rid of Emma."[35]

Thus, at the December 8 meeting, Emma vowed to prolong the discussion over the amendments, and to delay, especially, any decision on when they would be put before residents for a vote. To the uninformed and unaware, her position must have seemed downright silly. After all, she was the one who two years earlier had first proposed to modernize the city charter. Nonetheless, sensing that if the amendments were approved she could well fall to defeat, Emma pursued as long and as detailed a discussion of politics as had ever taken place in the council chambers. Bar none. Not even Mayor Miller's verbal odysseys. She spoke for the greater part of thirteen straight hours. She found fault with each and every amendment. She claimed that the amendment designed to improve the city's bookkeeping actually would increase a citizen's tax burden. She argued that another amendment would give unlimited powers to the city manager, Walter Seaholm. Emma already thought him incompetent. Most of all, Emma insisted that the vote on the amendments be postponed. Her change of heart was brought to her attention by Trueman

O'Quinn, former city attorney, who reminded her that only a year before she urged the eleven amendments be taken to the voters immediately. But Proposition 5 had not been part of the original eleven-amendment package.[36]

At the close of the meeting, the sides were firmly drawn, and the fight over the charter quickly became one between the business community, represented by Frank Erwin, and Emma and her allies. For the first time in memory, the *Austin American* and the *Statesman* did little to disguise their own favorites. And they helped give Emma enough rope to hang herself. In an interview with Wray Weddell, published on the front page of the *Austin American* on December 21, 1952, Emma revealed her plans to get a "balance of power" on the council in the forthcoming elections. With three positions rather than just two, she proclaimed, it would be possible for her finally to bring the Establishment to its knees.[37] The Establishment did not stand idly by. For the first time in its history, the chamber crowd and others in the business community consciously organized themselves for a political fight. Until now their forces had always relied upon the loose connections of an old-boy network to vie for positions on the council. Now they realized they were in for a spirited fight. And a mean one. In mid-December, Erwin announced the formation of a new citizens' group, the Good Government League of Austin. Their first meeting was chaired by Erwin, and attended, according to the paper, by more than 250 residents of Austin. Erwin informed the assembled crowd that the league would actively work to secure the passage of all thirty-two amendments, including Proposition 5.

If Emma's forces could have found tea to dump in Lake Austin they would have done it. The war over the charter, taxes, and the hegemony of the business forces in Austin got hotter and hotter. Erwin found an *American* reporter, and informed him that Emma's fight against the amendments was really intended to grab power for herself.[38] Emma fought back, arguing that the Good Government League was merely "a front organization for the boys in the back room."[39] The Good Government League deployed its forces quickly, and throughout the city. Longtime opponents of Emma appeared publicly to support the league, including Ed St. John, whom she had defeated in the 1948 campaign. A. C. Bull, a much-admired business-man, former president of the Austin Chamber of Commerce, and member of the charter revision committee, spoke out strongly for the amendments.[40] The large banks and lending institutions in the com-

munity gave their support to the revisions of the charter, in a half-
page advertisement in the *Austin American*.[41] The first real evidence
of a split in the black community of East Austin happened, too.
Everett Givens, speaking on behalf of black residents, claimed that
the majority would give their support to the passage of all charter
amendments. But a new group, known as the East Side Better Government Association, appeared and condemned many of the same
amendments as Emma had.[42] Through it all, Charles Green and the
papers sought to drum up support on behalf of the amendments.
Both papers ran a series of articles providing favorable coverage of
each amendment in detail. Headlines in the papers, such as "Charter
Amendments Gaining Support," were intended to scuttle Emma and
her allies.

The most deadly assault against the liberals came in a thinly disguised effort to get at Emma's friend on the council, Ben White.
Emma and Stuart always were able to sustain their pursuit of an issue
because they were financially beholden to no one. Bankers could
threaten to limit the charges of some white liberals, but the Longs
had independent income. And, therefore, they were unassailable.
Not so for Ben White. White was the plant superintendent at Austex
Chili, one of Austin's larger business firms. It just so happened that
Fred Catterall, Jr., head of the firm and also leading member of the
Austin Chamber of Commerce, sent a notice to all his employees in
late December. It said that the employees stood in danger of losing
their jobs if they participated in any political activities that meant
extended time away from the plant. This obviously was intended for
White's eyes only. White, not in the least intimidated, told a reporter
he had several other job possibilities. He also mentioned that he
planned to run again for his council seat in the spring.[43] The *Austin
American* was not so thinly disguised in its sympathies by now. In a
front-page article on December 31, 1952, it headlined, "Openly
Defiant, White in Race."[44] White soon was fired by Austex Chili.
This action created such an uproar, including a boycott of the chili
firm, that White was rehired. Within months, however, the company
simply retired him with a pension. He had worked for them for
thirty-one years.[45]

Emma's campaign against the amendments lost. All of them were
passed by the voters in an election held on January 31, 1953. Most
got through with wide margins, with the closest vote coming on
Proposition 5. This passed, fifty-nine to forty-one percent. The

middle- and upper-income areas of the city, like Tarrytown and Brykerwoods, went heavily in favor of the amendments. Dr. Givens proved mistaken about the black and brown vote. In East Austin the voters overwhelmingly went against the amendments, maintaining their allegiance to Emma once more. The fight was not yet over, however.

Emma now agreed to abide by the will of the majority. She and her aides had to reassess her electoral prospects in light of the new place system. After concluding she could still be victorious in the upcoming spring election, the Long advisors had to decide which place to enter. They wanted to prevent the business forces from putting their strongest candidate against her, and also from running a minority candidate against her who might divide the liberal vote. Emma did not let her decision be known until the last moment. Then, just at the stroke of midnight on March 4, the last day for filing, Emma declared for Place 1, running against the strongest of the business forces' candidates. Her opponent was Evans Swann, a very prominent businessman. Ben White entered the race for Place 2. His opponent was Gary Morrison, another member of Austin's business community. The battle lines in these races remained drawn as they had been for the charter fight. More money was spent to defeat Emma than had ever before been spent on any council race. Dr. Givens and several other members of the black community emerged from a small meeting to announce they would support a ticket of five candidates, led by Swann and Morrison. James Nash, a very wealthy businessman in Austin who rarely let his hands get dirtied by politics, made some strong recommendations on behalf of Swann. Swann himself spoke of his qualifications for office, and stressed that he was not particularly hungry for power, a remark obviously intended to malign Emma. The *Austin Statesman*, not to be indicted for objectivity or change of heart, wrote a whole series of articles in support of the Long and White opponents. Headlines paraded above them, announcing "Morrison Called Solution to Council Turbulence," or "Evans Swann Praised by Businessman Nash."[46] Emma, in contrast, received such notable treatment as the article that appeared in the *American* just days before the election. Purporting to provide a summary of her career, its headline read, "Political Career of Mrs. Long Has Been One of Storm, Strife," and it went on to single out the controversial moments of her career.[47]

Now the issue of the Longs' support of unions reared its head in

Austin politics. Frank Erwin, ever the charmer, went on local television to proclaim that Emma and Stuart were on the payroll of the Texas State Federation of Labor.[48] Therefore, he said, Emma was not an impartial member of the City Council, but, in effect, was paid by an unpopular group to press forward with its desires. Of course, no one had ever accused the bankers like the Bartholomews, father and son, of failing to take note of the interest of the banks in Austin. But the unions were something else. Emma and Stuart took to the offensive, and fought back. They noted that the current mayor of Austin, William Drake, was the head of Calcasieu Lumber Company, a firm that had done tens of thousands of dollars in business with the unions of the Texas Federation of Labor.[49] Stuart used his broadcasts on the radio to challenge Erwin's assertions. He collared a reporter in order to wonder why Erwin was going to such lengths in order to fight Emma. "Somebody," he said, "sure must be figuring on cutting a fat melon up there at city hall if it's that important to them to get rid of Emma. Because if they get rid of Emma, then there won't be anybody to tell the folks what's going on, and who's getting off with what."[50] The newspapers, not to be outdone, continued to wage war with Emma. The *American* had already intimated that Stuart ran Emma, and the *Statesman*, in its editorial just prior to the election, asked, "Who makes Mrs. Long's decisions in City Council? Is it Mrs. Long or is it her husband, Stuart Long? Or is it a powerful organized labor group working through them?"[51]

The people's candidates won in the election of April 4. Both Emma and Ben White, the only two incumbents to run for office were victorious. But Emma had created a tough and active opposition for herself, one that she would battle in each and every race from there on out. Other scars were left, too, personal wounds that took a long time to heal. Of greatest moment was what the fight told of Austin politics. The chamber crowd and the liberals were willing to fight their battles to the very end, the very bitterest end. The chamber crowd also was willing to toy with the law in order to fight their enemies on the council—whether it be the law of the community, or, as in the case of White, the law of the workplace. Whoever said that politics in America is conducted on the basis of impartial law alone would have learned much from living in Austin during the tempestuous days of 1952 and 1953.

Emma remained on the City Council until 1959, when she decided to save her sanity and withdraw for a time. "The phone kept ringing off the hook," she told me, "and I just wanted it to stop."[52] But politics was too much in her blood. She reentered the electoral arena in 1961, only to be defeated for office by a margin of sixty-three votes by Bob Armstrong. In 1963, she again ran, and this time won. She continued to serve on the council until 1969, when, once again, she was defeated. This campaign, which became her last hurrah, was one marked by almost as much viciousness as the 1953 race. It was occasioned by her and fellow council members' support of a special Fair Housing Ordinance in Austin. This story is so important to Austin's history that we shall examine it in detail in chapter 10.

Between 1953 and 1969, Emma brought her continuing concern for the little people to office. She cared about whether they would have the benefits of new and improved city services, and so pressed relentlessly for turning dusty roads into asphalt thoroughfares. She fought as hard as she could to ease the financial burden on homeowners for these costs, sometimes in a losing effort. She took to the hustings to press continuously for the fiscal responsibility of city government. Because she pursued this issue with as much passion and persistence as every other, she ultimately was responsible for the retirement of city manager Guiton Morgan, the firing of a second city manager, Walter Seaholm, and even played a role in the dismissal of a third one, Bill Williams.

Emma's style rarely endeared her to colleagues, who often found her windy and razor-sharp. She never was in the least reluctant to speak her mind, which led to many fiery words between her and council opponents. Consider this instance, just a year before Williams was fired from his post. The issue under consideration was the city budget:

Williams: I've talked myself hoarse over your voice tonight.

Long: You poor beat-up man, I know you're so abused.

Williams: I'm pretty well mauled by your tongue.

Long: If you don't like it, Mr. Williams, you know what you can do. You can resign. The people put me here, but you can leave any time.[53]

Sometimes, it seemed, that style did Emma more harm than good. In the 1959 council race, Emma and her allies engaged in some politicking even though she herself was not a candidate. Edgar Perry III, by all accounts a very generous and devout Christian individual, had been persuaded to run for office. Although he was an intimate of his grandfather, Commodore Perry, the younger Perry was by no means his clone. Emma and her forces did not fully understand that. Nor did they understand that the young Perry might have been on their side on different issues. He was a novice to politics and was eager simply to learn the terrain. But Emma contended that he was an obvious link to the Establishment, and a device for carrying on the dominance of the Commodore over the Austin skyline. Once the criticism took this tone, Perry immediately became her opponent, aroused by the tactics of "guilt by association." [54] It was not only the business community that occasionally played rough politics in Austin. Emma did, too.

Much legislation and much well-being for Austin came through the tireless work and many years Emma devoted to Austin politics. She helped to expand and improve the park system, and through her appointments got concerned citizens active in these programs as well as those on behalf of the library. [55] During the 1960s, she continued to press for the people, and to urge that blacks and browns in Austin be given a better shake. Adding to the decade of her previous effort, she concluded here sixteen years in office with a handsome legacy of legislation. Miles of paved streets, park lands dotting the landscape, better pay for police and fire personnel, a better transit system, these and other sorts of legislation are on the books because Emma helped to put them there. Still, when all is said and done, it is not her specific deeds that remain alive today in people's minds. Like the other heroes and heroines of our world, Emma Long has become important to Austin not so much for what she did as for what she has come to personify—the little people.

THE
DREAM PREVAILS

▬

9.

Shaping the Frontier

—

Plus ça change, plus c'est la même chose.

As THE OLD GENERATION OF URBAN ENTREPRENEURS
in Austin passed from the scene, owing either to illness or to resignation from office, a new generation was there to replace them. There
were perhaps some telling differences between the first- and second-
generation entrepreneurs. The vision for Austin and the appetite for
its growth, and their own, had been somewhat more circumscribed
in the case of the first generation. Long, Perry, and even Miller had
possessed ambitions for themselves as for the city, but those ambitions only stretched so far. They wanted the city to grow and to blossom, but they never wanted, it appears, to develop a full-scale
industrial empire.

In part, this may have sprung from their rural or small-town
origins, which limited the size of their appetites; in part, it may have
sprung simply from an ambition limited by the possibilities for industrial growth in Austin itself. Harboring few natural resources that
could be mined for their wealth and usefulness, set in a wooded, hilly
landscape, bedecked with rivers and lakes, Austin was a prisoner of
its environment, yet one that enjoyed its fate. But the dams had
changed all that. They had made possible a control of the rivers, and
industry that could use the electric power they harnessed. They had
made life livable in Austin and throughout the rest of central Texas.
Obviously, the community had reached a turning point, one might
even say a second stage in its industrial and economic potential. But
would that potential be realized? And would growth—the expansion

and enlargement of the community—be pushed forward? Those were questions that now awaited answers.

This chapter relates the story of the new generation of urban entrepreneurs, and how they sought to expand the dream for growth. It tells how a handful of men stirred up the community, and how they encountered some resistance along the way, particularly from the old, established businesses and banks in Austin. In the midst of the changes it depicts, the chapter portrays the threads of continuity that run throughout Austin history, from the vision of the future to the conscious efforts of the Chamber of Commerce to shape that vision.

C. B. Smith was one of the many recent migrants to Austin from up north, arriving in 1944.[1] He was by no means a newcomer and foreigner. He had been raised in Texas, and attended the university, graduating in 1928. After a brief position as a teacher in Houston, Smith became involved in the automobile business. He revealed great flair for salesmanship and organizational work, and by 1934 had become the Midwest sales manager for the Chevrolet division of General Motors. People in the higher echelons of the company were much impressed with Smith's work, and had great plans for him. The plans were interrupted by World War II. Several days after the Japanese invasion at Pearl Harbor, Smith received a call from William S. Knudsen, a former boss and president of General Motors. Knudsen asked whether Smith would be willing to come to Washington and take charge of the procurement for the tank division of the War Production Board, which Knudsen headed. Smith agreed, and spent the next three years working in Washington.

By 1944, Smith was ready to move on. His love of Austin and the university was a compelling memory, and led him to resettle in the small central Texas city. He had already purchased a Dodge-Plymouth dealership here in 1943, and so was set up to start work right away. But his profession did not interfere with his broader plans. Almost from the day he arrived in town, Smith started to move and shake people, hoping to dislodge Austin from its economic slumber. His main concern was to get some action going in town, the kind that could serve as a proper stimulus for business. He made visits to a number of civic leaders and business figures, hoping to persuade some of them of his plans for the growth of Austin. Among others, he spent some time with Ed St. John. St. John was an Austin native, who had spent most of his life in the community. Owner of an out-door advertising business, St. John was one of the more respected civic leaders, a devoted friend and helper to many groups, including boys' clubs and the like. St. John remembers that "C. B. was a live wire. . . . He wanted to attract industry to Austin. . . . We had so many conversations about it. He sold me on the idea of attracting in-dustry to Austin."[2]

And Smith sold many others as well. Many people were as im-pressed with Smith's argument as St. John. Many believed C. B. to be a man of great vision. Dave Shanks, an Austin newspaperman, and later editor of the *American-Statesman*, was much taken with Smith's plan and his salesmanship. "C. B.," he recalls, "was the first [person] to formalize and implement a scheme for the development [of Austin]. . . . He provided a blueprint [for what Austin would be-come]."[3] Not everyone in town was impressed by Smith's dream, nor by his effort to move and shake the community. Some longtime residents, especially some of the bankers and local businesspeople, en-sconced in positions of Austin power, took particular offense at Smith's call for greater industry. Many of them believed that industry meant smokestacks, tenement houses, and, as Smith himself put it, "a middle European woman, with a goose under her arm, getting on a streetcar."[4] Walter Long, the grey eminence in Austin industrial circles, was one who resisted Smith's call for new industry, and the two men eventually came to loggerheads. Smith eventually won out, and won out in a big way. He became head of the Chamber of Com-merce's Industrial Bureau. And Walter Long was forced to resign his position at the chamber, after a tenure of thirty-five years.

By the spring of 1948, C. B. had assembled enough allies in Austin business circles to set the stage for a new industrial recruitment or-ganization. The final stimulus was provided by the visit to Austin of Richardson Wood, an acquaintance of Smith's and an industrial con-sultant from the East.[5] He came to town at Smith's request. Wood, who had offices on prestigious Fifth Avenue in New York City, was well known for his successes in developing the economies of small American cities. During his stay in Austin, Wood spoke to a large gathering of Austin businessmen and a handful of women. He spoke to them about the importance of economic growth to a community, and of the many benefits that new businesses could provide. So effec-tive was his talk that C. B. invited him to provide a brief written analysis of the Austin economic situation, and its prospects for growth. Wood did so in the space of four intense workdays. Drawing on Smith and the usual handful of New Deal stalwarts, like Raymond Brooks and Max Starcke, both of the Lower Colorado River Authority, Wood urged that Austin seek to develop a large skilled and semiskilled labor force.[6] He thought the university could provide a good stimulus for growth. And, in a moment of great prescience, he observed that "small shops and design laboratories [of skilled workers] can grow out of the various departments of the university."[7]

No sooner had the ink on Wood's report dried than the *Austin American*, ever the ally of new ideas and good business, published a series of articles on the Wood visit, and the formation of a new industrial organization, headed by C. B. The organization was to be called the Austin Area Economic Development Foundation. Days later, the *American* went further, publishing an editorial that lauded the new growth campaign:

> This week Austin draws the blueprint of its future – a future of progress, growth, prosperity, and happiness – or a future of stagnation driving out the ambitious and ablest young people for lack of opportunities at home. . . . Diversity of small business and industry, a diversified and broadened payroll, the addition of many small businesses and industries which will be in the growing stage when a business recession comes – these are the acknowledged best insurance policies against the blight of hard times. . . .[8]

These were the sorts of arguments that Richardson Wood himself had made to the businesspeople and in his report. Moreover, appended to the bottom of the editorial was a pledge card. Readers were asked to fill out the card with their name, and to provide a financial donation to the new group. This was only the first of many plugs that the *American* would provide the foundation.

Some of the prominent members of the business community, particularly the New Deal allies, lined up squarely behind Smith's growing campaign. Ed Clark, whom Smith believed vital to the effort, provided a donation of $1,000, one of only several on that order.[9] Another New Deal ally jumped on the bandwagon, too, recruited through Smith's great flair for salesmanship. At a meeting of hundreds of residents, Smith was greeted with the appearance of a young man in the front row scribbling madly away in a bluebook. Smith was much impressed, and thought the man to be a stray university student. At the conclusion, Smith was standing to the side of the podium when the young man approached, breathlessly. "By God," he exclaimed, "that was some speech. I own a radio station in town, and I'm going to go on the air for thirty-six hours straight to talk about your campaign, and Austin growth." Soon thereafter the voice of John Connally could be heard on KVET, sounding much like a disciple of C. B.[10]

Eventually the foundation got together a sum of $150,000 to fund an all-out effort to attract new industry to Austin.[11] That was a most handsome kitty, probably something on the order of several times the amount that the Chamber of Commerce had in its entire annual budget. (As late as 1960, for instance, the chamber's total budget was only $35,000 a year.)[12] The money enabled the group to put together a full-time staff of office help and consultants, a recommendation of Richardson Wood. Frank Jessen, an engineering professor at the university, was hired as the principal director of the group's operations. Wood himself was hired as a continuing consultant, working out of his New York offices. And a consultant was also employed to work the Midwest region of the United States. Now the effort turned from selling Austin on industrial growth to selling industry on Austin. Wood took it upon himself to make a series of visits to key business firms throughout the Northeast. He sought out mainly technical and research firms, believing them to be the principal kinds around which the industrial architecture of Austin should be designed. Similar trips were taken by the representative in the Midwest, and by Jessen.

All these efforts were augmented by intense advertising and mail campaigns. A newsletter was begun in 1948, and distributed to all those people in Austin who had pledged money and become members of the foundation.[13] It was also sent to potential industrial recruits. Brochures were put together, heralding all the social and economic advantages of settling in beautiful downtown Austin. The foundation even managed to recruit the Missouri-Pacific Railroad to its side, drawing on its influence to act as a potential lure for industry. The railroad, which was the major line serving Austin and central Texas, produced its own advertisement for the industrial campaign, one that seemed quite telling about the essential theme of the effort.

After noting the new business spirit afoot in Austin, the flyer proclaimed:

> Surveys made for the [Foundation] have shown that Austin is ideally adapted as a site for research industries and those which can use the chemical-mineral resources which abound in the territory surrounding the city. To these industries Austin holds out an exceptional attraction—the super science laboratories and other research facilities of the University of Texas.[14]

And, rather incidentally, the advertisement happened to mention that Austin also possessed a good Southwest location, an "agreeable climate," and "ample power and water." It was these last qualities that most concerned prospective recruits.

Wood had informed C. B. and other foundation officials that Austin probably faced an uphill battle in selling itself to American industry. Its great strength in the postwar period was that it represented an industrial frontier, unbounded and ready to be seduced by the magic of American industrial profits. Not only Austin, but Texas as a whole had that image in the mind of America. But there were drawbacks to the frontier images. Untamed. Isolated. And, most of all, parched. No one from the North could possibly imagine that central Texas now possessed recreational rivers and lakes and a seemingly endless supply of water furnished by the dams. With a good deal of craftiness, C. B. embarked on one of the more glitzy aspects of the growth campaign. He got together a large quantity of local water, filled it into a 3,000-gallon truck, and shipped it to New York City.[15] There, across the street from the Mark Hellinger Theatre on Broadway, the city water commissioner, flanked by four delicious girls from the cast of Lil' Darlin' and members of the New York City Texas Club, heralded the arrival of the truck.[16] The story made headlines in the Austin American, and even hit the pages of the Houston Chronicle.[17] New Yorkers now knew that Austinites were not thirsty.

C. B. and the Development Foundation continued their industrial campaign for a full three years. All the while, people like Jessen worked fast and furiously to drum up new business. The payoff was not always easy to assess. The foundation did manage to convince Austin businesspeople of the need to press forward with new industrial growth. The membership roster eventually read like the Yellow Pages, and a businessperson was a nobody if unrecorded on the foundation's rolls. But the number of new businesses that came into Austin by the end of the organization's lifetime, in 1951, was rather small. The Ward Body Company, a firm that manufactured buses. Another small manufacturing firm. A store that made furniture. But, quality, not quantity, it seemed, was what counted. The one big fish that the foundation lured to Austin proved to be the model of what it sought — a technical research firm with potential jobs for graduates of the university. Jefferson Chemical Company chose to settle on the northeastern outskirts of Austin, sometime in 1949. The company specialized in research and products in the chemical industry. It was not much. But it was a beginning.

One of the people who worked with C. B. in the industrial campaign was J. Neils Thompson. Like Smith, Thompson had graduated from the university. Thompson was doing research work in industrial engineering for the State Highway Department in 1940 when he was asked to return to the engineering faculty.[18] At the time, few of the professors were engaged in research, and Thompson, who was a skilled research scientist, was believed capable of adding glitter and light to the College of Engineering. And, not so incidentally, also a few bucks. His role on the faculty soon turned to one of searching for research funds, to support his own work but also that of others on the staff. Thompson's main research interest was concrete and clay products. The federal government had by this time begun to pour more and more money into defense contracts, and Thompson began to take trips to Washington to lean on the federal government for money, much as Tom Miller had years earlier. His leaning worked. Within a short space of time he became an expert grantsman, able to secure monies easily from the government, and thereby keep his concrete research going.

Thompson quickly became known as one of the up-and-coming young salesmen for a bigger, and presumably better, Austin. His theme was that Austin could develop its industrial potential if it drew upon the strengths it possessed. What were they? Well, he argued, energy and materials represent two of three key ingredients for a potent economy.[19] The third is knowledge. And knowledge is to be found in the educational apparatus at the university. Use the university, he urged, to build the Austin economy. Develop research firms, and recruit electronics industries to Austin. Get high-tech industries, he said in speech after speech to local civic groups. But, of course, he did not say high-tech because no one said high-tech then.

By the mid-1940s, Thompson had a bright idea. The Magnesium Plant that the Department of Defense had constructed in Austin to purchase the surplus electricity of the Lower Colorado River Authority now lay unused. Just as well, some residents thought, unrepentant about their wishes to rid the skyline of smokestacks. Thompson wanted to turn the plant to a good purpose. Why not, he thought, use the shell of the plant as a facility for research and educational work at the university? He drummed up support among the higher-ups on campus, and then turned to the federal government to secure the link. Lyndon Johnson now reentered the picture. Working through Johnson, Thompson proposed to the government that it make the plant available for research work. Johnson and the government agreed. First, a long-term lease was effected that permitted the university to rent the facility. Then, in 1949, a purchase contract was created. The university would buy the facility over a twenty-year period.[20] Moreover, if the university agreed to do work that "would benefit the public," then the government agreed to waive the annual amount due on the sale. Thompson and the university consented to the terms. Soon the facility became the recipient of a large number of Department of Defense contracts, presumably testimony to the work it was doing on behalf of the public. Twenty years later, that arrangement would cause the university students political apoplexy. At the time, it seemed just right. For the university. For Thompson. For Austin.

While Thompson took to the hustings late in the 1940s to help C. B. gain industrial recruits, the new research facility was growing in funds, and in number of operations. It soon became home to work on the transmission of radio waves, on the use of radar, on problems of structural mechanics, and on military physics.[21] All the research was funded by the federal government, much of it by the Department of Defense, and some, like that in military physics, begun during the course of the war. By the early 1950s, the plant had changed its name to the Balcones Research Center—though many continued to know it only as the Defense Research Laboratory—was a thriving site of intellectual activity and defense funds, and foreshadowed the shape of the Austin economy.

Even the city tried to get into the act. In the aftermath of the city charter debacle, some city officials began to grapple seriously with the city's future. Members of the City Planning Commission, which had been officially called into existence just at the end of the war, were much concerned about the direction of city growth. Convened mainly to consider citizens' requests for zoning changes on property, and other questions of private property and public ordinances, the commission had become increasingly angered by what it perceived to be an indifferent City Council. At the council meeting on Thursday, February 4, 1954, the commission chairman, H. J. Kuehne, complained that the council ignored commission recommendations on zoning, annexation, and the like, and treated the commission much "like an ill-favored stepchild."[22]

Kuehne and his associates pushed the council to create a new master plan, noting that the most recent one had been the Koch and Fowler plan of 1928. Kuehne had the new city charter on his side. One of its measures called for a new city plan, to be initiated by the Planning Commission. Eventually the council and city manager Walter Seaholm acknowledged the wisdom of the Planning Commission's proposals, and Seaholm put a figure of $50,000 into the 1955 budget to cover the cost of preparing a new master plan.[23] Many throughout the community believed the city had taken the right step, including the influential former school superintendent R. W. Byram, who urged, moreover, that an outside firm be employed to develop the new plan.[24]

Months later, on February 7, 1955, a firm headed by Harold F. Wise of Menlo Park, California, was hired to create a master plan for the city.[25] Wise and his associates subsequently spent a great deal of time in Austin, assembling piles of economic and demographic information, talking with city officials, civic leaders, and other members of the community. The design of the plan grew slowly, and at various stages elements were submitted to citizens for their reactions. At each and every point of its creation, the master plan was nurtured not merely as a planning document for an urban center, but also a political document that could incorporate as many as the citizens' wishes as possible. By September 1956, more than eighteen months after they had been hired, Wise and his firm had a draft of the master plan available for inspection. Few details were to change between this version and the final report.

The 1956 master plan was an intriguing report.[26] If ever there were a document that clearly sought to promote industrial growth in Austin, and yet to forestall its many ramifications, this was it. Over one hundred pages long, the plan was filled with a variety of estimates of market size, transportation routes and uses, and land use patterns and recommendations. The heart of the document, however, was contained in a few pages, in which Wise and his associates made specific recommendations for the City Council to act on. The plan called for extensive industrial development in order to furnish employment opportunities for an expanding population.[27] It urged that the city seek to promote the growth of industry in certain specific geographical locales.[28] Wise and his associates spoke of the importance of setting aside districts of the city in which new industry would be encouraged to settle. Such a strategy had been used most successfully in nearby Dallas, and it had the benefit, among other things, of segregating industry from heavily populated residential areas. East Austin, in particular, was identified as prime industrial real estate, so once again it was urged that this apparent residential wasteland be demolished in favor of plants and factories.

So prescient were the planners that their report anticipated that the Austin population would reach something on the order of 370,000 by the year 1980, more than double its current size, and that unless long-term prevention steps were taken, the city would expect heavy traffic congestion along such thoroughfares as Mo-Pac Boulevard (yet to be constructed) and the road bordering Town Lake on the north.[29] By 1980, in fact, the size of the population had reached 350,000 and at rush hours there was heavy congestion on the road lying along the northern shore of Town Lake. But the foresight of the 1956 planners and many of their recommendations went unheeded. Why? When the plan finally was unveiled, it was met by mixed and divided reactions, including those of the council and Mayor Miller. Louis Goldberg, associate publisher of the *American-Statesman* and outgoing president of the Chamber of Commerce, said in early 1957 that he and other chamber members strongly endorsed the plan's call for industrial growth.[30] Yet, just one month later, Doak Rainey, a prominent member of the City Planning Commission, took exception to the entire design of the plan, claiming it to be a "utopia," and its recommendations to be far beyond the financial reach of the city.[31] Citizens, moreover, seemed to have been little involved in the actual implementation of the plan's proposals. Few copies even reached their hands, and fewer still seem to have been read. When a master plan was officially adopted by the City Council June 8, 1961, it was nothing but a shell of the Wise program, a few pages of trivial generalities. The failure of Austin to act on information contained in its master plan was a failure that would happen time and again in future years.

The city government effort, then, to shape the frontier of Austin seemed to have led nowhere. And the community was left to flounder, unprepared for its economic destiny. But one recommendation did meet with strong approval, at least in some quarters. Wise and his colleagues noted that a "strong chamber of commerce usually takes the lead" for the recruitment of industrial firms, and the development of industrial areas. "The chamber or its industrial committee takes stock, " the plan went on, "determines what facilities are available; what are needed; [and] what industries the community wants and can attract."[32] The next move would be up to the Chamber of Commerce.

Vic Mathias, handsome, smooth, and articulate, had been hired at the Chamber of Commerce in 1953. By 1956, he had been elevated to the post of manager, and had thereby become successor to the great tradition established by Walter Long.[33] Sometime in the spring of 1957, he paid a visit to John Stockton, director of the Bureau of Business Research at the University of Texas. The chamber, and Mathias, had taken the master plan's recommendations for prompt and extensive industrial growth in Austin seriously. Now Mathias turned to Stockton to get more specific recommendations.[34] The bureau had developed quite a nice reputation and a ready facility for accomplishing industrial surveys for individual Texas communities. They had done such surveys for Bastrop, for example, and also for Llano. Mathias wanted them to put together one for Austin.

Over the summer of 1957, Alfred Dale and Izumi Taniguchi prepared a detailed examination of the current industrial situation, and the economic prospects for Austin. By September, they had completed their work, and turned in the report to Mathias. Although the bureau generally took a cool stand on the actual implementation of its analyses, in this instance, Stanley Arbingast, associate director of the bureau, took a much more emphatic tone. In his cover letter that accompanied the bureau document, Arbingast wrote, ". . . the survey staff feels these suggestions need to be acted on as early as possible if the city is to secure new industry." Furthermore, he noted, building on one of the central arguments of the bureau survey, in Austin "one of the major handicaps to the attraction of more industry is the lack of a planned industrial district."[35] Just as in the case of the master plan, the bureau report made fascinating reading. It worked on the assumption that economic growth was, in and of itself, desirable, and that, among other things, growth produced new income in a community, and with it greater consumption, new stores, more economic vitality.[36] It recommended that a number of strong steps be taken to bring about such growth, and indicated the direction such steps should take. It argued that Austin should build on its strengths, and thus seek industry that could be linked somehow to the university. It urged the development of plants and firms in the electronics sector, thus echoing the sentiments of J. Neils Thompson. It also acknowledged the resistance to growth that was evident in many quarters in Austin, and so claimed that "a major, and probably the first priority . . . of any group taking the initiative in developing a program for economic development in Austin is to sell its importance to the Austin community."[37] Mathias now had the ammunition that he and the chamber needed.

Over the span of the next four years, Mathias began the "first priority" task outlined by the bureau report, selling the project to Austin. He was assisted in this effort by several prominent citizens, some of whom had been involved in the continuing campaign to shape the Austin economy. Ed St. John, J. Neils Thompson, C. B. Smith, as well as others like Joe Crow, worked together with Mathias to sell Austin on industry. A major challenge was to get the banks interested in new industry. The bankers' customary stance was to resist any ventures that involved the outlay of capital.[38] Too risky, they believed, too unlikely to put capital in Capital; or in Austin National; or in American National. Mathias had to convince the bankers that without the introduction of new industry Austin would probably turn to dry rot, losing out in the postwar industrial race to other Texas towns, such as Waco or Temple. While Mathias worked on the bankers, his fellow chamber members worked on other sectors of Austin.

Neils Thompson, who also helped sell growth to the bankers, turned most of his attention to the many civic groups and clubs, and sought to drum up enthusiasm among them for new industry.[39] He pointed out that the tax base of Austin was severely limited, and thus the city government and the chamber, as public enterprises, were limited in their ability to meet city needs, and provide city direction. He urged that new industry be brought in to enlarge the tax base, and to expand job opportunities for Austin youth, many of whom now were forced to move to Dallas or to Houston to secure decent employment. And he continued to press hard with his campaign to recruit electronics firms to Austin. Crow, a successful developer, now headed the Industrial Bureau of the chamber, and he hit hard at the need to develop industrial districts in the community.[40] Crow had observed the success of such districts firsthand in Oklahoma City, and had seen the financial worth of that community grow by more than $50 million in the postwar period just because of the development of such districts. And Ed St. John tried to drum up civic enthusiasm, in general, hoping to use his blue-ribbon image to promote an interest in the chamber's economic plans.[41]

By 1961, the work of the chamber had begun to pay dividends. A large-scale fund-raising effort took place that year, with the result that the chamber managed to raise over $100,000 for its economic growth campaign.[42] Mathias and the chamber could now set about in a serious manner to find new industry for Austin. The chamber put together a whole series of brochures on the city, just as C. B. Smith had done some time earlier, and began to advertise the merits of Austin far and wide. Neils Thompson sparked a new idea, encouraging local businesspeople and university faculty who made trips outside the state to visit potential industrial recruits and fan their enthusiasm for the city. The *American* and the *Statesman*, now under the influence of publisher Dick Brown, got involved in the growth campaign in a big way.[43] They not only published a series of editorials that backed the new Austin spirit for industry, but, throughout much of late 1961, Wray Weddell, Jr., a young newspaperman on the *American*, drafted a series of articles on growth. Appearing on the front page of the paper, the articles covered everything from new entrepreneurs in town to the work of Ed St. John at the chamber to the need to keep up with the Houstons.[44] Joe Crow continued his work with the chamber and industry, too, but now began to realize the fruition of some of his own efforts to shape the unbounded frontier of Austin.

Crow is one of those not-so-shadowy figures who appears and reappears throughout the effort to shape the Austin future.[45] This is no little coincidence. Crow wanted to do everything possible to get Austin moving in the postwar period. He had helped C. B. and the

Economic Development Foundation. He had been the principal supporter of the industrial district concept described by Harold Wise as
part of the 1956 master plan. He was concerned about the city, but
he also had his own business interests at heart as well. One might
even say he was an example of an emerging breed of entrepreneur in
Austin, a *market entrepreneur* rather than an *urban entrepreneur*, a
man who was as committed to the idea of growth, *per se*, as he was
to the idea of Austin. Crow was primarily a developer. He bought
and sold huge pieces of land throughout Austin, often long before
other people even recognized the land as valuable property. Crow
thought there were many such parcels in the vicinity of Austin that
were ripe for use as industrial sectors. During the period he was head
of the chamber's Industrial Bureau, he tried repeatedly to sell the concept to Austin businesspeople. He was constantly rebuffed.

His other pursuits also led to rebuffs. Crow believed that Austin
could use some new customer outlets, such as department stores,
shoe stores, grocery stores, and other sources to offer customers a
greater variety of merchandise. The Austin he saw was the same as
the one seen by blacks in the early 1950s. A few major stores dominated the landscape, and all were located on or near Congress
Avenue. Scarbroughs was the major store, towering over the small,
one-story buildings nearby. T. H. Williams, Yaring's, and a handful
of others also were present. Crow sensed that the community needed
something more, something new, and that if it failed to attract novel
business ventures it would soon lose out in the postwar financial race
to the likes of Waco, or Temple or—heaven forbid!—College Station.
Taking $5,000 of his own funds, Crow invested in a marketing survey
of the extent of consumer outlets in Austin.[46] What he found did
not surprise him. For a town of its size, Austin was store-short and
dollar-poor. He set about to change the situation, and also to make
a profit for himself. He embarked on the development of the first
series of shopping centers, or malls, in the city.

In 1955, he set about to purchase acreage near the municipal airport, just east of Interstate 35, which divides East from West Austin,
and cuts across the city. It took him about three years to assemble
a parcel of forty-two acres, a parcel that, once developed, would
become the site of Capital Plaza.[47] In the course of developing this
site, he had to bargain and barter with a group of ten different
property owners. His manner of purchasing the property was the one
he would always use, in this case as in the development of other

malls. He confronted the owner of a piece of property with the possibility of getting greater market value for the land. Crow needed the
full ten tracts to complete the site for the center, and the owner
wanted as much as he could get for his land. The deal took time, but
eventually was completed in 1958. At the site, Austin became home
to its first Montgomery Ward store, and to an outlet of the HEB
chain of supermarkets.

Naturally, downtown store owners were concerned. Their major
fear, Crow recalls, was simply competition. The town lacked business
vitality because it lacked an entrepreneurial spirit. "People in this
town just didn't understand business," Crow claims.[48] Anything
that smacked of risk-taking, anything that upset the status quo of
business, was to be condemned. The bankers and the downtown
store owners cut no corners in their efforts to cut out Crow, and the
Capital Plaza site. They even prevailed upon the good Mayor Miller,
who had by now entered the second period of his office-holding.
They urged the mayor to set certain zoning restrictions on the proposed site, thus preventing the development of a shopping center.
But Tom Miller and Ed Clark had recently pushed through a deal
of their own, permitting the city to sell forty acres of park land to
Sears for a new shopping center, Hancock Mall, and Tom was not
about to stand in the way of another illustration of good free enterprise.[49] Thus, he backed Crow's effort to acquire the property near
the airport, informing his fellow businesspeople that there was no
legal recourse to prevent the new shopping center.

Capital Plaza was only one of several centers that Crow started in
Austin. With similar savvy for selling and property acquisition, he
got earlier ventures off the ground, too, including the Lamar Plaza
Shopping Center, the first of the centers in town to offer rival outlets
to the downtown stores, and the North Loop Shopping Plaza. His
biggest catch, however, and one that followed shortly on the heels
of the Capital Plaza transaction, was the development of Highland
Mall, at its time a far-reaching and extensive array of stores that
matched the most expansive malls anywhere else in the state.[51] Here
he acquired over one hundred acres of land, and bought it all from
the heirs of one of the earlier actors of the Austin drama—Herman
Brown. The land acquisition here was not nearly so difficult. There
also was a special irony to the construction of the mall. Crow
managed to attract some really big outlets to this operation, including
Joske's, a major chain of department stores in Texas. Once Joske's

opened, it did a lot of good consumer business, so good that it effectively diminished much of the business at other nearby stores, including Sears at Hancock Mall. By this time, however, Tom Miller was dead.

Joe Crow's enterprising spirit was characteristic of the spirit that now began to multiply and accelerate in Austin. A momentum had evolved on behalf of the growth campaign, and ever greater numbers of people were jumping on the bandwagon. The chamber took the lead, but it was beginning to be as much of a representative body as a vehicle that promoted growth itself. To assist this effort, and to counter the failure of the city government to help effect plans for Austin's future, attention now was turned to the political arena once more. The hope was to create some kind of political alliance in town, involving the Chamber of Commerce, civic groups, and officials of city government itself, an alliance that would act in concert to shape the future of Austin.

The makings of that alliance probably first emerged in the early 1960s.[52] Several of the more adventurous and reckless young businesspeople in town decided to make their voice heard in the chambers of the City Council. One of the more outspoken was Hub Bechtol.[53] Bechtol had been a star athlete at the University of Texas, an All-American football player who had run alongside the likes of Tom Landry. Bechtol was as exemplary of the new economic spirit in Austin as anyone. A firm believer in free enterprise, he thought that no one should challenge the rights of private property. The business spirit was good for a community, he thought, and could help a community to grow, just as it would help the individual private investor. He carried on the spirit of Adam Smith with unparalleled enthusiasm and found allies in others in Austin, particularly among what he called the Shivercrats, friends and supporters of former Governor Allan Shivers. It was among this segment of the Austin social and economic community that the political alliance emerged. One of their first efforts targeted Emma Long in her return to the political trails in 1961, after a two-year absence. And the alliance was victorious, backing the candidacy of Bob Armstrong. Good old "landslide" Bob surprised Emma at the polls, and won by sixty-eight votes.

For several years, the alliance was an off-again, on-again affair, never clear about how to act, never certain how to defeat its foes

—whom it viewed as many of the growing number of East Austin minorities—but always hopeful of guiding the economic future of the community. By 1966, however, it had jelled. A formal association was created, known as the Greater Austin Association.[54] Under the leadership of C. B. Smith, Bechtol, Neils Thompson, and a host of others, including Clyde Copus, local builder, Bill Milburn, also a builder, Bill Youngblood, owner of the local Terminex outlet, and Hardy Hollers, lawyer, friend of C. B., and former opponent of Lyndon Johnson for political office, the group set about to provide a greater unity to the political and economic direction of Austin.[55] That it was moved by the spirit of business to influence the political shape of Austin is evident in some of the projects it considered. Hollers, for instance, in a private memorandum to C. B., suggested that the city charter should be updated. In particular, he urged that the council, Austin's representative body of citizens, be curtailed in its specific powers, its "actions . . . limited to laying down general principles, with details left to the City Manager and the departments of the city." He urged, further, that "the operations of a city such as Austin should be based primarily upon business principles rather than upon political considerations," and suggested another method for the election and tenure of the City Council members.[56]

Most of all, the Greater Austin Association had the purpose, if not entirely the effect, of cementing hegemony on behalf of growth. It regularly held meetings on matters of Austin's future, and encouraged brainstorming sessions about what goals the community ought to pursue.[57] It periodically would have its attention engaged by City Council elections, and some of its members, including Lester Palmer and Dick Nichols, found their way onto the council. But its financial and political support of candidates did not always secure its influence in the council chambers, as the vote on fair housing by Nichols soon would show. Nevertheless, it sought to do in the political arena what the chamber had embarked on in the economic one—to make Austin a grander and happier place. Its work was soon overshadowed by the greatest economic victory of all, one that would rank in the annals of Austin development history, alongside that of the coming of the LCRA.

In May 1966, a telephone call came to the offices of Lloyd Lochridge, an Austin lawyer.[58] Lochridge was a member of a respected Austin law firm, and scion of an old Austin family. His grandfather had been business manager of the university, and his father, before becoming a wealthy executive of the Sinclair Oil Company, had been an editor of the *Austin Statesman*.[59] The man on the phone was another lawyer, from New York City. He told Lochridge that he represented a national firm that was interested in locating a plant in Austin. Would Lochridge be willing to represent the firm in Austin? the caller asked. Lochridge, who did a variety of tasks for clients, agreed. The caller told Lochridge he would come to Austin to meet him, and the two men set a date for an appointment.

Some days later, the man appeared in Lochridge's office. He told Lochridge that he represented International Business Machines Corporation (IBM). Though Lochridge was not at all involved in Austin politics, he immediately realized the significance of the firm's move to Austin. It would put Austin on the map. The lawyer asked Lochridge to reveal nothing of the firm's identity. There was nothing particularly sinister or illegal in such a request. Most business firms do not want their identity revealed to the public when they are considering new plant sites. Such information could have all sorts of dire effects, from increasing land prices at possible physical sites to harming the firm's image if it chose not to locate in a particular community.[60] The IBM lawyer asked Lochridge to begin to assemble various kinds of materials about Austin. IBM was interested particularly in the water supply — shades of C. B.'s old nemesis — and in the availability of adequate electricity and power. It also was concerned about the cultural life of the city, and whether its employees would find an adequate array of concerts, plays, and other big-city highlights.

At roughly the same moment, a man about middle age and nondescript, walked into the Chamber of Commerce quarters. He presented himself as the representative of a major United States corporation. His corporation, he told the receptionist, was interested in Austin as a possible site for a new plant. The man was directed to the office of John Gray.[61] Gray, a somewhat stocky, voluble, and friendly figure, had just joined the chamber as its new director of industrial growth. The man told Gray of his purpose, and asked Gray to help him assemble a basic package of information about Austin. While he could not reveal the identity of the corporation, he did tell Gray his name was Gene Tunney. That name itself later proved a fiction. Gray, of course, was delighted at the possibility that Austin could secure a major U.S. corporation, and especially thrilled because this could be the jewel to crown the decades-long effort of the chamber to recruit new industry. Gray told his visitor that he would do everything to help. He also told him that until such time as the company revealed its identity, Gray would assign it the name the XYZ Corporation.

Over the next few months, while Lochridge worked to get information for the IBM Corporation, Gray was helping its alter ego, the XYZ Corporation. Gray took Tunney on various drives through the city, showing him the residential and commercial areas. He did not spare his visitor anything. He took him on tours of the old, rich residential sites in Tarrytown, but also the area of East Austin where the poor black and brown residents lived. He got packets of information from City Hall that told about city services, utility rates, and other such things. And he introduced Tunney to a realtor in town, with whom Tunney could go about the selection of possible physical sites. His name was Hub Bechtol.[62]

Bechtol was treated to a series of special mysteries in the visits of Gene Tunney. He was told that Tunney was only a fictitious name, as was the name of the company, the XYZ Corporation. But Tunney went so far as to park blocks away from Bechtol's real estate office, and often would call Bechtol from exotic cities and countries. However much he was intrigued, Bechtol's main job was to find pieces of property, and to help Tunney get other kinds of information on Austin. Bechtol took Tunney down to City Hall to meet Mayor Lester Palmer, an associate from the Greater Austin Association and a friend. Palmer, hearing that he was dealing with a possible big-time corporation in Austin, just about did somersaults, and made every city department head freely available to work with Tunney.[63] Over the course of perhaps fifteen or twenty visits, Bechtol took Tunney to different physical sites in Austin. All the while, Lochridge also was engaged in the same activity.

Someone even contacted Neils Thompson at the university. But Thompson was to learn the real identity of the firm. His old but continuing sales pitch on behalf of the electronics firms in Austin at last had found a ready audience. Thompson made a number of trips to the Lexington, Kentucky, offices of IBM, the division that was about to create a spinoff in Austin.[64] Time and again he told IBM of the importance of engineering and science at the university. He made one other point that probably was key. He noted that the university had already bred some free enterprise ventures of its own. The most notable one was Tracor, the creation of several men who had been engaged in engineering for the Defense Research Laboratory and who one day decided to turn their ingenuity into American profits. Tracor was not the only one of these new firms. There were at least, Thompson thought, thirty, possibly forty such firms in Austin.

IBM was nothing if not cautious in its efforts to decide whether Austin would become its newest home. And Austin, through the effort of these several individuals, was nothing if not comprehensive and aggressive in its effort to land XYZ. Over the next eight months, the two consorted with one another. For the most part, IBM held the upper hand, particularly since it could tantalize Austin with its possible treats, much as any prize fish. Finally, a decision was reached at the corporate headquarters in New York. Telegrams were sent to about 150 Austin citizens, including prominent bankers, businesspeople, and public officials.[65] The recipients were asked to attend a large party on Friday, December 9, 1966, at which an important announcement would be made. The telegram was signed "IBM Corporation." When Hub Bechtol received his telegram, he knew the months of mystery were over. At the gathering, the company officials announced their intentions. The corporation would build a new plant in Austin. The site had already been selected, a section of 400 acres lying in the northern section of the city, somewhat near the Balcones Research Center.[66] Mayor Lester Palmer, delighted with the news, offered the memorable observation that "it's a proud day for Austin when the XYZ Corporation turns into IBM."[67]

The decision by IBM was, indeed, momentous. IBM was the first major U.S. corporation to come to Austin. As John Gray later would say, "There were two key decisions in my eighteen-year tenure at the chamber. One of them was the decision by IBM."[68] Within the space of just a few years, other national corporations followed IBM's lead. Soon Austin was home to Texas Instruments, Motorola, and a number of related firms, some of which would act as suppliers to IBM. The chamber no longer had to engage in a furious advertising campaign for Austin, and could divert its advertising funds to other purposes. All the years of hard work, from that of C. B. Smith to that of John Gray, seemed to have paid off.

IBM was both an end and a beginning—and it was the shape of things to come.

10.

A Big Victory for
the Men of Property

—

. . . the Supream Power cannot take from any Man any part of his Property without his own consent. For the preservation of Property [is] the end of Government, and that for which Men enter into Society. . . .

John Locke
Second Treatise on Government

THE YEAR 1968 WAS A ROUGH-AND-TUMBLE ONE IN American politics. On March 31, President Lyndon Johnson told a stunned nationwide audience of his decision not to seek re-election. Johnson's presidency had reached its low point. The antiwar troops had gained an increasing large and vocal number of adherents. Many of the most youthful had rallied behind the banner of Eugene McCarthy, a distinguished and circumspect Minnesota senator who showed the historic audacity to challenge an incumbent Democratic standard-bearer. Only weeks before Johnson's announcement, McCarthy had won forty-two percent of the vote in the New Hampshire primary election, and twenty of the twenty-four convention delegates. Johnson obviously saw the handwriting on the wall. His announcement was soon overshadowed by other, more tragic news. On April 4, Martin Luther King, Jr., the inspirational leader of the American civil rights movement, was gunned down as he stood on the balcony outside his room at a Memphis motel. The night before, King had addressed an audience of striking garbage workers and their supporters. He counseled them to keep on with the fight, and spoke with eerie prescience of how he had been to the top of the mountain and had seen the other side. Riots broke out in many large urban centers on the evening of April 4. Many homes and stores were destroyed by crowds of distraught and angry black marauders. Even in Austin, where racial tensions typically were subdued, there was some restlessness. But Mayor Harry Akin, generally thought to be a friend of the black community, kept things calm and under control by walking the streets of East Austin, and talking to citizens in bars and in neighborhoods.[1]

The volatility of 1968 did not stop there. Just two months after the death of King, his heir-apparent among the white population, Robert Kennedy, was shot dead by an assassin, Sirhan Sirhan, in the kitchen of a Los Angeles hotel. Kennedy had just come from a crowd of cheering supporters who had gathered to hear his words of hope and praise at his California primary victory celebration. Bobby Kennedy had deeply touched the hearts of black Americans as had no white person before, or since. Tousled hair flying in the wind, Kennedy seemed enormously boyish, eager, and almost poetically impassioned about improving the lot of the black poor. In Austin on the day of his death, Arthur DeWitty, the much-respected and beloved leader of the Austin black community, told Bill Petri that black Americans had suffered a loss with the death of John Kennedy, but that Bobby's death took away their heart and soul.[2] DeWitty, whose health was poor, died himself only six months later.

The violence moved from Memphis to Los Angeles, and then stormed into the streets of Chicago in August as the Democrats held their national convention. Chicago proved to be a city gone crazy, America gone wild, a political party gone berserk. The Yippies, under the leadership of Abbie Hoffman, the Students for a Democratic Society (SDS), the Weathermen, a more radical faction of the SDS, and the police all came to serious and violent confrontations, which led to bloodied skulls, arrests, and what a study commission later would call "police riots." Television viewers, who had grown accustomed to the scenes of murder and violence in the far-away lands of South Vietnam, now could see violence up close, at home, in their very midst. Surely, no one will ever forget the bizarre montage of television images, in the the large quarters of the Democratic convention center, delegates milling about, and then, a split second later, downtown in front of the Conrad Hilton where bricks were being tossed, young men and women hit over the head, bloodied bodies being carted away in police vans across scattered shards of broken store windows. The night of Wednesday, August 28, was an extraordinary moment—scary, bloody, a nation entirely undone. Everybody blew his cool, from the handsome, otherwise dignified Connecticut Senator Abraham Ribicoff, who, hearing of the violence downtown, spoke of the Gestapo tactics in the streets of Chicago, to Chicago Mayor Richard J. Daley, whose thickly stretched neck veins seemed to balloon beyond the danger point and whose lips could be seen to excoriate Ribicoff with a whole parade of names.

It was a terrible time in America, and a terrible time in Austin, too. The intensity of battle and of emotion was high-pitched. It appeared as though the nation had reached the edge of civil war—blacks against whites, liberals against conservatives, young against old, Republicans against Democrats, the propertyless against the propertied. Showdowns were happening all across the land, and Austin proved no exception. In the spring, sandwiched between the violent deaths of King and Kennedy, Austin witnessed its own confrontation. It was a battle over open housing, a struggle almost as bitter as the fight over the city charter fifteen years earlier. Three liberals on the Austin City Council—Emma Long, Dick Nichols, and Mayor Harry Akin—pushed hard for open housing. They hoped to end discrimination in the sale and/or rental of homes to blacks, browns, and other Austin minorities. And they were faced by a tough opposition, organized and led by the Board of Realtors. Many angry words were exchanged between the two sides, and not a few friends turned into enemies overnight.

Why did the Austin battle become so heated? In part, it had to do with the volatility of the times. Austin's politics reflected the sheer craziness of America. But there was more to it. The battle over open housing was fought on different levels, and its outcomes had implications for other issues. For one thing, it was a struggle between the voices on behalf of the people and those on behalf of the Establishment, a battle that had begun in the mid-1940s with the firing of Homer Rainey. Blacks and browns were knocking at the doors of the homes next door, asking to be allowed not only to visit but to live there. They, too, wanted to share in the fruits of growth, which much of the rest of Austin now shared. The Establishment, the bankers and their allies, together with many other whites, were just plain scared.

But there was even more to it; the emotion would not have been nearly so intense had there not been some deeper matters at stake. It was also a fight over governmental intervention in the economy.

This was a fight, as we have seen earlier, that began during the first days of the New Deal, when Tom Miller, E. H. Perry, and Lyndon Johnson elected to go to the side of the New Deal, much against the advice of many other businesspeople in Austin. Now that debate had resurfaced, but in a fundamentally different form. What now was at issue was whether the federal and local governments could step in to redress the conditions of those Americans who historically had been prevented from achieving the good life. At root the gains for blacks and browns, which would prove not to be substantial in any case, were deeply resented by other Americans. In Austin, that resentment was directed not merely against minorities, but against the government as well. How dare the government invade the privileged realm of private property, many businesspeople exclaimed.

In a phrase, the fight in Austin was one of civil rights against property rights. On the one hand, those who worked for the civil rights of black and brown Americans wanted to extend the benefits of America, and of Austin, to all groups. On the other hand, those who fought for property rights took the time-honored point of view that a man's property was his to do with as he pleased—and no government could tamper with such a right. The winners were the men of property. They won for good. The New Deal in Austin came to an end with the victory over the Fair Housing Ordinance in 1968, not with the election of Ronald Reagan in 1980. Thereafter, the pendulum, which had swung between federal/local intervention, on the one side, and free enterprise/private property, on the other, swung clearly over to the side of free enterprise. The victory proved to be a signal one—historic, and an omen of the opening up of Austin to the wild, almost reckless development of property in the 1970s and 1980s. It proved to be a sign that the public was willing to tolerate government regulation only so far. Beyond that point, the government would never be permitted. Beyond that point, only the forces of private enterprise would be allowed to play.

In this chapter, then, we shall learn more about the continuing efforts to enlarge the Austin polity for all residents, brown, black, and white alike. We shall also learn about the confrontation over fair housing. Just as with every other important event in Austin, this one, too, must be seen in the broad sweep of history—the development of the dream, the implementation of the dream through the efforts of realtors and the holders of private property, the continuing attempt to make the benefits of such growth available to all groups in Austin, and, finally, the bitter showdown between the agents on behalf of private property and those on behalf of public rights.

To comprehend fully the origins of the fight over fair housing, we must recall one set of events, and learn of another. The first have to do with the growing momentum on behalf of growth, and the increase, in particular, of the political forces behind growth, such as the Greater Austin Association. These forces continued to expand and to gain a prominent hegemony over Austin politics in the late 1960s. They represented one important side of the battle, the forces essentially on behalf of private property. In the midst of their development, another set grew and blossomed. These were the social and political agents that would sponsor the alternative vision, that of integration, of civil rights, of justice for both majority and minority Americans. Here let us pick up the threads of our story about integration efforts.

During the 1950s and 1960s, the efforts to integrate Austin continued, stimulated in part by Hemann Sweatt's victory and the integration of the University of Texas. Arthur DeWitty and Bill Kirk remained in the forefront of this work, particularly the former. For much of this time, DeWitty worked within the black community. He spent countless hours listening to the complaints of his fellow black citizens, seeking to console them, helping to make them aware of the political channels through which their grievances might be redressed.[3] During this time, too, DeWitty helped to found the Travis County Voters League, a black group that sought to educate residents of East Austin about their political rights.[4] The league with the help of liberal Democrats, labored long and hard to get black voters to pay the poll tax, an anachronistic nuisance from the nineteenth century that cost anywhere from $1.50 to $2.50 and effectively prevented black, Hispanic, and poor voters from participating in elections.[5] The league became the device through which DeWitty and his black cohorts would seek to shape the black vote, and thus also became the target of many white candidates who sought the endorsement of the black community.[6]

DeWitty took the concerns of black Austinites before the City Council on many occasions during the 1950s, much as Everett Givens had done earlier. By this time, the career of Givens was on the wane, that of DeWitty on the rise. Givens had become for many black residents nothing more than an Uncle Tom.[7] Moreover,

DeWitty sought to redress black grievances against the system through emphasizing greater social justice and fairness, not material gains as Givens had years before.

A good example took place at the council meeting held on July 16, 1953. DeWitty appeared to complain about the unfair treatment Austin blacks had received at the hands of the police department. He informed council members of several recent cases in which blacks had been accused of raping white women and had been subjected to harsh physical mistreatment by police officers even before their cases had come to trial. Members of the white community who were accused of committing similar acts against black citizens, DeWitty continued, were treated far better. "We had a clear case of rape by a white man upon a twelve-year-old girl," he told council members:

> She was run into the streets absolutely nude. Upon examination by the doctors she showed evidence that she had been tampered with, but officers through the District Attorney's office persuaded the girl's mother to permit them to carry the child to John Sealy Hospital at Galveston and remained there for three days. Finally a report came back that the child is a victim of Illusionary Epilepsy. Despite the fact that the child is an A-class student and has no days absent on her card, the man went free. All of this adds up to tremendous mis-application of justice and cannot be ignored by any intelligent citizen. Such action gives cause for one to face the realities of a dual system of justice based upon one law.[8]

Time after time, DeWitty hammered home this theme of dual justice, hoping, in effect, to replace one vision for Austin with another.

Another episode took place on February 16, 1956, when DeWitty and a number of his East Austin colleagues, including Bill Kirk, showed up in the council chambers to inquire whether Jim Crow statutes were about to end in Austin. Earlier in February, Mrs. Howelen Bunton Taylor, a black citizen, had boarded one of the city buses and had refused to sit in the section assigned for "colored" riders.[9] Her effort was an obvious imitation of similar actions then underway in Montgomery, Alabama, where a bus boycott had begun under the leadership of a young black minister, Martin Luther King, Jr. In Austin, Mrs. Taylor had been arrested and taken to civil court. The case against her suddenly was dropped. The judge, Tom Blackwell, claimed he believed the 1954 Supreme Court decision that led to school desegregation effectively had invalidated the Jim Crow statute on buses.

The black residents supported the interpretation of Judge Blackwell, and argued that black riders in Austin should be permitted to
sit anywhere they pleased. Bill Kirk made the additional point that
it was a great inconvenience for him to have to sit apart from his
white friends once he boarded the bus.[10] But the council felt it
necessary to obey the state statute that upheld segregation on public
vehicles. Emma Long, the friend of Arthur DeWitty and the black
community of Austin, sided with the legal interpretation of the state
law, and claimed that even though the law might be regarded as
morally improper, it remained the law nevertheless.[11] DeWitty,
Kirk, and the other black residents were furious. Days later, DeWitty
warned Emma in his regular *Houston Informer* column that "all of
Travis County knows that without the Negro vote both Mrs. Long
and Mr. White would have gone off the Council in 1953."[12] The
buses remained segregated nonetheless.

By the early 1960s, the campaign to break down the racial barriers
in Austin had picked up, and the targets of the campaign had broadened to include restaurants and other eating places. Other actors
now became involved in attacks on segregation. A major episode
began in early 1963.[13] Black students at the Huston and Tillotson
campuses in East Austin decided to embark on an all-out effort to
defeat segregation in Austin's restaurants. Before they were able to
get their campaign underway, Bill Kirk intervened.[14] He decided it
would be best to settle the matter peaceably. Kirk got on the phone
and spoke to several Austin residents. He urged meetings among
blacks and whites, and asked their support for the effort to open
Austin's restaurants to all residents, regardless of color. Among those
people with whom he spoke were the Reverend Bob Bryan, a longtime friend and fellow civil rights activist, E. W. Jackson, a banker
and prominent businessman whose support was often sought in difficult community problems, and Harry Akin, the owner of the Night
Hawk Restaurants. Akin's voice was to prove the most important.
   Akin was a rather interesting anomaly in Austin, something like
Mayor Miller or E. H. Perry in previous epochs. He had begun his
adult life as an entertainer, and had hoped to make it big in Holly-
wood. He did not, however, and so made his way in 1931 to Austin,
where he decided to try his hand at something else.[15] He opened a
small restaurant on Congress Avenue, just south of the Congress
Avenue Bridge. This first establishment was small and had just a
couple of employees. The volume of business rose quickly, helped in

no small measure by a unique hamburger, the Frisco, so named because of Akin's affection for the California city.[16] Akin's affections also extended to other places, even to people. Thus, in 1932, much contrary to the practice of other Austin businesspeople, Akin hired a black man, Isaac Craig, to work in the kitchen as a cook.[17] Craig proved to be so exceptional that Akin soon made him manager of the restaurant. There was one problem, however. Akin sensed that his business would fall off considerably in this bastion of Old Dixie if Craig managed the business in the main quarters. Thus, for years Craig served as the manager of the restaurant from the kitchen. Akin and Craig only let this little story out years later, when both racial prejudice and the fires of civil rights confrontations had subsided.[18]

Akin received the phone call from Bill Kirk at a most propitious time. That spring he had attended a meeting at the White House, convened by President John Kennedy to discuss the racial crisis in America.[19] Akin was not only a successful restaurateur, but also had risen to become president of the National Restaurant Association. It was in that capacity that Kennedy had sought him out. Kennedy urged Akin and other officials of the Restaurant Association to do anything in their power to dampen the racial passions. He said restaurants, like other public facilities, should become open to people of all races, and that segregation had to be eliminated as the informal law of the land.[20]

Akin, already predisposed in the same direction, came back to Austin ready to do whatever he could to implement Kennedy's wishes. Meetings were held, with Akin, Kirk, Jackson, and Edmund Heinsohn, minister of the University United Methodist Church, in attendance.[21] The participants all agreed that it was important to bring about the integration of Austin's restaurants. Akin offered to take the first step. He informed the others that he would open his Night Hawk Restaurant near the university, at Nineteenth and Guadalupe, to any student who showed a university identification card.[22] Black UT students, in other words, could be served merely by showing their cards. Within a short space of time, Akin's steps were followed by similar actions at other Austin eating places. Only a few downtown restaurants held out. White's Pharmacy, at the corner of Sixth and Congress, long the scourge of black residents who had to gather outside to await transportation to East Austin, tore out its stools rather than serve black customers.[23] And Scarbroughs, which maintained practices of segregation through the early

1960s, completely shut down its restaurant.[24] Old Dixie was not dead yet.

At just about this very moment, the strongest attack yet on segregation in Austin emerged in other quarters. In March, the Citizens' Committee for a Human Relations Ordinance, comprised of a number of black Austin residents, decided to confront segregation head-on.[25] The members of the group concluded that it would be a good idea to develop a human relations commission in Austin, one that would seek to implement desegregation in the full gamut of Austin's public facilities, even its businesses. Obviously they were willing to tread on very dangerous, even sacred, territory. The group asked Professor Joseph Witherspoon, of the University of Texas Law School, to help draft a design for such a commission as well as an ordinance that would outlaw segregation.[26] Witherspoon had been through a couple of interesting civil rights cases in Austin. In the late 1940s, he had been a member of the group that successfully halted the practice of restrictive covenants designed to keep Jewish residents from living in Rollingwood, a suburb of Austin.[27] Witherspoon soon helped the Citizens' Committee to develop a plan to implement an ordinance similar to one recently passed in El Paso, Texas.[28] This ordinance imposed criminal penalties on any business that practiced segregation. Witherspoon believed the criminal penalties were too severe, thus incapable of enforcement through the court system. Instead he urged some kind of civil devices, and argued for an adjudicative process of persuasion and negotiation.

Witherspoon, the Citizens' Committee, and other people also held a series of public meetings at which they sought to hammer out the purposes and designs of their plans. The whole thing was a long, drawn-out affair, one that sought the opinions of many residents. Several workshop meetings were held with members of the City Council. The Citizens' Committee hoped to reach some kind of agreement with the council on a responsible and feasible ordinance. The council members listened closely to the concerns of the black residents. They heard the plans for an ordinance, and the advisabilty of seeking legal means to implement desegregation in Austin. But they also balked at the proposals. Their counterarguments were more or less the standard repertoire.

Some council members—but not Emma Long—argued that the problem of racial discrimination was a moral, not a legal, one. Therefore, it could only be solved as the moral enlightenment of the community improved.[29] Others noted that voluntary efforts to integrate public facilities were already underway, the most notable being that of the recent integration at Harry Akin's Night Hawk Restaurant and other eating establishments. But the most compelling argument dealt with the property rights of men and women in business. Several people claimed that the "use of law to compel businessmen or professional men serving the public generally to deal with the Negro is an unwarranted interference with the right of these people to conduct their affairs and to use their private property as they see fit."[30] This argument hit close to the genuine concerns of the business community.

After more meetings and discussion over the issue, a public meeting was held in the council chambers on the afternoon of December 19, 1963.[31] The meeting was long, packed with people, emotional, and noisy. Mayor Lester Palmer, a rather gentle person who was the manager of Calcasieu Lumber Company, a leading local business, presided. Witherspoon, speaking for the Citizens' Committee, presented a clear, powerful case. He relied on the many months of discussion to argue on behalf of a civil rights ordinance and a commission that would seek to implement the ordinance. It soon became clear to Witherspoon that the mayor and the city attorney had decided against an ordinance.[32] The city attorney, Doren Eskew, observed that such an ordinance would not be constitutional. His view, of course, ran counter to that of Witherspoon.

Toward the end of the meeting, Harry Akin rose and made the most courageous declaration of his life.[33] He told his fellow businesspeople that while he agreed with the sentiment on behalf of voluntary compliance with integration, this would no longer prove sufficient. Too many businesses in Austin still did not freely and openly cater to black and brown customers. Therefore, he argued, legal means must be used. He went on to say he believed that a human relations commission was the perfect solution, and that such a commission would provide an open and fair forum in which complaints about discrimination could be heard and resolved. Akin's outspoken stand did little to endear him to the businesspeople in the audience. Soon he, his restaurant, and even his family life would feel the effects.[34]

At the conclusion, Mayor Palmer and the other council members, urged on by Emma Long, decided to create a temporary human relations commission, consisting of seven members, with Akin appointed as chairman.[35] The purpose of the commission, according to the council, would be to conduct a survey of Austin business practices, and of its citizens, in order to determine the extent of segregation. For the next few months, this temporary commission met. It assembled a vast amount of information about discrimination in Austin. On March 12, the commission reconvened, together with members of the City Council.[36] Akin reported that he and his fellow commission members had discovered that there indeed was widespread segregation still present in Austin. Only somewhat more than half of the restaurants in Austin were integrated. Hotels and motels also heavily discriminated against blacks and browns. The facts obviously were pretty alarming, and seemed to indicate the plans of the Citizens' Committee and Joe Witherspoon ought to be implemented immediately. Akin and his commission members endorsed this strategy. But the council members—in particular, Mayor Palmer—were not at all convinced. Most, save for Emma Long, rejected the recommendation of Akin, and thus came out on the side of Austin's business community. It was a sorry day for civil rights in Austin. Something had to happen. It did.

Volma Overton, the head of the local chapter of the National Association for the Advancement of Colored People (NAACP), now moved to center-stage. Overton and a number of other members of the NAACP appeared before the council at its meeting of March 26.[37] Overton claimed that the El Paso Ordinance, which had been the basis for the original demands of the Citizens' Committee, was perfectly constitutional. Therefore, he argued, it should be enacted immediately in Austin. He maintained that no progress could be made unless Austin was able to enforce its demands for integration. Voluntary compliance, by itself, would not work. He hinted, moreover, that the NAACP was now prepared to take more radical action if the council failed to enact appropriate legislation. Mayor Palmer reacted with anger. He argued that the threat of pressure would do no good. He counseled patience, and urged that communications be kept open between the NAACP and the council.[38]

Palmer's counsel proved futile. At the council session one week later, Overton, Claude Allen, a white instructor at Huston-Tillotson, the Reverend Wesley Sims, Booker T. Bonner, a veteran of many civil rights demonstrations, and Arthur DeWitty all showed up in the chambers.[39] At 10 o'clock that morning, Volma Overton launched into a wordy tirade against prejudice and discrimination. He began

by reading from the work of John Howard Griffin, *Black Like Me.*
Griffin, a white journalist, had taken a drug that darkened his skin,
and then traveled throughout the South, pretending he was a black
man. He hoped to experience what it felt like to be black in America.
His story was not a pretty one. Overton used it to convey the years
of mistreatment that black people suffered in the United States. At
the afternoon session, and then well into the evening, the filibuster
continued. Allen took the floor and demanded the council pass an
ordinance even stronger than the El Paso one. On and on the talking
and reading continued, stretching beyond hours into days. Through
it all, most of the council members remained in the room. University
of Texas students appeared on the steps of City Hall, picketing on
behalf of the filibusters. The folksinger Joan Baez, who happened to
be in Austin for a concert, even came down to demonstrate her sympathy and alliance with Overton and others.[40]

By Thursday, April 9, the filibuster had gained statewide attention.
Nothing like it had ever happened before. Austin had come up with
its own brand of racial protest. Lester Palmer was now in the hospital, a victim of what the papers called extreme exhaustion.[41] Even
Volma Overton had taken ill. Mayor Pro-Tem Travis LaRue recessed
the regular council meeting, and then the Reverend Sims assumed
the mayor's place at the council table. He held forth as mayor pro-
tem, so declared, he claimed, by the NAACP. While the filibuster
continued, other segments of the community came into play. The
Daily Texan, for example, refused to endorse the filibuster, claiming
it to be far too radical.[42] Ironically, the conservative Austin Junior
Chamber of Commerce, under the leadership of Maurice Quigley,
decided to act on its own, and tried to corral 7,000 signatures on a
petition that demanded an antidiscrimintaion ordinance in
Austin.[43] For the next week, the demonstration dragged on. The
tempers and nerves of all participants soon gave out. By April 16, two
full weeks after it had begun, the filibuster came to an abrupt end.
Booker Bonner had taken over the regular council meeting scheduled
for that day. He was ruled out of order by Mayor Pro-Tem Travis
LaRue. Refusing to abandon his seat, Bonner was ejected from the
council chambers.[44] The meeting was then adjourned. That afternoon, the council reconvened for one minute, only to have LaRue
immediately adjourn the session. Soon thereafter, a spokesman for
the NAACP called a halt to the filibuster, but demanded some positive action from the council. Ten days later, the NAACP also held

a rally in Givens Park in East Austin, and all in attendance heard the speakers decry prejudice and discrimination in Austin.[45]

The council finally was prompted to act on May 13. Members had given in to the demands of the NAACP, and had established an Austin Human Relations Commission, something that Emma Long had supported all the while.[46] Its purpose would be to investigate and to settle civil rights problems. But there would be no penalties for the infringement of civil rights, as the El Paso ordinance ordered. Voluntary compliance and negotiation between disputants were all that was required. Overton and the NAACP quickly claimed that the Austin commission was a watered-down version of what they wanted, and therefore they could not support it. That was not the end of it. The council also appointed seven members to the new commission. They included the longtime civil rights proponent Edmund Heinsohn, and J. C. Kelam, an old friend of Lyndon Johnson who ran his radio station in Austin. The commission also included Virgil Lott, the only black appointee. Emma Long was upset at its composition, claiming it did not represent the full variety and body of Austin citizens. She thus refused to endorse the appointments. Only days later, six members of the commission resigned. The only one to remain was Virgil Lott.[47]

An uneasy peace now set in. Overton and the NAACP continued to press for some kind of commission. The council was divided. Its members hoped for a way to salvage its work. Lyndon Johnson gave them all hope. In July he signed a Civil Rights Act, the first far-reaching legislation on civil rights in more than a century. Palmer and his fellow council members expected this would free them from their dilemma. But the act provided for no specific measures of implementation. The matter in Austin continued at an impasse for the next two years.

The article was brief. Written by Stuart Long, it informed readers of the *Washington Post* that Austin had established a Human Relations Commission, as an arm of city government, on Thursday, October 5, 1967.[48] The article noted that the City Council also had declared itself in favor of an open housing ordinance. The report of this local event in the pages of the *Post* obviously was intended for the eyes of President Johnson, who was Stuart's friend, as well as for many of his critics who might have found political ammunition in Austin's failure to implement the Johnson civil rights policies. The action itself was highly significant. After three years of battling over how to proceed to implement integration policies, the Austin City Council finally had come up with a feasible plan. In large part the council's decision was the product of its new composition. In the April 1967 election, three liberal members were voted into office, a majority. They were Emma Long, Dick Nichols, a realtor, and Harry Akin. Akin was also elected mayor by his fellow council members.

The council charged the new Human Relations Commission with promoting an appreciation of the responsibilities of citizenship among all races, and with discouraging by all lawful means any attempt to abridge the rights of individual citizens.[49] The commission possessed its own executive director, Charles Miles, a veteran of many civil rights struggles, and a graduate of the University of Texas. It also had a very large board of directors, designed obviously to appease Emma and others who were concerned about its representation of the public. Tom Black, a local attorney and strong liberal, was the chairman. Others included Volma Overton, several Mexican American residents, Sue McBee, wife of an executive of the Tracor Corporation, and Jack Otis, professor of social work at the University of Texas. By and large, all the members of the commission were deeply committed to liberal policies, and willing to back any efforts to promote integration in Austin.[50]

Although the commission was intended to handle all manner of civil rights disputes, its *raison d'être* during the first year was to carry through with an open housing ordinance. The discussion of such an ordinance, and how it might work, fully occupied the energies of the Board of Directors. Month after month they met, seeking to develop an ordinance that would end discrimination against minorities yet also not offend the larger white public.[51] The board learned that discrimination in the sale and/or rental of homes in Austin and nearby communities was widespread. One estimate claimed that at least thirty different apartment complexes would not rent units to black or brown residents.[52] Officials at Bergstrom Air Force Base, just on the southern outskirts of Austin, often complained about this situation. They were concerned that many of their officers and servicemen simply could not locate suitable housing in Austin for their families. The situation so provoked Volma Overton that in August 1967 he wrote a letter of complaint to Robert McNamara, then United States secretary of defense. He told McNamara of the considerable segregated housing in Austin, asking that "the government impose off-limits housing sanctions on this area . . ." and that "further federal spending on construction at Bergstrom AFB be suspended until the Austin community takes steps to stop subjecting military personnel to discrimination in housing."[53]

All the while that the commission's board was meeting to draft a workable ordinance, two other events conspired to affect the outcome of its proposal. In Washington the federal government had worked out its own open housing ordinance. The ordinance, which had been enacted in January 1968, prohibited racial, religious, or other forms of discrimination in the sale and/or rental of property. Moreover, it provided that complaints of discrimination could be taken to the federal authorities, who, in turn, would seek resolution of the disputes through local courts. Finally, the federal open housing law would go into effect in three separate stages, the last stage to occur on January 1, 1970, when it became binding on the sale of private homes. At the same time, the Austin Board of Realtors, under the leadership of Hub Bechtol, was keeping a close eye on the development of the local ordinance. Bechtol and other officials of the Board of Realtors had put in an appearance when the City Council first created the Human Relations Commission in October, and they had then agreed in principle to an open housing ordinance for Austin.[54] Their interest in the nature of the local ordinance did not abate; in fact, as the moment of its presentation to the council drew closer, members of the Board of Realtors grew increasingly anxious.

The local open housing ordinance drafted by the Human Relations Commission differed from the federal law in two important respects. First, if and when passed, it would become immediately binding on local residents. Second, it called for all conciliation and adjudication to occur at the local level, thereby bypassing the time and effort required to work through federal officials.[55] Both measures obviously were designed to speed up the demise of the practices of racial discrimination in the sale and/or rental of Austin housing. The official Austin Fair Housing Ordinance was first presented to the City Council at its meeting of May 9, 1967. A number of prominent realtors were in the audience, including Bechtol, Nelson Puett, and George Sandlin. The council members listened to the arguments on behalf of the ordinance from members of the Human Relations Commissions's Board. They also heard comments from realtors in the audience, a number of them now opposed to its passage. When the vote was taken, the council passed the ordinance by a vote of three to two, with Long, Nichols, and Akin in favor, and Travis LaRue and Ralph James opposed.[56] The realtors were mad as hell. Nelson Puett told reporters that the proposed local ordinance "won't help racial problems. . . . This is just another skirmish between those who believe the government should own or control everything."[57] And Hub Bechtol added that "we [the realtors] are . . . dedicated to preserving the right of private property."[58]

Things turned quickly from bad to worse. All the racial tensions and political turmoil that had been submerged since the 1964 council filibuster now burst into the open with even greater fury. Bechtol and other officials of the Board of Realtors began to make noises about preventing the passage of the ordinance. The council, and in particular the three liberal proponents, moved to push the ordinance through. As is customary in any legislation enacted by the Austin council, there must be three readings, or decisions, taken on any single proposed ordinance. Two more readings were necessary to make the Human Relations Commission draft into a full-scale housing ordinance. A second reading was taken on May 16, and the ordinance passed again by the same vote of three to two. And just to make sure that no realtor would throw any wrench into the works, Emma, Dick, and Harry took the third and final reading the very next day.[59] The ordinance was now on the books. It would go into effect on May 27.

The Board of Realtors grew more furious. They let others know just how angry they were with a series of advertisements in the *Austin American*. They called the new ordinance "forced public housing."[60] They also decided to take an extraordinary measure. In the long history of Austin politics, there have been very few successful referenda. A referendum can occur only if a sufficient number of citizens proclaim their discontent with a council action. The Board of Realtors elected to go this route. More advertisements now appeared in the paper, asking citizens to support a referendum on the Fair Housing Ordinance. Emma was singled out as the devil in the debate. She was quoted as expressing her own fears over a straw vote on open housing.[61] The advertisements also repeated the long-standing concern of the realtors themselves. They said that unless "approximately 9,000 citizens sign the petition in the next few days some of your property rights will be gone forever."[62] Even announcers on the radio were roped into the campaign, with favorite radio personality Arlie Duff lobbying on behalf of the realtors' petition.[63]

The effect of this campaign was nothing short of remarkable. In the space of ten short days, the opponents of the ordinance had secured 27,000 signatures on their petition. The figure represented just under one-third of the Austin *eligible* electorate. It represented almost as many voters as would normally show up for a city election. No petition before, or afterward, would gain as many signatures. Obviously the Board of Realtors had struck a responsive chord in the public.

Within days virtually all of the 27,000 signatures had been confirmed as legitimate by the city clerk. In fact, only something under 1,000 of them proved to have been unregistered voters. Once they were certified, the petition took effect. The ordinance now became null and void. But the battle was by no means over. The council proponents, and many of their supporters, were as bitter as the Board of Realtors. Dick Nichols already had voiced his concerns, noting that Bechtol and Puett had put economic pressure on him, urging clients to discontinue real estate transactions with him.[64] The council continued to meet on the matter, and by mid-July had developed an alternative ordinance that contained certain revisions of the original. Once more, Emma, Dick, and Harry pushed through the revised Fair Housing Ordinance. Even this one failed to satisfy Bechtol and the Board of Realtors. Moreover, they claimed that the three liberals had played unfair because the new ordinance was not subject to public vote as the first one had been.[65] The three council members finally decided it would be best if voters were given a chance to voice their views in a public referendum on open housing. An election was held on October 19. Over 24,000 people showed up at the polls. Their final vote confirmed the view of the Board of Realtors. Austin voters turned down a Fair Housing Ordinance by a vote of 13,913 to 10,391.[66]

It was time for opponents to gloat, for proponents to concede defeat. Two days after the election, the council convened in its chambers. A large and noisy group of realtors was there to meet them. Akin spoke first. He said he made "no concession or accept[ed] no compromise where principles relating to the Ordinance are concerned." He also urged that the realtors adhere to the guidelines of the federal housing law.[67] Nelson Puett stood. He said he had a statement he wanted to enter into the record. He then told the council members and his fellow realtors that he had urged a public vote before the May passage of the first Austin Fair Housing Ordinance. He also took delight in the fact that the victory over the ordinance had been secured despite its endorsement by local television stations, the three council members, and even the local Council of Churches. He concluded by observing that it was a "glorious thing that the people of Austin were able to see what the issue was—the right to private property against those who wanted to dilute the rights of private property."[68]

The Board of Realtors, and all those who supported the system of free enterprise over government regulation, had won the battle. Months later, they also won the war. In April 1969, City Council elections were held. Three incumbents were voted out of office— Harry Akin, Dick Nichols, and Emma Long. Dick Nichols returned to run for office again in 1971 and was elected. But for Harry and Emma, the 1969 election was their last hurrah.

11.

Challenging the Dream

The liberals have evolved in fifteen years. . . . [Now we] are highly skilled at being able to acquire power. We're still growing up on how to use it. . . . The conservatives that we were fighting understood how to use it. . . . Old Tom Miller, he knew how to get power and how to use it.[1]

Robert "Peck" Young

FRIDAY, MAY 8, 1970: 25,000 PEOPLE CROWDED THE streets of downtown Austin, the largest outpouring of demonstrators ever to assemble on these streets. Marching ten abreast, they paraded down the Drag, greeted by cheers on one side of the street, and jeers on the other. They were there because of what happened four days earlier. On that particular Monday, on the grounds of Kent State University, there had been another crowd, one of marching, chanting students. They were rallying against the war in Vietnam, and against President Nixon's recent decision to invade Cambodia. Weaving up and down several hills on campus, the marchers finally faced a long line of very determined and very hostile National Guard troops. Something happened, something went wrong. Tear gas canisters flew, people screamed. Shots were fired from the rifles of the troops. As the white mists cleared, four students lay dead. Now, on Friday, people were marching in Austin. They had been easy to assemble. Many different sorts of people, who until then had stood on the sidelines, distant from yet distraught because of the constant battering of terrible news from abroad, joined the march. Four innocent students, like those attending the University of Texas, had been shot. The war had finally come home. Until the last hour, the council had refused a parade permit to the marchers. Then Jeff Friedman, a University of Texas Law School student, and several other students had managed to prevail over the council's wishes and to secure an injunction against their action from Federal Judge Jack Roberts.

Friedman was in the crowd that day.[2] A large, physically overpowering man, whose thick black hair barely disguised a receding hairline, he was thrust into the limelight of this event. Days earlier, at the first demonstration after the Kent State shootings, Friedman had intervened between student marchers and Austin police at the university entrance to campus on Nineteenth Street. The students had attended a rally on the grounds of the State Capitol and were on their way back to the safety of the campus. As they marched, they taunted the police, throwing rocks at them, calling them "pigs." It looked like all hell would break loose just as the students reached the university guard house. But Friedman, who had spent time observing Austin police at work and had become friends with a few officers, managed to calm everyone. He persuaded one of the officers, Captain George Phyfer, to ignore the students' taunts and, at the same time, convinced the students to retreat to the inner portions of the university grounds.

Another law school student was also among the marchers. Virtually the physical opposite of Friedman, Bob Binder remained in the background of that day's events.[3] In about a year's time, however, he would move directly to center-stage of the student community and become president of the UT student body. Binder was much like a number of other students, a recent convert to the antiwar, anti-Establishment cause. Child of a career military man, Binder had served several years in Vietnam as an officer. The war left deep scars on his soul, as deep, perhaps, as on anyone. While in the heat of battle, he wondered why "we were killing these innocent people. . . . They didn't know a Vietnam existed. They didn't know what electricity was . . . . They fished their fish up, they had their kids, they lived, they died."[4] Binder had not come up with a satisfying answer to the war and the killings, an easy rationalization. Saddened by the tragedy at Kent State, angered by what the National Guard did, Binder was on the streets, ready to fight against the established forces of Austin, and the nation.

Robert "Peck" Young and Dean Rindy were somewhere there, too, though in different parts. Young eventually found his way up to the stage at the Capitol where speeches were taking place.[5] He helped to keep a lid on the emotions, and was somewhat amazed when some crazed soul threw himself at his feet and started talking about how great the whole event was. Young was anything but crazed, a cool head and quick wit in times when cool heads and quick wits were needed. Unlike most of the other demonstrators, he was a native of Austin. His daddy grew up in Austin, worked as a sign painter, but also spent a lot of time engaged in local politics. Young took to politics easily. At Austin High School, he had been active in debate and school government, often taking on the more staid and affluent Robert Brooks, son of Max and Marietta Brooks. Max, of course, was the protégé of Commodore Perry.[6] Young's were the politics of the New Dealers and the Great Society, and he believed himself to stand as heir to the likes of Emma and Stuart Long, Creekmore and Adelle Fath, and others of the old populists. His heroes were Lyndon Johnson and, especially, Tom Miller, whom he remembered as the "people's mayor." During the course of the demonstration, he helped to shepherd marchers into some kind of organized parade. As he assisted and watched the marchers, "it crystallized in my mind . . . that if we could get 20,000 of these people to march, I didn't need but about 5,000 of them and I could — up a city election real bad."[7]

Rindy was less involved that day than Young, but equally moved by the mass of humanity.[8] A tall, thin, and handsome skeptic, who some years later would take the nickname of "Buck" and publish tough political satire in the pages of the *Austin Sun*, Rindy had developed into a critic of the war, and of Frank Erwin, too, the *major domo* and chairman of the University of Texas Board of Regents. Rindy thought that Erwin had a lot to do with all the students at the march, particularly since Erwin recently had engaged in such outrageous acts as bulldozing some students out of trees at nearby Waller Creek. Frank and the university had wanted to build some concrete enterprise there, and nothing, not even trees or students, would stand in the way. Two years down the road, Rindy would run an unsuccessful campaign for state representative. But he was snagged by the lure of political activism and, among other things, eventually joined Binder as a friend and a political consultant.

Elsewhere there were a few other notable figures among the many thousands on the streets. Roger Duncan, a young university undergraduate from a small Texas town, was somewhere, dodging police and enjoying himself enormously.[9] Duncan's greatest thrill was to move up and down alleyways, narrowly missing being captured by the authorities. He was a novice at politics, and not as totally caught up in the somber mood of the event as some others. It was the sheer excitement of it all that got to him. In two years' time, he would become active in the Travis County campaign on behalf of presidential candidate George McGovern, and shortly thereafter he would rise quickly to become the chairman of the South Austin Democrats. Ed Wendler, Sr., was also among the masses of demonstrators.[10] Roughly twice as old as most of the students, Wendler had an interesting career as a lobbyist at the State Capitol. And a lucrative one as well. At midlife, he decided to embark on a different pursuit altogether. He saw his own future in the future of young people and in liberal politics in Austin. And so he was there that day, on the front lines, showing his sympathy with the student cause. And, perhaps, anger at the senseless killings at Kent State as well. Also a hometown boy, Wendler was the director of the Texas Intercollegiate Students' Association, and soon would acquire two key protégés from among the Texas students of the 1970s—Gary Mauro, student body president at Texas A&M University, and Roy Spence, an illustrious graduate of the University of Texas. Wendler's brother, Ken, was also very active in local politics. The two men soon would emerge as the Cain and Abel of Austin, bitterly battling one another in a whole array of electoral contests. Ed Wendler was uncommonly canny, liberal, and obviously knew where the action was.

These several individuals were about to become key players in the Austin politics of the 1970s, and beyond. The demonstration that day was something of a turning point for them. Peck Young realized that students could be used as an effective political force to battle the conservatives. Jeff Friedman had been suddenly cast into a very visible place in the student community and would use it to his advantage. And Roger Duncan loved the political excitement. The march was more than a turning-point in the lives of these few people, however. It marked a turning-point, too, for Austin, and it set the stage for what would become an ongoing series of challenges to the dream of growth and expansion of Austin.

This chapter relates the story of these challenges, and how, in particular they culminated in the watershed council election of 1975, in which the majority of those elected were liberals. It also tells how challenge spread throughout Austin in the 1970s, springing up among students at the University of Texas, members of environmental groups such as the Sierra Club, and many, many neighborhood associations. No decade in the history of Austin has ever displayed so much popular discontent. Nor has any decade offered as much hope to those who have promoted the other dream for Austin, that of full-scale democracry. The challenges of the 1970s, though superficially different in content, were roughly the same in form – all were designed to impede, alter, or just plain water-down the Wooldridge dream of unlimited expansion for the city of Austin. The tale, in brief, is one of the continuing battle between the forces on behalf of expansion and those on behalf of the people.

The first challenge began on the University of Texas campus, developing almost naturally from the inner-workings of the Kent State demonstraton. Some students urged the university community to move in a radical direction, to attack the Austin establishment at its very core, at jobs, among the working classes. They included people like Jeff Jones, who would soon become a radical legend on campus, and Pat Cuney.[11] Others pressed for a moderate stance, to promote modest reforms within the city. Peck Young and Jeff Friedman stood in the ranks of these students. And they were the first to act. Young and Friedman, together with fellow university students Betsy Palmer, Margaret Moore, Dean Rindy, and a handful of others, decided in the late summer of 1970 to put the student body to good use.[12] Meeting in a small room of the Student Union, the group agreed on a simple strategy. They would develop a special effort to get the thousands of university students to register in Travis County as voters. The idea would be to use this constituency to win liberal seats on the City Council. An earlier effort to do the same thing had failed. But then the moment seemed inappropriate. Now the time was right. A new federal law was about to go into effect, lowering the nationwide voting age from twenty-one to eighteen years old. Now that the students had the franchise, they should do something with it.

The major obstacle that the campaign for student registration faced was one of establishing the legal residency of a student. Until that time, students had naturally been considered residents of the home and town where their parents lived. Young and Friedman realized that a certain latitude was evident in the interpretation of the law regarding voter's residence. Although the nominal criterion of a certain time of residence in a particular place could easily be met, the more important criterion had to do with whether a person would qualify as a permanent resident of a given locale. Could University of Texas students, in particular, qualify as permanent residents of Travis County? Friedman, using his newly acquired legal knowledge, set about trying to resolve the question in a manner favorable to the student registration effort. First, he realized that the matter boiled down to the "intentions" of a person.[13] The law read that a "student shall not be considered to have acquired residence at the place where he lives while he attends school unless he *intends* to remain there and to make that place his home indefinitely after he ceases to be a student." Thus, if students were willing to proclaim that they "intended" to remain as permanent residents of Travis County after graduation from the university, they would qualify as voters. The real key to the problem would be to secure the cooperation of Fritz Robinson, Travic County assessor-collector. If Robinson were to accept a student's declaration of "intentions" to remain a permanent resident of Travis County, the matter would be settled. Young and Friedman both consulted with Robinson, and managed to get his consent to accept students' declarations at their face value.

Once this issue was settled, the campaign to register students began in earnest. Working with demographic information on the student body, the registration project determined that a maximum figure of 15,000 could be registered to vote in Travis County. That was a sizable number, considering that in most local elections the total turnout had been an average of 35,000 voters in recent years. The registration campaign evolved over the next several months. Speakers were sent out to various locations across campus. Advertisements were put in the *Daily Texan*, and posters placed in strategic locations. The *Daily Texan* editorial board, which included some of the more radical campus voices, offered only indifferent help to the campaign.[14] But this proved no problem. Over 14,000 students eventually were registered to vote in Travis County, an increase of seventy percent over the previous student registration. Moreover, voter registration in other parts of the city was on a decline. Obviously, the students now stood a good chance of "— —ing up a city election real bad." But registration represented only the first step. Another, more important, one was to come.

Jeff Friedman decided sometime in the spring of 1970 that he would run for a seat on the City Council. A few other students had done so in the past, but no one was quite so serious about the effort as

Friedman. He did not think he would win, but he did believe he could bring some important issues to the attention of the local public.[15] He knew, as a result of the registration campaign, that students could be mobilized to take part in elections. He also had strong opinions on some important issues of the day. He wanted things to be better in East Austin for the browns and the blacks. He wanted the poor people to have better jobs and better housing. But he also wanted to defeat the forces of the Establishment. He wanted to bring down the rich and the powerful. In particular, he targeted the Greater Austin Association as his enemy. By running against the Association and all it stood for, and by running on a platform of strong liberal ideals, he thought he could mobilize a sizable segment of Austin citizens.

Friedman was not the only liberal challenger to run. There were a handful of others as well. The incumbent council, under the leadership of Mayor Travis LaRue, had been thought a travesty, even by conservatives.[16] Most members were regarded as racists, owing to the fallout over the 1968 fair housing campaign, and they had been perceived as generally incapable of city leadership. Among other things, they bungled the city bus service. They had brought in a firm to provide public transit, and it had employed some second-rate school buses. As it turned out later, the firm had secured the contracts as the result of a nice little Texas elk hunt they took council members on.[17] The liberals, of course, were up in arms about the council, and about LaRue, in particular. Oat Willie, colorful owner of a local dry goods store, ran for mayor. The position was now open for at-large election, previously having been determined only after election by the council members themselves. Pericles Criss was another liberal challenger who decided to run for office. Manager of a local movie theatre, Criss was thought by many citizens to be among the most enlightened and progressive of all the candidates. Several minority candidates also offered themselves. They included Al Mendez, a Chicano businessman, and Berl Handcox, a black man employed as a personnel manager by IBM.

Even the businessmen who ran in the 1971 council race represented some fresh blood. There were people like Dr. S. H. "Bud" Dryden, a local physician who was much admired by many people. Dryden, however, seemed to have very little knowledge about city politics. Then there was Dan Love, station manager of local radio station KHFI. Love was yet another novice to city politics, but displayed an increasing interest in what happened at City Hall.

The two most interesting business candidates were Roy Butler, proprietor of the local Lincoln-Mercury dealership, and Lowell Lebermann, a millionaire investor, and former University of Texas student body president. Butler chose to run against LaRue for the position of mayor. He had already served in at least one major civic position, as chairman of the Austin School Board, and had also been active in the campaign of conservative Democrat Lloyd Bentsen for the United States Senate. Initially Butler declined to run for the position, telling friends like former Governor Allan Shivers and banker Leon Stone that he wanted no part of the hassle that came with it. But his friends prevailed, particularly Bill Youngblood, owner of the local Terminex company.[18] Youngblood pulled a trick out of the hat of Tom Miller's supporters. He gathered a group of two to three hundred businesspeople at the Stephen F. Austin Hotel, and they collectively urged Butler to run for mayor. They were a very different group from those who supported Travis LaRue and who normally were associated with the Greater Austin Association. Although equally conservative in politics, they represented a younger cross-section of the business community. They were smoother, less bumptious. The did not swear so much. Some of them even professed sympathy with blacks.[19] And they also, many of them, were good friends of Lyndon Johnson, a man who always had wanted Austin to present a good face to the rest of the country. Lebermann was young. He had shown himself to be a very shrewd businessman, and was unsullied by any association with the more racist, redneck elements of the Austin business community. Moreover, Lebermann was likely to draw a sizable number of students into his camp simply because of his prominent role as an undergraduate at the University of Texas. The most important thing about Lebermann was that he provided the first true voice on behalf of environmental issues in the history of Austin politics. He professed a concern for preserving the greenery and for waterways, all those features of the community that had marked it throughout the years as such a distinctive setting. Soon he became known as the "green panther," and because of his claims forced other liberal council candidates, like Friedman, to acknowledge the importance of the environmental issues.

As the council races developed, Young, Friedman, and the students they had helped register to vote in Travis County played an ever more significant role in the campaign. Under Young's leadership, the principal members of the student organization, which now went under the name of the Student Action Committee, interviewed a sizable number of the candidates. Eventually they settled on a slate that they presented to their fellow students. The slate consisted of Roy Butler for mayor; Dick Nichols of fair housing fame, for Place 2; Jeff Friedman for Place 5; and Berl Handcox for Place 6.[20] Not one to leave any stones unturned, the group also worked with other liberal organizations in Austin to develop a unified front. Such groups included the West Austin Democrats, under the leadership of Philip White, University of Texas history professor.[21] Although their effort to help forge alliances was not always a happy or satisfying one—Friedman and Young, for example, came to believe that the old populists, such as Emma Long and the Faths, had become self-defeatists and were inept at winning electoral contests—the effect, at least, was to get other liberals to acknowledge the seriousness of the student effort. They were not the only ones to do so.[22]

On March 31, Sam Wood, editor of the *Austin American*, ran an editorial condemning the electoral campaign of the Student Action Committee at the university.[23] Wood and the *American*, plus many local businesspeople, had never quite recovered from the apparent chaos and disorder posed by the Kent State march. Wood wanted to advise Austin of the dangers of the student voice. He told his readers that the students might exercise the dominant voice at City Hall. Heaven forbid! His column, whose tone verged on the hysterical, concluded that "the *Statesman* believes Austin will accept the challenge of the students. This can be done one way, and by one way alone—vote Saturday. The alternative is to stay at home and move the 'drag' to Congress Avenue."[24] The effect was to generate unusual interest in the campaign in its waning days. When the final results of the election were tallied, including a runoff between Friedman and Wick Fowler—a local columnist and conservative who ran against Friedman on the platform that hippies were unfit to hold public office—the business sector of Austin had secured the majority of seats on the council. But Berl Handcox had been elected, the first black ever to serve on the City Council. And so had Jeff Friedman, the first student and the youngest person ever to serve.

The new challengers had secured a foothold in Austin politics. The council was an entirely new one from its predecessor. Butler had soundly defeated LaRue, thus revealing how unhappy the public was with the Old Guard. He now stood at the helm, and Friedman in the left wing ready to make a strong pitch on behalf of liberal causes.

While the populists plotted, the city of Austin was facing new and difficult problems, which would severely test the character of the community as well as the effectiveness of city government. The problems were those that represent a constant threat to the survival of any human community—those of energy. Austin had managed to solve its first battles with the environment by securing the handiwork and power of the dams. But such matters never die an easy death and, almost like the forces of politics, are always waiting in the wings to offer new challenges. Sometime in the late 1960s, city officials had realized that Austin could be in for trouble in acquiring a steady and adequate supply of fuel for its rapidly expanding commercial and residential population.[25] The dams had supplied much of the energy to keep the city alive until about 1960. Now the city had to make plans to shift to new sources. One possible source were coal-burning plants. Another was nuclear energy.

By 1970, a number of American cities already had developed nuclear plants capable of generating cheap power supplies. Austin, together with Houston Lighting and Power Company, the City of San Antonio, and the Lower Colorado River Authority, had taken some preliminary steps to scout out the possibilities for developing a nuclear generator to be worked as a joint venture among the several utility operations.[26] The investment in the preliminary project was cheap, something on the order of several thousand dollars, and had committed the city to nothing other than project estimates. A number of city officials were very much in favor of a cooperative nuclear venture, including the head of the City of Austin utilities division, R. L. Hancock. Hancock, a career utility man given to few words put in very technical lingo, believed firmly that nuclear power represented the wave of the future. Although he was aware of the possible dangers to the environment if a nuclear plant suffered from some such fate as the China syndrome, a major meltdown capable of creating catastrophic consequences, he believed that the dangers were far outweighed by the potential savings in cost from nuclear power.[27] There were a number of other local Austinites who also were deeply committed to the idea of nuclear power. As usual they came from the ranks of the technical staff at the university, and included such articulate spokespersons as John D. McKetta, dean of the School of Engineering.[28]

Within a year of the inauguration of the new council, it had become evident that some decisions would have to be made about committing the city to participation in a nuclear generating facility, alongside the other three utility companies. The council, led by Roy Butler, agreed to open the matter up to a public vote of the citizens. Friedman went along with the majority. Among the strongest advocates of joining the venture were Butler and his close ally, Bill Youngblood.[29] Both men tacitly accepted two notions that had reverberated throughout the long history of Austin: one, a progressive community is a community that must enlarge; and two, a progressive community is one that takes advantage of all the latest technical advances. But not everyone in Austin agreed with them. A number of local citizens decried Austin's possible entry into the joint project, claiming that nuclear power had as yet been untested in America, and that it could pose very serious dangers to the natural environment and to human beings.

The biggest surprise, however, originated in the quarters of the Lower Colorado River Authority (LCRA). Its engineers and staff, including manager Sim Gideon, had believed all along that nuclear power and the joint project were basically sound operations. But they had failed to communicate that message to the members of the LCRA Board of Directors.[30] When the board convened on Wednesday, September 6 to discuss the merits of the project, there was a good deal of disagreement. Several key proponents of nuclear power appeared, including McKetta. They presented a persuasive case on behalf of nuclear power. They claimed that there was little to fear from any potential dangers. But Bill Petri and other members of the board were unconvinced. Petri, in particular, grew very suspicious of the project. "Why," he wondered aloud, "had the board not been informed of the details of the preliminary plans?" "Why had no one bothered to keep us apprised of the negotiations all along until now?"[31] Angered by what he believed to be almost deliberate malfeasance on the part of the LCRA staff, Petri urged that the board reject any future participation in a joint venture for nuclear power. The majority of his fellow members concurred.

Unfortunately for Butler, Youngblood, and the City of Austin, the vote by the LCRA Board came only three days before the citizens of Austin would vote. Butler, firm in his commitment to the joint venture, took to the hustings in Austin, and tried to convince various citizens of the need to go ahead with Austin's participation. His strongarm tactics, however, upset a number of people. Sinclair Black, acting dean of the University of Texas School of Architecture and a member of the city's Board of Environmental Quality and Natural Resources, reported to the *American* that the mayor had convened a meeting of Black's board members and informed them that "even if you have any reservations about the power plant, vote for it because your vote will influence the rest of the community."[32] Several other citizens also went public with their dissatisfaction with the mayor's role in the vote.

Butler may well have anticipated what would take place at the Saturday elections. Although the vote was close, the majority of citizens decided to reject Austin's participation in the nuclear power project. Butler became so incensed at the outcome that he even phoned Bob Long, a friend of Bill Petri and a member of the LCRA Board, and yelled at him that "you and that sonovabitch Bill Petri killed our Austin election Saturday."[33] The failure of the nuclear power project was not the only problem that confronted Austin's uncertain energy future. The city also had a problem with its supply of natural gas. To say the least.

When it became evident to city officials that Austin would have to turn increasingly to other energy sources in the early 1960s, one of those to which they turned was natural gas.[34] It seemed in plentiful supply and, at least since the 1950s, it was becoming more and more popular as a substitute for fuel oil or coal, each of which was considerably more expensive. The natural gas was used by utilities to heat water in large boilers, which, in turn, was eventually converted into steam to produce electricity. An up-and-coming young Texas entrepreneur, Oscar Wyatt, had been one of the first to recognize the great financial opportunities in harnessing the natural gas produced in Texas oil fields, and selling it to various consumers. In 1962, a fight developed in Austin over which natural gas supplier would receive a city contract. For over thirty years, United Gas of Shreveport had furnished Austin's main supply of natural gas. Wyatt, and Coastal States, hired Austin attorney Frank Erwin, already well known in local circles for his role in the Emma and Stuart Long debacle of the early 1950s, to arrange an agreement with the City of Austin. United and one other firm competed for the bid. Coastal States, seeking to outdo its competition, agreed that it would furnish the city a supply of natural gas at a fixed rate for a period of twenty years. United would only guarantee a fixed rate for ten years. The city chose

Coastal States. By 1968, however, Coastal States claimed that the fixed rate was too rigid, that its suppliers were charging higher prices, and it requested that it be permitted to raise the rate to a figure of 20¢ per 1,000 cubic feet of natural gas. The city, at this point having no real alternative, complied.[35]

By the early 1970s, the supply-and-demand market situation of natural gas had changed once again. The prices of the supplies to Coastal States had begun to creep up, so Wyatt intimated. Moreover, because of the demand from its other customers, Lo-Vaca wanted to adjust the rate accordingly, and to increase the price charged to the City of Austin, as to its other customers. Don Butler, the city attorney, and R. L. Hancock became involved in the negotiations with Lo-Vaca.[36] Hancock was one of the few people well aware of the impending energy crisis in Austin. Butler, an aggressive attorney who had worked with public utilities for much of his professional life, tried to secure precise information on the needs and supplies of Coastal States. With no luck. Nature once more intervened to cause trouble. The winter of 1972–73 was a particularly harsh one for Austin, with temperatures hovering about freezing for long stretches of time. Several ice storms swept into the city, forcing residents to place unusually heavy demands for heat on the city's generators. For a period of time in January 1973, the University of Texas even had to close its doors because of the limited supply of electricity from the city. Meanwhile, Lo-Vaca continued to press Don Butler and Hancock, along with the council, to allow it to turn to the Texas Railroad Commission for some relief on the rates it was charging its customers. The energy outlook seemed especially grim for Austin.

While Coastal States was barely burning, and Austin officials were fuming, Jeff Friedman was struggling to get his fellow council members to act on behalf of liberal goals. It was an uphill fight, of course, since he faced a six-man opposition. Nevertheless, during his tenure he did manage to raise some key issues. At his urging, for example, the council considered the matter of utility refund contracts.[37] Such contracts were created in the post–World War II years as a means of inducing housing development in Austin. They guaranteed building contractors that the city would reimburse them for the construction of sewer and water lines connected with new construction. Originally they assured contractors of a one hundred percent refund, but then, as a result of the vast amount of money paid out by the city, they were scaled down to ninety percent of the builder's cost. By the early 1970s, residents had become increasingly vocal about the apparent inequities of the contracts, pointing out that they seemed to benefit new homeowners at the expense of current ones. The argument was that the monies generated by the city to pay the contractors came out of revenues from current residents, and thus the current residents, in effect, were subsidizing the costs of new housing. Friedman and his fellow residents got nowhere with their argument. Nor did Friedman get anywhere with his calls for the firing of Police Chief Bob Miles, whom he believed to be responsible for the sometimes harsh police treatment of Austin's minority citizens.[38]

Meanwhile, Roy Butler was showing himself to be a superb political infighter, a master at getting the council to do much as he wished, and an invariable opponent of Friedman. Bill Youngblood continued to remain behind the scenes, becoming an increasingly close ally of the mayor's. The duo slowly began to take on all the earmarks of another earlier city duo, that of Tom Miller and Commodore Perry. In a way, this should not have been surprising, especially to those familiar with Youngblood's background. Bill Youngblood had almost consciously fashioned himself into an urban entrepreneur.[39] In the early 1950s, just after his arrival in the city, he had become close friends with another young man, Edgar Perry III, grandson of the Commodore. With the aid of funds they borrowed from Commodore Perry, they embarked on several joint business ventures, including the Terminex Pest Control Company. Eventually Youngblood bought out the younger Perry and repaid the Commodore. Over time he also became a close friend of the Perry family, and dined regularly with them during their Sunday brunches at the Driskill Hotel. He even came to see himself as a member of the Perry family. Today, among the very few pictures hanging on the wall behind him at his Terminex office, there is one of the Commodore, wisely smiling and looking over Youngblood's shoulder — as though to be certain Youngblood is behaving in the appropriate urban entrepreneurial manner.

Friedman's efforts to get some policies through the council were effectively stymied by the Butler-Youngblood duo. But Friedman faced what he perceived as another formidable foe by 1972, the city manager, Dan Davidson.[40] Davidson, who had been serving as an assistant city manager in Austin until his appointment, was selected to replace Lynn Andrews, whom the council had fired. Davidson soon became known as a tough, no-nonsense administrator. He was all business, and thus pleased the likes of people such as Hardy Hollers, who only a few years earlier had urged his Greater Austin Association associates to create a council that was all business. Davidson also managed to develop a strong sense of loyalty within the city staff, a special quality for any city bureaucratic administration. If any city employee, particularly the higher-level figures, were under fire from a citizen, or from a council member, Davidson went to bat for him. City employees greatly respected and trusted him because of this trait.[41] Davidson also managed to develop a very effective working relationship with Mayor Butler, and became a good acquaintance and friend of Bill Youngblood. To the camp of challengers, however, Davidson's associations with the Butler-Youngblood duo, as well as with other business figures in the community, smelled fishy. Indeed, Friedman grew convinced that Davidson exercised inappropriate control over city affairs by telling people what he wanted them to hear.[42] Friedman's liberal supporters, especially the University of Texas students, were equally certain of this.

By early 1973, the elections for City Council offices had once again rolled around. The challengers offered candidates for every seat. The most interesting races involved Friedman and his opponent, Bob Gray, and Dick Nichols and his opponent, Bob Binder. Gray was a local building contractor who had become quite wealthy. His major claim to public prominence was that he was Roy Butler's next-door neighbor. While Friedman and his campaign strategist, the redoubtable Peck Young, sought to promote his liberal credentials over the course of the campaign, Gray characterized Friedman as nothing more than a hippie-radical.[43] Gray's advertisements were particularly clever and sinister. Friedman was displayed in jeans and a workshirt counterpoised to Gray, who was decked out in a business suit, and seated beside his happy, all-American family.[44] Friedman's bachelorhood also was attacked by Gray, as though bachelors somehow were unfit to hold public office. The campaign of Binder and Nichols was even more intense. For one thing, it divided the challenging community. Nichols was remembered favorably for his work on behalf of the Fair Housing Ordinance, and he also was perceived as a friend of the unions in Austin. Binder, however, had little more to his credit than his distinction as a former president of the University of Texas student body. And one other thing. Along with some other student leaders, Binder had appeared at an antiwar demonstration

convened when President Nixon spoke at the Lyndon Baines Johnson Library. There, according to a number of observers, Binder had
thrown his war medals on a fire. Today he denies the charge, but
during the course of the 1973 campaign his opposition singled it out
for attack.[45]

When the election results were tallied on April 7, all the incumbents had been re-elected to office, except for one. Binder had defeated Dick Nichols. Now there were two youthful challengers on the
council, and it seemed that the liberal community at last might be
able to make some genuine legislative inroads. Much would depend
on whether coalitions could be established between the Binder-
Friedman camp and figures like Lebermann and Handcox, each of
whom offered the promise, at least in theory, of going the right way
on issues of some importance to the challengers.

By the spring of 1973, the matters of Austin's energy supply had
reached a critical point. Hancock and Don Butler were well aware
how close the city was to a genuine crisis.[46] Lo-Vaca, which claimed
that its reserves were stretched to the limit, threatened possible
natural gas curtailments to Austin. Meanwhile, the city had purchased fuel oil from Lo-Vaca in order to help it survive the crunch.
With its control of both natural gas and fuel oil supplies, Lo-Vaca
Gathering clearly had the city over a barrel. One afternoon in May,
Hancock recalls, the situation had become so severe that he called
Don Butler into his office for an urgent meeting. Hancock told Butler
that the city only had enough fuel left for another one and one-half
days of full operations. Hancock felt the matter acutely. At his finger
tips, he realized, were the lives of many thousands of citizens. Who
should get fuel? Who should not?[47] They debated the question at
length. Within hours, they learned, the crisis could temporarily be
averted as there were some unexpected reserves of fuel oil near
Austin. But the city's energy picture obviously remained uncertain.
Even the citizens, alerted by some newspaper reports and occasional
brownouts, had begun to sense the problem.[48]

The council, aware of the urgency of the matter, began to search
for ways to resolve it. One long-term solution, of course, was to try
once again to hookup with the joint nuclear venture, headed by the
Houston Lighting and Power Company. Butler and Youngblood still
felt strongly in favor of this option.[49] The council agreed to hold
another public election in December to have citizens vote on whether

Austin should join the project. This time around, both sides took the issue far more seriously. Peck Young and Roy Spence, both of whom had a string of important electoral victories under their belts, were hired as strategists for the campaign on behalf of nuclear energy.[50] This move would ultimately anger many of Young's liberal friends, and help drive another wedge into the liberal camp.[51] A number of university faculty once again were called upon to support the drive for nuclear power. John McKetta reappeared to argue forcefully for the merits of the venture. He was joined by Herb Woodson, a recent addition to the engineering faculty, who carried impressive credentials as an authority on public utilities.[52] At various meetings throughout the city, Woodson presented very persuasive arguments for why the city should go with nuclear power, noting that the cheap cost of nuclear energy far outweighed any potential harms to the environment.

The forces on behalf of nuclear energy seemed to have lined up all the big guns on their side. But the challengers, who by now had become popularly known as the anti-Nuke forces, were not about to lie down and give up. Friedman and Binder both were somewhat skeptical of the nuclear project.[53] Binder was especially so. On a visit by the council to the Connecticut Yankee plant in Plymouth, Massachusetts, Binder took along a tape recorder to keep a permanent record of what he learned. The answers to his questions and those of other council members seemed to provide assurance about the possible dangers of a project. Professor Richard Wilson of Harvard University, in a response to one question, observed: " . . . if you went to the top floor of the Prudential Building in Boston, you'd get more radiation than you would from a nuclear power plant. People worry about this radiation, the designers worry about it and the general public worries about it. We should worry about it, but in fact . . . the radiation of all working nuclear reactors is fairly low."[54] Binder himself wondered about the potential costs of building such a plant, and whether the actual expense departed much from the projected one. He learned that the original cost estimate for the Connecticut Yankee plant had been a figure of $60 to $65 million in 1965, but by the time the plant actually was completed several years later it had cost over $200 million dollars.[55] When he inquired about why the cost overrun had been so large, he learned that the project engineers simply had not had sufficiently good information to make an accurate estimate of costs. Upon his return to Austin, Binder concluded that cost overruns were a genuine possibility in the project planned for Texas. In a prepared public statement, he announced that he would vote against the project, noting in particular that "nobody knows what our plant will end up costing Austin. $161 million is just the first amount [we in Austin] are asking for. No one is assuring us it won't go much higher. No one."[56] Roy Butler was furious over Binder's decision. Binder proved to be the only council member to vote against Austin's participation in the nuclear project when the matter came up for a council decision. Friedman, after some waffling, decided to go with the majority.[57] Butler was especially angry at Friedman because he had cut a deal with him, so he thought, that would have assured Binder's compliance with the nuclear project.[58] When Binder came out against the project, Butler held it personally against Friedman, fueling their antagonism toward one another.[59]

Binder was not the only voice urging Austin voters to reject the joint venture. The challengers were heavily represented, particularly by an assortment of regular Austin liberals. Ed Wendler, Sr., for example, came out strongly against Austin's participation, thus beginning the series of biblical contests in which he would battle his brother, Ken—or was it Cain?—over political questions. Ken, who by now was very active in the Travis County Democrats, was a strong supporter of the nuclear project; indeed, it was he who had convinced both Young and Spence to help concoct the strategy for the pro-Nuke forces.[60] Ed Wendler became the citizens' chairman of an antiproject group that took on the delightful name Citizens for Public Power.[61] Joining him were, among others, Steve Gutow, a University of Texas law student, and Dave Butts, another of the regular liberals among Austin's youth.[62] The challengers had one very special thing going for them. They were fresh from a victory that fall on behalf of Lloyd Doggett. Doggett, in the words of Gary Mauro, had scored the "upset victory of all time" when he defeated a conservative for the position of state representative from the congressional district that included Austin and Travis County.[63] Doggett was a strong, forceful liberal, with Lincolnesque features, and was deliberately seeking to carry on the grand Texas tradition of populism fashioned by the likes of Ralph Yarborough. Much as Emma Long had done years earlier, when she and her forces successfully employed the Travis County Democratic contingent for her first race, Wendler, Gutow, and their fellow liberals used the Doggett operation to try to defeat the nuclear project. Many of those who ranked among the members of this contingent, of course, were University of Texas students. Moreover, it was more than mildly ironic—and testimony to how very peculiarly the challengers were sorting themselves out in various contests—that one of the principal strategic architects of Doggett's victory had been none other than Peck Young.[64]

The challengers campaigned with the same amount of enthusiasm and vigor as the proponents of nuclear power. At the meetings where McKetta and Woodson spoke on behalf of Austin's participation, the challengers had their own array of speakers. Their best spokesperson, Gutow remembers, was Peggy Sackett. A housewife and mother, Sackett was especially effective in raising fears about the potential dangers entailed in a nuclear undertaking. She communicated the sense that she was uncertain about the technical aspects of nuclear power, and thus equally uncertain about what might happen if something were to go wrong. "I don't know about you," she told her audiences, "but I have a couple of children and I worry about what could happen to them." She left many other parents feeling the same way.[65]

By the time the election came around, on November 17, 1973, the community was well aware of the issues, many citizens were deeply committed to their own points of view, and Austin, particularly the people who otherwise challenged the dominant economic interests, was very divided on the issue of nuclear energy. When the votes were counted, the decision proved a narrow one. The proponents of the nuclear project had won this time, by 722 votes from among the more than 39,000 cast. Some people had more riding on the outcome than others—like R. L. Hancock. As election night wound down, and the votes kept coming in, Hancock became particularly nervous about the final tally. He, after all, knew how troubled Austin's energy future really was. When Young and Spence finally were able to assure him that the nuclear project would win, Hancock broke down. Tears streaming down his cheeks, he thanked Young and Spence for all their help. Once. Twice. Too many times.[66]

Days later, Don Butler and Dan Davidson traveled to Houston to put together the legal paperwork assuring Austin's participation.[67] They met with officials from Houston Lighting and Power, which served as the principal director of the overall effort. Butler was somewhat edgy. He himself was not at all certain that Austin could easily secure entry at this point because the work had proceeded so far

286   P O W E R , M O N E Y & T H E P E O P L E

along. After some lengthy discussions, however, he and Davidson worked out a contract with the other partners. There were some other matters that should have troubled them. *A lot.* Such as the fact that there was no bottom line to the projected cost of the plant, so that the bills could skyrocket, much as Bob Binder had predicted.[68] Or the fact that Brown and Root, which had never actually had complete charge of the constructoin of a nuclear power plant, was now the principal contractor for this one. Nevertheless, it surely must have seemed to the two men as though the whole tough question of energy was finally behind them.

Although the challengers had been dealt a setback on this issue, it was not sufficient to render their whole effort against the established economic forces – and the dream for unlimited expansion – null. It was still possible that Binder and Friedman could collaborate on efforts to promote the interests of liberals. But, again, it would depend on whether they could effectively link up with other voices on the City Council. Roy Butler had other ideas. Almost from the day they came on the council, Butler sought to isolate Binder and Friedman from the majority. One day, for instance, shortly after Binder took office, he learned in a telephone call from a friend that Butler was having lunch with the other council members at the Headliners' Club. It appeared, from what Binder could make out, that the purpose of the lunch was to decide which citizens to appoint to the Austin Planning Commission. Later that afternoon, Binder confronted Dan Love and asked whether such a luncheon had taken place. Love confirmed it. Binder was upset. He believed such a tactic went against the grain of the very purpose of the City Council, namely, that it was to serve as a representative and a deliberative body on matters of interest to the entire community. He also, of course, sensed what Butler was trying to do.

Binder and Friedman got together, and went public with their anger. They found Dick Ellis, a television reporter for Channel 7, the CBS affiliate in Austin, and told him what had happened. Then Ellis interviewed the several council members who had attended the luncheon. That evening the regular news broadcast headlined the Binder-Friedman complaint. Moreover, there was a certain humor in what appeared. Ellis asked Dan Love, "Was there such a luncheon, Mr. Love?" "Yes," he replied. "Was there such a luncheon?" Ellis asked Lowell Lebermann. "Yes," he replied. "Was there such a luncheon?" Ellis asked Berl Handcox. "No," he responded. Binder and Friedman had won the day.[69]

But by no means the week. On several different occasions, Butler would invite council members to his nearby ranch for various discussions. He, however, would not invite the two purportedly radical council members. Ultimately the antagonism between Butler and the Binder-Friedman camp became so intense that Butler resorted to what at best might be called, in those days at least, "dirty tricks." He threatened, for example, to expose an embarrassing youthful indiscretion of Friedman's aide, Ann Schwartz, hoping to get rid of her.[70] Schwartz only learned of Butler's tactic when Carol Fowler, an *Austin Citizen* reporter, called to inform her that Butler had just told Fowler the story. It never became public, thanks to Fowler's good sense. Moreover, for a period of several months, Schwartz became convinced that Butler had hired the Austin police to tail her and to dig up any dirt they could on her past. More and more, Butler was showing himself to be a real hardball operator.

The other problem that Binder and Friedman faced, as the challengers, was how to develop a program around which they could unite popular support, and from which they could press other council members for specific policies. That they seemed to have problems in coming up with such a program testified to the continuing difficulties that had haunted the populists' effort in Austin, ever since the days of Emma Long and her hardy band of supporters. But there was more to it than that. Binder and Friedman often did not see eye to eye on issues, even those that, to other observers, should have served as the basis of a common attack.[71] Binder, for example, began to feel that the limited pay of council members was a severe drawback not only to his continuing work on the council, but also to his ability to carry on his fledgling law practice.[72] Arguing that such low salaries would not permit adequate representation of the entire Austin body politic—virtually an acknowledged fact since all council members, including Emma Long, had until then some form of private wealth on which they could rely—Binder pressed his fellow council members for an annual salary for the council of $12,000. He tried to get Friedman to side with him in support of this measure, but Friedman would not, believing it was inappropriate for the council members to enact such a substantial pay raise for themselves.[73] Friedman won friends among the business community for his stand; Binder furthered his own image as a university radical.

All was not lost with the challengers' cause, however. Although Binder and Friedman failed to develop a solid alliance, cemented by some common vision for a better future, they could attack their opponents at certain vulnerable points. The one point most open to attack was the utility refund contracts that Friedman first had raised for discussion in 1971. The two men and their staffs – Schwartz and Young for Friedman, Dean Rindy and Amy Orum for Binder – produced a full-scale assault on this front.[74] Rindy generated the most detailed information.[75] In documents made public to the media, Rindy demonstrated that some of Austin's developers had grown quite wealthy on their refund contracts. His information also revealed that Austin banks often would purchase the contracts from building contractors, thus allowing the contractors to get about their business. The banks profited, too, for the contracts carried with them a guarantee of three percent per annum interest on the unpaid balance. Inasmuch as the city owed hundreds of thousands of dollars on unpaid contracts, obviously the banks could profit quite nicely. And Rindy's information revealed that they did. This new information kept the Austin pot boiling, and the challengers' cause alive.

Everything came to a head at a meeting convened by the council on the refund contracts on March 28, 1974.[76] The meeting occurred against the backdrop of a number of recent public charges, including a series of articles by Brenda Bell in the *Austin Citizen*.[77] Bell's articles made clear that the development segment of Austin was raking it in. Any number of speakers were scheduled to appear at the day-long session, but only a few held the floor at length. The first was Richard Baker, who appeared on behalf of the Austin Home Builders Association. Baker told the council that the home builders were very much in favor of continuing the refund contract program. The program, he claimed, helped to reduce the cost of housing to new homeowners, and thus promoted the expansion of Austin that, of course, everyone wanted. At the end of his very lengthy exposition, Binder asked him whether it was not true that he was on the Board of Directors of North Austin Bank.[78] Yes, Baker replied. "And, is it not also true," Binder queried him, "that your bank holds at least three major refund contracts?" Baker was uncertain. Binder's questions had raised doubts about the sheer impartiality of Baker's presentation. Baker, it seemed, was one of those who clearly profited from refund contracts. Mayor Butler, still a strong supporter of refund contracts as well as an equally tough opponent of Binder, rallied to the defense of Baker. He observed that there was nothing unethical in the bank's operations. But Binder's point stood.

Bill Youngblood naturally appeared at the meeting. And just as naturally he came out on behalf of retaining the refund contracts. Youngblood told the assembled crowd that "the refund contract is not the sole reason that Austin is the great place . . . to live, but it is part of making Austin the very successful city that it is at the cheapest cost to the taxpayer for this quality of life."[79] Youngblood's declarations were largely ceremonial and symbolic, an effort by an urban entrepreneur to anoint a particular program for growth. That was not the case, however, with the speaker who carried the day, Professor Michael Conroy of the University of Texas. Conroy, an expert in urban economics, had undertaken an exhaustive study of the utility refund contract program. Among other things, he discovered that there were few cities in America that had such a program at present, having abandoned it because it was outdated. But he also drove home the point that the refund contract program was inequitable to the community as a whole, and to older residents, in particular. He recapitulated the earlier argument that the refund contract penalized older residents for the benefit of the new ones. His information was powerful and systematic, as was his style of presentation. Everyone seemed impressed, except for the expected few— like Butler, Youngblood, and even Dan Davidson, who quibbled with Conroy over his facts. At the conclusion of the meeting, there was sufficient skepticism about the merits of the refund contract program that Lebermann successfully moved to appoint a council subcommittee to review the entire program. Over the next several months, study sessions were held about the program, and modifications eventually were made to it. By early 1975, it was terminated. Binder and Friedman, along with their fellow challengers, had another victory in their pockets.

But the sweet smell of success lasted only months. Then the two men were hit with the heavy artillery. Binder and Friedman had come to depend on their aides for help in assembling and digesting information preparatory to council deliberations. Bud Dryden did not require an aide, and the wealthy business figures, like Lebermann and Butler, did not really need one either. Butler, moreover, had taken an increasing dislike to Schwartz. What next happened, perhaps, should not have been unexpected. At the council meeting on September 19, 1974, as the council routinely went about its business of trimming costs on its latest budget, Dan Love made the surprise motion to eliminate the program of council aides. Butler commented that "the move seemed justified."[80] Binder and Friedman were absolutely stunned. Even Lebermann found the move "shocking." With little fanfare, the council voted four to three to disband the aides' program. Schwartz broke down, and ran out of the Council Chambers, muttering sweet somethings about Roy Butler.[81] This was the final blow. Nothing much more was accomplished on behalf of the challengers over the next months. But other forces were now astir in Austin, ones that would help to broaden the base of challenge and, ultimately, to furnish a real chance at developing an alternative vision for the future.

The early 1970s were a time not only for the small revolts of American youth. They were also a time when challenges to the normal routine of political life were breaking out everywhere. A large part of that broad movement of revolt took place in urban areas, and it concerned the struggle between individual homeowners and their perceived nemesis, the land developer. As Austin grew, these sorts of struggles now happened almost naturally in its wider residential environs. And with growing frequency. Developers had taken advantage of this little oasis in the Sunbelt, and sought to put up new apartment complexes, shopping centers, anything that might turn an eventual profit. Annoyed and angry citizens, believing their lives unjustly disrupted by the excavating rigs of the developers, took to the streets and to the homes of neighbors. In the vicinity of the University of Texas, for example, there emerged the Save University Neighborhood group, an organization founded to protect the integrity of the local university neighborhood against realtors and developers who, neighbors claimed, preyed on empty lots almost like vultures.[82] In West Austin, too, there grew another such group, the West Austin Neighborhood Association, which sought to further the interests of residents against the continuing threats of individual developers. (This particular association would later become the site of an attempted takeover by a cadre of developers who, hoping to profit from open neighborhood democracy, wanted to beat the neighbors at their own game.)

Elsewhere in Austin, much the same thing was happening. And the political scenario between the neighbors and the developers was always identical. Word got out of a developer who wanted to put up a building on a vacant lot. The developer approached the council for a zoning variance that would permit, let us say, commercial, or dense residential, construction. And the citizens, under the auspices of a newly organized neighborhood alliance, would appear before the council to do battle with the developer. All of this may have taken inordinate time and energy in the council chambers, but it also gave heart to those who hoped that Austin might someday see the dream of all the "little people"—as Emma Long's correspondent had called them—realized.

Joan Bartz, a resident of the University Hills neighborhood in Northeast Austin, was typical of those men and women who became involved in the broad neighborhood challenge to the development community.[83] So was her experience. Bartz moved to Austin in 1968 with her husband and family of several children. They had purchased a modest home in the University Hills area, hoping to remain there forever. One of the things that had especially attracted them to this particular site was the neighborhood park. It served as the meeting grounds for local residents, and helped to promote friendships and common neighborhood activities. The developer of the area, Walter Carrington, made a special pitch on behalf of the park. The pitch was enough to sell the Bartz family. Four years after they moved in, however, Carrington proposed to change the park into a site for multifamily condominiums. Joan Bartz was outraged. She believed Carrington had simply sold her a bill of goods. She got on the phone to city officials and tried to find out how to prevent Carrington from going ahead with his plans. A bitter fight ensued, pitting Bartz and her neighbors against Carrington. The issue dragged back and forth for months, then years, eventually winding up in the courts. And Joan Bartz and her neighbors prevailed, preventing the construction.

Bartz and her neighbors had learned an important lesson. They realized that if they wished to maintain the quality of their life and to protect their one major financial investment, their home, then they had to keep close track of what happened to their neighborhood. Soon neighbors came knocking at Bartz's door, asking for help with other local problems. What can I do about the problem with the sewer? one neighbor asked Bartz. What about the lack of police protection and the recent rash of crimes out here? another wondered. With some time on her hands and a growing interest in the problems of her neighbors, Bartz decided to help organize a local neighborhood group, the University Hills Neighborhood Association. She became its first head. The organization turned out to be unique among Austin's neighborhood groups, not merely for the degree of its vigilance, but because it was comprised of the whole ethnic array of local residents, from Southern whites to longtime black residents to Chicanos—truly a rainbow coalition.

Bartz eventually proved so effective at the neighborhood watchdog effort, as well as so much in demand outside her own locale, that she was invited to organize and to serve as head of a coalition of Austin neighborhood groups, the Austin Neighborhood Council. By the end of her tenure as its chair, the council included at least thirty of the over sixty neighborhood groups then active in Austin. As more problems of citizens came up, and as they were resolved by Bartz and her associates, a set of political maxims evolved. Today they read almost like Saul Alinsky's handbook of neighborhood organizing.

> Maxim 1: Learn your facts; do not take a City of Austin report as the gospel truth. Maxim 2: Be businesslike at council meetings, and leave your emotions at home (there is no one in the world more businesslike than Joan Bartz). Maxim 3: Don't back your opponent into a corner so that he gets egg on his face. Maxim 4: Work out all political details in advance with your opponent and allies. Leave absolutely nothing to chance. And Maxim 5: Realize that your neighborhood requires absolute and constant vigilance. This means keeping your eye on what is happening with local streets, police, fire facilities, parks, businesses, commercial development, schools, churches . . . the whole bit."[84]

Bartz soon seemed to abide by these maxims almost effortlessly, and to convey to friend and foe alike a ruthlessly straightforward, direct, and, "businesslike" attitude. And, because of it, she and her fellow neighbors and associates effectively threw a wrench into many a proposed development.

Austin city government did not prove entirely indifferent to what was occurring in its neighborhoods. Slowly it became obvious, as more and more citizens brought their complaints before the council, that a lot was brewing in Austin, and that the pot might soon boil over. One Austin official who took particular note of the goings-on was Dick Lillie, the director of city planning.[85] Lillie is one of the few former city officials about whom many people still say kind

things. He was friendly and open to suggestion. And this open attitude may have helped to bring about a virtually revolutionary program, the Austin Tomorrow Program. Sometime in 1972, Lillie had
the bright idea to involve the masses of Austin citizens in constructing their own plans for the future of Austin. The notion was to encourage Austinites to talk to one another about their individual
concerns and complaints, and then, from a set of common concerns,
to develop a new master plan for the city. Nothing like this had ever
been done before in the city's history. And, if it worked, it would
produce extraordinary results, possibly even a model for other
American cities.

Roy Butler, and the council, agreed to support the program. And
the federal government, through the Department of Housing and
Urban Development, gave a grant to the city to help provide for
costs. Council members were invited to nominate various citizens to
serve on the overall advisory board, known as the Goals Assembly.
The assembly's job was to provide general direction for the program,
as well as to pull together the different ideas and suggestions that
grew out of citizen meetings. Altogether, 250 citizens were appointed
to serve, although only about 180 would become active participants.
Not surprisingly, the woman who was appointed as its president was
Joan Bartz. Rumors floated about on the background and qualifications of other people selected.[86] Claims were made that Mayor
Butler and other wealthy figures on the council had selected only the
very rich and famous. Such an act, if true, violated the spirit of the
program, which was designed to represent the entire body politic of
the city. Nothing was ever substantiated on these claims, however,
and, when the assembly finally was constituted, it seemed to furnish
a good cross-section of Austin.

Although the concept surely was a good one, it perhaps was to be
anticipated that such an effort at participatory democracy, or, as its
opponents called it, "mobocracy," would run into problems.[87] It did.
Bill Youngblood, who became involved for a time, recalls that while
the meetings appeared at the outset to be useful, they would drag on
and on for many hours.[88] Boredom seemed to be the hallmark of
the small, intimate meetings of citizens, rather than the kind of
creative deliberations Lillie originally had desired. Even Bartz found
various difficulties in securing complete cooperation and participation from all the many citizens involved. While many neighborhood
residents seemed to take the meetings seriously, Bartz found that to

be far less true of the businesspeople. One encounter graphically portrays the reaction of many business leaders to the experiment. "A businessman came to me," Bartz recalls, "and he said, 'I just can't serve anymore, Joan.' And I said, 'What's the problem?' And he said, 'Well, I just don't see why we in the business community should have to sit down with a bunch of housewives and blue-collar workers and laborers, and have them sit there and tell us what's going to be good for the city for the next twenty years. After all, what do they know?' "[89]

Nevertheless, the program pushed forward. Eventually several thousand citizens took part, active in the hundreds of neighborhood sessions and citywide meetings. As the program reached its final stages, the Goals Assembly was divided into separate sectors, each one working on a major element of the plans for Austin's future. Some of the longtime populist challengers were very active at this point, including Dean Rindy and Peck Young.[90] Rindy, for example, helped to shape the environmental plans for the program.[91] After several additional months of work, a report finally was put together to present to the City Council for its deliberations. The report documented many of the concerns that citizens had been voicing among themselves as well as at council sessions about the rapid growth and expansion of Austin. The key points were these:

1. Uncontrolled growth is the number one concern of the Austin Tomorrow participants;
2. There must be more effective land use controls outside the city limits;
3. It is imperative that the city protect and preserve the many creeks, flood plains, historic buildings, and area lakes and rivers for the enjoyment of Austin citizens;
4. Development must be controlled in the city. . . . The city government should play a major role in deciding where development should occur . . . environmentally sensitive areas such as flood plains should not be built upon;
5. Austin creeks and waterways should be preserved as open spaces;
6. Developers should be required to set aside park lands in each residential development site.[92]

The recommendations were remarkable in themselves, quite apart from the broad democratic manner through which they had been achieved. For the very first time in the long history of Austin, they put into written, formal language the challenge that citizens were making to unbridled expansion. Before, growth had been merely a notion bandied about in talk, or used as a symbolic weapon around which neighbors could unite to battle developers. Now a set of clear proposals had emerged, ones that challenged the very core of Alexander Wooldridge's vision. Could such a program succeed, even with the apparent support of so many individuals? Or would it prove, in the end, to be merely another political ploy designed to appease an upset body of citizens?

As the Austin Tomorrow program wound down, the challenger's efforts were being revived in another arena. Sometime in late 1974, Steve Gutow recalls, he and fellow University of Texas student Steve Rosenbaum brought together a group of people active in the various neighborhood and liberal groups of Austin.[93] Their purpose was to create a broad coalition effort, a force that could prove effective in citywide politics. Gutow already had demonstrated that he could be an intelligent campaign strategist with his work in the 1973 anti-Nuke campaign. He remained a person deeply committed to a liberal program for Austin. Other liberals were there as well, including his friend Ed Wendler, Sr.[94] A number of questions were raised by the audience during the course of the meeting. Someone asked, "Well, what purpose will the group have?" Gutow responded, "It will serve simply as an umbrella organization, to bring all the liberals of Austin together."[95] Representatives of some groups did not see how they could possibly align themselves with others. Those who seemed particularly uncomfortable with one another were the members of environmental groups and the representatives from the black and brown minorities of Austin.

People departed after several hours, perhaps less sure of their common grounds with their challenger friends than they had been before. Nevertheless, what emerged from this meeting as from others that took place over the next couple of months was a powerful new alliance in Austin politics. It was named the Coalition for a Progressive Austin, and it was designed to help bridge the ideological differences among the various camps of challengers. It provided the challengers' answer to the Greater Austin Association. First and foremost on its agenda was the goal of rallying behind a slate of liberal candidates for the 1975 City Council elections. Bob Binder had already announced he would not seek re-election, so the challengers had to find a replacement for him. Jeff Friedman, on the other hand, had declared that he would not only run for City Council again, but that he would try for the position of mayor. This pleased any number of Austin liberals.

Eventually the coalition identified a handful of candidates who seemed to qualify as good, liberal challengers. There was Margaret Hofmann, a housewife very dedicated to the preservation of Austin's environment. Another candidate prominent on environmental concerns, and pushed to some degree by the Coalition, was Stuart Henry, an attorney. John Trevino emerged as the candidate from the Chicano community. He had run during the previous council election in 1973, and had lost. Jimmy Snell, a black insurance company official, was identified as the challenger to run as the representative of black East Austin. The slate was rounded out with Sandra Weinstock, an Austin resident who had been very active in the Austin Tomorrow effort, and Emma Lou Linn, a professor of psychology at St. Edward's University in Austin. Although all the candidates offered the promise of a serious liberal challenge to the dominant economic interests of Austin, each also possessed somewhat different goals.

Two measures ultimately were used to hold together the otherwise diverse slate of office-seekers.[96] The first was a more or less common alliance against the dominant economic interests of Austin, and, particularly, against rapid growth. But there were different degrees of commitment to the fight against growth. Figures like Weinstock, Hofmann, and Henry stood very committed to a program of limiting Austin expansion inasmuch as they were dedicated to preservation of the natural environment. Trevino and Snell, in contrast, ran on a platform of seeking economic and social improvements for the brown and black minorities of Austin. Neither man believed that such a program could succeed if there were limits placed on the city's expansion. The absence of a firm and total consensus among the challengers' slate thus necessitated the second measure, the time-honored device of political brokerage and negotiation.[97] Various figures from the coalition and the individual council races worked closely among themselves, unbeknownst to the Austin public. Gutow and Rosenbaum, for example, took charge of the effort at the University of Texas. They both drummed up support on behalf of the slate, and worked hard at fashioning a common theme for all the candidates, that of no-growth.[98] Peck Young, as usual, ran the campaign for Friedman, but he also carried on secret meetings with other campaign managers, such as Neil Reimer, who ran the Weinstock effort.[99] Roger Duncan by this time had emerged as a clear voice for liberal Austin, and he directed the effort for Hofmann, consulting often with the other political strategists.[100] In the midst of it all, Ed Wendler, Sr., finally grew into the role that would become his trademark thereafter in Austin politics, that of a broker and mediator among contending factions.[101] Wendler was in and out of the camps of the various challengers. His biggest task, he recalls, was somehow to develop an alliance between the challengers who represented poor East Austin and figures like Weinstock and Hofmann, who ran on platforms that seemed to commit them exclusively to the preservation of the natural environment.[102]

As the races developed in early 1975, it became more and more evident that the liberals had a good shot at gaining a clear majority on the council. But they needed some extra help. That help soon came from materials disclosed in a trial conducted eighty miles away in San Antonio.[103] A suit had been brought against Southwestern Bell Telephone Company by the family of T. O. Gravitt, the former head of the company in Texas, and James Ashley, another former company official. In October 1974, Gravitt had committed suicide, the apparent result of his termination by the company. Ashley himself had also been fired. Together, he and Gravitt's relatives were seeking to get Bell to come up with $29 million for damages that allegedly had been inflicted on them by the company. The suit maintained that a whole string of improper and illegal actions had been committed by Bell, including illegal campaign contributions and wiretapping. The outcome of this case, coupled with a handful of others, would lead to the eventual breakup of Ma Bell.

Depositions were taken by the Securities and Exchange Commission in the course of the trial. They revealed some of the improper actions taken by Bell. By January 1975, the information they contained had found its way into the headlines and pages of the *Austin American-Statesman* and the *Austin Citizen*.[104] The materials revealed, beyond any shadow of a doubt, that Bell officials had illegally sought to influence the actions of members of the Austin City Council with an eye to securing their compliance for telephone rate hikes. The information clearly indicted several of the more prominent businessmen on the council. Roy Butler, it was shown, had been the recipient of several small but illegal donations by local Bell official Bill Holman. They had been made in the course of Butler's 1971 campaign for office.[105] In statements he made to the press, Butler denied any knowledge of the exact nature of the contributions.[106] Dan Love also turned out to be the recipient of some special business from the company. Love took the matter much harder than Butler, and on January 22 he resigned his position on the City Council.[107] Dick Nichols had also been targeted for special attention by Bell officials. Not only had Nichols received some small contributions for his 1971 council race, but Bell had also used his real estate firm to purchase property on behalf of the company. Even Nichols' daughter, whom Ashley described to Holman in a tape-recorded conversation as "dumber than hell," was the recipient of a special promotion to first-line supervisor at the Austin Bell headquarters.[108] The disclosures became the talk of Austin. And the campaign of the challenging forces seemed to have gotten the shot in the arm it needed.

The elections for the 1975 council were held on Saturday, April 5. Three of the challenging slate were elected outright – Jeff Friedman, Emma Lou Linn, and Jimmy Snell. Stuart Henry was defeated by Betty Himmelblau, and Sandra Weinstock by Lowell Lebermann. The other two races produced runoffs. Margaret Hofmann was in the race against Bob Gray, Friedman's erstwhile 1973 opponent, and John Trevino was pitted against Jay Johnson.

Now the Coalition for a Progressive Austin flexed its political muscle. The effort among students on the University of Texas campus was intensified by Gutow and Rosenbaum. Young moved over from his successful campaign with Friedman to help direct the runoff campaign for Hofmann.[109] Wendler acted to mediate the differences between the Hofmann and Trevino camps, particularly to pacify the forces of Trevino, who had trouble with the antigrowth stance of Hofmann.[110]

When the votes from the runoffs were tallied, both Hofmann and Trevino had won. The challengers thus stood poised at a historic moment. Never before had the City Council had more than two voices of the people in its midst. It was about to experience a clear majority of five.

Almost from the day it was first seated, the Friedman council made headlines. Citizens jokingly referred to it as the people's council comprised of a Jew (Friedman), a blind man (Lebermann), a liberal (Linn), a conservative (Himmelblau), a Chicano (Trevino), a black (Snell), and a tree lady (Hofmann).[111] "Motley" would have understated its character. National and state media picked up on the victory of the liberals, and traced its roots to the events of the early 1970s, and to the University of Texas student body. Friedman himself, who was characterized as the "radical Hippie" mayor by one publication, seemed to be taken as the symbol for the entire council.[112] Liberal, it was proclaimed, and committed to the cause of the people. Austin and Friedman quickly were identified as among the most emancipated cities and mayors in the country, ranking alongside Madison, Wisconsin, and its chief executive, Paul Soglin. Friedman came to the attention of a whole raft of radicals and liberals throughout America, showing up on mailing lists and in demand for special reports on the Austin scene.[113] Barely thirty years old, Jeff Friedman once again was cast into the limelight, only this time he sat on a national stage of attention.

All of the hoopla surely must have put enormous pressure on the members of the council and on Friedman himself. The real trick, observers in Austin seemed to be saying, was whether a liberal majority could somehow enact policies that represented the will of the people. Would such policies follow the mandate laid down by the thousands of citizens in the Austin Tomorrow program? Dick Lillie, Joan Bartz, and other representatives of the program, in fact, turned in their report to Friedman and his fellow council members in June 1975. The symbolism must have been self-evident.[114] "Okay, you won; now take the people's program and enact it!" Friedman himself was keenly aware of the historic nature of this particular council, and sought in some early speeches to provide a posture for himself and his fellow liberals.

Friedman gave one speech before a friendly audience in Madison, Wisconsin, on June 13, 1975. His remarks set the tone for what he would pursue:

Unfortunately, many citizens interpret my position on [city] priorities as a 'no growth' stand, and I believe most of them are sincere in their inaccurate assessment. One of my biggest jobs will be to convince them that I am not opposed to new streets and highways, new sewers and water lines, nor new buildings and annexations. I am opposed to them at any cost, while

handicapping our 'People Programs' with a 'what's left' attitude. . . .[115]

I am extremely excited about the opportunity we have to
reorient priorities and place 'People's Programs' ahead of
'Paving Contracts.' The next two years will be the most 'people
oriented' leadership in the City's history. . . .

Friedman made clear that he wanted to promote the programs of the
people, but he also made clear that he was not genuinely opposed to
the growth of the city. In effect, he was seeking to water down the
proposals drafted by citizens through the Austin Tomorrow program,
as well as to take a stand in opposition to the more radical voices on
the University of Texas campus—including Steve Gutow, Jeff Jones,
and others—who had helped elect him and the other liberals to office.
It was a dangerous ploy, seeking the middle ground between the
people's camp and that of the reigning economic interests, in the
form of the bankers, the developers, and the real estate community.
But Friedman stuck to it.

The critical test for Friedman and his four fellow liberals on the
council came only eight months after the election. Under the regime
of Roy Butler, the city had successfully passed several important bond
issues. These elections, which were coming at a rising tempo as the
growth of the city seemed to outdistance its public services, were
almost as crucial to Austin's well-being as the regular elections for
council positions, perhaps more so. Pass the bonds, and city services
could be provided; vote them down, and the city would face countless problems in providing residents with adequate sewage disposal,
water treatment plants, decent highways, and other public facilities.
A proposed package of municipal bonds was scheduled for a vote by
the citizens in December 1975. (Many other cities, incidentally, do
not require public passage of general obligation bonds, in contrast to
Austin's practice. That such an electoral requirement is built into the
city charter has caused no end of consternation to many Austinites
who firmly believe that it greatly impedes the ability of the city to
keep pace with its growth. People divide on this issue, more or less
as one would expect—those who favor expansion would like to
bypass the vote by citizens.)[116]

Friedman, his close advisor Peck Young, and his administrative
aide Ann Schwartz—she, unlike Douglas MacArthur, had returned
—agreed to a program of planned, or controlled, growth for Austin.

They interpreted such documents as the Austin Tomorrow report to mean a design for the city that included controls over development, but not one that ruled out expansion altogether.[117] Many of Friedman's allies, however, had different ideas. Gutow and the other university radicals wanted to stop growth dead in its tracks. Theirs seemed to be a more primitive vision for the Austin future, a utopia perhaps rid of big capital and selfish economic gain at any price.[118] Others were suspicious of the bond package on entirely different grounds. Marilyn Simpson, for example, who would soon come to occupy a prominent position among neighborhood association activists, suspected that the bonds were not all they were cracked up to be.[119] On close inspection, she discovered that a couple of the more costly bond proposals, for water and wastewater treatment, seemed to include monies that would end up in other city coffers. She was angry and said so to the council and also to many of her friends.

Despite the difference within the ranks of the challengers, Friedman pressed ahead, hoping to convince his supporters that the bond package was a good deal for Austin. All of his fellow council members did the same. Figures like Trevino and Snell had already shown they had nothing against the expansion of Austin, *per se*, while others, such as Betty Himmelblau, were at root economic conservatives, and, thus somewhat inclined to support city spending on new public services. Friedman, however, was caught on the horns of a dilemma. He wanted the support of his friends, particularly those in the quarters of the university, but he also sincerely wanted to see that adequate services were provided for Austin's rapidly expanding population. The campus radicals, Friedman believed, already had shown so much strength in the April elections that it was necessary to get them on his side for the bond proposals. Thus, he agreed to cut a deal with them.[120] In return for a policy of their choosing, he wanted them to corral a big turnout in support of the December bonds. The deal was made, sometime in the summer, and the campaign on behalf of the bonds seemed virtually assured of success.

But then a wrench was thrown into the works. In early September, while Friedman and Schwartz were out of town attending a National Conference of Mayors, Friedman's close associate John Albach met with a group of students at the university. It included the usual bunch—Gutow, Jones, Pat Cuney. Albach told them that Friedman was planning to renege on his promise of support for their program, a claim that was patently false. They should be aware of this going into the fall campaign, Albach said. Albach never revealed to Friedman what he had done. But when Friedman and Schwartz returned, the tide of student sentiment clearly had turned against them, and the radicals, who had been a crucial base of their support only months earlier, now stood as their opponent.

So much for your friends. Even Friedman's enemies stood ready to make the bond election a disaster. It was a curious position for them, inasmuch as the passage of the bonds, especially the $162 million intended for the water and wastewater bonds, would have satisfied their program for the city. Yet many of Austin's leading business figures wanted Friedman's People's Council to fail, and to fail in a big way. By the fall, complaints were already making the rounds of the city. Letters to the editor of the *Austin American-Statesman*, for example, demanded the recall of the council.[121] The mood of the business community was reflected in comments made by Dave Shanks in his *Austin Business Review*, a report that found its way into the hands of many businesspeople. He wrote: "What's happening in politics? Well, there's a great deal of uneasiness within the business community – to say the least. Never before has the business segment been so isolated in terms of influence in city politics. . . . Some say things are going to get worse. Others say they can't get worse."[122] Friedman tried to get leading business figures to endorse the bond package. He contacted Roy Butler, and asked for his public support. Butler refused.[123] Many leading businesspeople seemed to take Butler's position. On the other hand, Bill Youngblood, ever the urban entrepreneur, willingly agreed to endorse the bonds, and to push hard for them among members of the business community.[124]

Throughout the fall, the campaign on behalf of the bonds was waged. Friedman and the other council members took the whole matter very seriously, and worked as vigorously for the bond proposals as earlier Butler councils had. The split within the challenging community, which had earlier been evident in the tenuous links between the environmentalists and the minority camps, continued, even deepened. Ed Wendler, Sr., decided to remain comparatively quiet in his support for the bonds, apparently not wishing to offend his radical friends. Days after the election, Friedman wrote Wendler, acknowledging his silent affirmation, "as I am aware of the difficult personal situation it . . . created for you."[125] His brother Ken, however, was a strong public advocate of the bonds, finding no such divided loyalties among his friends in the community.[126] The council members sought to get as many of the challengers on their side as possible. Joan Bartz, for instance, was recruited to write a statement in support of the bonds. It appeared as a guest editorial in the *Austin American-Statesman* and noted, among other things, that the "Ongoing Committee for Austin Tomorrow . . . has endorsed the proposed C.I.P. [Capital Improvements Project] bond program . . . and found it to be compatible with the 'Goals for Austin' established by citizens through extensive neighborhood participation."[127]

The more radical challengers, however, ended up carrying the day. Although nine of the twelve bond proposals were passed by the December 4 vote, the two that had been targeted for defeat, Proposals 11 and 12 on water and wastewater, did not pass. In effect, a peculiar political alliance had defeated the principal bond package, one composed of radical challengers and growth-oriented business figures. The day after the election, this was brought home by Bob Sneed, a higher-up in the ranks of the Travis County Democrats, who called Gutow on the phone and told him, "I never thought I'd see the day when you and Nelson Puett [the realtor] would be on the same side of an issue."[128] Probably no one else in Austin did either. Years after this election, another realtor, George Sandlin, would sit across his desk from me and crow about the failure of the Friedman council in this election.[129] But he would not admit that it was a failure constructed by deep design.

Had the Friedman council successfully passed the entire 1975 bond package, it might have undercut at least one major segment of its support among the public, but at least it would have established political momentum for itself. That it did not was taken as *prima facie* evidence of its failure, and the failure of the challengers, to provide leadership for Austin. Friedman himself came under heavy attack, especially from the university quarter, for not carrying through with an effort on behalf of the "people." When asked about his inability to furnish direction, he told a reporter that it was a "matter of style," and that he preferred the more open, democratic method.[130] What he left unsaid, of course, was that he preferred that style to the one he had experienced under the reign of Roy Butler.

In the months that followed the December defeat of the bonds, the council seemed unable to come up with any earthshaking policies, or program, something that would truly mark its historic charcter.

Instead, members set about a course of what might best be called
"government by personal idiosyncrasy." Margaret Hofmann, who
seemed to epitomize this style, got on a high horse about a leash law
for dogs and the protection of the trees. Roger Duncan, her aide, did
produce a sensational report about the ongoing nuclear project, now
known as the South Texas Nuclear Project, which revealed the many
problems that beset it.[131] The report would soon help to propel an
effort that led Austin citizens to vote against further participation in
1981; yet, by that time, the cost of participation for the city alone had
run more than five times the original expectation. Bob Binder had
been right. Emma Lou Linn also expressed concern with the cost for
the nuclear project, but failed to come up with a systematic liberal
program herself. And Trevino and Snell, the other liberals, seemed
to spend much of their time just learning the ropes of council affairs.
Perhaps the only thing that the liberals could unite on was their displeasure with the work of city manager Dan Davidson, but even in
this case they were unable to effect his removal. The voice of the
people, when given the opportunity to speak, had gotten a severe
case of laryngitis.

Although the Friedman council came up virtually empty-handed,
the efforts of the challengers would not abate. Others took up where
they left off. The Austin Tomorrow report eventually became the
basis of a new Austin master plan; and although key elements of the
plan were not adhered to in detail by future City Councils, at least
it furnished some general directions in which the city should
move.[132] Among other things, for example, a Barton Creek
Watershed Ordinance was enacted that would serve to protect this
historic natural waterway through the city. Neighborhoods remained
a visible part of the Austin landscape, and the Austin Neighborhood
Council experienced a renaissance under the tireless leadership of
Marilyn Simpson. New leaders also arose from within the ranks of
the citizens, people like Helen Durio, who would give new voice to
the environmental concerns of many Austinites. New organizations
arose, too, such as the Zilker Park Posse and the Save Barton Creek
group, associations that would furnish a citywide alliance for preserving Austin's greenery and waterways. Austin's mayor in 1986,
Frank Cooksey, for example, was a former president of the Save Barton Creek association, and was elected to office through the strong
and vigorous efforts of the challengers.

Yet the early 1970s, and the Friedman years, if they may be called that, also left the challengers and their allies with some important lessons. Most of all, the populist challengers found it hard to derail the dream for growth and expansion because they could not unite themselves behind another common vision for the Austin future. It is one thing to decry the position of your opponent; it is quite another to provide an alternate blueprint for a better world. Thus, growth today continues unimpeded, unaffected in the long run, it would seem, by the defeat of the water and wastewater bonds in December 1975. History and culture, moreover, were very much on the side of those who promoted the vision for expansion and growth. After all, they had the benefit of a string of victories for a period of almost a century, so it would be hard to derail them in the space of just a few years.

There were other lessons, too. Not only did the challengers lack the funds to help finance their causes, but they also did not know how to play hardball politics. That seems to have been the bane of the liberal challengers throughout modern Austin history. They can yell and they can swear, but they cannot defeat someone like Roy Butler at his own game. Or, as Peck Young has put it, the challengers are only now beginning to know what to do with power.[133]

Yet one more lesson suggests itself from the Friedman years. When the Fair Housing Ordinance went down to defeat in 1968, the New Deal came to an end in Austin. The ramifications were many. But the most important one seems to have been that the action in Austin moved away from the public arena of city government to the private arena of business and industry. Tom Miller and the many New Dealers had been able to use the government not only to provide services for the poor and the needy, but also to construct Austin. The impetus for that expansion had shifted virtually unnoticed from government to business. The challengers of the 1970s, many of whom still were working within a New Deal frame of mind, thought that if they gained the reins of government, they could bring Austin growth to a halt or, at least, manage it. In retrospect, a number of them now realize that they could not, and, of course, did not.[134] The business of growth in Austin, in fact, had become the growth of business.

12.

Tales of the Land

—

I wanted some land. I wanted to own something of my own. . . . Of course, everybody does.

                                                                    Emmett Shelton, Sr.

If a town grows, and if you stagnate or quit growing then you are dying, then what do you do? . . . You have to use the land. I am not convinced that, even though I'm an environmentalist, the land is set aside for the animals. Man has to use the land. Man even improves the land.

                                                                          Chuck Stahl

I had Redbud Trail built up there, so [Paul Wakefield, Van Kennedy, and I] went up there to take a drink of whiskey [after we had lost the election], and I showed 'em my fence lines, and was telling 'em about my dreams and about the land I had bought and what I was going to do with it. And Paul Wakefield made this remark: He says, "Emmett, let's call it the anti-sonovabitch association, and let's just have nothing but residences on it, and have nobody that's a sonovabitch that he can't buy it. That's the only restriction. . . ." I tell that story to a lot of people, that worked fine as long as I was on my first sales, but I said a lot of you folks have got in under the wire on the re-sales. . . .

                                                                    Emmett Shelton, Sr.

IF THERE IS ONE THING THAT PEOPLE IN THIS PART OF world cherish, apart from the river, the lakes, and the wide open skies, it is the land. The terrain here has a special feel to it, a sense that marks it off from that in most other places in America. There are the remarkable hills, undulating and winding along the horizon. There are the many juniper trees, the live oaks, the Spanish oaks, the yaupons, the mountain laurels, and more, all of which decorate the hills, and all of which give that unique, purplish cast to the landscape at dusk. All of these things and more create the distinct topography that is called Austin and that, even to Texans who hunger for the land so much that they want to conquer and to dominate it, single out this setting as worth unlimited affection as well as the name "home" for growing numbers of Americans.

So wonderful is this land that when the great economic boom came to Austin, beginning in the late 1970s and lasting through the mid-1980s, much of the new wealth came from the sale of it. The great business of Austin became that of land deals, the trading of land, all designed to make the most profit in the shortest space of time. The favorite jokes of the Austin scene were about how many developers and real estate brokers worked in the city. One joke had it that you could shake a tree, and five of the six people who fell out would be real estate brokers. The joke, indeed, was more than fiction. It is said that the roughly 200 or so people who sold land and housing in Austin back in the early 1980s had quadrupled to more than 800 by the great land boom of 1983 and 1984. Thousands of acres and millions of dollars traded hands in this period, leaving the city with literally dozens of new millionaires, and far too many Jaguars, Mercedes, and BMWs to count.

The rush to buy and to sell land, however, profoundly violated the sense of intimate community as well as the sense of public trust that had taken told of Austin residents. Spurred on by the infusion of huge amounts of cash into the Austin real estate market, the land boom made it evident that this physical setting is not public property, that the community is not a public trust, and that in the end, when all is said and done, private property always reigns victorious over the common good. That violation, that tearing asunder of the nature of community in Austin, has subsequently produced a set of conflicts over the meaning of land for the city, a set of conflicts that more or less overlap with the traditional ones between liberals and conservatives, but that fuel them with an energy of uncommon strength and vitality.

Today there exist, in fact, two very different meanings that people in Austin attach to the land, two very different ways in which people construe it, and much of the rest of nature, in general. If one does not understand these two different modes of belief about land here, then one cannot fathom much of what happens in the city itself. On the one hand, there are those people who today define the land purely and simply in terms of modern-day capitalism, that is, as a commodity. To them, the land in and around Austin has meaning only insofar as it can be sold, and it can bring them a profit, perhaps of considerable proportions. The land to these folks is by no means a public trust, nor part of a common setting; instead, it is private property and, thus, something that can be bought and sold. On the other hand, there exists another group of people, who possess an entirely different conception of the land. To them, humans and nature possess a special kind of relationship, one of balance, a harmony that must not be disrupted by the senseless abuse of land. To this group of people, the land is to be preserved as much as possible in its natural, primitive state, and equally as much to be used for the enjoyment of the broad public rather than simply the large-scale developer, or even the private landowner.

Both groups, those who view land as a commodity and those who view it as a public trust, share a belief in the sanctity of private property and private ownership because both groups live under the same economic system, that of modern capitalism. The crucial difference between them, however, the difference that animates their struggle and that today creates in Austin such a profound degree of tension, is that members of the former group wish, quite simply, to turn as much land as possible into a source for their own private gain, whereas the latter wish to preserve as much land as possible in a public trust, believing that the very foundations of this Texas community rest ultimately and intimately in the character and quality of the land itself.

This last chapter in our story of Austin, then, is about the land, and about how it has been claimed, and about the men and women who have sought to claim it. Much of our story is about the land boom that hit the community in the 1970s, and then sent it skyward in the 1980s, but some of it is also about some earlier tales of the land, and about how certain sections of the city actually came to be created. There are, in fact, countless tales to be told here about the land, wonderful stories about monies made and monies lost, about people who sought to develop their own small dreams in a place called Austin. All of them, of course, cannot be told, but there are enough to provide a clear sense of how the land of the city was developed, and how vast Texas-sized fortunes grew in the wake of those developments.

We shall learn more than the stories of the land here, however. We shall also learn about that new breed of entrepreneurs who emerged in Austin to take the lead in the expansion of the city. Joe Crow, whom we read about in an earlier chapter, was a precursor of this figure, the *market entrepreneur*. The market entrepreneur is a social type, a role that people fulfill. He, or she, is a figure who takes risks and seizes opportunities, much as the urban entrepreneurs do, but who is primarily consumed with turning a profit rather than constructing a public place. In a phrase, whereas the urban entrepreneur, someone such as Tom Miller or Walter Long, sought to take risks in order to fashion a greater public entity, the market entrepreneur takes risks in order to create a greater private fortune. Both figures can contribute to the expansion of a community, but the former do so through actions taken on behalf of the place itself, whereas the latter do so through actions taken on behalf of themselves. Furthermore, to the extent that the city of Austin has grown rapidly in recent years, the growth has come about precisely because of the energy and the number of market entrepreneurs who have come to dominate this particular setting.

Just as not all urban entrepreneurs turn out to be of a piece, however, so, too, it is with the market entrepreneurs. There are important variations among them, nuances evident in a greater hunger for money among some, a greater willingness to promote the public good among others. Nevertheless, we must not mistake the nuances for true differences in character: as land developer, and market entrepreneur, Fred Purcell, put it: "I'm in the business because I'm a capitalist. I like to make money."[1] Moreover, the true market entrepreneur is a person who takes considerable risks, whose life is put on the line with each and every project, and whose back is almost always up against the wall. In Austin, in the late 1970s and early 1980s, the occupational group that came closest to this intense risk-taking mold were land speculators and developers. Many of them have told me, in the course of our interviews, how absolutely frightened they are by the risks, how tense a life they lead when they are living constantly at the edge, how precarious their existence seems, knowing their whole world rests on the success, or failure, of the next development down the road. If there are millions to be made in this world of the market entrepreneur, there also are millions to be lost, and the failed dream has, more often than not, resulted in abandoned families, endless bouts with alcohol, and even long stretches of time in the hospital. All of this may explain why the life of the market entrepreneur usually is one that can only be led by young people, individuals who have the fortitude to withstand the downturns, yet also the hunger to want to get rich, almost at any price.

To tell the stories of the land and its use in the creation of modern Austin, we shall follow the route of two major thoroughfares that now cut across the city, Mo-Pac Boulevard, or Loop 1 (hereafter referred to as Mo-Pac), and Capital of Texas Highway, or Loop 360 (hereafter referred to as Loop 360). Both these roads are fairly recent additions to the city's network of highways. Mo-Pac, in fact, is still in the process of construction. The choice to let these two roads serve as the vehicle for our tales is by no means a random one. Alongside both of them, one today can find some of the major residential and commercial developments in Austin. Moreover, the very creation of these projects is intimately connected to the construction of the two roads themselves. For instance, the very prestigious and affluent Rob Roy and Davenport Ranch residential developments, which lie on the western edges of the city, would not have been possible without the access afforded their residents by both Mo-Pac and Loop 360. The same holds true for Northwest Hills, another very fancy residential area of the city. Finally, the story of these two roads, but particularly Mo-Pac, represents almost a condensed version of the development of land, and the struggles over its meaning, in modern Austin. By traveling the route of these roads, in effect, we also shall travel through some of Austin's most memorable and most difficult times.

As originally envisioned by city planners, Mo-Pac, so named because it runs alongside the Missouri-Pacific Railroad tracks, was to extend across Highway 183 to FM 1325 (Burnet Road). Today it actually ends at Highway 183, but someday that strip of road will be finished, and with good reason, too. For out here, in the northwest quadrant of the city, between Highway 183 and FM 1325, lie some of the most visible signs of the Austin industrial future. Texas Instruments Corporation, which came to Austin largely through the recruiting efforts of the Chamber of Commerce's John Gray and Vic Mathias back in 1968, sits astride Highway 183, and today employs more than 3,000 workers. Just behind it, lying adjacent to FM 1325, are the Balcones Research Center Laboratory, which J. Neils Thompson had a hand in developing, and the quarters of IBM, whose location here heralded the great boom in Austin's industrial future back in the late 1960s.

But the major story out here is that of the Microelectronics and Computer Technology Corporation, or MCC as it is commonly called. MCC, which has offices along both Highway 183 and FM 1325—the latter property part of a gift from the University of Texas—brought international prominence to Austin back in 1983. More than that, its arrival in the city helped to stimulate the great speculation in land. The story of how MCC came to Austin is by now an old one; it has been told so many times that to repeat it here, in great detail, would be tedious at best. But the outlines are interesting because they reveal so much about how the city and the state have gone about the process of recent industrial growth. MCC is designed as a consortium of private technology firms in America, and is intended to compete with Japan, and other industrial nations, in the race to develop artificial intelligence, otherwise known as the fifth generation of computers.[2] The conception of a consortium of private firms, working hand-in-hand in the United States to develop new industrial apparatus, is a pioneering one, the brainchild of William Norris of Control Data Corporation.[3] The man, however, who has made it all go until now is Admiral Bobby Ray Inman, former deputy director of the Central Intelligence Agency. Inman was hired in February 1983 as the chief executive officer and president of the new corporation. His job was to create the organizational structure for the firm and to locate the headquarters for its plant. Inman was said to be brilliant, was a graduate of the University of Texas at the uncommonly young age of nineteen, and rose through the ranks of the Central Intelligence Agency extraordinarily fast, becoming, among other things, the only civilian admiral in the agency's history.

Through a stroke of good luck, Austin ended up on a list of cities that competed for the location of MCC's headquarters in early 1983.[4] Officials of the fledgling company invited the representatives of fifty-seven cities across the nation to a gathering in Chicago, held on March 18. The purpose of the meeting was to enable the MCC officials to identify a handful of cities from among which they eventually would choose the site for their operations. This open, public process of site selection was unusual among American corporations, but, in a sense, it was fitting for such an unusual corporate undertaking. Governor Mark White and other Texas officials made a brief presentation at the meeting on behalf of the state, and then representatives of several individual cities, including Dallas and Houston, each made twenty-minute deliveries of their own. John Gray, head of the economic development arm of Austin's Chamber of Commerce, and Ben Streetman, a recent high-level recruit to the University of Texas Department of Electrical Engineering, attended the meeting on behalf of the city.[5] Gray decided, in the days just before his presentation, that he would give his standard, industry-luring delivery—that is, that he would try to show MCC how Austin, and its special institutions like the University of Texas and high-tech firms such as the Tracor Corporation, met the needs of the new technology consortium.[6] Gray's presentation, as usual, was thorough, but not the very best, as Admiral Inman later noted.[7] The best delivery was that of San Antonio Mayor Henry Cisneros, who gave a full-scale multimedia presentation, with slides, reinforced by his typically smooth and high-powered oratory. Nevertheless, when the MCC officials got together after presentations by all fifty-seven cities, they decided to include Austin as one of the final four, mainly because it housed the University of Texas and thus, they felt, had the potential for developing an intellectual training grounds so necessary to MCC's own expansion.

Three other cities also were included in the final four. They were Atlanta, San Diego, and Raleigh-Durham, North Carolina. Each of these sites held considerable appeal. Atlanta, of course, is a booming industrial and financial empire of the Southeast, as well as being home to such good technical universities as the Georgia Institute of Technology. Raleigh-Durham is the site of the Research Triangle, which includes a number of fine private research outfits as well as two outstanding universities, Duke and the University of North Carolina at Chapel Hill. San Diego also has its own parade of intellectual and industrial centers, including a superb branch of the University of California, and, of the four cities, probably the very best climate and physical setting. Notably, too, all four of these cities are located in the Sunbelt, a general factor that seemed to enter into the formula that Inman and his colleagues used in identifying potential locations.

Within the space of four days in May 1983, MCC permitted itself to be wined, dined, and generally cajoled by people in each of the four cities. Each place brought out its big guns, but those of Austin clearly seemed the biggest. By the time MCC officials set foot in Austin, the city's presentation did not include merely local officials, but was an orchestrated effort by major state figures to lure MCC here. Governor White had been persuaded that the economic future of the state lay with the development of a strong high-technology base of operations and he, in turn, helped to corral a number of other prominent state leaders including computer magnate Ross Perot, Houston banker Ben Love, former Governor Allan Shivers, and multibillionaire Perry Bass. Also included were a number of close friends and associates of the governor, among them, Pike Powers, an attorney and his administrative assistant, and John Watson, an Austin developer.

MCC ultimately selected Austin for its site of operations. No one, it appears, is quite sure why. Neal Spelce and Howard Falkenberg, local advertising firm officials, came up with a comparison, by residents, of the quality of life in each of the four cities, which, on balance, favored Austin.[8] Some people say this information had much to do with the final decision by MCC officials. Others, of course, point to the University of Texas, including Admiral Inman himself, who wanted MCC to choose a place in which there was a good second-class university that would be willing to devote enormous resources to both its computer science and its electrical engineering programs.[9] But, clearly, the biggest thing going for the city of Austin was the complete financial package worked out by Texas leaders and by the university itself. The University of Texas, under the leadership of President Peter H. Flawn, committed itself to $15 million worth of endowed faculty chairs for thirty new faculty positions in computer science and electrical engineering; adding an income of $1 million each year for research in these areas; grants totaling $750,000 a year to support seventy-five graduate students in these areas; $5 million for the purchase of new equipment; and a nominal cost for leasing portoins of its Balcones Research Center facility. The entire package was worth, on final tally, many millions of dollars, and far outstripped that offered by the other cities. In fact, when informed that MCC had selected Austin to be its headquarters, Atlanta Mayor Andrew Young scornfully commented that Austin simply had "bought" MCC.[10]

Nothing has ever put Austin on the map as the coming of MCC did—not even Tom Miller or Lyndon Johnson. Following the May

1983 announcement, the hoopla was enormous, comparable perhaps only to the time when Harold Ickes announced to the citizens here that the New Deal was about to pour $17 million into the construction of dams on the Colorado. People started referring to John Naisbitt's *Megatrends* book, which had been on the bestseller list for over a year and which had identified Austin as one of the great high-tech centers of the twenty-first century, as though it were the Bible.[11] Naisbitt even was invited to the city in order to provide further prognostications for his newly won disciples. The atmosphere was electric. Newspapers from across the country, including ones as distant as the *Milwaukee Journal* and the *Wall Street Journal*, started singing the praises of the Texas hill country, while Peter Flawn and the University of Texas made the front pages of the *New York Times* in an article about millions for endowed chairs.[12] Austin truly had made the big time, and was, in the words of many of its boosters, on its way to becoming a "world-class" city. Alexander Wooldridge would have been proud of it.

What the arrival of MCC did, in fact, was to excite an interest in real estate that had begun about 1978 or 1979 as well as to reinforce the industrial directions of the city that had been molded by people like J. Neils Thompson and John Gray. Land values were most vulnerable to the news, however, and in the period of 1983 through early 1985 they shot through the roof. Austin land appraiser Jim Frederick is the bearer of many tales about this period.[13] In October 1983, for instance, just months after the MCC announcement, property near the projected MCC quarters on FM 1325 sold for about $1.80/square foot. Three months later, it sold for $3.08/square foot, an incredible rise in the cost of acreage.

Frederick also recalls that people came into Austin from everywhere, some making honest deals, some fraudulent ones. There was the case of man who put down a hot check, in the amount of $50,000, to buy the option on a piece of property. He was not found out until he had already made more than $1 million by flipping the land (selling it to other buyers), and could cover his hot check. New businesses also began to enter Austin at an ever increasing rate: in the year following MCC's announcement, it was reported that the Austin area had gained a net total of 32,000 new jobs, making it the fastest-growing job market in the entire nation.[14] As one looks back at these tales today, of course, they seem almost mythical. The land market has cratered, as they say, and the increase in the number of new jobs has dropped drastically. The economy is in something of the doldrums due, in no small measure, to the effects of the downturn in the broader Texas oil market. Nonetheless, MCC helped to secure the industrial future of Austin; and while the promise, no doubt, lies in a further reach of history than many, especially land speculators, ever expected, it is a promise that most assuredly will come true.

While MCC represents the most prominent and recent addition to the line of enterprises that lie in and around the northern end of Mo-Pac, the oldest story, perhaps, begins just a mile or so down the road, south of its intersection with Highway 183. If you are driving here, and heading south, then just to your right lies a large stretch of several thousand acres that has come to be known as the Northwest Hills section of Austin. And it is here, on this property, that the early foundations for residential growth and for the construction of Mo-Pac truly lie.

As usual, there are a set of individuals who occupy the center of this particular tale of Austin expansion. Among them are names familiar to the real estate community, people like Wallace Mayfield, Tom Bradfield and his father, and Donald Cummings, Tom Bradfield's partner. Mayfield, and the Bradfields, and Cummings all helped to begin the tremendous residential building boom that took place in Austin, and their efforts began back in the 1950s. The Bradfields and Cummings, for example, built a number of residential units in an area now known as Highland Hills, property that bordered some of the land owned by Commodore Perry.[15] They, thus, became some of the first developers to risk construction in the hills of Austin, a venture that could have flopped but did not. The major figure in this particular tale, however, is a man by the name of David Barrow, Sr. Along with his son, David, Jr., and associate Chuck Stahl, David Barrow helped to develop the major part of the residential construction in the flatlands and rolling terrain of Northwest Hills. And Barrow also is primarily responsible for the eventual construction of Mo-Pac, as well as a good deal of the Austin planning that took place in the 1950s and 1960s.

Barrow, Sr., was a man of considerable integrity and honesty, a good church-going Presbyterian. He also probably possessed one of the shrewdest business minds in recent times in Austin. He was born and bred here, attended Austin High School, and then set about making a career for himself, first as a railroad clerk, then as a key official with the State of Texas Insurance Commission – when he retired from it he was deputy commissioner – and then in the last twenty years or so of his life, when most men spend their time playing golf or fishing, developing much of the Northwest Hills acreage.[16] He was raised in a family of four boys, and each and every one achieved remarkable success and fortune. One of his brothers, Edward, joined with Gus Wortham of Houston to found the American General Life Insurance Company, which now is worth at least a couple of billion dollars. Another, Slim, went on to become the chief executive officer of Humble Oil Company (Exxon), and a third, John, joined with David in the land development business. All the brothers – but especially David, Edward, and John – remained very close to one another throughout their lives. Once Edward started making money in the insurance business, he and David created the Austin Corporation, which served as the vehicle for purchasing and developing property in Austin.

Why David decided to spend his autumn years going through the hassle of land development remains unclear. He was always a very athletic person, had lettered in baseball at Austin High, and loved the out-of-doors.[17] But, it seems, his favorite love was the land itself, particularly the rugged northwestern territory. As Chuck Stahl, his business associate, remembers, David, Sr., was "very, very sensitive about the land. . . . He walked the land every day, and he worked six and seven days a week. He was on the land virtually all the time. . . . [and he] knew virtually every rock outcropping in the hills."[18] Sometime in the early 1950s, Barrow, Sr., began his residential undertakings with purchases of a few pieces of property along Balcones Drive, in what is now known as the Edgemont section of Austin. Soon thereafter, he moved into the Mount Bonnell area, somewhat nearby, into land that overlooks the Colorado, and developed a few other properties. Then, gradually, he began to develop the land further into the hills.

As David, Jr., and Stahl tell the story, David, Sr., at the start had no real designs for something that would be called Northwest Hills.[19] What he did believe was that the upper-end, affluent growth of the city was apt to take place in the northwest quadrant of the city, and that if one were to build for this segment of the population, one had to be prepared to develop the hilly terrain. Barrow, thus, set about on a gradual course to acquire the property in these parts, and to do so only on a piecemeal basis, picking up a few parcels of land

here and there, developing them, and then moving farther northward, out into the more rugged land.

The owners of much of this property at the time were M. E. Hart,
a Canadian who made his money in gravel pits and who spent six
months of the year living in Austin (Hart Lane is now named for
him), and a Captain Knox. Barrow, Sr., made a deal with Hart to
buy the land on a rolling option. This meant that he had the first
option to Hart's property, but would purchase it only a piece at a
time, and at the current market price. Both men stood to gain from
the deal. Barrow did not have to put up much money, and Hart sold
his property at an ever increasing price owing to the value created by
Barrow's new developments.[20] Ultimately, Barrow, Sr., his several
associates, and partner Edward, came to own 2,500 of the nearly
3,500 acres in the northwest quadrant. Their project also turned out
to be no overnight prefabricated set of row houses. The first houses
in their scheme were finished sometime in the late 1950s, and the
final properties are just now being completed.

The designs for this land by Barrow, Sr., were unique for the time.
When architects Stahl and Barrow, Jr., first put together something
like a grand plan for the hills, their conception was of a new
town, almost.[21] The shape of the town turned out to be in the
image of Austin itself. Hence, they pictured the eastern boundary
of Northwest Hills would be like the southern boundary of early
Austin, with Balcones Drive—which now runs alongside the property—as the counterpart of the Colorado River. They further pictured something like a downtown to the area, again in a comparable
location to the downtown of Austin. Thus, Far West Boulevard,
which runs on an east–west course, leading on the eastern end
into Mo-Pac Boulevard, was conceived to be roughly comparable to
Congress Avenue in downtown Austin.

When now seen in its broadest design, the scheme of Stahl and
Barrow, Jr., for these hills is very impressive, including not only
homes, but schemes for rail transportation, and even a plan for Far
West Boulevard to empty into Airport Boulevard, lying miles away
in the southeastern sector of the city. As the residential developments unfolded during the 1960s and 1970s, much of the scheme
came true. Unfortunately, as Stahl now points out, few residents of
the area, and probably even fewer of the city, ever came to recognize
the grand design, owing to the reserved manner in which Barrow,
Sr., conducted his business.[22]

But Barrow, Sr., himself came to be very well known and highly respected in the leading social and political circles of the city. As he became ever more involved in the land development and residential construction business, he also became more visible to the city leaders, people like Tom Miller. He soon came to be called on to serve in various civic capacities, the most important of which was as a commissioner on the newly revised City Planning Commission in 1955.[23] And it was on this commission, in his role as its chairman from 1957 through 1966, that Barrow, Sr., would leave his greatest mark on the planning of modern Austin. Just to show how different the 1950s were from the 1980s, today many hundreds of people in Austin—not to mention such critical periodicals as *Third Coast*— would be going over the life and times of Barrow, Sr., with a fine-tooth comb, and would probably be down at the City Council chambers noisily lobbying for his ouster. But no one did so back in the 1950s, nor even in the mid-1960s, and Barrow, Sr., was left to walk the fine line that separated his activities as an urban entrepreneur from those of his work as a market entrepreneur. The actual dilemmas created thereby for him, it would now seem, must have been experienced more deeply than those of virtually any other prominent figure in Austin at the time.

One of the most important decisions that confronted the City Planning Commission back in the mid-1950s had to do with the construction of Mo-Pac Boulevard, also known then as Railroad Boulevard. The original designs for this road had been fashioned in 1944, just at the time when the federal government, in preparation for a postwar era of growth and prosperity, had undertaken plans for a great interstate system of highways.[24] In Austin, a city planning engineer by the name of G. S. Moore had been hired to work up a long-range scheme for Austin's own system of roads and thoroughfares. Moore's plan called for such things as the relocation of the major railroads to the eastern sector of the downtown area, even though, in so doing, he realized that such a project might conflict with the continuing effort to "encourage negroes to continue to live here."[25] Moore's scheme also included a design for a boulevard that would run alongside the Missouri-Pacific Railroad tracks (to be vacated), what is now called Mo-Pac. The boulevard, as he designed it, bears a remarkable similarity to today's highway. It began roughly in the area where Highway 183 runs, followed alongside the path of the tracks, cut across the river on the western edge of Zilker Park, and then ended somewhere south of the city limits, just about where it terminates today. Moore strongly urged the development of such a road inasmuch as he believed it would encourage the industrial and residential growth of the city, something, of course, that Austin desperately needed.[26]

Nothing much more was heard of Moore's grand design until the early 1950s, when the city officials, like Tom Miller, began to recognize the need for such a north–south thoroughfare. In March 1950, the City Council agreed to begin work on something like a Railroad Boulevard. Taylor Glass, who served then as mayor of the city, even recalls that he went to Houston to talk with Missouri-Pacific officials about the purchase of some of the railroad's right-of-way.[27] By the time that Harold Wise and his company put together a master plan for Austin in 1956, city officials were sufficiently committed to the new highway that a Mo-Pac Boulevard was part of Wise's plan for thoroughfares. But it was only a scheme and design, and given the controversy that met Wise's master plan when it was unveiled, evidently it was an idea whose time had not come.

The slow, almost tortured fashion in which the city seemed to be developing its plans for a Mo-Pac Boulevard annoyed David Barrow, Sr., and many of his fellow developers in the northwest area. Barrow, Sr., it was clear, was deeply interested in a boulevard that ran alongside the railroad tracks.[28] And with good reason, too. The residents who lived in the northwest quadrant of the city typically worked in downtown Austin. In the 1950s, and well into the late 1960s, their only manner of transportation into this area was to travel east of the hills to Lamar Boulevard, or, if necessary, even farther, to the interstate, Highway 35. As more and more people came to live in the northern sectors of the city, Lamar Boulevard, along with some more minor routes into the downtown area, became increasingly clogged with rush-hour traffic. Barrow, Sr., realized that the access both to work and to home must be made much easier. Not only would this help the current residents, but it would also promote further growth, and, of course, home sales, in Northwest Hills.

So, David Barrow, Sr., and several of his fellow developers in the hills spent time talking about how to get city officials out of the clouds and down to earth, particularly the earth around the railroad tracks. For years, several of them, including Mayfield, the Bradfields, and Donald Cummings, had gathered once a week just to talk things over and have friendly chats.[29] As time went by, more and more of their discussion focused on how to get the boulevard built along the tracks. The men even went so far as to invite Jac Gubbels to join their friendly gatherings, the explicit purpose being to learn how to get such a road constructed.[30]

Gubbels, it just so happened, had been a longtime landscape architect for the State Highway Department, and had inside knowledge on how one went about securing help from the Highway Department for roads like the one they dreamt of. At one point, sometime around 1960 or 1961, Gubbels advised the men that if they wanted the boulevard to be built anytime soon, then they should have an origin-and destination study done by the city. Such a study, he said, would reveal how much actual traffic was carried daily and weekly by the current roads, such as Balcones Drive. Further, if the traffic was as heavy as they claimed, Gubbels told them, then there should be no problem in securing not only the action of the city, but also help from the State Highway Department as well.

The study was done. And it did, in fact, reveal the need to provide better roads to handle traffic, particularly rush-hour traffic, than the current ones.[31] Barrow, Sr., all the while, made sure not only that the cooperation of the State Highway Department was secured, but that the city, through the auspices of the Planning Commission, continued to press for the construction of the boulevard. Careful study of the minutes of the Planning Commission, during the time that Barrow, Sr., was chairman, reveals that he periodically pressed the issue of its development, and that, generally, his fellow commissioners were receptive to his encouragement.[32] Barrow, Sr., exercised great control over the commission, owing in no small measure to the respect he engendered among the other members. Eveything he wanted he got. This is clearly evident in the decisions that the commission took on questions of ordinances and zoning regulating Barrow's own property. Although he was legally prevented from voting on these matters, careful study again reveals that on every such question the commission always decided in favor of Barrow, Sr.[33]

Finally, in 1966, through the efforts of Barrow, Sr., and others, the State Highway Department agreed to join the City of Austin in constructing Mo-Pac Boulevard.[34] The city itself already had done some of the initial work, including the construction of an underpass at Enfield Road and the purchase of some of the right-of-way from the Missouri-Pacific Railroad. The State Highway Department agreed to build the road in segments, the first part stretching from just north of the river in downtown Austin to Northland Drive. To complete the plans, the Highway Department also convened several public hearings, including one on February 6, 1968, at which the last approvals were made for the road, and members of the public were permitted to voice their opinions.[35] State and local officials showed up in large numbers for this meeting, including David Barrow, Sr., in his capacity as chairman of the Regional Planning Commission for the City of Austin.

The story of Mo-Pac Boulevard, thus, is partly the story of David Barrow, Sr., and partly the story of the growth of Northwest Austin. Just like so many other events in the city's history, moreover, this one grew to a scale far exceeding the original expectations, even of David Barrow, Sr. To cite but two examples: state highway engineers in 1974 anticipated that the most heavily traveled segments of Mo-Pac would reach a figure of about 45,000 cars, on the average, per day by 1990. In fact, in 1985, these stretches of road already had reached a figure of 100,000 cars.[36] Likewise, the newly opened section of Mo-Pac that runs across Barton Creek, south from Loop 360, was expected to carry 18,000 cars per day by 1990. In the days after it opened in 1986, it carried 38,000 cars.[37]

On the northern edge of the northwestern hills, straddling Mo-Pac Boulevard and Steck Lane, is one of the first office park developments in the northwest quadrant of the city. It is called West Park, and was developed by two men, Walter Vackar and Frans Posse, in 1980. Although its story is not one of the most important or extensive about land and Mo-Pac, it nevertheless furnishes some insight into how the land and building boom came to Austin, and, most especially, how foreign investors provided some of the money for the boom.

Walter Vackar is a handsome and smooth-talking Texan.[38] He also is one of the new breed of market entrepreneurs active in contemporary Austin. Like so many other Austinites, Vackar came to the city to attend the University of Texas and, except for one year after college, has remained in Austin ever since. In 1969, with his degree in architecture in hand, he entered into a four-man firm, consisting of Tom Shefelman, David Minter, and Alan Taniguchi. Taniguchi himself was a longtime Austin resident, whose father, Isamu, had developed the renowned Zilker Park Gardens into one of the highlights of the Austin nature scene. The men worked well together, and put up some very attractive homes, for a period of several years.

At the inspiration of Vackar and Minter, the firm also embarked on a few development projects of its own, including a small set of duplexes on Bluebonnet Lane, just blocks from Zilker Park. By 1976, it had become clear that Vackar and Minter were more interested in development projects than Shefelman and Taniguchi, and so they went their separate ways. Within the space of a couple of years, the two made a small bundle for themselves by creating several commercial projects in Austin. By the late 1970s, they, too, parted ways, and Vackar embarked on a career of commercial projects on his own.

At this point, Vackar started looking for investors who would be willing to go in with him on his projects. Although he had made some money, the projects of interest to him required substantial cash, more than he himself could scrape up. One evening, at a dinner party, he met a man by the name of John Krone. Krone, it just so happened, was head of the foreign investment department of Lomas and Nettleton, a major U.S. investment outfit. Vackar explained to Krone that he needed some cash to help finance his projects. By coincidence, Krone had just been talking to a Belgian investor, Frans Posse, who was looking around for places in the United States where he could invest some cash. Posse had found, apparently, that other Sunbelt cities, like Phoenix, did not interest him very much, and was on the lookout for a city that had some of the rugged ambience of European villages and towns. Krone told Vackar about Posse. He also informed him that while Posse was not a big investor, nothing like the mutual fund or union operations in Europe, he, nevertheless, might have some money to put into Vackar's projects.[39]

Vackar and Posse finally met in Austin, and struck up an immediate friendship. Vackar had the talent and interest in architecture, and in developing commercial ventures, while Posse had the money. Their first project together was the West Park office complex. It took a couple of years to complete and, like David Barrow's Northwest Hills residences, it was something of a risk since Mo-Pac Boulevard did not yet stretch this far and the area itself was fairly undeveloped. Posse also showed himself to be far more than a small investor, at least by Austin standards. When the time came to put up the cash for the initial plans and bank loans for the project, he was able to come up with a tidy $1 million in hard cash.[40] Not bad for a European civil servant who retired at the age of fifty. With the completion of West Park, Vackar and Posse moved on to other commercial ventures. Their most successful, perhaps, was a set of buildings that lie roughly at the intersection of Mo-Pac Boulevard and Highway 183, known as The Echelon. These tall, graceful, all-glass structures have gained the attention of many a passerby, and also earned the two men awards for architectural elegance and sensitive environmental landscaping. Plus, it just so happens, they furnished MCC with its first temporary quarters in the city of Austin.

Vackar and Posse are no longer partners. Posse, it appears, also has fallen on hard times. A recent article in the *Austin American-Statesman* reports that he has filed for bankruptcy on one of his projects.[41] Vackar, on the other hand, has turned out to be one of the most prosperous of all the city's newly rich land developers. Today he is in the midst of a major commercial/residential project located only miles from the northern tip of Mo-Pac Boulevard. Known as the Lakeline project, it covers 400 acres of very valuable property and, at present, is worth about $100 million. When completed, Vackar estimates, its residential and commercial operations will be worth somewhere in the neighborhood of $1 billion.[42]

Just south of the Northwest Hills residential sector sits Allandale, a small, lower-middle- to middle-class setting of Austin. The area was developed in the late 1940s and early 1950s, during the postwar building boom, by Tom Bradfield and his father, and was named for George Allan, from whom the Bradfields purchased it.[43] Starting roughly at this stretch along Mo-Pac, and extending all the way across the Colorado River, into Zilker Park, there are a series of stories about citizen dissent and unhappiness with land development and even the construction of Mo-Pac Boulevard itself. These stories complement those told in the preceding chapter, on challenges to the dream, but they go further, revealing how the dissatisfaction erupted over the the very meaning of land, and the environment, to Austin residents. And they demonstrate something of the historical origins of the one view of land in Austin, as something that should be preserved in as natural and primitive form as possible.

Back in the 1950s and even late into the 1960s, no one thought much about the expansion of Austin at all. Everyone, as we have learned earlier in this book, somehow took growth for granted. It brought in new jobs, it gave graduates of the university an opportunity to remain in the city, it helped provide more money to the

Austin economy, and it furnished a way of civilizing this otherwise outlying stretch of the American frontier. But there were a few people who raised issues about what expansion might do to Austin, and they started raising them somewhere in the mid-1960s. There were a few groups that did so, like the Sierra Club.[44] Members of the club wondered what all the new residential developments, such as those in Northwest Hills, might do to the wonderful hills and trees of the city. Then there were others who raised questions, most notably a woman by the name of Roberta, or Bobbi, Dickson (Crenshaw).

Bobbi Dickson Crenshaw is an Austin institution venerated almost as much as Emma Long.[45] She has argued on behalf of environmental issues for years, when virtually no one else was prepared to do so. Her links to Austin run wide and deep. As a young woman, still at the university, she married Malcolm Reed, the brother of Dave Reed. Dave Reed was the partner of Edgar Perry. The marriage between the young woman and the considerably older man—she was not yet eighteen years old, and he was somewhere in his early seventies—caused much commotion among the stodgy ranks of Austin society, but it also led Bobbi to have her first taste of politics. She got to know Tom Miller a bit, and also became acquainted with the Commodore and other famous figures on the Austin scene. After Reed died, she married another older man, Fagan Dickson, a prominent Austin attorney and Texas assistant attorney general.

About this time, she also started to get interested in environmental issues in the city. In the mid-1950s, she was nominated by Emma Long, and appointed by the City Council, to serve as a member of the Austin Parks and Recreation Board.[46] She revealed herself to be a person of imagination and energy while serving on the board. For example, although today Lady Bird Johnson gets most of the credit for having planted a number of flowering trees alongside Town Lake in downtown Austin, it was Bobbi Crenshaw who first put up trees and other shrubbery here. Using considerable funds of her own, as well as a number of her own hands, as she calls them, she had almost 350 trees and shrubs planted on the river's shores between Congress Avenue and First Street.[47] Even now one may go down to this stretch along the shore of the River, just at the northwest side of the Congress Avenue Bridge, and observe her beautiful handiwork. Eventually, in the 1960s, Bobbi was named to serve as the chair of the Austin Parks Board. And soon her work and opinions gained her so much fame that she was appointed to the National Parks and

Recreation Board, there becoming familiar with a number of important American environmentalists.

At the open hearing on Mo-Pac Boulevard, held on February 6, 1968, with David Barrow, Sr., among others in attendance, Bobbi was one of the few people to take issue with the plans. Her concern was characteristic. She wondered what the new boulevard, but especially its proposed links into the downtown area, would do to the natural setting along the lake. She worried that this special feature of the Austin setting would be ruined, that it would become another victim to the expansion and so-called progress of the city. She told other congregants at the meeting that "First Street . . . is an extraordinary street . . . the only street . . . that can offer amenities to city living which [would] preserve it for those who don't want to drive on an expressway and for those who want to preserve the aesthetic value of [our] downtown."[48]

Within the space of just a few years, Bobbi's concerns became those of many Austin residents. By 1972, encouraged by the growing number of neighborhood organizations led by people like Joan Bartz, the citizens' expression of the potential harm by growth and, particularly, by the proposed new segments of the Mo-Pac Boulevard had grown virtually into a firestorm of dissent. Many of Bobbi's neighbors, in the Tarrytown area of Austin, which lies just south of Northwest Hills along Mo-Pac, echoed her sentiments. Together, a number of them, including Bobbi herself, put together an unusually thoroughgoing report on the state of living in this section of Austin, and what harm might be done to it by the completion of the new road.[49] They actually gathered information on the projected daily flow of traffic, purportedly demonstrating that many cars ultimately might end up along the small residential drives of the neighborhood. Many West Austin residents believed that the traffic not only would endanger their children, who played on the streets and walks, but also would do eventual harm to the trees and flowers that decorated their beautiful landscapes. Some people took a different view of the protests, including members of the State Highway Department who believed the objection to be nothing more than concern with so-called property values by the homeowners. Regardless of its roots, however, the dissent grew and grew, and the call for environmental preservation to the neighborhoods bordering the proposed Mo-Pac Boulevard became widespread.

By the time the Friedman council reached office in 1975, a large stretch of Mo-Pac had been completed, and many neighborhood residents were giving vent to their anger about it. To many of them, of course, it must have seemed as though the new council was an answer to their problems, if not their prayers. The Allandale neighborhood was the source of some of the pleas to Jeff Friedman and his fellow council members. One resident wrote: "as a citizen of the community who will be greatly affected by the opening of Mo-Pac, I loudly protest against the terrible injustice that should never have gotten this far. I realize that it is a hard climb to the top of the mountain on which stand the few wealthy controllers, but with a city council made up of a majority of members willing to help the people, I believe we have gained a few footholds."[50]

Allandale itself already had witnessed some earlier concerns about what development and the construction of roads like Mo-Pac would do to the environmental quality of the area. In early 1974, Dr. S. J. Lerro wrote Bob Binder, who then served on the council, to note his worry over the developments now occurring on the northwestern edge of the city: "I wish to emphasize that the city of Austin has rapidly changed the ecology in northwest Austin in permitting the building of a large shopping area here [Northcross Mall] and other commercial properties without immediate effective planning [on how] to handle over 300 to 500 per cent increase in peak water runoff as a result of urban development."[51] Lerro noted, specifically, that the growing amount of impervious land cover in the area, especially the large parking lots associated with the mall, coupled with the earlier developments of Northwest Hills lying just above Allandale, threatened potential flooding to the homes of many residents.

Lobbied strongly by environmental and neighborhood spokespersons, the Friedman council acquiesced, and decided to do what it could to prevent Mo-Pac Boulevard from ever becoming a full-scale highway. In what must today stand as one of the more idiosyncratic and memorable actions by this council, the members agreed to shut down the ramps that led into the recently completed segments of the road. Thus, the ramps that fed into Mo-Pac from Thirty-fifth Street, Westover Road, and Enfield Road all were closed off.[52] The council members expected that in so doing they would insure that no downtown traffic could thereby disturb the local neighborhoods, like that of Tarrytown. The amount of anger engendered on the other side was enormous, including outraged editorials in the *Austin American-Statesman*.[53] The land developers, the real estate brokers, indeed, the entire business community, which, on other matters, already had lined up squarely against the Friedman council, took the ramp closing as yet another sign of the so-called no-growth attitude of the council. Suits were threatened, and some City of Austin officials, such as Joe Ternus, head of the Transportation Department, even considered resigning because they believed the action by the council to be illegal.[54]

Ultimately the council, under considerable pressure from the State Highway Department and the city staff, reversed its decision, and opened the ramps to traffic. But the concerns over the harm posed to the natural environment by the road, and by developments along it, did not subside. Just a few years later, in 1978, Tom Bradfield and Don Cummings, who had helped to construct Allandale homes, and who both had taken a hand in some of the original lobbying by land developers for the construction of Mo-Pac, sought to get the City of Austin to approve their plans for the use of 108 acres of land they owned adjacent to Zilker Park, bordering what was projected to become part of the extension of the road just south of the river. The two men proposed to put up some commercial projects, including office buildings.[55]

By now the forces to preserve the natural environment had become far more sophisticated in the quality of their arguments and in the effectiveness of the public expression of them. Citizens appeared in large numbers to argue against the Bradfield and Cummings plans, noting the potential harm to the Barton Creek watershed by the proposed large-scale development.[56] The city staff had its own problems with the proposal, and ultimately spent years working through it in order to insure that the project did not actually threaten harm to the land, and to the creek. Bradfield and Cummings eventually got the project through, but not without considerable cost to themselves.[57] Indeed, this little fiasco came to exemplify many of the market entrepreneurs versus citizen standoffs that stamped the decade of the 1970s. For their part, those who challenged the project, the neighborhood groups as well as the environmentalists, won a victory of sorts, inasmuch as the controversy produced new organizations, not the least important of which were the Zilker Park Posse and the Save Barton Creek Neighborhood Association.

More than anything else, what this particular series of episodes of struggle over the land came to reveal to Austinites, and to students who seek to make sense of this wonderful place, is how deeply divided the community actually is. And the division, to reiterate a theme established at the outset of this chapter, is essentially over how to think about the land. While, of course, it is easy, in a sense, to agree with the market entrepreneurs that growth and expansion may be good for the city, those who wish to protect the land against environmental dangers are not entirely out-to-lunch, as their critics claim.

Only seven years after he wrote his letter of concern to the Friedman council, Dr. Lerro's nightmare of urban runoff indeed came true, and with a fury that residents will never forget. On the Memorial Day weekend of 1981, and then again just one week later, there were several floods that hit the city of Austin. To those today who know the history, they can only be compared to some of those savage floods along the Colorado River, torrents of water that eventually brought about construction of the dams. And like those same floods, there were lives lost, thirteen Austin residents altogether falling prey to the unleashed waters. Ironically, one of Austin's most beloved environmentalists, Helen Durio, lost her life in that flooding. The worst of the damage happened along the shores of Shoal Creek, which at its northern end runs parallel to Mo-Pac. It was along here that several people drowned. In addition, there was also considerable property damage, totaling many millions of dollars. Some months after the flooding, a report on its causes revealed that, in fact, the force and amount of water sweeping into the creek had been partly the result of all the new ground cover, of asphalt, associated with commercial and residential growth in this section of the city.[58] In brief, those who wish to preserve, indeed to save, the natural environment seem to have truth on their side, too.

Just south of the Bradfield-Cummings tract, on the other side of Mo-Pac, another land story took place in the first half of the 1970s. It concerns the development of the Barton Creek Square Mall that now sits at this site, and it reveals something of the topsy-turvy world of the market entrepreneur, and also how city government has sought, sometimes unsuccessfully, to protect the land, and the rivers, from possible harm.

For more years than many people can remember, the land out here had been held by the Dellana family of Austin. There were many, many acres of property, and much of it had been devoted to grazing pasture for cattle. It was somewhat hilly, but not nearly so much as the land in the northwest sector that had been developed by David

Barrow, Sr. Sometime in 1973, local developer Sid Jagger, who had made a name and small fortune for himself by constructing a number of apartment complexes in Southeast Austin, alongside Riverside Drive, decided he wanted to do a big multi-use project in this area.[59] So Jagger began to buy up parcels of this land, purchasing the largest piece from the Dellana family, and several smaller pieces from other nearby property owners. At the time, Jagger was looked on with favor by many Austin residents. To the developers, he seemed to be a great success story, someone who had created very lucrative residential dwelling units. To the liberal community, especially environmentalists, he was a darling, too, someone genuinely concerned with how development projects would affect the character of Austin land and water.[60]

Jagger put together what the planning community refers to as a conceptual scheme for his project. What such a scheme does is to lay out, in broadest outlines possible, how the land will be used. What the scheme does not do is to commit the developer to any specific plans, thereby allowing him, or her, a free hand once approvals for the project are obtained from city government. Jaggers' conceptual scheme called for some pioneering ideas, at least in Austin. As the scheme portrayed it, the site would include a dense, central area of commercial and industrial enterprises, an adjacent area of apartment and condominium complexes, and then, at the outer edges of the development, many single family homes with fairly good-sized yards.

Jagger lobbied every concerned party hard for his scheme. He had to go before the Austin Transportation Committee, chaired by Senator Lloyd Doggett, in order to get its approval. The committee was not convinced that the scheme was a good idea for the land, especially given the proposed extension for Mo-Pac Boulevard. Thus, one day, Jagger appeared in the offices of Walter Vackar, and asked him, in his capacity as a trained architect, to do a sketch of how Mo-Pac Boulevard could be built so that there would be no possible conflict with his own plans for the land. Vackar drew up such a plan, in the space of a couple of days, and weeks later learned that it had turned the trick, at least for Jagger's approval by the Transportation Committee.[61] Jagger also wanted the City of Austin to annex the parcel of 412 acres so that he could benefit from various city utility services. Thus, he had to lobby city departments and commissions in order to gain their consent for his proposed development. The scheme was presented, for example, to members of the City Planning

Commission, and although reservations were expressed about the possible hazards to the nearby Barton Creek watershed, on the advice of Dick Lillie, head of the City Planning Department, they gave their approval.[62] On January 2, 1975, after spending a couple of years developing the entire package of land, together with securing the consent of various interested parties, Sid Jagger and his property were given the stamp of approval by the Austin City Council, and annexed into the city limits.[63]

Jagger, who seemed to be a man of his word and who had persuaded a whole raft of people, from city planning commissioners to concerned residents, about the merits of his work, became a turncoat within months of the City Council action. In March 1975, Jagger sold the entire parcel of land to Melvin Simon, out of Indianapolis, Indiana.[64] Melvin Simon is one of America's most prominent mall developers, and Jagger's sale of the property to him meant that in yet another way Austin had become tied into the broader national marketplace. But to many residents, the sale to Simon meant no more than that Sid Jagger was a man who did not keep his word. He had never informed the members of the city staff, not to say to the City Council, that he was dickering for a sale to Simon while he was in the midst of dealing with them. The City of Austin had approved one conceptual scheme in order that the land be annexed into the city, and now Jagger had gone and sold the property to someone else.[65]

When Jagger later was questioned about the sale, he complained that he had fallen on hard times, and that he had been compelled to sell the land in order to save his own neck.[66] There may have been some truth to his point, inasmuch as the real estate market of 1975 Austin was, indeed, at an ebb, comparable in some ways to today's market. But careful study of the transaction documents between Jagger and Simon reveals that Sid Jagger made, at least, several hundred thousand dollars from the sale, though the amount probably was far less than he ever expected to earn from his proposed projects.[67]

While several voices were raised in protest of the sale, they did not deter Jagger from turning the property over to Simon. And once Simon got hold of it, he developed it along far different lines than Jagger ever had proposed, or possibly even envisioned. What he created, in the end, was a very tightly packed set of buildings squeezed into a two-story mall, surrounded by literally acres and

acres of asphalt parking lot. Many people today are vocal about
the development, including Walter Vackar. Vackar refers to the
mall as "ugly as sin."[68] But, because of the times, Simon did not
escape the clutches of the environmentalists and the city government
altogether. The head of the Sierra Club at the time, Ken Manning,
who today is in the employ of a large developer in Austin, and his
colleague, Joe Riddell, pressed Simon and his corporation to take
various environmentally sensitive measures. Their effort also prompted the City of Austin, through its newly appointed director of environmental planning, Maureen McReynolds, to stipulate a number
of environmental measures that the mall would have to take in order
to safeguard the nearby Barton Creek watershed.[69]

Nonetheless, given the earlier decision to annex the land by the
city, as well as the lack of clear procedures for enforcement at the
time, Simon and the mall got out of the situation relatively un-
harmed. Yet, unfortunately, the environment itself does not appear
to have done so. The City of Austin required that Simon build a set
of several detention and sedimentation ponds surrounding the mall
site, to collect the water that runs off the parking lots after a rain,
filter out any pollutants, and then gradually permit the cleansed
water to be absorbed into the ground. Claire McAdams, a current
member of the City of Austin's Water and Wastewater Commission
who completed a doctoral dissertation on the development of the
mall some years ago, recently told me that the ponds are not being
properly maintained, and that, in fact, huge chunks of chemical
sludge have been found at their bottoms—where there should be no
sludge. The City of Austin, however, is not in a position to do a
thing about the lack of maintenance, she also said, because it lacks
any way to enforce its original environmental covenant with
Simon.[70]

Walter Vackar may complain about the aesthetics of Barton Creek
Square Mall, but he does so only in a soft voice. For good reason.
In 1983, Vackar decided to buy the piece of property, thirty-five
acres, that lies alongside Mo-Pac just north of the mall site. The value
of this land, owned by Melvin Simon, had risen considerably since
the mid-1970s when it was sold to Simon by Jagger. Vackar decided
that he wanted to do another commercial project on the site, something that adhered to his own aesthetic standards and yet also something new, for him at least, in the Austin scheme of things.[71] So he

set about trying to figure out how to lay his hands on the property. He found it almost impossible to negotiate the sale because he could not locate the Simon representative in Austin. Finally, he got hold of Steve Matthews. Matthews was the local broker for Sid Huberman, and Huberman, who lived in Dallas, was an intimate friend of Melvin Simon. One day, Matthews gave Vackar a call and asked him whether he would be willing to buy the land outright. In a matter of seconds, Vackar, who had grand designs for the site, said, "Yes, I want the land." Only hours later, he learned, Simon was willing to sell it, and Vackar responded by offering a figure of $6 million, contingent on getting the necessary city approvals for the land. Simon said fine.[72]

Vackar set about designing a development for the site. The project that he fashioned, working with the local architect David Graeber, was one of several office buildings set at varying heights. The design seemed to fit naturally into the landscape, but the city staff got fidgety, forcing Vackar to modify his plans somewhat. While the city staff and Vackar were engaged in working out the details for the project, Melvin Simon was contacted by another interested party, who offered him $7 million for the property. He got back in touch with Vackar, and said, "Look, we've made a handshake deal on this, and I don't want to go back on my word, but can you come up with another $300,000 for the land?" At this point, Walter Vackar was not sure what to do. So, like any good market entrepreneur, he consulted his financial advisor, an economics hotshot whom he had recently hired. "No, Walter, don't do it," the advisor told him. "Blow it off, the land isn't worth the price." And Vackar, like any good market entrepreneur, decided not to take the hotshot's advice.[73]

It was a good thing, too. Vackar eventually bought the property from Simon, and proceeded full steam ahead with the construction of his office buildings. Then, just months later, in the middle of the great land boom, he was contacted by another party who expresesd interest in the land. Vackar had already put some money and a good deal of his own time into the development, including his work with the city staff and several hundred thousand dollars for plans, checking the place out for utilities, and the like. Thus, he figured, he had an investment of about $8 million. "What will you give me for the land?" Vackar inquired of the party. "How about $25 million?" came the response. Now Walter Vackar is not a dumb man, by any means. He quickly realized that he would stand to make quite a handsome amount of money—in fact, it was of a magnitude that probably would make it one of the largest in Austin at the time. So Vackar took the money—$20 million in cash, the remaining $5 million in the form of a note—and ran.[74] And today he is working on his Lakeline project, putting in trees and other pieces of architectural and environmental apparatus on the property, his financing aided in small measure by the sale of the thirty-five acres of land. And, by the way, the developer of the huge mall site for Lakeline is—that's right—Melvin Simon and Company.

We now head west, out Loop 360, deeper into the hills that surround the city. Loop 360 was part of the broad network of highways envisioned by the City of Austin and by the State Highway Department, back in the 1950s. No one is quite certain who put Loop 360 on the map, or when it began. The best guess, perhaps, is that of Orville Miller, who became the State Highway Department's chief engineer for the road. Miller reckons that the topic of a Loop 360, skirting the western perimeter of the city, was first brought up at the meeting convened by Tom Miller at the Night Hawk Restaurant in the mid-1950s. The group included several state officials, plus Miller. Over a breakfast of ham and grits, Miller said, in his customary way, "Boys, we got to have a road there," and the State Highway Department boys agreed. That was that.[75] Whether Orville Miller is right or not, we cannot tell for sure, but, in any event, an outer loop for Austin was part of the city's highway plans by the late 1950s, and appeared on charts prepared by Harold Wise for the master plan in 1957, and on maps of the State Highway Department as well.

The concept was rather simple—merely an extension of the plan that involved Mo-Pac. The idea was to create a highway on the western edge of Austin that would furnish a full outer loop to the city, connecting to Ben White Boulevard on the south (named for the longtime councilman), to Highway 183 on the north, and winding up on the east with Ed Bluestein Boulevard (named for the chief engineer of the local division of the State Highway Department).[76] At the time, the notion was that this western portion of the loop would provide something like a circumferential road, as they are called in the East, a road that permits travelers to skirt the city, driving through its outer environs where few residents live. Indeed, planners in the later 1950s thought that, at most, there would be 12,000 cars on the road by about 1990.[77] Of course, as in all such things that urban planners have envisioned for Austin, the estimate was entirely wrong. In fact, as Orville Miller recalls, the day after Loop 360 was fully opened in 1982, it carried almost 20,000 cars.[78]

Only several blocks from where the road intersects with Mo-Pac, at the spot where Barton Creek Square Mall is found, there lie a series of residential developments, most on the left as one faces west. These are named the Lost Creek subdivision of Austin, and were developed by another market entrepreneur, Dick Rathgeber. Just beyond this property, out of sight from the road, are the Estates above Lost Creek. This project was developed by Ben Barnes and John Connally. The project, like Barnes and Connally themselves, is on the rocks today, another victim of the 1986 real estate market that has bottomed out in Austin. Also, in this same vicinity, are a series of buildings that lie adjacent to Loop 360, on both the right and the left sides of the road. It is little known to Austin residents, but within the walls of these buildings are the offices of some of Austin's most prominent land developers, including Walter Vackar, John Lloyd, Fred Purcell, and Gary Bradley. In effect, this has become developers' row. But these small tidbits are by no means the most fascinating story in these parts of Austin.

One-half mile from developers' row lies the junction of Loop 360 and Bee Caves Road. Within the vicinity of this intersection, about two miles west out Bee Caves Road, and about two miles north on Loop 360, lies a major piece of Austin land development. It is called Rob Roy Ranch, and has been witness to some of the most interesting tales about land in Austin.

Much of this property once was owned by Emmett Shelton, Sr. Shelton is something of a minor legend in these parts, perhaps as characteristic a Texan as one can find. Now eighty-two years old and virtually blind, Emmett walks with the vigor of a man half his age, and rattles stories off like a cowpoke around a campfire. Emmett grew up in Austin, along with a set of brothers that included Polk and John. All the boys went on to become lawyers, even entering into practice with one another. Polk also became quite famous in these parts just for challenging Lyndon Johnson for the congressional seat left vacant by the death of James Buchanan. The Shelton boys were a more conservative lot than many Austin politicians, certainly a good deal more so than Edgar Perry, Ed Clark, or Tom Miller. Polk, when running against Johnson, for example, took out against FDR for packing the Supreme Court, while Johnson supported FDR all the way. By the late 1940s, all the Shelton boys had become close friends with the more conservative political bigwigs in Austin, including Allan Shivers, and Emmett himself went on to work with Shivers in a number of different campaigns, including one against Emma Long.[79]

Emmett was the one Shelton boy who got involved in land. He loved the land around Austin and, shortly after his graduation from the University of Texas Law School, he bought his first piece, a parcel of 145 acres in the Westlake Hills area, near the intersection today of Loop 360 and Bee Caves Road.[80] He raised a few hogs on it, and kept it pretty much because he simply wanted to own property. Emmett's first big purchase of land came about, it happens, because of Lyndon Johnson and the New Deal work on the Colorado River.[81] A year or so after he had been elected to office as Tenth Congressional District representative, Johnson was back in town, trading small talk with the boys. One day, while in the Shelton law office, he happened to mention to Emmett and John that the property alongside the Colorado was going to become very valuable since some of the New Deal fellows, like Harry Hopkins, were putting together a lot of money to build dams on the river. Lyndon urged Emmett and John to buy some of the land there, and to do it soon, before others realized the land boom was about to happen.

Emmett and John decided to do so. Everett Looney, a local lawyer, happened to be in the office while Lyndon was telling his story and offered to put money into the deal if he could be an equal partner with the Sheltons. The Sheltons, since they had little money themselves, agreed. Because he knew the land out in the western hills so well, Emmett said he would figure out which property would be the most valuable. He eventually set his sights on a large parcel of 1,800 acres that bordered a large stretch of the river. The land was owned by the Roy girls, Addie and Jessie. Their father, Cal, and brother, Rob, had lived on the land back in the early part of the 1900s, and had worked it as a cattle ranch, though there were few cattle that could be raised on the hilly property. Emmett got in touch with the Roy girls in Houston, and asked them whether they would be willing to sell him the land. They said they really had very little interest in it, and so happily agreed to the sale.[82] All they wanted, they said, was $125 in earnest money, and that would permit Emmett, John, and Everett Looney to have the option on the land for a year.[83]

The year passed, and another payment was due the Roys. Emmett was living a relatively meager existence at the time, still suffering, like many others, from the poverty of the Depression years, and had little to his name but the small piece of property in the hills, and his profession as a lawyer. He and John, who was equally broke, realized that they would be unable to make the payment. Thus, they asked Looney whether he would be kind enough to take the property off their hands. Looney was more than willing to do so. He and his new law partner, Ed Clark, bought the land from John and Emmett simply by paying them the amount of the earnest money, $125. They got the 1,800 acres worth, then, about $18,000, and soon paid off Addie and Jessie Roy. The trade, in effect, brought no profit for the Shelton boys. Nothing ventured, nothing gained. The Looney-Clark purchase soon became a steal, to say the least. A few years later, when the Episcopal Diocese of Texas was looking for some property to serve as the site for its planned private school, Ed Clark, who sat on the board of the diocese, offered to sell them 400 acres of the Roy land. The diocese bought it for $40,000 or $100 per acre, leaving Looney and Clark with a handsome profit of $90 per acre, or $36,000 all told.[84]

The Roy land continued to be held by Looney and Clark until the early 1970s, when a series of events led to its sale, and to the creation of what today is known as the Rob Roy Ranch Development. Two new men now enter the story of this land, two men who have come to stand out as prominent contemporary examples of Austin's market entrepreneurs. Gary Bradley and John Wooley were recent graduates of the University of Texas when they met back in the early 1970s in Austin. Both were hungry, both wanted to get in the fast lane, and both had decided that the way to the big bucks was through the buying and selling of land.[85] When they first met, each had already done some deals, creating syndicates of doctors and lawyers who would purchase a piece of property as a long-term investment. Bradley was working for Doug Dewey, one of a handful of land speculators in Austin in the early 1970s, a man who specialized in creating relatively lucrative investments for small groups of Texans. Dewey was quite the salesman, a good person to serve as hero to Bradley and Wooley. Dewey once bragged, for example, that he was able to sell Lem Scarbrough, of the Scarbrough store family in Austin, a big piece of property every year just by taking him out in his Porsche 914. Doug would pocket $60,000 annually from his sales to Scarbrough.

However clever a salesman Doug Dewey was, he was not clever enough to realize that the Austin real estate market was about to bottom out. Gary Bradley and John Wooley were just at the start of their promising money-making schemes when the hard times hit in 1973, and both survived the next couple of years with a small deal here and there. Nothing big, to be sure. Just large enough to keep a little bread on the table and the beer still flowing in downtown Austin pubs. Sometime in 1976, with the market in real estate still at its ebb in Austin, Wooley remembers that the two men had just seen a story on *Sixty Minutes* on CBS.[86] It was a story about São Paulo, Brazil, and about how wonderful the living was there, with its white sand beaches and beautiful women. Wooley and Bradley started talking seriously about departing Austin for São Paulo, perhaps going into a bank down there as they had to Austin National, taking out a small loan, and doing a few land deals. Then, just as they were on their way out of town, so Wooley recalls, they said to one another: "Hell, let's just try one more deal in Austin."[87]

They learned that there was some property for sale out in Westlake Hills. It was rugged and rocky countryside, and so should come cheap. Bradley also imagined that it would make wonderful land on which to build homes since it possessed some of the most beautiful views of the hill country. So the two men set about trying to buy the land. Now there were several different pieces of property for sale, some on the south side of Bee Caves Road, and others, the Roy property, in particular, on the north side. Their first target, Wooley recalls, was the southern property, once owned by a syndicate put together by Doug Dewey. An engineer was hired to survey the land, and to figure out where the best spots were for drilling wells. While in the process, he mentioned to Wooley one day that the land on the northern side seemed much more suitable for building homes than the southern portion.[88]

Thus, Bradley and Wooley began to pursue the purchase of this property, the Roy land. They learned that it had passed through several hands on the way from Looney and Clark to its present owners. They also found out that Looney and Clark were about to foreclose on the property inasmuch as the most recent holders, one of whom was a relative of Stanley Marcus of Neiman-Marcus fame, had, like so many other investors, fallen on hard times. Figuring that the land was a bargain, selling then for $3,000 an acre, they flew off to New York City, where they called Mickey Shenen, Marcus' relative, and found out they could have the 1,100 or so acres for only about $3 million. But that was not the good part of the deal. All it took to secure an option on the property that would hold it in their hands for a year while they undertook their plans was $100 in earnest money.[89] It had to be the cheapest as well as the best land investment in modern Austin history.

With the parcel of Roy property in hand, Bradley and Wooley eventually created a development of about 2,000 acres. The story does not end there, however. Both men now ran head-on into city government, and into the labyrinth of procedures that today give land developers such headaches in Austin. Although the Friedman council had gone down to defeat, the notion that city government must somehow put a hold on commercial and residential developments in Austin had not disappeared. Many elements of this new attitude on the part of the Austin city administration were beneficial to the community, to its residents, and certainly to the natural beauty spots. The environmental safeguard attempts, spearheaded by people like Maureen McReynolds on the city staff, and urged by groups such as the Sierra Club, no doubt helped to preserve the Austin environment in the long run. But there was another attitude that Bradley and Wooley confronted, namely, the attempt to put strong, virtually inflexible, regulations on the land developed in the hills west of Austin, in Westlake Hills.[90] What Bradley and Wooley were proposing to do with their residential construction in the hills, in fact, was seen as a pioneering project, by some accounts, yet a very harmful one, by others.

For the next two years, Gary Bradley lobbied the city staff and the City Council to get approvals for the Rob Roy Development. The chief problem seemed to lie in what the engineers and architects had proposed for roads in the project. Inasmuch as the terrain was so very hilly and steep, it seemed difficult, at best, to build roads of the usual width approved for city streets. It also seemed impossible to put in gutters and drainage measures of the typical kind required by the City of Austin. Thus, Bradley and Wooley requested that city officials make allowances for their project, and permit them to have narrower roadways and modified gutters.[91]

But the city staff balked, particularly people like Joe Ternus, head of transportation. Ternus, for example, argued that city regulations must be followed almost exactly.[92] Bradley recalls, moreover, that he must have spent on the order of 2,000 hours of his time just down at City Hall and in various meetings with city officials trying to get approvals for the project. Of these days John Wooley remembers that money talks or, at least, whispers to some City Council members. Wooley says he and Bradley "became important to them because [we were] a source of funds. . . . We were making $1,000 to $5,000 contributions." Moreover, Wooley says, Ed Wendler, Sr., who by 1977 had become Austin's version of New York City's power-broker, Robert Moses, would tell them whom to give money to, and also advise them on how to gain personal access to these figures. (It is rumored, incidentally, that, at the time, Wendler would charge people $1,000 a shot to get in to see his prize pupil on the council, Richard Goodman.)[93] In the end, Wooley learned that "once you started being a significant campaign contributor, you never got a 'no' vote on anything that was [a] reasonable [request]."[94]

After much lobbying by Bradley, and money-giving by the two men, the whole issue boiled down to a vote by the City Council on a Thursday in August 1979. Bradley and Wooley, who today are no longer partners and have not spoken to one another for about three years, recall the event almost identically.[95] The question before the council was whether the City of Austin would approve the variances on the city regulations for roadways and gutters. The decision was by no means a simple one, in part because members of the city staff were adamant that the variances not be allowed.

Several council members, including Richard Goodman and Ron Mullen, who by now had become friends of Bradley and Wooley, thanks, in part, to the campaign contributions, agreed to vote in favor of the variances. Mayor Carole McClellan had elected to side with the city staff. Lee Cooke, who would have been the decisive vote in favor of the development, at the last moment had to leave the council chambers for another engagement. Thus, it looked as though the fortunes of the two men, not to say the project, were doomed. When the vote came, it was four to two in favor of the variances, but a minimum of five votes was required. Wooley appears to have taken the defeat more stoically. Bradley, with perspiration soaking his shirt, stared daggers at Councilperson Betty Himmelblau, who had voted against the request. Then, as the council was about to turn to another matter, Ron Mullen leaned across to Himmelblau and said, "You know, Betty, you've just bankrupted those two boys." Seconds later, Himmelblau changed her vote. And Rob Roy was a step closer to reality.[96]

From there, the completion was a piece of cake, almost. The initial development loan on the project was from First City Bank. If the vote had not gone the way Bradley and Wooley had hoped, the bank would have called in the loan. It did so anyway. Eventually, however, another local financial legend, Austin National Bank, and its land officer, Guy Bodine, were willing to underwrite the financial end of the Rob Roy deal. Bodine and the bank both thought that while Rob Roy was a pioneering concept for Austin, set out in the western hills, it eventually would come to be accepted by residents, particularly those at the upper end of the income scale.[97] Nevertheless, the sale of the property to homeowners, they thought, might take place over a long period of time, perhaps five, ten years, even longer. Fate, however, intervened, just as it had with the Himmelblau vote, and just as it had with the initial purchase of the property for a measly sum of money. In December 1979, while Bradley and Wooley were in Hawaii undergoing emotional decompression from their adventures with Rob Roy, the Austin Independent School District finally decided, after a delay of almost twenty years, to integrate the schools and to do so through widespread busing. Bradley and Wooley lucked out, to say the least, for the Rob Roy Development was in the Eanes School District, and thus escaped the pitfalls of this new ruling.[98]

The Rob Roy land now sold like hotcakes. In the month following the busing announcement, Bradley recalls, he would take his jeep out to the property, where nothing but beautiful vistas and piles of rocks lay, and in the space of a single day sell four or five, even more, pieces of land.[99] Doctors and lawyers, especially, took to these hills, readily turning over a check for $10,000 just to hold a piece of property. Within that first month, Bradley and Wooley must have made a couple of million from the sale of lots, enough to pay off their loan with the bank. Eventually the two men, not yet thirty years old, still wet behind the ears, gained many millions of dollars from the sale of the Rob Roy land.

While the story of Rob Roy, more or less, ended, certainly the tales of Gary Bradley and John Wooley did not. Both men, in partnership, also sold the City of Austin 200 acres of scenic land on Lake Austin, keeping a little over 100 acres for themselves, and making a nice profit of about $1 million in the deal.[100] Today that acreage is known as Commons Ford Park, and will probably rank eventually as one of the prettiest of the city parks. They have become very wealthy men, and each has set out on an entrepreneurial course different from the other. Wooley today, besides other investments such as prize blocks of downtown land, is also the owner of the Schlotzsky's eating establishments, a chain of small restaurants across the south-western rim of the United States.[101] Bradley, besides his twenty-five percent interest in the Houston Rockets basketball team, has pursued new residential projects.

Bradley's most current, and certainly most ambitious, project is known as the Circle C Ranch Development, and lies south of Austin, in Travis County.[102] Consisting of 4,500 acres of land, it will become the most complex residential property ever developed in these parts. The project involves four separate municipal utility districts, for example. Such districts, which were the brainchild of Ed Wendler, Sr., in Austin, provide a way in which residential developments can bypass the City of Austin in securing utility and water services. Critics point out that they furnish a device that ultimately will lead to an urban sprawl around Austin that resembles that of Los Angeles, or Houston. But for Circle C, they also furnish a means to create virtually a self-contained new city. Circle C, in a sense, also brings our story of land and Mo-Pac in Austin almost full-circle, to the days of David Barrow, Sr., and Northwest Hills. Gary Bradley is now in the process of getting a donation of about $30 million in land from property owners whose land lies between the city limits of Austin and the Circle C Ranch. The reason is simple. The State Highway Department has agreed that if the property owners will donate that land to the state, it will extend Mo-Pac Boulevard 5.5 miles into Travis County.[103]

Our story continues as we make our way farther along Loop 360. About a mile or so from the Rob Roy Development, we come to a bridge that stretches high above Lake Austin. The bridge is very special, constructed unlike any other metal structure spanning the water. It is a suspension bridge, with high curving arches, and requires no concrete beams for support in the water. It is made from Korean steel, and cost the state about $11 million, more than the entire Loop 360 roadway itself.[104] Most people believe the cost was well worth it. The bridge seems to fit naturally into the rocky cliffs along here, and provides uninterrupted views of the lake on either side of it. But the bridge also has contributed more than merely an aesthetic addition to the landscape. It, like the road itself, has helped to accelerate the growth of Austin, particularly here, in the western hills. As Joe Ternus, now director of transportation for Espey Houston and Company, an engineering firm, and formerly director of transportation for the City of Austin, comments: "When that bridge was built the whole character of West Austin changed because you now had a complete road that went from Highway 183 to Lamar Boulevard. . . . That bridge connection truly helped to spur a lot of growth in West Austin."[105]

Once across the bridge, we enter the western boundaries of the Northwest Hills section of Austin; in effect, we are beginning to travel almost parallel to Mo-Pac Boulevard, which runs on the east. The first major thoroughfare to intersect Loop 360 at this point is FM 2222, one of the most scenic but also one of the most dangerous roads in these parts, accounting annually for a number of otherwise avoidable automobile accidents and deaths. Just north of the junction of these two roads lies another brief story that helps further to illustrate the wealth and volatility associated with land in and about Austin.

Kathlene King is a young woman who ranks among the most prominent and successful real estate developers in today's Texas. A former graduate student in sociology at the University of Texas, like other modern market entrepreneurs she is a recent player in the game. She is shrewd, wily, and comes across principally as a gentle Southern belle. Her work as a graduate student at the university taught her how to prepare for sales, how to figure out the proper way to price land, how to put together a marketable package for a buyer—in general, how to make a smart deal. King started small, working up a tiny development of several acres on Lake Travis back in 1979, when she was on the mend from injuries suffered in a serious automobile accident.[106] She only wanted to do a minor project, hoping to sell a couple of acres to another buyer, and then to use the profit to build her own place on the remaining land. She did the project easily and quickly, and found, like so many others who have turned into land developers, that "doing a project" was, in fact, exciting and satisfying. And something she wanted to do a lot more often.

From this adventure, then, she moved on to others. She got in touch with a friend at a real estate firm of McLester and Grisham and told him that she wanted to learn the trade.[107] The Austin market had not yet reached its peak, so she was welcomed aboard, and got her first taste of what it took to create big projects, of apartment complexes, for example. At the start, she did mostly high-density developments, investigating what it would take to find land for a large apartment or condominium complex, and learning what kind of parties might be interested in financing them. It was only a matter of time until she had put together some real good deals—so good, in fact, that by 1984 she should claim a profit of $2 million.[108]

Sometime in 1983, Kathlene learned that a parcel of land at the junction of Loop 360 and Spicewood Springs Road was tied up in court, but that it might become available at a fairly cheap price. Together with a group of several other real estate investors, King tried to buy the property. Her intention, like that of her fellow investors, was to do a land flip, which simply means taking an option on a piece of property, putting down a certain small amount of cash, and then holding the land, typically for a very short period of time, until it can be "flipped" to another buyer. The transaction takes relatively little up-front money and can make a lot for an investor, but, naturally, is looked down upon by many people, even many in the financial community. At the time that King and her associates sought to get the Loop 360 property, many pieces of land were starting to flip in Austin. The King deal turned out to be one of the more typical, and also one of the more successful. She and her partners managed to get the property out of its court entanglement, and to purchase it for $3 million. Only a month and a half later, after they closed their deal, another buyer came along, and offered to buy the piece of property from them. The sale price—$16 million—gave King and her partners a handsome profit of $13 million.

For our final tale, we turn now onto FM 2222, and head west, out to Lake Travis, and Mansfield Dam, where much of our story about Austin has occurred. The view along this road is truly wonderful and, even though one is only minutes from downtown Austin, it sometimes feels as though one is in an entirely different world. It was a story from another world, in fact, that took place on acreage on the northern side of this road, just miles from the Loop 360 intersection, where the Beard Ranch lies today. The Beard Ranch turned out to be the setting for not the most profitable land deal in Austin, but surely one of the most bizarre.

Fred Purcell once was a dentist in Austin.[109] Today he ranks as one of the most successful market entrepreneurs in land sales. Purcell is in the game for money, and for no other reason. Unlike Walter Vackar, for example, he is not really interested in developing some aesthetically satisfying complex, and unlike Gary Bradley he is not absorbed with leaving his mark on the civic landscape. He and some others, like John Lloyd, are principally after the big bucks, and they are as responsible for driving the Austin economy forward today as anyone else.

In the late 1970s, Purcell started doing some land deals in Austin. His first was a project along Lake Austin, the Woodlands, where he bought about twenty acres of land, developed some homes, including one for himself, and then made a nice tidy profit through sales.[110] His next was a project to help locate new grounds for the Austin Country Club, which was searching for property on which to construct a new golf course. Purcell, a golfer, and a couple of other golfing buddies, set out to find the most attractive and also the cheapest property in Austin at the time. They identified several pieces, and the one that seemed to offer the best deal was the Beard Ranch, on FM 2222. Consisting of about 1,000 or so acres of land, the property could be had for about $3,000 per acre, a reasonable price for property in Austin, and a great one in Texas, considering that land values in cities like Dallas were in the range of $10,000 to $15,000 an acre for premium property.[111] So Fred and his partners made a deal, thinking that they had found just the right spot for the new Austin Country Club. Unfortunately for them, however, the club elected to move to Davenport Ranch, just on the other side of the lake, directly across from Rob Roy. The partners decided to opt out, but Fred, thinking that the land might indeed become valuable, decided to stick with it.

About this time, Purcell was contacted by John Lloyd.[112] Lloyd was himself a fairly recent arrival in Austin, a recruit originally from Iowa who was an architect by trade and a capitalist by ambition. Lloyd had already made a few deals, including the La Costa complex of residences, a hotel and businesses at the intersection of Highway 290 and Interstate Highway 35 in Austin, plus a handful of others. Lloyd told Purcell that he was working on behalf of some Canadian clients, people that Lloyd now refers to as the "killer Canadians."[113] Purcell told Lloyd to come by and he would show him some slides of the Beard Ranch, revealing what a really sweet deal it was. The men met, Lloyd liked what he saw, and he got back to his Canadian clients, advising they pick up the piece of property. The men whom Lloyd represented, it turns out, included Max Kugler, who presented himself as the agent for Ivanhoe Savings Corporation of Canada, a branch of the Steinberg Grocery firm, and, like the firm itself, over-flowing with cash that could not find a profitable site for investment in Canada.[114]

Purcell agreed to make the deal. He sold the land to Kugler for a figure of $3.5 million, assuring himself a profit of $500,000.[115] After a couple of months of dickering, and working out the formal arrangements, the transaction was completed, and Fred moved on to his next deals. Four months after the sale, he was phoned by David Orr, an Austin attorney who worked for the firm of McGinnis, Lochridge, and Kilgore. Orr informed Purcell that he was collecting some information about the sale for his client, who, it turned out, was the Ivanhoe Savings firm of Canada. As Purcell learned more from Orr, the details of a rather strange transaction became clear.[116] Purcell discovered that the Canadian representative in Austin for Ivanhoe, Max Kugler, apparently had made more than a handsome profit for himself on the Beard Ranch.

As Purcell and Lloyd both tell the story, Kugler had made up some fictitious transaction that listed a Bonnie —— as the owner of the property, instead of Purcell. Bonnie —— was, in fact, someone that Kugler had met one night when he and his Canadian partner first arrived in Austin to make the deal. Then, instead of telling the Ivanhoe folks that the price tag for the land, owned by Purcell, was $3.5 million, they claimed it was $7 million. The difference between what they would pay Purcell and what they would get from Ivanhoe for the land, $3.5 million, represented a handsome little profit.[117] And also a big lie.

At this point in the tale, things become somewhat blurred. What seems to have happened is that people started suing one another for various alleged misdeeds. Purcell, for example, sued Kugler and others because, he claimed, he had been misinformed of the actual sale price to Ivanhoe; Ivanhoe sued Kugler, too, because he had tricked them out of a lot of money. Other suits piled up, one on top of another, forcing the whole matter to come to trial in Austin in 1980. One of the witnesses in the trial was Ralph Ordauer, the president of Ivanhoe Savings. Ordauer came down to Austin from his home in Canada and testified about what he knew of the transaction. Two weeks after his testimony, Ordauer was found shot to death in Canada. The suits of various parties were quickly dropped. John Lloyd remembers the time as pretty scary, and Purcell recalls that everyone was a little uptight because of what happened.[118] No one is quite sure about who bumped Ordauer off, but it was learned later that Max Kugler had close ties to the killer, who apparently was a hit-man out of Chicago.[119] Austin land deals, indeed, had truly made the big time.

Today the Beard Ranch remains in the hands of Ivanhoe. Its value, of course, has increased since 1980. John Lloyd informed me that last year he offered Ivanhoe $22,000 per acre, but they turned him down, thinking the price too low.[120] Fred Purcell has become a very wealthy man—he owns a great deal of the property in the general vicinity of Lake Travis where 3M Corporation is building a new research site—but he, like others, has been hurt by the downswing of the Austin real estate market. John Lloyd seems even more ambitious, but, at the same time, his fortunes have ebbed. He has been forced to start selling the homes he developed in Rob Roy on the Creek, land he purchased four years ago, from Bradley and Wooley, for half their current asking price.[121] And Max Kugler, one of Austin's first Canadian land investors, has gone into partnership with Dick Rathgeber, a wealthy land man in Austin, and the Chamber of Commerce's 1986 Man of the Year—which makes both Lloyd and Purcell chuckle about the "killer Canadians."[122]

The tales of the land are endless in and around this city, and they could be spun on and on until the longhorns come home. Many people have profited from the land boom that hit Austin beginning in the late 1970s and continued until a year or so ago. Many people also have hit the skids, and some, like several of the land speculators in Austin during the mid-1970s, probably will never recover. Some people, nonetheless, have managed to survive well, very well, indeed, including most of the market entrepreneurs talked about here.

So have other people, too, especially Ed Wendler, Sr., who, in the past decade, since he broadened his interests from liberal causes to the development game, has been as powerful a figure in Austin as one can find. Two of our market entrepreneurs have laid it on the line with me, and told me precisely how much they paid Wendler for his services. Gary Bradley, for one, who today bears a bitter grudge toward Wendler over a number of things, says that he agreed to pay Wendler $150,000 just as "insurance money" to make certain that no one, especially Wendler himself, disrupted the deals that Bradley was making for Circle C Ranch.[123] Bradley delivered $50,000 of that amount up front, in hard cash, as a down payment, and while he was on vacation in Europe, Bradley expected that Wendler would protect his interests. On return, Bradley found out that Wendler had not done so and that, in particular, Wendler's other developer clients were getting the same, or better, treatment down at City Hall. Ed Wendler, Peck Young—our liberal activist from the 1970s—and lobbyist-lawyer David Armbrust also were made wealthy men by Walter Vackar. Vackar recently informed me that he paid the three men, and their firms, something on the order of $500,000 over a period of two years just to get lobbying done at City Hall for Lakeline.[124]

Of course, Ed Wendler would not be rich today if city politics in Austin were not so confused, so virtually Byzantine, and if, perhaps the City Council and the city staff were more easily persuaded of the goals and ambitions of the market entrepreneurs. But city government, since the days of Jeff Friedman and his fellow populists, has become a thorn in the side of the developers in Austin; and, although expansion will continue on and on, as it has for more than a century, it still costs a pretty penny to get projects through city government today. But we must save that story for another time.

Lying on the eastern edge of the Beard Ranch property is the Texas Tumbleweed Restaurant, long a landmark to Austin steak lovers. If you stand here, on its parking lot, at the top of the steepest hill in these parts, and survey the land around it, you can see acres and acres of undeveloped countryside, and literally thousands of trees and shrubs, even some deer. Despite the growth of Austin, despite the Wooldridge dream of January 1, 1888, the land remains uncivilized and wild. But will it be so fifty years from now?

Epilogue:
I Hear America Singing

I hear America singing, the varied carols I hear,
Each singing what belongs to him or her and to none else,
Singing with open mouths their strong melodious songs.
Now I will do nothing but listen,
To accrue what I hear into this song, to let sounds contribute toward it.

Walt Whitman
Leaves of Grass

GROWTH. CHANGE. MUCH OF THIS BOOK HAS BEEN about these things. How the city of Austin has mushroomed, how it has expanded from a small, allegedly sleepy university community to something on the order of a booming metropolis. The change and the expansion have happened for a number of reasons, some of them cultural, such as the dream, some of them personal, such as the pursuit of wealth and power by bare handfuls of people like Lyndon Johnson. Over the course of the century and one-half during which these things have come about, the residents of Austin have been buffeted about, their lives left to the fates that conspired to create a new Austin. I have not told the whole story of many of these residents, those who constitute the community itself, except insofar as their lives were implicated in the manufacture of the dream, or in the steady and continuous conflicts that seemed to have absorbed what we call the city of Austin. I have put their words into my rendering. Now it is time to right the balance, and to let them tell how it feels to live in a place so dramatically transformed.

In the course of my oral histories with many residents of Austin, I routinely asked them what they thought of the growth of the community, how they pictured the future, what they thought of relations between blacks and whites, whether life next year, the year after, or many years down the road, would be any better. Their answers were variously interesting, disheartening, uplifting, surprising, but all revealed a sense of attachment to Austin. Most of these residents, after all, had lived through many decades of growth, and so they brought a special sense of time and place to my inquiry. It is hard to summarize their thoughts into a few simple words. But there is a thread that runs throughout most of what they voiced. It is a sense, almost, of a paradise lost, of a regret that the community to which they were bound—and which bound so many others in a common life and purpose—that this community is gone. These are people who are caught, like all of Austin, in the great transition today from wilderness to civilization, and most wonder and are worried about what civilization—progress, industry, and all the rest—will do to them and to their children. Listen to them, for they are the voices of Austin, and of America, singing.

A black man, mid-thirties, from Clarksville—

> Austin is becoming like all the Northern cities that died, and they have become concrete jungles, full of concrete and water and asphalt. . . . The Chamber of Commerce did a good job of selling Austin, Texas, but they did one thing wrong. They forgot to prepare for the type of growth they wanted, and the type of quality of living. The people love the quality of living here, that's why they came here. . . .
>
> You see I have a hang-up. I love trees and I love greenery. I've lived where you have the concrete jungles. And the most beautiful thing that anyone can have and possess is the trees and the vegetation that God has given us. We are now in the process of desecration of this whole continent. Every time they build something they cut down trees. Trees hold the stuff in the soil, they keep us from having the floods. . . .

A former city councilman—

> The pursuit I now see seems to be money. It seems to be how much have you got? How well are you doing now? Do you live on Cat Mountain [an exclusive neighborhood], do you have your Mercedes? . . . I remember when Ray Mariotti [for-

mer editor of the *Austin American-Statesman*] wrote his finest editorial, the finest in his eyes I think, the most I ever saw him wax eloquent on something. . . . He was talking about some group of businessmen dining at the new club in the MBank, and he looked out the window, and he saw, corner to corner, this long line of limousines, a bunch of big black limousines, and he thought that was when Austin had made the big time. And I remember a time in the early seventies that someone wouldn't have been caught dead getting out of a limousine in this town. . . . If you go to Aspen [Colorado], they spend their time making the city, money is very much on display there, but not so much that they won't take care of the natural beauty that surrounds them. . . .

An affluent man, related to a scion of old Austin—

Back in those [earlier] days you could walk down Congress Avenue, and you knew half the people. Today I can walk down Congress Avenue and never see a person I know. . . .

A longtime woman resident, former legal secretary—

Something tragic has happened to things now. You know, we used to have this home, we never locked the doors. The manager is always after us to keep this door locked. . . . I'm afraid the downtown is going to be dead. . . . I went downtown the other day, and I was amazed. You couldn't see the Capitol. You could always drive down there, park the car, and walk until dark. And the last time I ever did that, we saw a policeman and he said we shouldn't be there, it was too dangerous.

A native Austinite, and federal judge—

I was a little disappointed with Austin about school integration. . . . And there is another area that Austin has to deal with . . . you can't restrict development in East Austin to the amount of revenue you derive from that area. You're going to have to go in that area and try to clean it up. . . . One of these days the new element coming into Austin is going to do it. The old Establishment did not. . . .

A female city planner—

I don't think we'll ever be the same. . . . I think we had more

than some cities. . . . We're very fortunate in that regard; but
we also had more to lose. . . . I can see this city being a half
million. . . . I sort of like driving through town, or walking into
an office building, and having people speak to you, and for me
to know them, and for them to know me. I don't like the idea
of strangers. . . . I once heard someone say, "I've been here
seven years so I'm a native Austinite now." To me it was
almost offensive. . . . I am not a native Austinite and I don't
consider myself one, but I consider someone who's been here
for just seven years an upstart. . . . I almost want to say—why
don't you go back. . . .

One of the urban entrepreneurs—

I think we've got the best chances now with this current
Chamber of Commerce going ahead and getting things done.
You see we're anywhere six or ten years behind . . . we didn't
have the water, and the sewers . . . I think we've got a chance
now. . . . [But] everything is high. Your taxes are just going to
eat you up here. I think we're going to have some rough going
here. . . . It depends on how the taxes go. Crime is coming into
this town, it's bad. . . .

A black woman, resident of East Austin—

Let's face it, you can change laws but you can't change the
hearts of people. You have some good wholesome white people,
and you have the other kind in both races. You just have to
face it, you cannot change their hearts. . . .

A university faculty member who helped to shape industrial
projections—

I would still argue that if you can introduce [business] activity
into the system that's improving the general welfare of the local
population. . . . I would argue that it could have been done in
Austin much better than it has. . . . It was not very fashionable
in [the fifties] to use the word "plan." I think you can retain
the important attributes of the city providing that you . . .
manage . . . the growth. . . . [In the fifties] people felt that whatever problems came up we could solve them. . . . In retrospect
that was the one blind spot we all had—that we never sat

down to consider the consequences of the population growth.
. . . We were still living in the era where growth and progress
were good. . . .

A native Austinite and political strategist —

What we want is Austin to be developing . . . for the benefit
of the entire community. We don't have to ruin Barton Springs
to have a dynamic enough city. . . . We don't have to [mess up]
the hill country so we can have enough job opportunities that
my daughters don't have to leave here to find a job. We don't
have to screw up our watershed for our lakes . . . to give us our
drinking water so that we can provide jobs for the handful of
blacks that are left, and the increasing number of Mexican
Americans. I mean they ain't mutually exclusive goals. . . . We
can do [everything] well . . . Austin's had explosive growth.
We're always going to have explosive growth. We're in the Sunbelt, it'a national trend, we're a beautiful city, we're the capital
of the biggest damned state in the Sunbelt. I don't care if we
erected machine gun nests at the edge of town, Austin would
expand to some extent. People would just slip past them at
night when [we're] not watching. There is always going to be
an expansion of the community. The question is — is it going to
be an expansion that is destructive?

A longtime woman resident, active in liberal politics —

I'm frightened now more than I used to be. . . . Many of my
friends are, too. . . . Now there are rapes and killings, just a few
streets over. . . . And this Seven Eleven, they killed a man
there. Just two or three blocks from here. . . . And taxes are
just going up, up all the time. That makes me feel like I ought
to go and move out in the country. I don't like the cities. . . .
Austin feels a lot different than when I first lived here. . . .
[But] growth is coming, there's no keeping it away. . . . it's going to get worse and worse . . . and I have no solution.

A longtime resident and former liberal activist —

I always thought of segregation and the British in India as
two things I would not live to see changed. And it's wonderful
that I was wrong.

A very wealthy land developer—

There has never been a big city planned by a democracy.

An architect and developer—

The city policies are creating sprawl. The policies are designed to limit it, but they actually permit only the wealthy to
live in the western part of Austin. . . . [City officials] don't
want anyone to work or live around Loop 360, so where will
growth go? . . . [The people in control] really are trying to stop
growth. Starting with the Friedman council they have been trying to stop growth. . . .

A black official of a local institution of higher education—

I think the future [of growth and race relations] can be rosy.
. . . It depends on whether the young whites and young blacks
who come to Austin are willing to get to know one another
and sit down and talk and listen. . . .

I think that's the key. Getting people to talk and to listen to one
another.

Methodological Appendix

———

THIS BOOK DRAWS UPON A WIDE VARIETY OF SOURCES of information, and it is most appropriate that I briefly describe the nature of these sources as well as some of the methods that went into the book's analyses. To begin with, I relied very heavily on a reading of the Austin daily newspapers of 1930 through 1965, and of 1980 through 1985. My longtime research assistant, Poopak Taati, helped me greatly with this particular phase of my work.

During the early period of our study, we found there were two regular dailies, the *Austin American* and the *Austin Statesman*, both published by the same company. Later the papers became combined into a single daily paper, the *Austin American-Statesman*. Rather than reading both the *American* and the *Statesman*, I chose to examine only the former. In order to determine whether its coverage of events and people was roughly the same as that of the *Statesman*, I made random comparisons of the two papers for the same day. These comparisons revealed that the two papers dealt with a particular event in almost identical ways, and thus assured me that reading only the *American* would not create any special bias to my coverage of Austin.

Although this work absorbed enormous amounts of time, stretching over a period of at least two years, it proved invaluable. It helped me, for instance, to identify prominent Austin figures, such as Tom Miller and Commodore Perry, to understand the importance of some of their public activities, and to realize the significant role of the Chamber of Commerce in the creation of modern Austin. This research also first suggested to me the role that visions and dreams played in the city's growth; indeed, it was these words and symbols that were routinely splashed across the pages of the *Austin American* whenever any major pronouncement was made about the growth or development of Austin. For laypeople as well as scholars interested in urban history, I would recommend this kind of patient study of the newspaper, but only if one has the luxury of good eyesight and many, many hours of spare time.

To supplement this research into the newspapers of Austin, I also conducted a number of personal interviews as well as oral histories. These took place over a period of about four years, from 1982 through 1986. A handful of the interviews also were done by several students of mine, including Todd Crossett (who conducted an invaluable interview of former city manager and Tom Miller confidant Guiton Morgan, shortly before Morgan's death at the age of eighty-three), John Palmer, Charles Ojo, Keith Householder, Diane Maya, and Erin Chen. Prior to this phase of my work, I had some experience in conducting interviews during my years of study and training as a sociologist. Yet I had never actually been trained to do extensive oral histories, and thus had to invent and develop my techniques as my work progressed. Altogether, I completed something on the order of 170 interviews and oral histories, supplemented by another 10 or so by my students. Many of these engagements lasted for two, three, even four hours. In the case of my work with Emma Long, who became a continuous source of information as well as a very dear friend, I can honestly say the interview lasted for a period of about four years, give or take a few weeks. With the completion of this book, all these histories have been donated to the Austin History Center, and now are available for other students of Austin.

The format of my oral histories always was more or less structured about a series of very specific questions, many of which originated from my reading of the newspapers, some from earlier interviews. The format, however, was a very loose one, and I let my informants guide me into new, sometimes very unexpected, areas. My style of conducting an oral history eventually matured, so that in time I had created a very specific manner of interviewing people. When the oral histories worked best—and I reviewed a number of them in the process of engaging in some self-criticism and improvement—I let my informants speak continuously. Occasionally I would provide some simple probes, redirect their questions, or repeat something they had said. I provided no evaluations or judgments about the content of their information. My approach, perhaps can best be summed up as that of a patient listener, someone genuinely interested in what a particular informant had to say—as, of course, I was. I never sought to antagonize an informant—after all, each person was doing me the favor of furnishing information for this project—yet I also did not shy away from asking very direct, sometimes very embarrassing questions.

It may also be helpful to add that whenever I conducted a personal interview, or an oral history, I routinely asked my informant if he, or she, possessed any personal documents relevant to the history of Austin. This inquiry sometimes produced very startling and unexpected treasures, including the many wonderful files of Walter Long, made available to me through the great generosity of his daughter, Janett K. Fish. Long's files, among other things, contained a number of oral histories that he himself had done in the late 1950s and early 1960s, and these not only proved helpful to my work but have since been donated to the Austin History Center for the benefit of other historians of early Austin. Through a similar inquiry, I was also able to procure and to use the files of Emma and Stuart Long (no relation, incidentally, to Walter). These files contained many useful personal documents as well as newspaper clippings that Emma had made of the Austin papers from the late 1940s through the late 1960s; these clippings were used to supplement the independent reading that Taati and I had undertaken. In general, enough helpful, sometimes fascinating, materials resulted from this strategy that I would highly recommend it to anyone who undertakes this kind of historical research.

This research also drew freely on available diaries, personal correspondence, census materials, city plans and statistics, and the few published documents on the history of Austin. I used diaries as a means of gaining further understanding of the character of such people as Edgar Perry and Alexander Penn Wooldridge. Here, I must note, I am particularly grateful to Edgar Perry III for permission to use materials from an unpublished diary of his grandfather, the Commodore. Much of the personal correspondence I used came from the wonderful and virtually inexhaustible archives of the Lyndon Baines Johnson Library in Austin, and it was developed in large part in conjunction with my research on the history of the Lower Colorado River Authority. The archivists at this library were most helpful and friendly. Other personal correspondence as well as documents came from the Barker History Center of the University of Texas, and a few materials, particularly City of Austin documents such as council minutes, came from the offices of the city clerk of Austin.

Far and away the most helpful archivists and most useful written materials for this research are located at the Austin History Center. This relatively new center is intended to house all important materials relevant to the history of Austin, and it already has made a magnificent start with guidance from its first curator, Katherine Hart, and for the past eleven years from its second curator, Audray Bateman. Audray has proven to be exceptionally helpful to my work. She not only has furnished guidance to particular written materials, but also has alerted me to people who could furnish me with information about the history of Austin. She is aided by a delightful staff that includes, or has included, Linda Zezulka, Mae Schmidt, Carlos Lowry, Nancy Byrd, Mary Jo Cooper, and Francis Moore. This history center, I must add, also contains the only available microfilms of the Austin newspapers, and thus proves an invaluable reference site for any determined historian of the city.

Lay readers might wonder how, with this multitude of information, I decided what constituted historical truth, and what did not. First off, there is no simple kind of historical truth that appears in this account. Rather, there are different kinds of statements made about history, some cast at very different levels of abstraction. At the broadest level, for instance, I propose my very general scheme to interpret the long history of Austin growth. My claims about the forces that figures into Austin's development over this period are based upon an interpretation, or concocted answer, to the question: why did the city of Austin grow? The particular answers I came up with, such as the role of the dreams, or the federal government, are ones that derive not from some obvious historical truth, but from the way that I put the data of history together. Another analyst may well put it together differently than I.

At seemingly more concrete levels of abstraction, such as where I talk about persons involved with growth and call them either *urban* or *market entrepreneurs*, again I have engaged in interpretation. No one actually called Tom Miller an urban entrepreneur, for example (though they did call him many other names); nor did anyone refer to Joe Crow as a market entrepreneur. Yet I identify them as such to isolate and to identify the role they played in the creation of modern Austin. Both terms refer, in other words, to social roles that were intimately connected to the growth of the community. Other

statements that are made in the course of this history are less obviously interpretive, but still are open to various readings by different
students of history. With regard to my claims about individuals and
their motivations, as to the unfolding of political events, here, too,
I have placed certain interpretations on the raw facts, putting them
into a kind of meaningful ordering. About the only things that may
be indisputable in this history, in brief, are the names of people and
the dates of happenings. The rest has been constructed, as interpretations, from the many sources of information and insight on which I
relied.

Let me conclude this brief discussion of my methods by making a
few comments about the nature of this type of social history. When
historians undertake this kind of work about urban areas, they, typically, are interested in the host of people and events that make a
place unique and special. As a sociologist, I, too, was interested in
these matters, but I also constructed this history in somewhat different, one might even say broader, terms. For me, the history that I
have written of Austin is the story not merely of this singular Texas
town, but also the story of a city that has grown dramatically during
the course of the twentieth century and that, in the course of this
growth, has experienced some severe internal struggles. The issues of
growth displayed here are put the way they are because of my more
general interest in questions of urban expansion. The same holds true
for the matters of the role of the federal government and the manner
in which blacks and browns have been treated in Austin. These sorts
of developments are ones that can be found in many other American
cities in the twentieth century. By having focused on them in Austin,
and by having shown how they played a part in the life of this city,
I hope that I may have said something not only about this place but
about many others as well.

To social scientists, this general approach is known as the analysis
of a case study, or a single case. One might examine a single case of
an organization in order to understand organizations better, or a
single family to comprehend family dynamics better. For me, the
study of Austin became a way in which I could better comprehend
the nature of a city and, in particular, a city that has undergone the
ups-and-downs, even sideways, of expansion. Many social scientists
today disapprove of this approach, just as they disapprove of any
work that sets about understanding the history of an institution, a
community, even a nation. For such social scientists, the only way

to understand a phenomenon is to assemble a very large number of cases – sometimes on the order of hundreds, if not thousands – and to study such cases over a very short period of time. I have come to believe, as have a handful of my colleagues in the social sciences, that this approach can furnish only so much knowledge about the world in which we live. In addition, I believe, we must return to our roots, as it were, to the intensive examination of the single case, in order to arrive at a level of insight and knowledge unavailable to the mass analyst. To the extent, then, that his book on Austin works, in furnishing readers with some new understanding of the history of American cities during the course of the twentieth century, as of Austin itself, it will restore, I hope, the intensive study of single cases to their honored and privileged place in the repertoire of social scientific research strategies.

Notes

Chapter 1

1. These lines are from comments made by Johnson shortly before his death. He was speaking about the hill country of Texas. The remarks now are included as part of the recordings for the tour of the Johnson Ranch outside of Johnson City, Texas.
2. City of Austin files.
3. Members of the University Student Geological Society, *Economic Geology of the Central Mineral Region of Texas* (Austin: University of Texas at Austin, 1974), pp. 90–91.
4. Wilburn Oatman, *Llano: Gem of the Hill Country* (Hereford: Pioneer Book Publishers, 1970), p. 64.
5. Ibid., pp. 73–78.
6. Robert Penniger, *Fredericksburg, Texas: The First Fifty Years*, translated from the original German by Charles L. Wisseman, Sr. (Fredericksburg: Fredericksburg Publishing Company, 1971).
7. Interview with Mrs. Nelda Kubalah, March 9, 1983.
8. Mary Starr Barkley, *History of Travis County and Austin, 1839–1899* (Waco: Library Binding Company, 1963), chapter 3.
9. Interview with Janett L. Fish.
10. Frank Brown, "Annals of Travis County and the City of Austin from Earliest Times to 1875" (unpublished, 36 vols., at Austin History Center), chapter 2, p. 6.
11. Oatman, *Llano: Gem of the Hill Country*, p. 135.
12. Tillie Badu Moss Fry, "A History of Llano County, Texas," thesis (Austin: University of Texas, 1943).
13. Brown, "Annals," chapter 3.
14. Fry, "A History of Llano County," pp. 56–60.
15. Penniger, *Fredericksburg, Texas: The First Fifty Years*, pp. 73–79.
16. Walter Long interview with Edna Besserer Kuse, March 8, 1962.

17. Brown, *Annals*, chapter 30, p. 65.
18. Fry, "A History of Llano County," pp. 52 and 53.
19. Brown, *Annals*.
20. Ibid., chapter 13, p. 8.
21. Ibid., passim.
22. Fry, "A History of Llano County," pp. 43–44.
23. Walter Long interview with Carl Widen, pp. 1–3.
24. Austin Chamber of Commerce minutes, December 27, 1927.
25. There were not in Austin and the nearby area reports of widespread lynchings as in South Carolina or elsewhere in the Deep South. Nor were there reports of slave revolts or other evidence of the mistreatment of blacks by whites. But Walter Long's interviews provide firm evidence, in the early twentieth century, of considerable tension between black and white residents of Austin and Travis County. The interview done with Judge David J. Pickle, on October 20, 1961, reveals that Judge Pickle and two other men, Ben Pierce and Charlie Hamby, "met John R. Shillady, who was Secretary of the National Negro Association and we contacted him on the corner of Brazos and 6th Street. He was here apparently advocating social equality of the Negros [sic] and Whites. We gave him a pretty sound thrashing, using no weapons, and directed him to leave town."

The interview with Pickle continues, with Walter Long asking a question: "Did you do the thrashing?" Pickle then responds, "Together with the others I did, and gave a statement to the newspaper that I took full responsibility for it. There were never any arrests or anything else in connection with it." The interview with Judge Pickle and an interview with Thurlow B. Weed provide reports of two additional serious incidents involving whites and blacks in or near Austin in the early twentieth century. The first is a report of a possible lynching of a black man for the rape and murder of a white girl near Manor. The incident took place in 1904, and the man was immediately brought to trial, found guilty, and executed. Because of rumors associated with this case, it was thought that there might be some violence, so guards were camped for a time on the grounds of the Capitol. The other incident occurred just after the "thrashing" of Mr. Shillady by Judge Pickle and his friends. Apparently there was a good deal of talk, as a result of this confrontation, that blacks would take up arms and retaliate against the whites. The home guards, a group of local militia men, were called up in Austin, to stand ready in case mobs of blacks, rumored to be organizing and with arms, entered the city. A meeting took place among some black and white men, at the Capitol, including Judge Pickle and the Texas adjutant general, and the battle never took place. (Walter Long interviews. Judge David J. Pickle, October 20, 1961, 14 pages; Thurlow B. Weed, October 20, 1961, 5 pages).
26. Austin Chamber of Commerce minutes, August 11, 1925.
27. *Austin, Texas: The City of the Violet Crown* (Austin: Templeman & Reissig, Publishers, 1917).

28. Walter Long interview with Carl Widen, pp. 23 and 24.
29. Alexis de Tocqueville, *Democracy in America*, 2 vol. (New York: Random House, Vintage Books, 1948).
30. Brown, *Annals*, chapter 3, p. 33.
31. Interview with Mrs. Nelda Kubalah.
32. Oscar Haas, *History of New Braunfels and Comal County, Texas; 1844–1946*, (New Braunfels: Oscar Haas, 1968), chapters 2–4.
33. Walter Long interview with Max Bickler, March 29, 1962.
34. Walter Long interview with Mrs. Edna Besserer Kuse, March 8, 1962.
35. Walter Long interview with Max Bickler, March 29, 1962.
36. *Mercantile and General City Directory of Austin, Texas 1872–1873*, by Gray & Moore (Austin: S. A. Gray, Book & Job Printers, 1872).
37. Ibid., p. 9.
38. *Morrison's & Fourmy's General Directory of the City of Austin for 1881–1882.* (Austin: Morrison & Fourmy Co., 1881).
39. Gillespie County Historical Society, *Pioneers in God's Hills: A History of Fredericksburg and Gillespie County People and Events*, 2 vol. (Austin: Boeckmann-Jones, 1960).
40. Brown, *Annals*, chapter 3, p. 33.
41. Georg Simnel, *Conflict and the Web of Group Affiliations* (Glencoe: Free Press, 1955).
42. Long interview with Kuse.
43. Long interview with Bickler.
44. Walter Long interview with Charlie Morrison, March 8, 1962.
45. Long interview with Widen.
46. Walter Long interview with Oswald Wolf, May 10, 1962.
47. Long interview with Bickler.
48. Ibid.
49. Ibid.
50. Long interview with Widen.
51. Long interview with Bickler.
52. Brown, *Annals*, chapter 33.
53. Long interview with Wolf.
54. Long interview with Bickler.
55. *Directory of the City of Austin, 1903–04* (Galveston: Morrison & Fourmy Co., 1903).
56. Long interview with Widen.

Chapter 2

1. Howard P. Chudacoff, *The Evolution of American Urban Society* (Englewood Cliffs, N.J.: Prentice-Hall, 1981), especially pp. 39–41.
2. Kenneth W. Wheeler, *To Wear a City's Crown: The Beginnings of Urban Growth in Texas, 1836–1865* (Cambridge, Mass: Harvard University Press, 1968).

3. Chudacoff, *Evolution*, pp. 40–41.
4. As quoted in Charles N. Glaub, "Visions of Metropolis: William Gilpin and Theories of City Growth in the American West," *Wisconsin Magazine of History*, vol. 45, number 1 (Autumn 1961), at p. 28.
5. Ibid.
6. Chudacoff, *Evolution*, p. 40.
7. Minutes, Austin Chamber of Commerce, July 15, 1914.
8. Ibid.
9. "Major Wooldridge, 72 Years, Today. The Man Who Made Austin Beautiful," *Austin American*, April 13, 1919.
10. *Austin Statesman*, day and month unknown, 1919 (A. P. Wooldridge Papers, Barker Texas History Center).
11. Anthony F. Wallace, *Rockdale* (New York: Alfred A. Knopf, 1978).
12. *Austin Statesman*, January 1, 1888.
13. Ibid.
14. Ibid.
15. Ibid.
16. Ibid.
17. Ibid.
18. Ibid.
19. Ibid.
20. "Our Water Power," *Austin Statesman*, June 23 or 25, 1889.
21. *Austin American-Statesman*, July 9, 1933.
22. *Austin American-Statesman*, January 1, 1935.
23. Ibid.
24. Ibid.
25. *Austin American*, June 7, 1935.
26. *Austin American-Statesman*, Buchanan Dam Edition, July 29, 1937.
27. *Austin American-Statesman*, June 5, 1938.
28. Ibid.
29. Ibid.
30. Ibid.
31. *Austin American*, January 1, 1941.
32. Ibid.
33. Ibid.
34. *Austin American*, May 25, 1941.
35. See, for instance, the *Austin American* issues of April 3, 1942, on the Chamber of Commerce; of January 28, 1944, on the City Planning Commission; and of September 10, 1944, on plans to expand the university.
36. *Austin American*, November 21, 1948, second section.
37. Ibid.

Chapter 3

1. See, for instance, "The Modern Prince," in Antonio Gramsci, *Selections from Prison Notebooks* (New York: International Publishing, 1971), pp. 123–205.

2. The matter of leadership, and why leaders lead, is a very subtle one, discussed in my unpublished manuscript, "Leadership; or the Organization of Compliance."

3. Edward Clark interview, May 12, 1983; Emmett Shelton, Sr., interview, May 5, 1983.

4. *Austin American*, October 25, 1959.

5. Janett L. Fish interview, February 10, 1983.

6. Miss Ruby Lee Ransom and Mrs. Jim Tatum interview, April 22, 1983.

7. Walter K. Long interview, March 17, 1983.

8. Walter Ewing Long, "Biography," mimeographed, personal papers.

9. Long, "Biography."

10. Fish interview.

11. See, for example, Minutes, Austin Chamber of Commerce, August 3, 1920, and April 4, 1922.

12. Minutes, Austin Chamber of Commerce, March 6, 1928.

13. Ibid.

14. Barker Texas History Collection, Chamber of Commerce Documents, National Recovery Administration papers (Box JT 2091).

15. Walter E. Long, *Wings Over Austin* (n.p., 1962).

16. Fish interview.

17. Clark interview.

18. Fish interview.

19. Minutes, Austin Chamber of Commerce, February 2, 1927.

20. Minutes, Austin Chamber of Commerce, June 1, 1943.

21. Minutes, Austin Chamber of Commerce, June 4, 1940.

22. Walter E. Long, "Autobiography of a Fool," Autumn 1949, mimeographed, p. 19.

23. Fish interview; also see Long, "Autobiography of a Fool."

24. Long, "Autobiography of a Fool," no page number.

25. Ibid.

26. Emma Long interview, June 3, 1981; Edgar Perry III interview, April 20, 1983; Clark interview.

27. Clark interview.

28. Ibid.

29. Floylee Hunter Hemphill, "Mayor Tom Miller and the First Year of the New Deal in Austin, Texas," M.A. thesis (Austin: University of Texas, 1976), p. 3.

30. For documentation on this, see, for instance, Minutes, City Council, City of Austin, May 11, 1933.

31. Walter E. Long interview with Oswald Wolf, May 10, 1962.

32. Shanks quote in Hemphill, "Mayor Tom Miller," p. 2.

33. Hemphill, "Mayor Tom Miller," p. 6.

34. Trueman O'Quinn interview, May 10, 1983.

35. The distinction here is due to the insight of Max Weber, "Politics as a Profession," in Hans H. Gerth and C. Wright Mills (editors), *From Max Weber: Essays in Sociology and Social Psychology* (New York: Oxford University Press, 1958), pp. 77–128.

36. *Austin Daily Dispatch*, March 19, 1933.

37. Clark interview.
38. Emma Long interview.
39. Clark interview.
40. Ibid.
41. Ibid.
42. See biographical sketches in the biography file on Robert Thomas Miller at the Austin History Center. Also noted in interview with Emma Long, Edgar Perry III, and Edward Clark.
43. *Dallas Times Herald*, March 25, 1959.
44. Biographical materials, Austin History Center.
45. Files, City of Austin, Austin Dam.
46. Ada Simond interview, April 19 and 27, 1983.
47. Clark interview.
48. Todd Crosset interview with Guiton Morgan, June 23, 1982.
49. Clark interview.
50. Biographical materials, Austin History Center.
51. Clark interview; Perry III interview; Shelton, Sr., interview.
52. *Austin American*, March 31, 1935.
53. *Austin Statesman*, March 29, 1939.
54. Taylor Glass interview, May 21, 1982.
55. Biographical materials, Austin History Center.
56. Emma Long interview.
57. Emma Long interview; Perry III interview.
58. Clark interview.
59. There are many indications of this, including correspondence of the mayor, in the Lyndon Baines Johnson Library in Austin. See, for instance, the letter from Miller to Wirtz of April 15, 1940; Alvin J. Wirtz correspondence, Box 5, Tom Miller to Alvin Wirtz, April 15, 1940.
60. Clark interview; Glass interview. Also *Austin American*, January 25, 1938.
61. Minutes, Austin Chamber of Commerce, February 9, 1941.
62. *Austin Statesman*, February 16, 1939.
63. Emma Long interview.
64. A. Garland Adair and E. H. Perry, Sr. (collaborator), *Austin and Commodore Perry*, Texas Heritage Foundation (Austin: Steck Co., 1956), p. 225.
65. Clark interview.
66. Edgar Perry, Sr., unpublished memoirs.
67. Ibid.
68. Perry III interview.
69. Edgar Perry Scrapbooks, Austin History Center.
70. Adair and Perry, *Austin and Commodore Perry*, pp. 200–202.
71. Ransom-Tatum interview; also Perry, Sr., unpublished memoirs.
72. "Who's Who in the Party," Edgar Perry Scrapbooks, volume 3, Austin History Center.
73. Perry III interview.
74. Adair and Perry, *Austin and Commodore Perry*, p. 214.
75. Ransom-Tatum interview.
76. Lady Bird Johnson to Edgar Perry, February 26, 1942, Edgar Perry Scrapbooks, volume 1, Austin History Center.

77. Edgar Perry Scrapbooks, Austin History Center.
78. See, for instance, the various letters between Wirtz and Johnson in the Alvin J. Wirtz correspondence, Lyndon Baines Johnson Library.
79. Perry III interview.
80. Ibid.
81. Ibid.
82. Ransom-Tatum interview.
83. Perry III interview; Ransom-Tatum interview.
84. Ransom-Tatum interview.
85. Perry, unpublished memoirs.
86. Max Weber, *The Protestant Ethic and the Spirit of Capitalism*, translated by Talcott Parsons (New York: Charles Scribner's Sons, 1958).
87. Perry, unpublished memoirs.
88. Ibid.
89. Perry Scrapbooks, Austin History Center; paper, month, and day unidentified.
90. Long, "Autobiography of a Fool." Also, see Minutes, Austin Chamber of Commerce, for various indications of the same.
91. Ransom-Tatum interview.
92. Ibid.
93. Walter E. Long, "The Century Class: Principles of Business Organization Applied to a Bible Class," mimeographed, 1946.
94. Miller Biographical Materials, Austin History Center.

Chapter 4

1. Ralph Yarborough interview, September 20, 1983.
2. *Austin American*, April 7, 1940.
3. Speech, Alvin J. Wirtz at the dedication of Tom Miller Dam, Austin, April 6, 1940, papers of Alvin J. Wirtz, Box 18, LBJ Library.
4. *Austin American*, April 7, 1940.
5. Statement before House Sub-Committee on Appropriations, Lyndon Baines Johnson, February 9, 1938, Papers of Lyndon Baines Johnson, House of Representatives, 1937–1949, Box 178, File 1940, Colorado River Authority, Marshall Ford Dam Appropriation.
6. Comer Clay, "The Lower Colorado River Authority: A Study in Politics and Public Administration," doctoral dissertation (Austin: University of Texas, 1948), pp. 33–35.
7. Ibid.
8. Tom Ferguson interview, November 15, 1983.
9. Ibid.
10. Clay, "The Lower Colorado River Authority," pp. 19–20.
11. Daniel W. Mead, *Dam and Water Power Development at Austin, Texas* (Madison, Wisconsin: Daniel W. Mead and Charles V. Seastone Consulting Engineers, 1917), p. 48.
12. Ibid, pp. 41–53.
13. Ibid, p. 113.

14. Ibid, p. 7.

15. Ibid, p. 8.

16. Report, S. S. Posey to E. C. Bartholomew, October 1, 1915, Austin, Texas, City of Austin files, The Austin Dam.

17. See the very excellent discussion of this and other events connected with dams on the Colorado in Walter E. Long, *Flood to Faucet* (Austin: Steck Company, 1956), see especially chapter 4.

18. Ibid, p. 31.

19. Ibid, p. 35.

20. Clay, "The Lower Colorado River Authority," p. 61.

21. Ibid.

22. Ferguson interview, November 15, 1983.

23. Long, *Flood to Faucet*, pp. 60-64; Clay, "The Lower Colorado River Authority," pp. 71-75.

24. Clay, "The Lower Colorado River Authority," p. 75.

25. Interview with Beverly Randolph, November 5, 1983.

26. Speech, Tom Miller at dedication of the Alvin Wirtz Dam, June 15, 1952, files of John Babcock.

27. Letter, Alvin Wirtz to Carl White, April 2, 1941, Papers of Alvin J. Wirtz, Box 18, Wirtz-LCRA Miscellaneous correspondence, LBJ Library.

28. Water Right Permits, Item 31, LCRA Supporting Data, Appendix A, LBJ Library.

29. Clay, "The Lower Colorado River Authority," p. 77.

30. Ibid, pp. 77-80.

31. Ibid, p. 80.

32. Ibid, p. 79.

33. Ibid, p. 78.

34. Randolph interview, November 5, 1983.

35. Ibid.

36. Ibid.

37. Clay, "The Lower Colorado River Authority," pp. 79-85.

38. Ferguson interview, November 15, 1983.

39. Long, *Flood to Faucet*, pp. 50-74.

40. Interview with John Babcock, October 4, 1943.

41. Clay, "The Lower Colorado River Authority," p. 88.

42. Ibid.

43. Ibid.

44. Memorandum, Henry Hunt to Harold Ickes, Subject: Colorado River Project (Texas), April 26, 1935, Papers to James Buchanan, Barker History Center, University of Texas.

45. Long, *Flood to Faucet*, p. 50.

46. Randolph interview, November 5, 1983.

47. Ferguson interview, November 15, 1983.

48. Letter, James Buchanan to Alvin J. Wirtz, June 26, 1934, Papers of James P. Buchanan, Barker History Center, University of Texas.

49. Ferguson interview, November 15, 1983.

50. Ibid.

51. Papers of James P. Buchanan, Barker History Center, University of Texas.
52. Ferguson interview, November 15, 1983. There remains, however, much dispute over this matter. See Clay, "The Lower Colorado River Authority," p. 111.
53. Ibid.
54. Babcock interview, September 27, 1983.
55. Letter, Walter Woodward to James Buchanan, November 21, 1934, Papers of James P. Buchanan, Barker History Center, University of Texas.
56. Telegram, James Buchanan to Walter Woodward, November 8, 1934, Papers of James B. Buchanan, Barker History Center, University of Texas.
57. Telegram, James Buchanan to Walter Woodward, November 9, 1934, Papers of James P. Buchanan, Barker History Center, University of Texas.
58. Ibid.
59. Long, *Flood to Faucet*, p. 86.
60. Ferguson interview, November 15, 1983.
61. Long, *Flood to Faucet*, penned note on p. 86 of personal copy.
62. See, for these items, Papers of James P. Buchanan, November 1934, Barker History Center, University of Texas.
63. Telegram Ray Lee to James Buchanan, November 20, 1934, Papers of James P. Buchanan, Barker History Center, University of Texas.
64. Letter, James Buchanan to Harold Ickes, November 24, 1934, Papers of James P. Buchanan, Barker History Center, University of Texas.
65. Memorandum, Henry Hunt to James Buchanan, December 3, 1934; and letter, James Buchanan to Harold Ickes, December 4, 1934, Papers of James P. Buchanan, Barker History Center, University of Texas.
66. *Austin American*, May 17, 1935.
67. Letter, Alvin Wirtz to James Buchanan, August 17, 1935, Papers of James P. Buchanan, Barker History Center, University of Texas.
68. Randoph interview, November 5, 1983.
69. Telegram, Raymond Brooks to Charles Marsh, August 16, 1935, Papers of James P. Buchanan, Barker History Center, University of Texas.
70. Telegram, James Buchanan to Roy Fry, August 24, 1935, Papers of James P. Buchanan, Barker History Center, University of Texas.
71. How the LCRA Acquired Its Properties in 1935, LCRA Supporting Data, Appendix A, LBJ Library.
72. See Long, *Flood to Faucet*, personal copy, penned note, p. 82. Long claimed Wirtz received $75,000 in legal fees from Morrison.
73. Minutes, Austin Chamber of Commerce, February 4, 1936.
74. *Austin American*, February 23, 1937.
75. Ibid.
76. Interview with Creekmore Fath, November 29, 1983.
77. Interview with Edward Clark, April 12, 1983.
78. *Austin American*, April 11, 1937.
79. Ferguson interview, November 15, 1983; interview with Jim Gideon, October 11, 1983.

80. Ferguson interview, November 15, 1983.
81. Letter, Tom Miller to Lyndon Johnson, May 21, 1937, City of Austin files.
82. Letter, Goodall Wooten to Lyndon Johnson, May 24, 1937, Papers of Lyndon Baines Johnson, House of Representatives, 1937–1949, Box 169, Colorado River Authority, Tom Miller Dam, LBJ Library.
83. Letter, E. H. Perry, Sr., to Lyndon Johnson, May 23, 1937, Papers of Lyndon Baines Johnson, House of Representatives, 1937–1949, Box 169, Colorado River Authority, Tom Miller Dam, LBJ Library.
84. Letter, Fritz Engelhard to Lyndon Johnson, June 4, 1937, Papers of Lyndon Baines Johnson, House of Representatives, 1937–1949, Box 169, Colorado River Authority, Tom Miller Dam, #3, LBJ Library.
85. Gideon interview, October 11, 1983.
86. Letter, John Page to J. J. Mansfield, Papers of Lyndon Baines Johnson, House of Representatives, 1937–1949, Box 185, 1941, LCRA, Marshall Ford Dam Construction, LBJ Library.
87. Telegrams, Lyndon B. Johnson to Tom Miller and to Herman Brown, July 21, 1937, Papers of Lyndon Baines Johnson, House of Representatives, 1937–1949, Box 167, Marshall Ford Dam #1, LBJ Library.
88. Clark interview, April 12, 1983.
89. Letter, Ray Lee to Lyndon B. Johnson, November 30, 1937, Papers of Lyndon Baines Johnson, House of Representatives, 1937–1949, Box 167, Marshall Ford Dam # 3, LBJ Library.
90. Ferguson interview, November 15, 1983.
91. Letters, Fritz Engelhard to Morris Sheppard and to Tom Connally, March 4, 1938, Papers of Lyndon Baines Johnson, House of Representatives, 1937–1949, Box 169, Colorado River Authority, Fritz Engelhard, LBJ Library.
92. Letter, Lyndon Johnson to Franklin D. Roosevelt, September 3, 1940, Papers of Lyndon Baines Johnson, House of Representatives, 1937–1949, Box 178, 1940, Colorado River Authority, Marshall Ford Dam Appropriation, LBJ Library.
93. Letter, Lyndon B. Johnson to George Brown, February 3, 1940, Papers of Lyndon Baines Johnson, House of Representatives, 1937–1949, Box 178, 1940, Colorado River Authority, Marshall Ford Dam Appropriation, LBJ Library.
94. Ferguson interview, November 15, 1983; Babcock interview, September 27, 1983.
95. Letter, Carl White to Lyndon B. Johnson, January 10, 1940, Papers of Lyndon Baines Johnson, House of Representatives, 1937–1949, Box 178, 1940, Colorado River Authority, L. B. Johnson, Personal, LBJ Library.
96. Letter, R. N. Elliot, Acting Comptroller General of the United States, to Secretary of the Interior, July 11, 1940, Papers of Alvin J. Wirtz, Box 19, Wirtz Correspondence, LBJ Library.
97. Fath interview, November 29, 1983.
98. Reprinted in *Austin American*, September 2, 1938, editorial.
99. Ibid.

100. Letter, Charles Hackett to Lyndon Johnson, Papers of Lyndon Baines Johnson, House of Representatives, 1937–1949, Box 169, Colorado River Authority, 1938 Flood, LBJ Library.
101. *Smithville Times*, August 11, 1938.
102. Telegram, Smithville citizens to Lyndon Johnson, Papers of Lyndon Baines Johnson, House of Representatives, 1937–1949, Box 169, Colorado River Authority, 1938 Flood, LBJ Library.
103. Babcock interview, September 27, 1983.
104. Babcock interview, October 4, 1983.
105. Letter, Lyndon B. Johnson to Clarence McDonough, March 16, 1938, Papers of Lyndon Baines Johnson, House of Representatives, 1937–1949, Box 171, Colorado River Authority, Power 4, Municipalities, LBJ Library.
106. Babcock interview, October 4, 1983.
107. See Papers of Lyndon Baines Johnson, House of Representatives, 1937–1949, Box 171, Colorado River Authority, Power 4, Municipalities, LBJ Library.
108. Speech, Lyndon B. Johnson, August 16, 1938, Papers of Lyndon Baines Johnson, House of Representatives, 1937–1949, Box 171, Correspondence and Issuances, LBJ Library.

Chapter 5

1. On some of this history, see Walter E. Long, *From a Magnesium Plant to a Research Center* (copyright 1962 by Walter E. Long).
2. *Austin American*, January 13, 1938.
3. Tarnish on the Violet Crown, Radio Address of Lyndon Baines Johnson, KNOW, January 23, 1938, Papers of Lyndon Baines Johnson, Statements of Lyndon B. Johnson, Box 2, LBJ Library.
4. Ibid.
5. Lorraine Barnes, "Does Austin Have Slums?" *Austin American-Statesman*, January 16, 1938.
6. *Austin American-Statesman*, January 23, 1938.
7. Ibid.
8. *Austin American*, January 28, 1938.
9. Interview with Lorraine Barnes, June 27, 1984.
10. *Austin American*, January 28, 1938.
11. Ibid.
12. *Austin American*, March 10, 1939.
13. Ibid.
14. Interview with Edward Clark, May 12, 1983; interview with Taylor Glass, May 21, 1982.
15. Glass interview, May 21, 1982.
16. Ibid, p. 5.
17. *Austin Statesman*, June 23, 1933.
18. *Austin Statesman*, June 29, 1933.

19. See the various articles by Raymond Brooks beginning with the July 2, 1933, issue.
20. *Austin American*, June 14, 1934.
21. *Austin American*, July 31, 1935.
22. *Austin American-Statesman*, July 19, 1936.
23. *Austin Statesman*, March 29, 1939.
24. *Austin American*, June 13, 1933.
25. *Austin American*, March 4, 1934.
26. *Austin American*, June 3, 1933.
27. Data furnished by the Austin History Center staff.
28. Mattye Gallagher-Reuter, *Our Friend, the President* (copyright 1933), Barker History Center, Chamber of Commerce files on the National Recovery Act, JT 2091, p. 8.
29. Ibid., p. 18.
30. *Austin American-Statesman*, January 27, 1934.
31. *Austin American*, March 31, 1935.
32. Ibid.
33. *Austin Statesman*, February 16, 1939.
34. *Austin American*, April 1, 1939.
35. Ibid.
36. Ibid.
37. *Austin American*, April 4, 1939.
38. *Austin American*, April 8, 1941.
39. Glass interview.
40. *Austin American*, March 4, 1947.

Chapter 6

1. The entire description of the university, save for a few spots noted, came from an interview with Venola Schmidt on February 21, 1984.
2. Interview with Wendell Gordon, March 1, 1984.
3. Gordon interview.
4. R. H. Montgomery, *The Brimstone Game* (Manchaca: Chaparral Press, 1949).
5. Ibid., p. 17.
6. See also interview with Reverend Bob Bryan, May 25, 1984.
7. Schmidt interview.
8. Interview with Creekmore Fath, February 21, 1984.
9. Fath interview; Schmidt interview; interview with David Miller, March 20, 1984.
10. Miller interview.
11. Interview with Walter Firey, April 26, 1984; also see, "In Memoriam: Robert H. Montgomery," by Professors Carey C. Thompson, C. Wendell Gordon, and Clifton M. Grubbs, distributed to the General Faculty at the University of Texas on November 30, 1979.
12. Firey interview.
13. Miller interview.

14. Interview with Homer Thornberry, February 28, 1984.
15. Henry Nash Smith, Horace Busby, and Rex D. Hopper, *The Controversy at the University of Texas, 1939–1946*, 3rd ed. Austin: University of Texas, Student Committee for Academic Freedom, Students Association, 1946), p. 18.
16. Ibid, p. 5.
17. Ibid., p. 7; see also *Texas Spectator*, October 4, 1946.
18. Smith et al., p. 7.
19. Ibid., p. 8.
20. Ibid., p. 10.
21. *Dallas Morning News*, March 17, 1942.
22. Ibid.
23. Gordon interview.
24. Ibid.
25. Ibid.
26. Ibid.
27. Smith et al., p. 6.
28. Gordon interview.
29. Ibid.
30. *Austin American*, October 22, 1944.
31. Smith et al., p. 11.
32. Ibid.
33. *Austin American*, November 2, 1944.
34. Ibid.
35. Smith et al., *The Controversy*, p. 13.
36. Ibid., p. 13.
37. Ibid., p. 13.
38. Ibid., p. 20.
39. Ibid., p. 21.
40. Firey interview.
41. Miller interview.
42. Horace Busby, "The Era of Hostility," *Daily Texan*, May 28, 1946.
43. *Austin American*, September 21, 1947.
44. Gordon interview.
45. Thornberry interview.
46. *Texas Spectator*, February 8, 1946.
47. Gordon interview.
48. See *The Heavy Load: Anti-Labor Laws Passed by the 50th Texas Legislature* (Austin: Texas Federation of Labor, 1947).
49. Fath interview.
50. See Hart Stilwell, *The Herman Brown Story* (Austin: n.p., 1951).
51. Thornberry interview; Fath interview.
52. See the *Colorado River Authority* files, Papers of Lyndon Baines Johnson, House of Representatives, 1939–1947, LBJ Library.
53. Unidentified informant.
54. Ibid.
55. Schmidt interview.
56. *Austin Statesman*, April 24, 1950.

57. Interview with Henry Holman, February 13, 1984; interview with John McCully, February 16, 1984.
58. Fath interview.
59. *Texas Spectator*, March 15, 1946.
60. Unidentified informant.
61. This synopsis comes from several sources: *Texas Week*, volume 1, number 17 (December 1946); and the interviews with Fath, Holman, and McCully.
62. Ibid.
63. Interview with Helen Spear, February 7, 1984.
64. Unidentified informant.

Chapter 7

1. Interview with Janie Harrison, May 25, 1983.
2. *Austin American*, August 31, 1949.
3. U.S. Bureau of the Census, Census of the United States, 1950.
4. *Austin American*, November 5, 1949.
5. *Austin American*, November 9, 1949.
6. *Austin American*, November 5, 1949.
7. *Austin American*, November 11, 1949.
8. Ibid.
9. Report with cover letter, April 1, 1950, Economic Research Agency, Madison Wisconsin, from files of Emma Long.
10. *Austin American*, May 5, 1950.
11. Interview with Ada Simond, April 19 and 27, 1983.
12. William B. Hamilton, *A Social History of Austin*, Bulletin of the University of Texas, Number 273, Humanistic Series, Number 15 (University of Texas, March 15, 1913).
13. *Austin American*, January 13, 1938.
14. *Austin American*, November 11, 1949.
15. Interview with Janie Harrison, together with *A Pictorial History of Austin, Travis County, Texas' Black Community, 1939–1920* (The Black Heritage Exhibit, Delta Sigma Theta Sorority, Inc., 1976 Bicentennial Project).
16. *A Pictorial History*, p. 9.
17. Ibid., p. 11; Reverend Jacob Fontaine III with Gene Burd, *Jacob Fontaine* (Austin: Eakin Press, 1983), pp. 42–45; plus Harrison and Simond interviews.
18. *A Pictorial History*, p. 11.
19. Interview with Ada Simond.
20. *A Pictorial History*, p. 7.
21. *Housing Pattern Study of Austin, Texas* (City of Austin, 1977), p. 10, files of Austin History Center.
22. Koch and Fowler, Consulting Engineers, *A City Plan for Austin, Texas*, 1928 (reprinted February 1957 by Department of Planning, City of Austin). My deepest thanks to my colleague Joe Feagin, for having brought this signal document to my attention.

23. "City Planning, Zoning and Race Segregation," An Address by Major E. A. Wood, no page, files of Walter Long.
24. Koch and Fowler, p. 57.
25. Interview with Ada Simond.
26. U.S. Bureau of the Census, Census of the United States, 1940.
27. The reconstruction here is based on various and sundry sources. They include the interviews with Ada Simond, Janie Harrison, Dr. John Q. Taylor King, on August 15, 1984, and Louis Schwartz, on January 17, 1985. Also, the description here relies heavily on the Austin *City Directory* of 1907, 1918, 1927, and 1937; and on the *City Register*, which contains property valuations on all land in Austin, of 1907, 1917, 1927, 1937, and 1941. The *Directory* and *Register* are in the Austin History Center.
28. The description here of Dr. Givens is built from various interviews and oral histories.
29. Interview with Louis Schwartz.
30. Assorted interviews.
31. *City Register* of 1917 and 1937.
32. Interview with James Wright, no date recorded.
33. Interviews with John King, and with W. Astor Kirk, August 29, 1984.
34. Interview with Ada Simond.
35. Interview with Louis Schwartz, plus assorted interviews.
36. Interview with Ada Simond and Janie Harrison.
37. Interview with James and Eva Marie Mosby, May 10, 1984.
38. Interview with Father Francis Webber, May 14, 1984.
39. Ibid.
40. Interview with Ada Simond.
41. Interview with James and Eva Marie Mosby.
42. *Austin American*, March 10, 1939.
43. *City Register* of 1907, 1917, 1927, 1937, and 1941, files of the Austin History Center.
44. Interview with Ada Simond.
45. Unidentified informant.
46. Economic Research Agency report, April 1, 1950.
47. Interview with Janie Harrison.
48. Interview with W. Astor Kirk.
49. Interview with Father Webber.
50. Interviews with John King and with Volma Overton, April 30, 1984.
51. Interview with Volma Overton.
52. Ibid.
53. Assorted interviews.
54. Interviews with Ada Simond and Eva Marie Mosby.
55. Assorted interviews.
56. Interview with Eva Marie Mosby.
57. Assorted interviews.
58. Interview with John King.
59. Interview with Dr. B. E. Conner, May 18, 1984.
60. Ibid.

61. Assorted interviews.
62. Interviews with Dr. Conner and with Mary Holman, February 23, 1984.
63. Minute Book 7, City of Austin, p. 206.
64. Ibid., p. 216.
65. Ibid.
66. Minute Book 10, pp. 63, 108.
67. Ibid., p. 484.
68. Minute Book 13, p. 164.
69. Interview with John King.
70. Minute Book 14, p. 29.
71. Ibid.
72. Ibid., p. 98.
73. Ibid., p. 162.
74. Minute Book 18, p. 263.
75. Minute Book 20, p. 33.
76. *Crisis* (May 1950): 288–332.
77. *Texas Spectator*, December 13, 1946.
78. *Dallas News*, November 21, 1946.
79. *Texas Spectator*, December 13, 1940.
80. *Texas Spectator*, December 20, 1946.
81. *The Crisis* (May 1950): 288–320.
82. *Texas Spectator*, December 20, 1946.
83. Sweatt *v.* Painter, 339 U.S. 629 (June 5, 1950).
84. This portrait of Arthur DeWitty has been constructed from assorted interviews.
85. Interview with Reverend Bob Bryan, May 25, 1984.
86. My copies of DeWitty's columns from the *Informer* come, in fact, from Emma Long's personal files.
87. Much of the following description of Kirk's activities in Austin is based on assorted interviews, with people like Dr. King, plus the personal interview I did with Kirk on August 29, 1984.
88. *Austin Statesman*, August 15, 1951.
89. *Houston Informer*, November 3, 1951.
90. *Austin American*, December 28, 1951.
91. Interview with Judge David Pickle by Walter Long, October 20, 1961.
92. This event is reported in Minute Book 9 of the City of Austin, p. 493.

Chapter 8

1. Long personal papers, letter from A. Wayne Hodges, August 20, 1952.
2. Interview with Emma Long, June 12, 1981.
3. Virginia Durr talk, LBJ Library, May 1984.
4. Interview with John McCully, February 16, 1984.
5. Dinner with Emma, March 1982.
6. Interview with Henry and Mary Holman, February 23, 1984.
7. Long personal papers, letter from Estella Davis, December 27, 1951.
8. Interview with Creekmore Fath, November 29, 1983.

9. Assorted interviews.

10. Long personal papers, letter from "Your friend," January 28, 1952.

11. Interview with Edith Hicks, January 31, 1984.

12. Ibid.

13. Ibid.

14. Ibid.

15. Interview with Stuart Long by Chandler Davidson, June 1976, Texas Oral History Program, Rice University.

16. Ibid.

17. Holman interview.

18. Fath interview.

19. Fath, Holman, and Long interviews.

20. Card, Long personal papers.

21. Interview with Judge Homer Thornberry, February 28, 1984.

22. *Austin American*, September 15, 1949.

23. Interview with I. W. "Stormy" Davis, May 24, 1984.

24. Holman interview; also see *San Antonio Light*, February 13, 1949.

25. Interview with Janett L. Fish, February 10, 1983.

26. Emma Long personal communication, December 9, 1984.

27. Long personal papers, letter from W. Astor Kirk, December 3, 1951.

28. *Austin American*, January 25, 1950.

29. Stuart Long Oral History, Rice University. In all fairness to Mr. Clark, I must report that he confessed to have no specific memories of the circumstances under which Stuart was fired by KVET. In an interview I did with him on May 12, 1983, he reported to me that he believed the firing was due to "Stuart's views about labor," and that John Connally probably fired him (interview with Edward Clark, May 12, 1983).

30. *Austin American*, February 24, 1950.

31. Long personal papers.

32. Emma Long personal communication, December 9, 1984.

33. *Austin American*, October 20, 1950.

34. In a personal communication (December 2, 1984), W. Astor Kirk informed me that there were at least two different intentions at work in the effort to create a new system of choosing council members. One, and probably the main, intention was to get rid of Emma. But also, because of the recent interest and success of black candidates, notably Harry Lott and Arthur DeWitty, there was an effort to develop some kind of system that might either aid or hinder minority representation on the council. As Kirk now recalls, some people in the black community of Austin felt that the old at-large system was the better device for securing minority representation, whereas others believed a district-system, in which the city was apportioned into geographical voting areas, would have been preferable. Discussion of the latter method soon was dropped after it had been taken up and sponsored by Kirk, mainly because of lack of support among members of the revision committee.

35. Interview with Jean Lee, February 2, 1984. Also, in the interview I did with Emmett Shelton, Sr., he told me that Frank Erwin was chosen by the bankers as sort of a front man to run the Good Government League.

Shelton did not remember which bankers, in particular, had a hand in the choice, but he seemed to think that E. W. Jackson, former head of the Steck Company and a director of the Austin National Bank, was one of those who wanted to get rid of Emma, and may have been behind the formation of the Good Government League (interview with Emmett Shelton, Sr., May 5, 1983).

36. See *Austin American* and *Austin Statesman*, December 9, 1952.
37. *Austin American*, December 21, 1952.
38. Ibid.
39. *Austin American*, December 22, 1952.
40. *Austin American*, January 23, 1953.
41. See Emma Long personal files.
42. *Austin American*, January 11, 1953.
43. *Austin American*, December 31, 1952.
44. Ibid.
45. Emma Long personal communication, December 9, 1984.
46. *Austin Statesman*, April 2, 1953.
47. *Austin American*, April 1, 1953.
48. *Austin Statesman*, April 3, 1953.
49. Interview with Emma Long, September 15, 1984.
50. *Austin Statesman*, April 3, 1953.
51. *Austin American*, April 2, 1953, editorial.
52. Interview with Emma Long, June 1982.
53. *Austin Statesman*, August 24, 1966.
54. Interview with Edgar Perry III, April 20, 1983.
55. Interview with Helen Spear, February 7, 1984.

Chapter 9

1. Interview with C. B. Smith, July 17, 1985.
2. Interview with Ed St. John, July 30, 1985.
3. Interview with with Dave Shanks, July 23, 1985.
4. Smith interview.
5. Interviews with Smith, St. John, and John Stockton, September 9, 1985.
6. Richardson Wood, "Outline of a Plan for the Further Economic Development of Austin, Texas," March–April 1948, files of Austin-Travis County History Center. Also, see the report of Wood's talk in *Austin American*, March 25, 1948, editorial page.
7. Ibid.
8. *Austin American*, April 21, 1948.
9. Smith interview.
10. Ibid.
11. Ibid.
12. Interview with Vic Mathias, July 24, 1985.
13. See various copies of *Austin and Industry*, the monthly newsletter of the foundation, files of Austin-Travis County History Center.
14. *Austin and Industry*, vol. 1, no. 2 (1948).

15. Smith interview.
16. Telegram to C. B. Smith, Sr., December 30, 1949, files of C. B. Smith, Jr.
17. *Austin American*, December 29, 1949; *Houston Chronicle*, December 29, 1949.
18. Interview with J. Neils Thompson, August 6, 1985.
19. Thompson interview.
20. Thompson interview; also, see the report "31 Years of Research, 1946–1977, Balcones Research Center, the University of Texas at Austin."
21. "31 Years of Research, 1946–1977."
22. *Austin American*, February 5, 1954.
23. *Austin American*, September 14, 1954.
24. Ibid.
25. *The Austin Master Plan*, Preliminary Report, Number 1, Program Status, Barker Texas History Center.
26. Draft Copy, *The Austin Master Plan*, September 30, 1956, files of Emma Long.
27. Ibid., p. 64.
28. Ibid., pp. 64–65.
29. Ibid., p. 64.
30. *Austin American*, January 9, 1957.
31. *Austin American*, February 24, 1957.
32. *The Austin Master Plan*, p. 64.
33. Mathias interview.
34. Ibid.
35. Cover letter to Bureau Report, "Possibilities for Industrial Expansion: Austin, Texas," Bureau of Business Research, The University of Texas at Austin, September 23, 1957, files of Austin Chamber of Commerce.
36. Ibid., p. iv.
37. Ibid., p. x.
38. Interviews with Mathias, Smith, Thompson, plus assorted others.
39. Thompson interview; see also *American Statesman*, July 7, 1960, editorial.
40. Interview with Joe Crow, July 31, 1985.
41. See, for example, *Austin American*, August 11, 1961.
42. *Austin American*, August 24, 1961; Thompson interview.
43. See the following issues of the *Austin American*: April 2, 1960; July 7, 1960; August 10, 1961; August 11, 1961; August 16, 1961; August 17, 1961; August 19, 1961; August 20, 1961, August 22, 1961; August 23, 1961; August 27, 1961; September 24, 1961; December 8, 1961; and December 15, 1961.
44. Ibid.
45. Crow interview.
46. Ibid.
47. Ibid.
48. Ibid.
49. Crow interview; see also the newspapers of September and October 1954; end of October 1959.
50. Crow interview.
51. Ibid.

52. Interview with Hub Bechtol, July 22, 1985.

53. Ibid.

54. Smith interview, plus Smith file papers.

55. Names shown on letterhead of Greater Austin Association stationery.

56. Letter from Hardy Hollers to C. B. Smith, Sr., March 3, 1966.

57. Bechtol interview; Smith interview; Smith papers of 1966 and 1967.

58. Interview with Lloyd Lochridge, August 22, 1985.

59. Memorandum prepared by Edmunds Travis, files of Sam Wood.

60. Assorted interviews.

61. Interview with John Gray, August 1, 1985.

62. Gray interview; Bechtol interview.

63. Bechtol interview.

64. Thompson interview.

65. Bechtol interview.

66. Assorted interviews.

67. Assorted interviews.

68. Gray interview.

Chapter 10

1. Interview with Glen Castlebury, August 23, 1985.

2. Interview with Bill Petri, October 25, 1985.

3. Interview with Charles Miles, October 28, 1985.

4. Biographical newspaper clipping, Austin–Travis County Historical Center.

5. Interviews with Emma Long, plus assorted interviews.

6. Petri interview, plus Long interview.

7. Miles interview.

8. Arthur DeWitty statement before City Council, July 16, 1953, personal papers of Emma Long.

9. Transcript of City Council meeting, February 16, 1956, personal papers of Emma Long.

10. Ibid.

11. Ibid.

12. *Houston Informer*, February 25, 1956, personal papers of Emma Long.

13. The exact dates of the beginning of this episode are difficult to determine. I have had to reconstruct the times from very different sources of information, including interviews with W. Astor Kirk, Reverend Bob Bryan, and others.

14. Kirk interview, August 29, 1984.

15. Harry Akin biographical file, Austin–Travis County Historical Center.

16. Ibid., plus Petri interview.

17. Ibid., plus interview of Leila Jones (Akins) Tinstman and Robert Tinstman, September 25, 1985.

18. Akin biographical file.

19. Harry Akin, "With Deliberate Speed," *Restaurant Management* (December 1963), 18 and 22.

20. Ibid.

21. Kirk interview, plus interview with Reverend Bob Bryan, May 25, 1984.

22. Ibid., plus Kirk interview.

23. Bryan interview, plus assorted other interviews.

24. Ibid.

25. Interview with Joseph Witherspoon, October 23, 1985. Also see the excellent source materials on this period of Austin history in Joseph Parker Witherspoon, *Administrative Implementation of Civil Rights* (Austin: University of Texas Press, 1968), pp. 38–92.

26. Witherspoon interview.

27. Ibid.

28. Ibid.

29. Witherspoon, *Adminstrative Implementation*, p. 56.

30. Ibid.

31. Ibid.

32. Ibid.

33. Ibid.

34. Tinstman interview.

35. Witherspoon, *Administrative Implementation*, p. 61.

36. Ibid., pp. 61–62.

37. Transcript of City Council meeting, March 26, 1964.

38. Ibid.

39. *Austin American*, April 4, 1964.

40. Ibid.

41. *Austin Statesman*, April 9, 1964.

42. *Daily Texan*, April 12, 1964, editorial.

43. *Austin Statesman*, April 10, 1964.

44. *Austin Statesman*, April 16, 1964.

45. *Austin American*, April 27, 1964.

46. *Austin American*, May 13, 1964.

47. *Austin Statesman*, June 4, 1964.

48. *Washington Post*, October 6, 1967, personal files of Emma Long.

49. Austin Human Relations Commission, First Annual Report, October 1967 to October 1968.

50. Miles interview.

51. Various minutes of Human Relations Commission meetings, personal files of Charles Miles.

52. Report in Long files.

53. Letter from Volma Overton to Robert McNamara, Secretary of Defense, August 3, 1967, Harry Akin personal files.

54. Stuart Long article in *Washington Post*, October 6, 1967.

55. *Fair Housing Ordinance*, Austin, May 1968.

56. *Austin American*, May 10, 1968.

57. *Austin American*, May 15, 1968.

58. Ibid.

59. Special news release to Capital Press Corps, May 17, 1968, Long personal files.

60. Long personal files.

61. Long personal files, advertisement.

62. Ibid.
63. Interview with Hub Bechtol, July 22, 1985.
64. Newspaper articles, Long personal files.
65. *Austin American*, July 16, 1968.
66. Transcript of Special Council Meeting, October 21, 1968, Akin personal files.
67. Ibid.
68. Ibid.

Chapter 11

1. Interview with Robert "Peck" Young, December 12, 1985.
2. Interview with Jeff Friedman, December 17, 1985.
3. Interview with Bob Binder, December 11, 1985.
4. Binder interview.
5. Young interview.
6. Interview with Pat Cuney, June 11, 1986.
7. Young interview.
8. Interview with Dean Rindy, December 18, 1985.
9. Interview with Roger Duncan, January 23, 1986.
10. Interview with Ed Wendler, Sr., February 21, 1986.
11. Cuney interview.
12. Young interview; also Robert Young, "The 1971 City Election Project," (University of Texas, Department of Government, Honors Paper, July 1971).
13. Ibid., pp. 27ff.
14. Young interview.
15. Friedman interview.
16. Assorted interviews.
17. Young interview.
18. Interview with Bill Youngblood, January 7, 1986.
19. Assorted interviews.
20. Young, "The 1971 City Election Project," p. 55.
21. Interview with Philip White, January 10, 1986.
22. Young and Friedman interviews.
23. *Austin American*, March 31, 1971, editorial.
24. Ibid.
25. Interview with R. L. Hancock, January 10, 1986.
26. Ibid.
27. Ibid.
28. Interview with Bill Petri, January 19, 1986.
29. Youngblood interview.
30. Petri interview.
31. Ibid.
32. *Austin American*, September 8, 1972.
33. Petri interview.
34. Interview with Don Butler, January 8, 1986; Hancock interview; Paul

Burka, "Power Politics," *Texas Monthly* (May 1975): 69–97.
35. Butler interview.
36. Butler and Hancock interviews.
37. Friedman interview; *Austin American*, November 22, 1971.
38. Friedman interview.
39. Youngblood interview.
40. Friedman interview; interview with Dan Davidson, February 6, 1986.
41. Interview with Glenn Weichert, no date.
42. Friedman interview, plus other interviews.
43. Gray advertisement, *Austin American*, March 23, March 24, March 25, March 26, March 27, and March 28, 1973.
44. Ibid.
45. Binder interview, plus others.
46. Butler and Hancock interviews.
47. Hancock interviews.
48. Interview with Ann Schwartz, June 5, 1986.
49. Youngblood interview.
50. Young interview.
51. Ibid.
52. Interview with Herbert Woodson, June 16, 1986.
53. Friedman and Binder interviews.
54. Binder files.
55. Ibid.
56. Binder, press statement, November 14, 1973.
57. Friedman interview; plus Schwartz and Young interviews; also private memorandum on the Nuke to Friedman, Mayors' Collection, Austin History Center.
58. Schwartz interview.
59. Ibid.
60. Young interview.
61. Pamphlet, *Citizens for Public Power*, private files of Steve Gutow.
62. Interview with Steve Gutow, December 23, 1985.
63. *San Antonio Express News*, November 30, 1975, Insight.
64. Young interview.
65. Gutow interview.
66. Young interview.
67. Butler interview.
68. See *South Texas Participation Agreement*.
69. Binder interview; *Austin Citizen*, June 15, 1973.
70. Schwartz interview.
71. Binder and Friedman interviews.
72. Binder interview.
73. Binder and Friedman interviews.
74. Rindy interview.
75. See, for example, Rindy documents on the refund contracts, Rindy personal files.
76. Minutes of City Council, March 28, 1974.
77. Brenda Bell articles, *Austin Citizen*, December 7, 11, and 14, 1973.

78. Council minutes; Binder interview.
79. Council minutes.
80. *Austin American-Statesman*, September 19, 1974; Schwartz interview.
81. Schwartz interview.
82. Cuney interview.
83. Interview with Joan Bartz, January 12, 1986.
84. Ibid.
85. Various interviews; plus interview with Dick Lillie, September 11, 1986.
86. Assorted interviews.
87. Bartz interview.
88. Youngblood interview.
89. Bartz interview.
90. Interviews with Dean Rindy and Peck Young.
91. Rindy interview.
92. *Austin Tomorrow Goals: Community Needs and Priorities* (Austin: City of Austin Planning Department, May 7, 1975).
93. Gutow interview; and interview with Steven Rosenbaum, December 23, 1985.
94. Gutow and Wendler interviews.
95. Gutow interview.
96. Gutow, Young, and Wendler interviews.
97. Wendler interview.
98. Gutow and Rosenbaum interviews.
99. Young interview.
100. Duncan interview.
101. Wendler interview.
102. Ibid.
103. Don Butler interview.
104. See Mike Cox and Larry BeSaw, "City Officials Allegedly Got Bell Contributions," *Austin American-Statesman*; articles by Brenda Bell and Carol Fowler in *Austin Citizen*.
105. *Austin American-Statesman*, January 15, 1975.
106. *Austin American-Statesman*, January 18, 1975.
107. *Austin American-Statesman*, January 23, 1975.
108. Ashley-Holman transcript, Wilson Moore and Associates, Court Reports, San Antonio, personal files of Don Butler.
109. Young interview.
110. Wender interview; also Gutow and Young interviews.
111. Assorted interviews, plus undated newspaper articles.
112. *San Antonio Express News*, November 30, 1975, Insight.
113. See the various pamphlets and documents in Friedman files, Austin History Center.
114. Assorted interviews.
115. Friedman speech, June 13, 1975, Madison, Wisconsin, Friedman files, Austin History Center.
116. Youngblood interview.
117. Friedman, Young, and Schwartz interviews.

118. Gutow and Cuney interviews.
119. Interview with Marilyn Simpson, January 9, 1986.
120. Schwartz and Cuney interviews, plus confirmatory interviews.
121. See *Austin American-Statesman*, October 21, 1975, and immediately prior issues.
122. *Austin Business Review*, September 17, 1975.
123. Friedman interview.
124. Friedman and Youngblood interviews.
125. Jeff Friedman to Ed Wendler, Sr., December 12, 1975, Friedman files, Austin History Center.
126. Jeff Friedman to Ken Wendler, December 11, 1975, Friedman files, Austin History Center.
127. *Austin American-Statesman*, December 2, 1975.
128. Gutow interview.
129. Interview with George Sandlin, Sr., July 29, 1985.
130. Mike Kelley, "A City Council under Siege," *Austin American-Statesman*, September 7, 1985.
131. "Economic Implications of the South Texas Nuclear Project," A report presented by Margaret Hofmann, March 30, 1976, research provided by Roger Duncan, administrative assistant.
132. Lillie interview.
133. Young interview.
134. Cuney and Schwartz interviews.

Chapter 12

1. Interview with Fred Purcell, February 4, 1986.
2. Diane E. Downing, "Thinking for the Future: The Promise of MCC" (Austin, August 1983), no pages indicated.
3. Ibid.
4. Interview with John Gray, August 1, 1985.
5. Ibid.
6. Ibid.
7. Downing, "Thinking for the Future."
8. *Fort Worth Star-Telegram*, Sunday, June 26, 1983.
9. Kelly Fero, "Bobby Ray to the Rescue," *Third Coast*, vol 3, number 5 (December 1983): 72–82.
10. *Fort Worth Star-Telegram*, June 26, 1983.
11. John Naisbitt, *Megatrends* (New York: Warner Books, 1982).
12. *Milwaukee Journal*, Sunday, March 25, 1984; and *New York Times*, April 17, 1984.
13. Interview with Jim Frederick, January 8, 1986.
14. Gray interview.
15. Interview with Tom Bradfield, January 28, 1986.
16. Interview with Chuck Stahl, December 9, 1985; and interviews with Stahl and David Barrow, Jr., September 9, 1986.

17. Stahl interview, December 9, 1985.
18. Ibid.
19. Stahl and Barrow, Jr., interview, September 9, 1986.
20. Stahl interview, December 9, 1985.
21. Ibid.
22. Ibid.
23. Minutes of City Planning Commission, January 7, 1955.
24. G. S. Moore, "A Brief Outline of Transportation in Austin—As It Relates to the Plan of the City," March 1, 1944.
25. G. S. Moore, "Place of Transportation in Austin City Plan Visualized," *Austin American-Statesman*, March 26, 1944.
26. Ibid.
27. Interview with Taylor Glass, May 21, 1982.
28. Interviews with Stahl and Barrow, Jr.; phone conversation with Kay Gurley, Barrow, Sr.'s former secretary, October 9, 1986.
29. Interview with Stahl and Barrow, Jr., September 9, 1986.
30. Ibid., plus Stahl interview, December 9, 1985.
31. Ibid.
32. See City Planning Commission Minutes, October 8, 1957; January 24, 1958; and July 31, 1962.
33. See City Planning Commission Minutes: February 8, 1955; January 10, 1956; October 16, 1956; November 13, 1956; December 11, 1956; January 15, 1957; February 21, 1957; March 12, 1957; June 11, 1957; July 2, 1957; July 30, 1957; January 7, 1958; February 18, 1958; January 20, 1959; May 12, 1959; June 9, 1959; April 5, 1960; August 23, 1960; May 16, 1961.
34. Minute Order, Texas State Highway Department, October 28, 1966.
35. Minutes, Public Hearing on Loop 1, February 6, 1968.
36. District Highway Traffic Map, Texas State Department of Highways and Transportation, District 14 (1985), and Highway Department reports on Loop 1, Planning and Research Division Projections, June 21 and June 28, 1974.
37. Interview with Roland Gamble, district engineer, State Highway Department, September 17, 1986.
38. Interview with Walter Vackar, September 30, 1986.
39. Ibid.
40. Ibid.
41. *Austin American-Statesman*, October 25, 1986.
42. Vackar interview.
43. Bradfield interview.
44. Interview with Dick Lillie, former Austin planning director, September 11, 1986.
45. Interview with Roberta Dickson Crenshaw, October 2, 1986.
46. Ibid., plus interviews with Emma Long.
47. Crenshaw interview.
48. Minutes of Public Hearing, February 6, 1968.
49. Projected Impact on Mo-Pac Expressway on the West Austin Inner City, June 9, 1975, in Friedman papers, Mayors' Files, Austin History Center.

50. Letter from Diane Carr and Barbara Weismann to Austin City Council, September 17, 1975, in Friedman papers, Austin History Center.

51. Letter from Dr. S. J. Lerro to Bob Binder, January 26, 1974, Binder personal papers.

52. Council action of July 1975.

53. *Austin American-Statesman*, August 4, 1975.

54. Interview with Joe Ternus, October 6, 1986.

55. Bradfield interview.

56. The private papers of Marilyn Simpson, longtime Austin activist and former head of the Austin Neighborhood Association, fully document this period.

57. Bradfield interview.

58. *Austin American-Statesman*, n.d.

59. Sid Jagger would not permit himself to be interviewed. Most of the details here came from the unpublished book by D. Claire McAdams, "Mall Environment Degradation: Issues of Conflict among Powerful Actors," and from an interview with her on October 6, 1986.

60. McAdams interview.

61. Vackar interview.

62. Minutes of City Planning Commission, November 12, 1974.

63. Documents in private papers of McAdams.

64. Land Transaction Records, in McAdams papers.

65. McAdams interview.

66. Ibid.

67. Figures recorded in land sale notes, McAdams papers.

68. Vackar interview.

69. McAdams interview.

70. Ibid.

71. Vackar interview.

72. Ibid.

73. Ibid.

74. Ibid.

75. Interview with Orville Miller, September 22, 1986.

76. Ibid.

77. Ibid., plus State Highway Department records.

78. Ibid.

79. Interview with Emmett Shelton, Sr., May 5, 1983.

80. Interview with Emmett Shelton, Sr., October 2, 1986.

81. Ibid.

82. Ibid.

83. Ibid., plus letter from Jessie Roy to Emmett Shelton, Sr., October 2, 1939, Shelton personal papers.

84. Shelton interviews, May 5, 1983, and October 2, 1986.

85. Interviews with Gary Bradley, September 25, 1986, and with John Wooley, January 11, 1986.

86. Wooley interview.

87. Ibid.

88. Ibid.
89. Bradley and Wooley interviews, plus interview with Guy Bodine, October 9, 1986.
90. Bradley interview.
91. Bradley and Wooley interviews.
92. Bradley and Ternus interviews.
93. Unidentified sources.
94. Wooley interviews.
95. Bradley and Wooley interviews.
96. Bradley interview.
97. Bodine interview.
98. Bodine and Wooley interviews.
99. Bradley interview.
100. Bradley and Wooley interviews.
101. Wooley interview.
102. Bradley interview.
103. Ibid.
104. Orville Miller interview.
105. Ternus interview.
106. Interview with Kathlene King, February 7, 1986.
107. Ibid.
108. Ibid.
109. Purcell interview.
110. Ibid.
111. Ibid.
112. Ibid., plus interview with John Lloyd, September 29, 1986.
113. Lloyd interview.
114. Lloyd and Purcell interviews, plus interview with Rudy Robinson, January 9, 1986; plus Mike Cox article, *Austin American-Statesman*, September 26, 1980.
115. Purcell interview.
116. Ibid.
117. Ibid.
118. Lloyd and Purcell interviews.
119. Unidentified source.
120. Lloyd interview.
121. Ibid.
122. Lloyd and Purcell interviews.
123. Bradley interview.
124. Vackar interview.

Index
